An Empire takes shape

EARLY AMERICAN HISTORY

An eighteen volume series reproducing over three hundred of the most important articles on all aspects of the colonial experience

EDITED WITH INTRODUCTIONS BY
PETER CHARLES HOFFER
UNIVERSITY OF GEORGIA

A Garland Series

AN EMPIRE TAKES SHAPE

Selected Articles
on the Origins
of the Old English Colonial System

EDITED WITH AN INTRODUCTION BY

PETER CHARLES HOFFER

Garland Publishing, Inc.
New York & London
1988

Library of Congress Cataloging-in-Publication Data

An Empire takes shape.

(Early American history)
1. United States—History—Colonial period, ca. 1600–1775.   2. Great
Britain—Colonies—America—History.   I. Hoffer, Peter C.   II. Series.
EI88.5.E46   1988   973.2   88-4086
ISBN 0-8240-6232-9 (alk. paper)

The volumes in this series are printed on
acid-free, 250-year-life paper.

Printed in the United States of America

CONTENTS

Pennsylvania, 1676–1683"
The Pennsylvania Magazine of History and Biography, 105 (1981), 373–392

PREFACE

The subtitle of this volume derives from George Louis Beer's pathfinding work on the origins of the English colonial system.[1] Beer's achievement was one of discovery, or rather, re-discovery. He and his successors in the "imperial" school unearthed the massive correspondence of the Lords of Trade and their successors, the Board of Trade, as well as the secretaries of state, and the committees of the Privy Council relating to the colonies. These colonial office memos, rulings, reports, and orders taught Beer and his colleagues what their revolutionary forbears well knew—that the Empire was a thriving enterprise throughout the seventeenth century.

If the imperial school can be faulted, it is for the thoroughness of its reconstruction of the apparatus of the first empire. To regard the first Stuarts' unwieldy collection of advisory councils, special interest lobbies, placemen administrators, customs collectors, vice-admiralty judges, forest surveyors, and not the least venal and incompetent of them all, the royal governors, as a system, much less a bureaucracy, is to give greater authority, direction, and coherence to imperial policy than it attained until the reign of William and Mary.

Successive generations of historians have added layers to our understanding of that first empire. To view it as merely an economic enterprise is to lose sight of the political authority, cultural standards, religious influences, and educational ideas that pulsed through the arteries of empire. The extent to which the empire was an informal structure, a network of kin, sect, and commercial house, is now apparent as well. These "irrational" (using the language of Max Weber) ties of empire gave day to day purpose to colonial

ix

business, church, and social activity. They remind us that the empire was a conglomeration of people, not just a mercantile experiment or a military frontier.

While the early Empire as a whole went through a number of stages of development, from Elizabethan trading posts and early Stuart proprietorships through Cromwell's first forays into naval imperialism, to Charles II's sponsorship of the Navigation Acts and his brother James II's attempts to reorganize the imperial administration, it never lost its overwhelmingly private character. Private individuals in the mother country and private individuals in the colonies directed the course of Empire, more than any central agency, much less a central authority. In later years, after the Glorious Revolution, a clearer idea of the value of Empire and its proper utilization would emerge in England. A true imperial bureaucracy would evolve. The trials and tribulations of this second Empire are traced in Volume Fifteen of this series.

One generalization does hold for the scholarship of both the first and the second old Empires. The most significant studies of imperial affairs appeared more often in book form than in article form. This was true in the first half of the century, as the multi-volume works of Beer himself, Herbert Levi Osgood, Charles McLean Andrews, and their successor, Lawrence Henry Gipson demonstrate.[2] It remains true of the more recent work of Thomas C. Barrow, James Henretta, Michael Kammen, Stanley Katz, David Lovejoy, Alison Olson, Jack Sosin, and Stephen Webb.[3] The continuing stream of these works does not preclude the appearance of first rate articles in the future, but the shape of this body of scholarship does suggest that the vast scope and complexity of research in the old Empire often demands greater length than journal editors will allow.

Peter Charles Hoffer
University of Georgia

Notes

1. George Louis Beer, *The Origins of the British Colonial System, 1587–1660*, (New York, 1908); *The Old Colonial System, 1660–1715* (2 vols., New York, 1913).

2. Herbert Levi Osgood, *The American Colonies in the Seventeenth Century* (3 vols., New York, 1904–07); *The American Colonies in the Eighteenth Century* (4 vols., New York, 1924); Charles McLean Andrews, *The Colonial Period of American History* (4 vols., New Haven, 1934–38); Lawrence Henry Gipson, *The British Empire Before the American Revolution* (15 vols., New York, 1936–70).

3. Thomas C. Barrow, *Trade and Empire: The British Customs Service in Colonial America, 1660–1775* (Cambridge, Mass., 1967); James Henretta, *"Salutary Neglect": Colonial Administration under the Duke of Newcastle* (Princeton, 1972); Michael Kammen, *Empire and Interest: The American Colonies and the Politics of Mercantilism* (New York, 1970); Stanley N. Katz, *Newcastle's New York, Anglo-American Politics, 1732–1753* (Cambridge, Mass., 1968); David Lovejoy, *The Glorious Revolution in America* (New York, 1972); Alison G. Olson, *Anglo-American Politics, 1660–1775: The Relationship Between Parties in England and Colonial America* (New York, 1973); Jack M. Sosin, *English America and Imperial Inconstancy: The Rise of Provincial Autonomy, 1696–1715* (Lincoln, Nebr., 1985); Stephen Saunders Webb, *The Governors-General: The English Army and the Definition of Empire, 1569–1681,* (Chapel Hill, 1979).

THE BOARD OF TRADE AT WORK

To the student of colonial history few English institutions offer more of interest than the one which, in name at least, presided over the destinies of the English establishments in North America, the Board of Trade and Plantations. The full story of its activities remains to be written, but in the course of investigations to that end many details of its inner life, scarcely less important and often much more interesting than the record of its public acts. have come to light. It seems not without value to bring these together to form a picture of the Board as a living, working body. For it is particularly true of the old British administrative councils that their internal history is often hardly inferior to their external career in importance. This is peculiarly true of the Board of Trade. It is proposed in the following study to describe as well as may be, what in an individual would be called, its private life.

"They had", says Roger North in his *Examen*, writing of a Restoration Council of Trade, "a formal Board with Green Cloth and Standishes, Clerks good store. a tall Porter and Staff and fitting Attendance below and a huge Luminary at the Door. And in Winter time when the Board met, as was two or three times a Week or oftener, all the Rooms were lighted, coaches at the Door and great passing in and out as if a Council of State in good Earnest had been sitting." Though these words were applied to an earlier establishment they are full of suggestions of the later and greater Board. Beginning its career in the spring of 1696 without precedent or traditions beyond such as were derived from these earlier bodies, the new Board of Trade had neither meeting-place nor employees, material assets nor order of procedure. By the second quarter of the eighteenth century it had become a fixed and elaborate institution. with the outward look of "a Council of State in good earnest", so that North's half-humorous description no doubt well fitted the later board to which he was accustomed. To trace some of the s▓▓s by which its complex organization was evolved, and to give a g▓▓pse of its inner life, its character and membership, is the purpose of this paper.

One of the first requisites for a new establishment like this was a meeting-place. In the royal commission issued in May, 1696, the persons therein named were directed to " meet together at some con-

venient place in our palace of Whitehall which we shall assign for
that purpose or at any other place that we shall appoint for the execution of this our commission ".[1] Though the place was thus named
by the king, the details were left to be arranged by the commissioners
themselves. For the first few meetings they occupied a room at
Whitehall, adjoining the apartments which, late in July, were
assigned for their permanent use.[2] The Board in a body officially
inspected the rooms,[3] and spent considerable time discussing them,
corresponding with the Treasury, the Lord Keeper, and even the
king,[4] and interviewing Sir Christopher Wren who was then surveyor of the royal works.[5] As a result the office was fitted up in
the course of the summer. It was occupied, however, only about a
year and a half. On January 4, 1698, occurred the Whitehall fire,
in which the Plantation Office, along with others, was destroyed.[6]
By prompt action on the part of the secretary and clerks, the papers
were probably all saved with the exception of a bundle relating to
Africa.[7] The secretary, William Popple, took the books and papers
to his home in Essex Street and there the meetings were held for
about two months.[8] During this time, as before, the Board negotiated with Sir Christopher Wren[9] about the fitting up of the office.[10]
In March permanent quarters were provided in that part of old
Whitehall which had been commonly known as the Cockpit, and
which about this time was remodelled for the Privy Council Office.[11]
By 1718 the Board had outgrown this location and was asking for
repairs and the building of a new room,[12] but no change was made

[1] Board of Trade Journal (B. T. J.), vol. IX., p. 1.

[2] *Ibid.*, p. 25.

[3] *Ibid.*, p. 12.

[4] *Ibid.*, pp. 11, 13.

[5] *Ibid.*, pp. 7, 8, 9.

[6] B. T. J., X. 391.

[7] B. T. Calendars, 66, contains an inventory of books and papers of the
Plantation Office. Against one of them is the memorandum. " This bundle of
African papers was lost in the fire at Whitehall Jan. 4, 1697/8 ".

[8] B. T. J., X. 391–446.

[9] *Ibid.*, pp. 397–398.

[10] Even minor details were discussed at the Board. In one case the secretary
was instructed to write for "locks, grates and tongs " for the rooms of the Board
of Trade. B. T. J., X. 415.

[11] John Timbs, *Walks and Talks about London.* The word Cockpit was used
only a few weeks. After May 30, 1698, the Board's papers were all dated at
Whitehall, but there was no change at this time.

[12] B. T. J., XXVII. 65. In July, 1720, this demand was increased to two
rooms, and from this time till 1736 requests for repairs were frequent. The complicated interrelation among parts of the British government may be illustrated
by the fact that these requests were addressed at different times to the Lord
Chamberlain, the Lords Justices, the Lords of the Treasury, and the Board of
Works. The decision seems to have been that the Treasury was the proper
authority. *Ibid.*, p. 181 ; XXX. 270, 283, 288 ; XXXI. 328, etc.

till 1723. In that year the Commissioners of Trade were asked to vacate their office in favor of the Bishop of London[13] and were assigned to other apartments in Whitehall. Here they worked without interruption for nearly twenty years. In 1742 the building which they occupied was sold to the "Commissioners for Erecting a Bridge at Westminster", who demanded a rental of £120 annually and refused to lease the place for longer than a year and a quarter in advance.[14] The Board paid rent till the summer of 1746, when a new office was fitted up in the Cockpit over the Treasury.[15] Here —and it was probably true of earlier buildings as well—the clerks and under officers "resided in the attick story" above the rooms of the Board of Trade.[16] No doubt this was in order to have them ever at hand, for their office hours were many and long. By 1774 the Board's lengthy reports and accumulated material had again outgrown the available space. On November 5, a petition was sent to the Treasury asking "either that the other state papers now kept in the rooms adjoining to these apartments on the South may be removed or that some other place within His Majesty's Palace of Whitehall may be appointed for carrying on the business of this department ".[17] As this is the last trace in the Journal of the housing of the Board, the situation, most likely, was not relieved till the dissolution in 1782.

In spite of these repeated changes, the general arrangement of the Plantation Office must have been similar throughout. With the exception probably of the first temporary location, it always consisted of four rooms or groups of rooms. The Council Chamber, where formal meetings of the Board were held, must have been of considerable size, as it was usual to give audience to a number of people at one time.[18] Here the commissioners seem to have sat around a table, each having his own place according to a definite order of precedence.[19] Communicating with this room from one side was that of the secretary, and from another side the waiting-room or rooms[20]—for there were at times several of them—

3

[13] B. T. J., XXXIII. 194.

[14] *Ibid.*, vol. LI. pt. I., p. 75.

[15] *Ibid.*, LIV., 49.

[16] *Ibid.*, LXVI. 197.

[17] *Ibid.*, LXXXII. 69.

[18] *E. g.*, March 26, 1737, when a "great number of Quakers" attended the Board. B. T. J., XLVII. 98.

[19] The names of the Lords of Trade always appear in a fixed order. When a name was omitted from the Commission, all below it were advanced and the name of the new member placed at the end of the list, except that a peer's name took precedence of others.

[20] B. T. J., XXXVIII. 235.

where witnesses, petitioners, and visitors of all sorts had to wait till formally admitted to the Board. Besides these[21] there was the clerks' room, which was most carefully guarded from outside intrusion. It was furnished with a separate desk for each clerk[22] and facilities for the constant drafting, copying, and assorting of documents.

It will be seen, then, that the Colonial Office was an establishment of considerable size and orderly arrangement. The Board of Trade which occupied this office was likewise well organized. It consisted at the outset of eight active and eight honorary members. The honorary or ex-officio members, the Chancellor, President of the Council, Keeper of the Privy Seal, Lord Treasurer, Lord High Admiral, two Secretaries of State, and Chancellor of the Exchequer, were required to attend the Board only on special occasions.[23] On the active members, two[24] lords and six commoners, devolved therefore the responsibility of office. The member first named in the commission—and this was always a peer—was the president. Three members were to constitute a quorum for the transaction of business, while all letters and representations must be signed by five. This last requirement was lowered to four in 1697.[25] From 1707 to 1712 only seven active members were named, and from 1712 to 1717 the Chancellor of the Exchequer was omitted from the honorary list. Otherwise the constitution of the Board was unchanged until 1768, when the newly established Secretary of State for the Colonies became ex-officio president, and only seven members were appointed by name. From 1779 to the dissolution in 1782 there was a separate president, thus making up the usual number of active members apart from the Secretary of State.

The Board seems to have had full authority over the time and frequency of its own meetings;[26] and if the number of them is any

---

[21] It is clear that there must have been also, especially in the Board's later years, a room or group of rooms used for storing the immense mass of books and papers that had accumulated. Curiously enough, the Journal makes no mention of such rooms.

[22] B. T. J., LVI. 100.

[23] "And we do hereby further declare our royal will and pleasure to be that we do not hereby intend that our Chancellor [etc.] . . . shall be obliged to give constant attendance at the meetings of our said Commissioners, but only so often and when the presence of them or any of them shall be necessary and requisite and as their other public service will permit." From the Commission, B. T. J., IX. 1. It is printed in *N. Y. Col. Doc.*, IV. 145.

[24] After 1714 and during short intervals before that time, only one lord was appointed to the Board, the other members being commoners.

[25] B. T. J., X. 233.

[26] E. g., on June 25, 1696, the Board decided to meet every Monday at 4 p. m. and every Wednesday and Friday at 10 a. m. (B. T. J., IX. 7) and on June 23, 1702, it decided to meet Mondays and Wednesdays at 4, and Tuesday, Thursday, and Friday at 10 (*Ibid.*, XV. 97).

indication, it must have been, during the first few years of its history, a very efficient public servant. In the first ten years it was not uncommon to meet eighteen, twenty, or even twenty-four times a month, and the average per month for a whole year was sometimes as high as eighteen or nineteen. By the middle of the century this average had been lowered to the neighborhood of ten, the Board's zeal having somewhat abated. After 1768 there was a more marked falling off, due possibly to the decrease of the Board's authority and its dependence on the Secretary of State for the Colonies.[27] Not only were the meetings less frequent in the winter, but it came to be customary to indulge in a vacation in the summer or autumn. As early as the '30's it was common to adjourn[28] for a month, and as time went on this was increased to two months and even three during which no effort was made to hold any meetings whatever. Perhaps this may throw some light on Edward Gibbon's admission that " our duty was not intolerably severe and that I enjoyed many days and weeks of repose without being called away from my library to the office ".[29]

In attendance as well as the number of meetings the Board made a good beginning. At first the average attendance ranged from four to six with a " full Board " on special occasions. In this as in other particulars enthusiasm waned toward the middle of the century, though it was somewhat renewed again at the end of the period. As early as 1708 there was some difficulty in getting enough members together to transact business,[30] and in 1709 the Earl of Sunderland ordered that enough members to form a quorum should be always in town.[31] When this was not the case a special summons was sometimes sent to the absentees who happened to be at the

5

[27] In 1774 the Board met, on an average, about twice a month, the lowest figure that it ever reached. Even this compares favorably with the Committee of Council for Trade and Plantations from 1675 to 1696, which met seven times a month during only one year, five times a month during one year, and the rest of the time from four times to a little more than once a month. Dr. Andrews says (*British Committees, Commissions, and Councils of Trade and Plantations, 1622–1675*, p. 78) that the Council of Trade held forty meetings in the year 1661. The Board held 35 meetings in 1774, 100 in 1767, 135 in 1749, 162 in 1730, 189 in 1715, and 230 in 1697.

[28] Adjournment might be for the " usual recess " in the summer or for other reasons. On March 7, 1768, the Board adjourned till April 12, " on account of the approaching general election ". B. T. J., LXXVI. 58. As most members of the Board were members of Parliament, they probably needed this time to look after their interests in the country.

[29] *Memoirs of Edward Gibbon* (ed. Henry Morley), p. 176. Gibbon was a member of the Board from July 14, 1779, to the disestablishment in 1782.

[30] B. T. J., XX. 35; XXI. 225.

[31] *Ibid.*, XXI. 234.

least distance from London.[32] A few times in 1733 Martin Bladen was left to uphold, alone, the dignity of the office.[33] So far as appears in the Journal the " Secretary acquainted the Board "[34] as usual of the business to be transacted and all the routine was gone through as though a quorum had been present.

The fact that anything at all could be done with only one member present is due, no doubt, to the constant attendance of the employees. Through them the Plantation Office was a permanent and continuous establishment which was always at work even when the Board itself did not meet. It is necessary, therefore, to glance at the office force and see just how it was constituted. The secretary was the most important official next to the commissioners themselves. At the first meeting that the Board ever held, June 25, 1696, it was decided to have a secretary and William Popple was appointed to that office.[35] Although this appointment was made by the Board, all following secretaries were named by the crown, while the Board continued to choose the other officials. In the first few weeks, employment was given to three clerks, two messengers, two doorkeepers, and a " necessary woman " or janitress, while two stationers were engaged to furnish paper under the Board's patronage.[36] In 1701 another clerk was added.[37] By 1708 the office staff consisted of a secretary at £500, a deputy secretary or chief clerk at £100, and seven clerks, two messengers, a doorkeeper, and a janitress, at from £80 to £30, the total amounting to £1150 a year.[38] After removing to the new office in 1724 the Board felt the need of a porter to attend at the door. The request was granted by the Treasury and the new officer installed at £40 per annum.[39] In 1730 the Board asked for and obtained still another official known as the solicitor and clerk of reports, at £200.[40] For over thirty years this position

[32] B. T. J., XL. 176.

[33] *Ibid.*, XLIII. 112, 114, 127, 128.

[34] After reading the Journal's frequent repetitions of this formula one is tempted to reverse the familiar story told of Bladen that when he applied himself to the business of the office, his friends in derision called him " Trade " and his colleagues " the Board ". See *Dictionary of National Biography*, art. Martin Bladen.

[35] B. T. J., IX. 7.

[36] *Ibid.*, pp. 8, 11.

[37] *Ibid.*, XIV. 194.

[38] *Ibid.*, XX. 22.

[39] *Ibid.*, XXXIV. 115, 190. In 1733 the secretary reported that disorderly persons were in the habit of causing disturbance in front of the office at night. The Board therefore petitioned the Secretary at War for a sentinel to station at the door. B. T. J., XLIII. 13. I failed to find any evidence in the Journal that this officer was appointed.

[40] B. T. J., XL. 204; also, *Calendar of Treasury Books and Papers*, 1729–1730, p. 437.

stood next in rank to the secretaryship and served as a stepping-stone to that post. In 1764 the deputy secretary was promoted to second place at £300, while the solicitor at £150 stood between him and the clerks. At the same time the number of clerks was raised from seven to nine, and all the salaries increased.[41]

There were, then, at the end of the period, at least fifteen persons—some of them with considerable salaries—directly under the Board's control. Besides these there was a law-officer who must be counted a part of the establishment, though his position was on a higher plane than that of the other officials, and his attendance was only occasional. The reason for such an office was this: all colonial laws had to be examined by the Board of Trade and submitted by it to the king with a recommendation for their confirmation or repeal. Also many colonial questions were considered on which a technical legal knowledge was necessary. To obtain a legal opinion, it. was at first customary to consult the attorney-general and the solicitor-general, sometimes separately and sometimes jointly. In order to make their work more systematic, they were, in November, 1698, asked to divide the field between them.[42] By 1718 the amount of business had outgrown the available time of either. It was, therefore, decided to appoint one of His Majesty's counsel-at-law to respond to all legal questions of the Board except those of the greatest importance, which were still to be referred to the attorney or solicitor.[43] This office was held by four persons: Richard West,[44] who was a playwright as well as a lawyer, held it from 1718 to 1725: Francis Fane, himself a member of the Board at a later time, from 1725 to 1746: Matthew Lamb, at one time a member of Parliament for Peterborough, from 1746 to 1770: and Richard Jackson,[45] whose remarkable knowledge won for him the title " Omniscient Jackson ", from 1770 to the end of the Board's career in 1782.

The employees of the office, especially the clerks, were subject to rules[46] devised by the Board itself and varied from time to time. The hour at which they were to report for duty was sometimes eight o'clock, sometimes later, but there was always provision for an

7

[41] B. T. J., LXXII. 348. The ninth clerk seems never to have been appointed, though the eight served for some time.

[42] B. T. J., XI. 278.

[43] *Ibid.*, XXVII. 133, 203.

[44] West is said to have attended the Board twice a week and received three guineas for every attendance. *Cal. Treas. Papers*. 1720–1728, pp. 114. 313. He resigned this office in 1725 to become Lord Chancellor of Ireland. See article Richard West in *Dict. of Nat. Biog.*

[45] For details of Jackson's life. see *Dict. of Nat. Biog.*

[46] Such rules may be found in B. T. J., XXIV. 341: XXXVII. 183: XXXVIII. 235: XLI. 124: XLV. 66. 260: L. 30: LVI. 100: LXXII. 541: etc.

afternoon and, if necessary, an evening session, subject to the call of the secretary. In any case clerks were expected to be at work regularly without reference to meetings of the Board, in order to prepare business for such meetings. No clerk could leave the building without permission of the secretary, and before leaving it each one must turn over to that officer all books and papers in his desk to be locked up for safe keeping. The strictest vigilance was maintained to prevent documents from falling into the hands of persons for whom they were not intended. To this end, papers were not allowed to leave the building without permission of the Board, and the clerks while on duty were forbidden to communicate with anyone from outside, except through the agency of the secretary. Two rules were made to prevent the corrupting of clerks—that they should not act as agents for the plantations,[47] and that "no clerk should presume to demand money of any person for business done in this office".[48] This latter seems not to refer to extraordinary attendance at the Board or the copying of papers for private persons, for which fees could legitimately be taken. The Privy Council issued an order August 12, 1731,[49] settling a schedule for such fees, and this was hung up in the office and referred to during the remaining fifty-one years of the Board's history.[50] The penalty for violation of rules was dismissal from employment, and it was one not infrequently resorted to. It might be inflicted directly by the Board, or by the secretary, who had authority to suspend clerks for neglect of duty and submit his action afterwards to be sustained or reversed by the Board. The two most interesting cases of dismissal are those of Bryan Wheelock and John Lewis. Wheelock was expelled July 13, 1714, for charging Arthur Moore, a member of the Board, with improper correspondence with the court of Spain.[51] He was, however, soon reinstated and promoted to the office of head clerk,[52] which he held till his death in 1735. Lewis was accused in July, 1769, of having written treasonable letters to persons in America advising continued opposition. Testimony was taken of the other clerks and, being convicted of the charge, he was dismissed.[53]

[47] On May 1, 1724, Anthony Sanderson, a clerk, asked permission to act as agent of Massachusetts, till the dispute with the governor be settled. It was refused as inconsistent with the above rule. B. T. J., XXXIV. 107, 110. This incident is referred to in a letter dated May 24, 1724, from John Colman in London to his brother in Boston, giving an account of a hearing before the Privy Council on a complaint brought by Governor Shute against the House of Representatives of Massachusetts. Printed in *Collections of the Massachusetts Historical Society*, first series, V. 32–35.

[48] B. T. J., XXIV. 341 ; XL. 202.

[49] *Ibid.*, XLI. 230.

[50] *Ibid.*, LXXXVIII. 32.

[51] *Ibid.*, XXIV. 263.

[52] *Ibid.*, p. 341.

[53] *Ibid.*, LXXVII. 120, 132.

When, for any reason, a clerk left the service, all below him were promoted and the new appointee placed at the foot of the list. It was not uncommon for a clerk who had grown to old age or infirmity in the service of the Board to be retired on the whole or a part of his salary. This was done as early as 1714.[54] In 1764 the plan was adopted on a large scale.[55] Lord Hillsborough represented to the Chancellor of the Exchequer the need of more clerks and of higher salaries. As a result the Treasury made an additional grant of £1715 per annum to be used as the Board should see fit. The Board thereupon created two new clerkships,[56] raised all salaries, and allowed the deputy secretary and four clerks to retire on a pension for life.[57] As pensions reverted they were to be applied to still greater increase in salaries.

The appointment of officers, as time went on, was reduced to a definite system of patronage. The president gradually acquired the right to fill the first vacancy after he came into office, while the other commissioners took turns in naming a candidate, and their nominations were always accepted. This method was in use until 1764. On July 4 of that year, the same day on which the pensioning system was arranged as already noted, the Board adopted a "civil-service reform" of its own making.[58] By this each candidate for a clerkship was to present a specimen of his writing and write another specimen "in the outer room". The members of the Board still took turns in suggesting names, but each must be examined as to the qualifications of his candidate, and must withdraw during the discussion that followed. If the election failed he was not to lose his turn to nominate. In practice the applicants seem also to have undergone some sort of examination,[59] and several clerks served a week or more on probation without salary before being admitted to

[54] *Ibid.*, XXIV. 341.

[55] *Ibid.*, LXXII. 348.

[56] We have already seen that only one of these positions was ever filled. See above, note 41.

[57] It must be owned that many people seem to have looked upon employment in the Board's office as a means of livelihood, rather than a post of duty. The commissioners did not easily desert their servants. In July, 1781, the secretary, Richard Cumberland, came back from a mission to Spain and Gray Elliot, who had acted in his absence, was thus thrown out of office. On July 13 the Board recommended him to Lord North for employment. B. T. J., LXXXIX. 270. On the 18th an answer was received that North had no vacancy for Elliot but would " certainly make no difficulty " in allowing £250 in contingencies of the Board till he could be provided for and would " consider himself as obliged to the Board " if they could save this amount from their expenses. *Ibid.*, p. 279.

[58] B. T. J., LXXII. 348.

[59] *Ibid.*, p. 444.

regular employment.[60] By 1779 these details had been dropped and the old method of appointment resorted to.[61]

A study of the names and relationships of the Board's employees might produce some curious results. Some families stood in high favor with the colonial department, and acquired a remarkable ability for getting their names on the waiting list.[62] The Popples are the best illustration of this. The Board of Trade's first secretary, William Popple, who by the way was a nephew and protégé of the poet Andrew Marvell and had himself a slight place in literature through his translations,[63] left his office in turn to his son William[64] and his grandson Alured,[65] the family holding it continuously for forty-one years. But that is not all; in 1737, the year in which Alured Popple of the third generation resigned the secretaryship to become governor of Bermuda,[66] William Popple the third, another member of the family and a dramatist of some note, entered the Board's employ as solicitor and clerk of reports.[67] This post he held till 1745 when he went to Bermuda to succeed Alured as governor.[68] Not only this but Alured himself served an apprenticeship as a clerk for five years before being made secretary[69] and his brother Henry was a clerk for a few months in 1727.[70] The Popple family, therefore, spent sixty-three years in one capacity or another in the service of the Board of Trade.

The only family that can at all rival the Popples is that of the Pownalls. John Pownall entered the Board's service as a clerk June 24, 1741.[71] He became solicitor and clerk of reports in 1745,[72] joint secretary in 1753,[73] and secretary in 1758,[74] holding this office

[60] B. T. J., pp. 457, 467; LXXIII. 130.

[61] Ibid., LXXXVII. 210.

[62] Ibid., XXX. 336; XXXII. 64.

[63] Dict. of Nat. Biog. His most famous translation was that of Locke's *Letter on Toleration.* He was associated with Locke at the Board of Trade.

[64] B. T. J., XIX. 165.

[65] Ibid., XXXII. 100.

[66] Ibid., XLVII. 186.

[67] B. T. J., XLVII. 106. According to an article in the *Dictionary of National Biography*, William Popple III., who was clerk of reports, was the only son of William Popple II., the Board's second secretary, and was a "relative" of Alured. It is very clear from the Journal that Alured and Henry were brothers and were sons of the second William. B. T. J., XXXII. 64. 100; XLIII. 161; XLIV. 174. Who the third William was I do not know. though I had supposed him to be Alured's son. He is spoken of in Pope's *Dunciad*—"Lo P-p-le's brow tremendous to the town". *Dict. Nat. Biog.*

[68] B. T. J., LIII. 63.

[69] Ibid., XXVI. 223.

[70] Ibid., XXXVII. 83.

[71] Ibid., L. 67.

[72] Ibid., LIII. 63.

[73] Ibid., LXI. 153.

[74] Ibid., LXVI. 238.

till 1776[75] and thus completing thirty-five years of uninterrupted service. Though he did not bequeath his office to his descendants as Popple had done, two of his family, George[76] and John Lillington Pownall,[77] held clerkships. Besides these two conspicuous families there are a number of other persons on the office staff, whose similarity of names makes one stop and wonder how these people were related and how they came by their posts.[78] A few of the Board's employees seem to have been old and infirm at the time of appointment, and at least three were retired on a salary after from four to six years' service.[79] On the other hand, many spent years and even a lifetime in the Board's employ. A dozen men served twenty-five years or more—some of them much more—and one of them, Samuel Gellebrand, first as clerk and later as deputy secretary, gave fifty years of his life to the Board of Trade.[80]

Employment in the Colonial Office must have served as a good training for other posts in the government service—unless indeed it was simply a stepping-stone to further patronage. Whatever the explanation, several of the Board's servants were chosen for work in allied fields. We have already seen that Alured and William Popple were called away from the Board's service, in 1737 and 1745 respectively, to become governors of Bermuda. In 1711 Bryan Wheelock, then only a clerk, accompanied Sir John Copley on a mission to Italy,[81] and in 1717 another clerk, William Hoskins, was chosen by John Chetwynd, himself a member of the Board, to attend him on a similar mission to Spain.[82] In 1761 John Pownall the secretary left his work to go to Ireland with Lord Halifax[83] who was then Lord Lieutenant. In 1765 Silvester, the clerk of reports, gave up his position because he had been appointed agent " to the intended new government in Africa ".[84] Again on May 7, 1776, Ambrose Serle, the clerk of reports, was given leave of absence without pay to become under-secretary to the " Commission which Lord Howe

[75] *Ibid.,* LXXXIV. 6.

[76] *Ibid.,* LXXX. 192; LXXXIII. 47.

[77] *Ibid.,* LXXVIII. 15; LXXX. 192.

[78] There were three Serles, two Hills, two Wrights, two Griffins, two Sedgwicks, and two Grays.

[79] Maurice Carrol, 1708–1714, and Daniel Cuchow and Robert Green, 1760–1764, all clerks.

[80] B. T. J., XX. 22; LXVI. 149.

[81] *Ibid.,* XXIII. 79.

[82] *Ibid.,* XXVI. 276. Chetwynd was envoy extraordinary and plenipotentiary to Madrid. *Ibid.,* p. 250.

[83] B. T. J., LXIX. 300.

[84] *Ibid.,* LXXII. 154. This was Senegambia. A plan to establish a government there was discussed at intervals in the first half of 1765, and by August the agents of the government were negotiating with the Board.

took to America ".[85]   Also Richard Cumberland, the Board's last
secretary, was sent secretly in 1781 to help negotiate a Spanish
treaty.[86]

These specific instances serve to illustrate the close relation between the Board of Trade and Plantations on the one hand, and the
great world of colonies and trade on the other.   Indeed unless their
position was purely a sinecure as some have maintained, the men in
this office must have had an excellent opportunity to become familiar
with colonial questions.   This was especially true of the secretary
who figures as a very considerable personage.[87]   He seems never to
have had a vacation.   He and at least some of his clerks were always
at their posts to receive communications and prepare business for
the meetings of the Board.   He opened the Board's letters;[88] he
transacted routine business, such as transmitting accounts to the
Treasury, without waiting for orders;[89] he interviewed petitioners
and visitors of all sorts, afterwards reporting their visits; he received
innumerable communications in his own name and answered many
of them, submitting his answer, however, for the Board's approval;
he had the custody of all papers and the supervision of all clerks.
If Mr. Penn postponed his attendance on the discussion of the
Pennsylvania boundary, it was the secretary that received and reported the message.   If the Board wished to interview certain men.
it was the secretary who found out in some way that they were or
were not in town.   If the Lords of the Treasury or the Commissioners of Customs sent a message, it was usually delivered in the
morning before the Commissioners of Trade had arrived, but the
secretary was always there to receive it.   He abstracted lengthy

[85] B. T. J., LXXXIV. 78.   Serle is classified as a " Calvinist writer ".   He
was the author of the *Christian Remembrancer, Christian Husbandry, The Church
of God*, and other works.   From 1776 to 1778 he accompanied the British army
to America and during part of that time had control of the press in New York.
Dict. Nat. Biog.

[86] B. T. J., LXXXIX. 260.   Cumberland was a dramatist, beginning his literary career at an early age.   According to the article in the *Dictionary of
National Biography*, he owed his preferment to the favor of Lord Halifax.
According to that article, the latter made him " *his private Secretary in the
Board of Trade* " and as the office was " nearly a sinecure " he " amused himself
by studying history and composing an epic poem ".   The Journal contains no
record of his being a clerk in the office before his appointment as clerk of reports
in 1765. and Halifax had not been a member of the Board since 1761.

[87] His influence with the Board may be shown by an illustration.   On
December 17, 1746, the Board adjourned till January 11 following.   On December
23, the secretary called a meeting to receive a petition from the Bristol merchants against the edict of the French king.   B. T. J., XLVI. 189.

[88] B. T. J., IX. 309.

[89] The president of the Board also, at times, transacted business alone during
a recess.   For an illustration of this see Westmoreland's action, February 20,
1728.   B. T. J., XXXVIII. 43.

documents for the Board's convenience; procured books and papers for its use; summoned men to appear at its session; investigated various commercial projects; kept himself informed about the sailing of ships and other matters of interest. In fact everything that was done or said was passed in some way through the hands of this ever present secretary. Every detail from the misdemeanor of a clerk or the need of having a wall of the office whitewashed, to important matters of policy, was brought to the notice of the Board by this same official. It is a temptation to feel that the secretary of the Board of Trade must have been a really learned man on the subject of the colonies, or else the most mechanical worker in the kingdom.

It has been seen that the Board's establishment became constantly larger, and it naturally follows that it became also more expensive. The salaries of employees amounted to something like £800 in the earlier years and by the end of the period had reached £2000. But this was only one source of expense. The Commissioners themselves were drawing a salary of £1000 each.[90] Besides this there was the cost of housing, light, heat, materials, and postage. For the whole they were dependent on the Treasury. Curiously enough, no systematic arrangement was made at first to furnish the Board with funds. George Stepney reported, December 31, 1697, that he had paid for the new commission in which his name was inserted, to the amount of £70, out of his own pocket, and asked to be reimbursed from the Treasury.[91] In the following April some of the employees were believed to be in actual want, their salaries being one year in arrears.[92] In February a novel arrangement was resorted to. The secretary received from the Treasury £150 in Malt Lottery tickets of £10 each, and was ordered to "sell these as best he can".[93] In May one Mr. Berry presented a bill for maps, and the secretary was ordered to give him a malt ticket and the rest in money; but the secretary being entirely out of the latter, was sent out into the city to dispose of more tickets.[94] Indeed the malt tickets continued to be

[90] The Journal contains no statement of the amount of salary received by the Lords of Trade. From the Treasury Papers we know that in 1730 it was £1000 each, and it is not at all likely that this would decrease. Moreover, Edmund Burke declared in 1780 that the salary was £1000. On the other hand, Edward Gibbon wrote, "I was appointed one of the Lords Commissioners of Trade and Plantations and my private income was enlarged by a clear addition of between £700 and £800 a year". *Memoirs of Edward Gibbon* (ed. Henry Morley), p. 276. See *Calendar of Treasury Books and Papers*, 1729–1730, p. 407, and *Works of Edmund Burke*, II. 109.

[91] B. T. J., X. 386.
[92] *Ibid.*, XI. 17.
[93] *Ibid.*, X. 424.

the chief source of supply throughout the year. Even when they were gone, the Board received a somewhat precarious support at the hands of the Treasury,[93] the salaries being frequently in arrears.[94]

It gradually became the custom to send to the Treasury every quarter—at Lady Day, Midsummer, Michaelmas, and Christmas—an itemized account which, besides the clerks' salaries, included the secretary's account for incidentals, the stationer's bill, and a bill for postage. To this was added once a year a bill for " wood and coals " or " wood, coals and candles ".[97] The bills were prepared and presented by the secretary and were frequently gone over, article by article, and signed by the Board before being sent to the Treasury. The amounts varied greatly from year to year. In 1708 this quarterly bill, apart from salaries, was £506 1d., of which £266 11s. 2d. were for postage. In the reign of George I., the bills were ranging between £400 and £900 and by 1730 had reached £1200. For some years accounts were not kept in detail. By 1763 the cost of maintaining the office had grown to £2098 4s., and this too, in spite of the fact that since 1746 all correspondence of the Board had been sent free of postage.

For years postage was a real burden. As early as October, 1696, William Blathwayt, in delivering a package of letters from the plantations, said that if free postage was not allowed as for the late Committee of Trade and Plantations the charge would soon amount to £500 per annum.[98] This estimate was somewhat exaggerated and produced no result. The Board asked for free postage in 1697,[99] but it was not granted, and bills from the Post-Office were frequently received[100] in spite of the fact that the quarterly estimate of expense always included an account with the postmaster. The charges on one box of papers from America, in the summer of 1746,

[93] B. T. J., XI. 55.

[94] Though a part of the government, the Board appears in some respects more like a private organization. Thus it paid for its own commission—evidently a fee for passing the commission under the seal. It paid for statutes, copies of bills before the House of Commons, etc. Judging from the Journal, each branch of the government paid every other branch for service done as though all had not been parts of one great whole.

[95] B. T. J., XXIII. 316; XXXIII. 128; XXXIV. 20; XXXV. 191. In 1769 the Board was in debt. B. T. J., LXXVII. 1.

[97] Besides the bills presented by the Board, the Treasury paid a good many fees presented individually. The attorney-general and solicitor-general before 1718, and after that the counsel-at-law, were paid for each attendance. So also were clerks of the Council and various servants and messengers. After the appointment of the counsel-at-law the Treasury decided that the attorney's and solicitor's fees should be taken out of the incidental expenses. B. T. J., XXX. 326. *Treas. Papers*, 1728–1730, p. 114.

[98] B. T. J., IX. 192.

[99] *Ibid.*, X. 127.

[100] E. g., ibid., XIII. 244; XXXIX. 28, 240.

was "upwards of £30".[101] To this the Lords of Trade objected,
and it was probably as a result of their complaint that the king[102] in
November issued a warrant to the Postmaster General[103] freeing
from postage all letters of the Board of Trade. In 1764 an act of
Parliament was passed to "prevent frauds and abuses in the sending
and receiving of letters and packets free of postage".[104] By this act
the officers and departments that were exempted from postage, including the Board of Trade and Plantations, were required to
authorize two persons each in their respective offices to endorse
letters. The Board of Trade appointed for this duty Richard
Rogers the deputy secretary and Silas Bradbury the clerk of reports,
and decided on a form of endorsement as follows:[105]

15

	On His Majesty's Service
	R^d Rogers
Office of	to Mr. Thos. Styles
Trade and	at
Plantations.	Portsmouth.

All letters and packages authorized by the Board were supposed to
be superscribed according to this model.[106]

The importance of postage as an item of expense is not so surprising when one considers the large amount of written matter
which found its way to the Board by post, and this is only part of the
immense mass of manuscript material preserved in the office. When
Burke made his celebrated attack on the Board he ridiculed its 2300
volumes of reports[107] and very likely this was not exaggerated. The
Journal alone from 1675 to 1782 comprises ninety large volumes.[108]
Perhaps a brief description of the Board's system of book-keeping
will throw some light on its methods. The transactions of each
meeting were reported, supposedly in full, in the Journal, the account containing the date and place of meeting, the names of those

[101] *Ibid.*, LIV. 71.

[102] *Ibid.*, p. 85.

[103] In October, 1755, the Postmaster General wrote to the Board that he had
provided vessels for regular monthly correspondence with the colonies. B. T. J.,
LXIII. 303.

[104] 4 Geo. III., c. 24.

[105] B. T. J., LXXII. 182.

[106] There was at a later date some controversy as to whether or not the Lords
of Trade were individually entitled to exemption under this act. B. T. J.,
LXXXVIII. 179.

[107] *Parl. Hist.*, XXI. 235.

[108] I have seen only the manuscript copies in the Historical Society of
Pennsylvania. I understand that they are an exact reproduction of the original,
not only in subject-matter but in paging, division of volumes, etc.

present, and usually a detailed report of all that took place. The last is, for the most part, naïve and straightforward and makes the reader feel that he has almost been present and watched the Board at its work. A vast army of men and women throughout these eighty-six years appeared at the Plantation Office and either made complaints or furnished information on some phase of the colonies or trade. Such complaints and information, when given orally as they frequently were, were reported in the Journal, often in the minutest detail, and plentifully sprinkled with quotations from the speaker's own words. In this way, not only the general heads of colonial business, but also in great measure the personality of the visitors, is preserved for the student. There were times when many details were omitted, owing no doubt to neglect. Especially at times between 1730 and 1740 it was not uncommon to make a more perfunctory and less picturesque account of the day's proceedings, but in the main, description is full. To the secretary, with the help of the clerks, was entrusted the compilation of reports and it was necessary to impose some check on them. To this end it was decided on December 20, 1714, that henceforth the minutes of each meeting should be read at the next meeting, and before being entered in the Journal should be signed by the commissioner highest in rank who should be present at the reading and had also been present when the business was transacted.[109] This rule was re-enacted from time to time.[110] and was for the most part adhered to, to the end of the Board's career.

But the Journal was, as we have seen, only a small part of the Board of Trade papers. To this must be added innumerable documents in the form of petitions, complaints, depositions, letters, narratives, etc., which in one way or another were introduced into the office, besides the bulky colonial correspondence which[111] was kept up more or less regularly throughout the entire history of the Board. All this material from whatever source was filed away in sections arranged according to subject. There was a bundle—or collection of bundles—for each colony; one marked " Proprieties " dealing with matters peculiar to proprietary governments; one called " Plantations General " having to do with matters of general colonial concern; a bundle on Trade, doubtless with subdivisions; and a miscellaneous one which included, among other things, all papers referring to the internal affairs of the Board itself. When one considers

[109] B. T. J., XXIV. 341.

[110] *E. g., ibid.,* XXXVII. 183: LVI. 100.

[111] This was at times in duplicate, the originals being sent to the Secretary of State.

16

that the series "Plantations General"[112] alone occupies thirty-one large folio volumes, and "Proprieties"[113] twenty-four of the same sort, it is possible to imagine the extent of the whole collection. The Board's method of book-keeping, at its best, involved marginal notes. In the margin, opposite each reference to papers, was an abbreviated word, indicating the department in which such papers had been filed. Besides this there was, during part of the period, an exact citation to the series, bundle, and number of paper within the bundle. As time went on the clerks became more careless about this and at times it was omitted altogether. Some papers referred to more than one colony and of these duplicates might be made by the clerks, and a copy filed in each of several bundles. This is not the only case of duplication. In December, 1699, a fire in the Cockpit caused some fear that the disaster of the previous year might be repeated. Fearing the destruction of the records the Board thought seriously of having them all transcribed in order to keep duplicates in a separate place, and ordered a "competent number of sacks" for carrying them away.[113] The only evidence of such duplication is found in certain entry books in a series called Trade Papers.[114] Perhaps want of funds defeated the project. In a few isolated cases the Journal, for no apparent reason, contains two copies of the same minutes.[115]

The Board of Trade not only accumulated papers of its own, but started life with a considerable stock-in-trade bequeathed from previous councils, commissions, and committees of like purpose. The continuous Journal for some reason begins, not with the forming of the Board in 1696, but with the appointment of the committee of Privy Council which took the place of the disestablished Council of Trade and Plantations in 1675. Before that time the records were somewhat fragmentary. In July, 1696, the books and papers of the Plantation Office which were in the hands of Povey, a clerk of the Privy Council, were, by an order of Council, turned over to William Popple, the secretary of the new Board.[116] Blathwayt presented further papers in 1703.[117] In 1707 an effort was made to

17

[112] According to the Pennsylvania transcript.

[113] B. T. J., XII. 302.

[114] On authority of Dr. C. M. Andrews.

[115] Thus at the beginning of volume XXIX. there are a few pages that duplicate others at the end of volume XXVIII., and cover the minutes of July 21, 22, 24, 28, 29, 30, and August 4, 5, 1719. December 18, 1735, and February 4 to April 18, 1777, are duplicated, and December 30, 1777, duplicated and enlarged.

[116] B. T. J., IX. 33.

[117] *Ibid.*, XVI. 137. Blathwayt also had been a clerk of the Privy Council but was now a member of the Board of Trade, having been named in the first commission in 1696.

purchase colonial papers that had been preserved in private hands, but this seems to have failed.[118]

Besides official documents, a large amount of printed and illustrative material was acquired by purchase and otherwise. A few illustrations will suffice. In March, 1697, "on suggestion that some of the public printed newspapers sometimes contain matters of fact that may be useful to be known for the service of this commission", it was ordered that one of each be taken.[119] In July, 1738, a copy of Rymer's *Foedera* was bought for the office.[120] In 1734 Henry Popple, the secretary's brother, having published a set of maps of the British Empire, a subscription was made for the Board, and one also for each governor in America.[121] Many maps both published and unpublished were received by gift and purchase. Indeed the collection of books and maps which graced the shelves of the Lords of Trade must have been a considerable one and one also which would be of great interest to-day. These books were not only used by the Board itself but were to a certain extent given circulation. It was common for books and maps to be lent to outsiders, a receipt being taken by the secretary[122] and a description of the missing article sometimes tacked up in the office.[123]

It does not appear that the Board followed any set rule of procedure, but in the general character of its routine and methods of business there is sufficient uniformity to admit of a fairly accurate description. After a new commission had been received internal affairs of the Board were always considered first. The commission was formally read and the new members, if in town, "took their places at the Board". If not in town at that time a new member

[118] In May, 1698, the Board, hearing that Mr. Henry Crisp had books of entry and papers of the Council of Trade of 1662–1663, ordered the secretary to ask him to bring them to the Board. On May 10 he answered that he had never seen any papers of the Council of Trade of 1662, but had heard that some such papers, in the hands of his father-in-law, Mr. Duke, who was secretary of that Council, were burnt in the Temple. He promised to find out about this and also to bring papers of the Royal Fishery of that time of which Duke was secretary. B. T. J., XI. 48, 53. He seems not to have come back, but in June, 1707, the Board received a letter from one Crisp, whom I take to be the same man, offering to sell books and minutes of the Council of Trade, 1660–1668. The Board refused to buy the books without seeing them and there was no result. *Ibid.*, XIX. 284, 296.

[119] B. T. J., X. 20.

[120] *Ibid.*, XLVIII. 73.

[121] *Ibid.*, XLIII. 161 ; XLIV. 174. *Cal. of Treas. Books and Papers*, 1731–1734, pp. 419, 576.

[122] E. g., *ibid.*, XXIII. 257.

[123] *Ibid.*, LXXXVIII. 29. The Board not only lent but also borrowed. In September, 1697, it was determined to ask Mr. William Bird of Lincoln's Inn for the use of his complete set of Virginia laws. *Ibid.*, X. 261.

would be formally admitted later and his admission noted in the
minutes. After the reading of the minutes, rules were frequently
adopted similar to those already considered in connection with the
clerks, new clerks were appointed if necessary, and in fact anything
might be presented and discussed which had to do with the office
itself.[124] Whatever time was left at this session was devoted to the
question of colonies or trade that happened to be most pressing. On
ordinary days such matters were taken up at the outset. If a petition had been received from merchants or colonists, it was presented
by the secretary and considered by the Board. In most cases the
Commissioners would not feel prepared to decide on such a petition
without further information. They would, therefore, set a day for
the discussion and order the secretary to summon persons to be
present at the hearing. The subject might be suggested orally instead of by written petition. A large number of matters that came
up for discussion were introduced in this way: "the Secretary acquainted the Board" that a certain man was without and wished to
be heard. He was called in to state his case, and his information,
be it trivial or important, was recorded in the minutes. He was
then instructed to "put what he had to offer in writing". Perhaps
a day was set for the further consideration of his demands, at
which time he not only brought in a written statement, but most
likely brought with him several other men to corroborate his asser-
tions. A "hearing", whether the result of a written petition or an
oral request, was often a lengthy affair, and involved the testimony
of various persons.

If a letter was received from a colonial governor,[125] together with
the voluminous enclosures which always accompanied such letters,
this too was presented by the secretary and read. The enclosed
papers also might be read through, which in some cases must have
been a heroic proceeding. In any case they were disposed of in the
proper bundles, and usually a list of titles or descriptions preserved
in the minutes. If the papers included copies of laws—and nearly
every packet did include some—these were dispatched to the attorney-general or solicitor-general or, after 1718, to the Board's special

[124] Even the most trivial matters were brought to the attention of the Board.
Thus at one time the "necessary woman" presented a bill of £10 for "mops and
brooms" which the Board considered too high. B. T. J., XI. 393.

[125] Such letters, as well as petitions and other papers, might as a rule either be
sent directly to the Board by post, or be sent first to the Privy Council or Secretary of State, and transmitted to the Board for consideration. The procedure
within the Board itself, *i. e.*, the presentation by the secretary, etc., was the same
in either case.

counsellor, to be reported upon from a legal point of view.[126] In the later years when laws came in great numbers the counsel-at-law frequently attended the Board, and a whole session—or more than one—was given to a single set of acts, each being carefully read and passed upon.[127] In either case, when the legal report was made, which was sometimes done promptly and at other times after a very long delay,[128] the Board prepared a representation to the King in Council incorporating the legal advice, and sent it with the laws themselves for the final action of the king. After consideration in the Council, which usually[129] resulted in confirming the Board's judgment, the laws were returned to the Board with an Order in Council approving or disallowing them as the case might be. This decision was reported to the colonial assembly by the Board of Trade.

When a new governor was appointed for a colony directly under the crown, his commission and instructions were prepared by the Board and approved by the king. In the case of a proprietary governor, the commission was issued by the proprietor, but the instructions were prepared by the Board and imposed through the proprietor on his appointee.

Whatever the business in hand every document[130] went through three stages. First, the subject was considered and the substance

[126] Legal advisers were not the only ones consulted. Questions were frequently submitted to the Lords of the Treasury, Lords of the Admiralty. Navy Board, Board of Ordnance, Commissioners of Customs, and other parts of the government on matters pertaining to these respective offices. Messages were constantly being sent back and forth. Indeed the administration was a perfect network of separate but related authorities.

[127] For an illustration of this see B. T. J., XLV. 94. Comments were written after each law—"no objection", "to lie over", etc.

[128] Thus on June 22, 1699, the secretary reported that the clerk of the solicitor-general had brought to the Board certain acts of Massachusetts, passed before the establishment of this office, with no report on them. They were ordered sent back to the solicitor for his opinion. B. T. J., XI. 102. The Board also was sometimes responsible for delays. On November 29, 1728, they discussed a New Jersey act for a partition line, etc., and "considering that it had lain by above nine years in this office and no objection had been offered" they ordered a representation for confirming the act. B. T. J., XXXVIII. 265.

[129] Of course the Board's decisions might be reversed or modified, or a law or report might be returned for reconsideration. I believe, however, that if the total number of laws considered could be brought together, it would be found that in a large majority of cases the Board's decision was affirmed.

[130] At first there seems to be a distinction between a report and a representation. The latter was the more formal paper addressed to the King in Council, while a report was less formal and was addressed to the Committee of Council. As time went on and the committee came to act in place of the Council, the two words were used more or less interchangeably. Thus on June 29, 1731, the Board signed what in the text is called a representation, but in the margin, a report. B. T. J., XLI. 169. Communications to the Secretary of State were usually called letters.

of the letter or report agreed upon—a process which was sometimes adjourned from day to day and occupied the greater part of several sessions. At last the Board ordered the letter, outlining to the secretary the points which it was to involve. The actual composition fell to the secretary who presented a first draught to the Commissioners for inspection. If satisfactory it was "approved and ordered to be transcribed". It was then delivered to a clerk to be put into final form, and having been "transcribed fair" was presented to the Board again for signature. Two classes of papers constituted exceptions to this rule: many of the less important letters having been ordered and approved by the Board, were signed by the secretary[131] and sent off without waiting for another meeting; and commissions and instructions for colonial officers, having been transcribed, were sent to the king for his signature.[132] In many cases a number of days might elapse between the stages of this process, while if there was need of haste they might all be performed in one day.[133]

Many questions of dispute were argued pro and con, before the Board; and on such occasions both parties attended with "Counsel learned in the law". The hearing which ensued sometimes lasted for days and had the semblance of a trial, with testimony and legal battles over technicalities which would do credit to a modern court.[134] In cases of appeal the Board itself had no jurisdiction. When once a decision had been rendered in the colonies, there was no appeal except to the king. The Board however could give such a case a preliminary hearing when asked to do so by a reference from the King in Council.[135]

[131] Or the deputy secretary might sign letters in rare cases. See a letter from Samuel Gellibrand, deputy secretary, to John Hamilton, August 23, 1743. *N. J. Archives,* VI. 153.

[132] The Board might prepare other papers for the king's signature. Thus in March, 1700, the Board was ordered by the Council to prepare the draught of an Order of Council, whereby the king could approve an agreement between New York and Connecticut over the boundary. B. T. J., XII. 410.

[133] This preparing of reports was not the only duty that occupied the clerks in their outer room. Many papers from the colonies were copied and duplicates sent to the Secretary of State, Lords of the Treasury, Commissioners of Customs, and others. Then, too, when a petition was being heard before the Privy Council, the petitioner would frequently ask the Board for copies of papers in its possession bearing on his case, and the request was often granted. It was in such cases as this that the clerks were entitled to fees for extra work.

[134] On February 9, 1720, the solicitor-general gave an opinion that the Board had power to administer the oath to witnesses. B. T. J., XXX. 80–83. It might be noted also, that the Board seems to have had a seal. On June 9, 1720, this was considered. His Majesty's engraver had presented a plan, and this had been sent to Sunderland, then first Lord of the Treasury, who "thought it very proper", and then to the king who ordered it engraved. *Ibid.,* p. 191.

[135] B. T. J., XXXII. 167.

The Board's methods might involve a division of labor. Thus in 1697, considering that it was impossible for all the "voluminous papers sent from the Plantations" to be read at the meetings, it was decided to divide up the field. Philip Meadows was to give special attention to Virginia and Maryland; William Blathwayt, and in his absence, John Locke, was to look after Jamaica, Barbados, and the Leeward Islands; to Abraham Hill fell New England, New York, and Newfoundland; while John Pollexfen was expected to care for the Proprieties, the charter colonies, and trade in general.[136] All papers relating to these subjects were to be read by the persons to whom they were assigned and the important parts extracted for consideration by the Board. This was simply a refinement of the process of extraction, since that was one duty that the Board performed for the Privy Council. The plan, however, was short-lived. Another method sometimes resorted to was that of having each member draw up an independent report on some subject, and compiling a representation from a comparison of these separate plans. This was done in 1697 in connection with the English and Irish trade, and John Locke's scheme being "pitched upon" was considered in detail.[137]

Though the work of the Board was, as a rule, performed by the seven or eight members appointed by name, these never forgot that an equal number of high state officers belonged in theory to their institution. When a new Secretary of State was appointed, or a Chancellor of the Exchequer, or any other officer included in the Board's list, a letter was at once dispatched to inform him that he was "a member of this Commission".[138] When a matter of special importance was to be dealt with the ex-officio members were summoned by letter.[139] They seldom stayed to the end of the meeting. If Secretary Vernon, for instance, and several others came down to the Board, as soon as the important subject was disposed of they withdrew, whereupon the Board ordered a letter to Secretary Vernon, informing him, as Secretary of State, of what had been done at the Board of Trade. These meetings of "extraordinary Board" were usually held at night. Moreover the Commissioners of Trade might be summoned to a joint meeting with the Privy Council or

---

[136] The Earls of Bridgewater and Tankerville seem to have escaped this by their titles. John Methuen, the eighth member, was in Portugal and did not return while his name was included in the Commission of Trade. He never took his place at the Board. B. T. J., IX. 348. *Hist. MSS. Comm., Portland*, III. 576.

[137] B. T. J., X. 207, 214.

[138] *E. g., ibid.*, XIII. 288.

[139] *Ibid.*, X. 424; XXIV. 16.

with a committee of Council.[140] At the close of such a conference, they adjourned to their own room and continued the session alone, perhaps to put into effect the decisions of the joint meeting, but always to take some account of them in their minutes. On the other hand the conference might take place at the Plantation Office. At one time a meeting of " Cabinet Council "[141] was held at the Board, and again word was received that the Committee of Council had " appointed a meeting at this Board tomorrow ".[142]

Under peculiar conditions the Board might devote its sessions to a special purpose. Thus after the treaty of Utrecht many days were given up wholly or in part to the examining of debentures and delivering them to claimants of land in Nevis and St. Christopher. As many as fifty debentures were sometimes delivered in one day, and this must have brought a constant stream of ill-assorted visitors. In 1749–1750, when the settlement of Halifax was being arranged for, the Board of Trade appeared at times more like a business office than a department of government.[143] Chauncey Townshend, a merchant who took the contract to furnish provisions, was in almost constant attendance. To the Board came men who wanted to furnish clothing, medicines, ploughs, and other commodities for the settlers. It was the Board that appointed physicians and surgeons, ministers and schoolmasters, the man authorized to erect saw-mills, and so on, through the almost endless detail. Here arrangements were made for transportation and the proper ventilation of ships. Here, too, came every settler that wished to sail, giving an account of his circumstances and the size of his family, and receiving from the clerk of reports a certificate admitting him on ship-board. It must have been a motley crowd indeed, which in those days thronged the Cockpit, in answer to the Board's advertisement of advantages published in the *London Gazette*.

Through its supervision over trade the Board came into close touch with the seafaring man from everywhere: the merchant from India, Africa, Muscovy or the Levant, the Newfoundland fisherman, the West Indian slave-trader, the dealer in Canary wines or Irish linen or American staves, all came to the Board to tell their stories. Not only did the Lords of Trade solicit information from the merchants, but the merchants solicited attention from them. If a man

[140] *E. g., ibid.,* XIV. 446; XV. 104; XVII. 8; XXXIX. 263; XLI. 287; LIX. 74, etc. On July 1, 1702, the Board received a letter from Mr. War, with the queen's will that the Board attend her at committee at St. James, to-morrow at 11. *Ibid.,* XV. 115.
[141] B. T. J., XI. 68.
[142] *Ibid.,* XXII. 417.
[143] *Ibid.,* LVII., LVIII., *passim.*

23

wanted a patent for an invention, or protection for an industry, he
had to produce some proof that he was able to make use of it. To
the Board of Trade came not only his testimonials—and they came
in great numbers—but also his demonstrations. For example, in
August, 1696, during a discussion of the linen trade, Mr. Furmin
displayed the model of a spinning-wheel of his own invention which
could be manipulated "by a girl of ten".[144] Various were the bundles of merchandise that found their way into the Colonial Office.
A box of clothing, sent to New York for the soldiers during Lord
Cornbury's administration, and returned as unfit for use, was
brought to the Board and publicly opened.[145] Samples of wool were
now and then received, and specimens of copper. Thomas Lowndes
was fond of sending certificates of the goodness of his salt,[146] accompanied by boxes of it by way of illustration.[147] John Plowman,
who asked for a patent for curing sturgeon in 1720, produced a
box of fish at the Board to show the merit of his method.[148]

Not only were boxes of merchandise sent to the Board, but the
living curiosities that came to town were looked upon as belonging
to its province. Thus in 1697 when five Mohawk Indians were
brought to Plymouth among French prisoners, the Board was closely
concerned in their care. Two of them made a visit to London for
the purpose of sight-seeing and these were presented to the Board
of Trade.[149] In 1730 an African trader, Bulfinch Lamb, and his
black interpreter, Captain Tom, attended the Board and presented a
letter from the Emperor of Dahomey.[150]

Perhaps the most picturesque scene that ever took place in the
council chamber of the Board of Trade was the consummation of a

[144] B. T. J., IX. 51.
[145] *Ibid.*, XVI. 131.
[146] *E. g., ibid.*, LIII. 118.
[147] *Ibid.*, LI., pt. 2, p. 46. Thomas Lowndes is a curious illustration of the
sort of peculiar personality with which the Board had at times to deal. He was
constantly appearing with a proposal, a request, or a complaint. In 1734 he
objected to a land-grant in South Carolina, claiming that he had a conflicting
grant. He emphasized this claim by making personal charges against Popple in a
stilted paper called " Thomas Lowndes' protest against the Lords Com^rs declared
Prepossession in favor of their Secretary ". It is amusing to note the seriousness
with which the Board considered this paper and resolved "to have no further
correspondence with the said Lowndes ". A few months later he wrote again at
length, asserting that Popple had helped to cheat him out of £60. He said that
if he did not abhor " disserving his country " he could show a " neighboring
nation how to deprive Great Britain of a valuable branch of trade without
infringing any treaty ". This epistle was honored with a set of five resolutions
by the Board. *Ibid.*, XLIV., *passim.*
[148] B. T. Plant. Gen., L. 5.
[149] B. T. J., X. 66.
[150] *Ibid.*, XLI. 117. *Cal. of Treas. Books and Papers*, 1731–1734, p. 88.

treaty with seven chiefs of the Cherokee Nation in September, 1730.[151] On the seventh, the chiefs and their interpreter attended, together with Colonel Johnson, the agent for Indian affairs, and Sir William Keith, governor of South Carolina. The members of the Board present that day were Thomas Pelham, Martin Bladen, and James Brudenell. They had taken care to have Sir William Keith prepare beforehand the form of a treaty with its imagery and phraseology modelled after Indian ideals. They had also asked for and obtained from the War Office the attendance of two sergeants and twelve grenadiers. When all were assembled one member of the Board, by means of an interpreter, read to the Indians the treaty, which was in part as follows:

25

Now the great King of Great Britain bearing love in his heart to the powerful and great nation of the Cherokee Indians, his good friends and allies, His Majesty has empowered us to treat with you here, as if the whole nation of the Cherokees, their old men, young men, wives and children, were all present. And you are to understand the words we speak as the words of the great king, our master, whom you have seen, and we shall understand the words you speak to us as the words of all your people with open and true hearts to the great king. . . . He takes it kindly that the great nation of the Cherokees sent you hither a great way to brighten the chain of friendship between him and them and between your people and his people; that the chain of friendship between him and the Cherokee Indians is like the sun which shines here and also upon the great mountains where they live and equally warms the heart of the Indians and of the English. That as there are no spots or Blackness on the sun so is there not any Rust or Foulness in this chain and as the great King has fastened one end of it to his own breast he desires you will carry the other end of the chain and fasten it well to the breasts of your nation. . . . And here upon we give four pieces of white cloth to be dyed blue.

The next article regulated trade between the Indians and the people of Carolina. The following articles stipulated, among other things, that the Indians were to keep peace with the English and make war on their enemies, that they were to refuse to trade with any other nation and were to return fugitive slaves. At the end of each article presents were given, including large quantities of ammunition and " six dozen hatchets, twelve dozen spring-knives, four dozen brass kettles and ten dozen belts ". Samples of all these articles were stowed away somewhere in the office and were shown to the Indians at the close of the interview. They expressed their approval and promised to give an answer in two days.

The second conference, on the ninth, must have been as imposing as the first. The soldiers attended as before. The Commissioners of Trade, who, this time were Bladen, Brudenell, and Paul Docinin- ique, found themselves addressed as follows ·

[151] B. T. J., XL. 226-237.

We are come hither from a dark, mountainous place, where nothing but darkness is to be found, but are now in a place where there is light. . . . We look upon you as if the great King George was present, and we love you as representing the great King, and shall die in the same way of thinking. . . . We look upon the great King George as the Sun and as our Father and upon ourselves as his Children, for though we are red and you white, yet our hands and hearts are joined together.

Having finished this speech the spokesman of the Cherokees walked to the table, and, laying down upon it a bunch of feathers as a symbol of his good-will said:

This is our way of talking, which is the same to us as your letters in the Book are to you; and to you, Beloved Men, we deliver these feathers in token of all we have said and of our agreement to your article.

This incident not only adds a touch of color to the picture, but also illustrates fairly well one phase of the Board's position. A treaty of peace with the Cherokee Nation might vitally affect the happiness and welfare of the colony of Carolina, and was therefore by no means beneath the dignity of the government. But the Privy Council could hardly be expected to exchange scalping-knives for feathers or pronounce a speech like the one above, in Indian terms. Such a duty must be delegated to a subordinate authority, and that authority was the Board of Trade. Indeed the treaty-making power of the Board is here displayed at a low ebb, for it had a part in negotiations of much greater importance. The point to be noted here is that the Board of Trade stood between the King in Council on the one hand, and the outlying portions of the empire on the other. As a result of this position it could, and did many times, give advice and submit policies, but at all times it furnished information. That such information was needed there can be no doubt. In those days reliable knowledge of remote corners of the earth was not easily accessible as it is to-day. Travel was slow. Modern methods of communication were not invented and printed material was expensive and scarce. There was considerable ignorance, even in government circles, about the British possessions. For example, the Commissioners of Customs asked the Board at one time if Campeche was an English plantation[182] and at another time if Annamabore was a "colony, territory or place belonging to His Majesty".[183] Such questions the Board was expected to answer.

By close connection with colonists and merchants the Board kept its finger, so to speak, on the colonial and commercial pulse, and helped to diagnose disorders for treatment by a higher power. That

---

[182] B. T. J., XXXVIII. 37.
[183] *Ibid.,* LXXXIII. 47.

the touch was always acute or the diagnosis always correct, no one can claim. That the contact was of much value can hardly be denied. Dropping the figure, the Board of Trade and Plantations was the one place at which all elements of the ever-growing British Empire could come together on common ground. Here came the British merchant from any corner of the globe to describe his trade or display his wares. Here came the wealthy proprietor to defend his boundaries or the lowliest colonist to settle his dispute; the Indian chief to make peace, or the foreign settler to arrange for his emigration. To this same place all papers regarding the colonies were likely in the end to find their way—books, maps, descriptions, primitive newspapers, pamphlets, anonymous letters, anything that could add a touch to the Englishman's knowledge of the New World across the sea. Here too could come or send, the Commissioners of Customs or of the Treasury, the Navy Board, or Lords of the Admiralty, to gather such information as the Board had been able to collect. Surely nothing could be more useful in theory than just such an information bureau as the Board of Trade. But it is difficult to look constantly at such masses of minute detail and still see things in the large. The Board had the power of a subcommittee coupled with the outward form of a Council of State; perhaps it is not surprising that while the colonies were growing into prominence and colonial questions were becoming acute, it was losing its grasp and was settling down into a more and more formal and expensive institution.

MARY PATTERSON CLARKE.

27

COLONIAL APPEALS TO THE PRIVY COUNCIL. I

THE rise of the king in council to the position of a court of last resort for colonial judicial appeals is a subject of much interest for the student of American constitutional law.[1] Not only did the Privy Council come to sustain a relation to the colonial courts analogous in a general way to that which the United States Supreme Court bears to the state courts in our present system, but at least three cases appealed to the English tribunal involved the important principle of American jurisprudence which accords to the judiciary the power of declaring invalid an act of a subordinate legislature.

The appellate jurisdiction of the king in council secured important advantages both to the colonist and to the crown. To the colonist, it represented a means of relief from arbitrary proceedings of colonial courts, which were sometimes swayed by local prejudices rather than controlled by considerations of law and justice. To the crown this appellate control afforded a means of preventing important changes in colonial law without the consent of the mother country; and it also served the purpose of correcting judgments given in the colonial courts to the disadvantage of the crown.[2]

I

The legal status of appeals from the American colonies was fixed by three classes of enactments: (1) regulations of the home government affecting appeals, as expressed in orders of the king in council and in commissions and instructions to the colonial governors; (2) colonial charters and grants from the crown; and (3) laws passed by colonial legislatures affecting

[1] This study is confined to appeals from the British colonies that later formed the thirteen original states of the United States.

[2] According to a representation sent to the Council of Trade in 1715 by the king's orders, the home government believed that the system of appeals "contribute[d] very much towards keeping Governors and Plantation Courts in awe." Colonial Records of North Carolina, II, 161.

appeals.   This threefold arrangement does not denote that each
set of regulations had its own special and peculiar functions to
perform; it signifies rather that, in a fashion characteristic of
British colonial administration, three organs were concerned in
dealing with conditions that might better have been regulated
by one.

The first general regulation of the matter by the crown was
the order in council of January 23, 1684, that no appeals should
be admitted thereafter from the colonies without " sufficient
security . . . to prosecute their appeals effectually and to stand
the award of his Majesty in council thereupon." [1]   This order
specified no definite amount of security; it is evident that the
sum was to vary with the importance of the case.   The order
of 1684 also failed to mention a money value which a case
must involve before it was subject to appeal. [2]   But the commission issued to Thomas Dongan as royal governor of New
York, on June 10, 1686, named such a minimum amount in the
case of New York.   It also traced the main lines of all later commissions and instructions to colonial governors in respect to
appeal to the crown by announcing four principles or rules of
procedure: (1) "The matter in difference" must exceed the
value of £300 sterling; (2) the appeal must be made within a
fortnight after the decision of the colonial court; (3) security
must be given by the appellant to answer such charges as should
be awarded in case his appeal should not be sustained; and
(4) execution of the decree of the colonial court should not be

29

---

[1] Acts of the Privy Council of England, Colonial Series, II, no. 123.

[2] Three regulations of the king in council, applying however only to individual
colonial governments, preceded the general order of 1684. The commission of John
Cutt as governor of New Hampshire in 1679 and Cranfield's New Hampshire com-
mission of 1682 had designated £50 as the minimum value in an appealable case;
N. H. Provincial Papers, I, 373–382, 433–443. An instruction of 1682 to Lord
Culpeper, governor of Virginia, had specified a value of £100; Calendar of State
Papers, Colonial Series, America and West Indies, 1681–85, no. 384; Hening's
Statutes, III, 550–551. Professor H. L. Osgood notes that the commission of Joseph
Dudley as president of the temporary government of Massachusetts, September, 1685,
named £300 as the necessary amount; The American Colonies in the Seventeenth
Century, III, 384. A complete collection of governors' commissions and instructions
might perhaps show other instances.

suspended by reason of the appeal to the king in council.[1] This last provision worked an injustice in a number of cases and was modified after the year 1727, as will be noted later. The commission issued to Sir Edmund Andros as governor of New England in May, 1686, and his second commission of April, 1688, repeated these instructions and seemed to point to a definite policy of fixing £300 as the minimum amount for appealable cases.[2]   In 1689, however, a general instruction to the colonial governors forbade them to allow appeals to the king in council unless the estate or matter in question amounted to the value of £500 sterling.[3]   This instruction was probably meant for the island colonies and other possessions of England which were far wealthier than her American continental colonies, for the £300 rule is specified in a number of accessible commissions and instructions from 1690 down to 1730.[4]   To this rule, however, there were two temporary exceptions.   In New Hampshire, appeals were allowed to the king in council from 1692 to 1698 when the amount in dispute exceeded £100 sterling.[5]   In New Jersey, from 1702 to probably 1758, the minimum amount was fixed to exceed £200 sterling.[6]

Differentiation of the general class of appeals into particular

---

[1] New York Colonial Documents, III, 377–382.

[2] N. H. Provincial Papers, II, 1–10; N. Y. Colonial Documents, III, 537–542.

[3] N. C. Colonial Records, II, 161.

[4] Commission of Governor Sloughter of New York, January 4, 1690; N. Y. Colonial Documents, III, 623–629.   Commission of the royal governor, Lionel Copley, of Maryland, June 27, 1691; Maryland Archives, VIII, 263–271.   Commission of Benjamin Fletcher as governor of New York, March 18, 1692, and his commission as governor of Pennsylvania, June 27, 1692; N. Y. Colonial Documents, III, 827–833, 856–860.   Commissions of the Earl of Bellomont as governor of New York, June 18, 1697, and as governor of New Hampshire, of the same date; *ibid.* IV, 266–273; N. H. Provincial Papers, II, 305–312.   Commission of Governor Joseph Dudley of New Hampshire, April 1, 1702; N. H. Provincial Papers, II, 366–375.   Instructions of Governor Hunter of New York, December 27, 1709; N. Y. Colonial Documents, V, 124–143.   Instructions of the royal governor, George Burrington, of North Carolina, December 14, 1730; N. C. Colonial Records, III, 90–118.

[5] N. H. Provincial Papers, II, 57–62, 63–69.

[6] Instructions to Cornbury, November 16, 1702, in Grants and Concessions of New Jersey, 619–646; and to Morris, April 14, 1738, in N. J. Colonial Documents, VI, 15–51.

classes of cases with varying amounts necessary for the appeal began almost at once. The lack of a complete set of governors' instructions prevents an adequate statement respecting the first class of special causes: "all cases of Fines Imposed for misdemeanors." The first instruction in regard to such cases appeared as early as 1690, but the material accessible would indicate that throughout the period only three provinces were affected, namely, New York, New Jersey and North Carolina. Instructions to the governors of New York in 1690 and 1709 granted permission for appeal to the king in council "in all cases of Fines Imposed for misdemeanors, Providing the Fines so imposed exceed the Value of Two hundred Pounds."[1] In the case of New Jersey, instructions to the governors in 1702, 1738 and 1758 fixed the minimum amount in such cases at £200 sterling.[2] In North Carolina, instructions to the governors in 1730 and 1754 placed the minimum sum at £100 sterling.[3] The object of these regulations was evidently the prevention of extortionate penalties at the hands of the colonial officials; and their purpose, the protection of the subject. An examination of the cases appealed shows that few, if any, cases in this class were appealed.

31

In 1712 a question arose respecting a class of cases in which this time the home government had a particular interest. A controversy had arisen as a result of the anomalous religious situation then existing in New York. Upon the death of Mr. Urquhart, rector of the parish of Jamaica, Long Island, in 1710, Governor Hunter had inducted into office Mr. Thomas Poyer, a person duly qualified according to the royal instructions. But Poyer was kept out of the parsonage house and glebe by the Presbyterians, who laid claim to the property. Poyer was

unwilling to seek his remedy at Law, being apprehensive that if a Cause of the Church should be Tryed and Judged by Dissenters, he

---

[1] N. Y. Colonial Documents, III, 685–691; V, 124–143.

[2] Grants and Concessions, 619–646; N. J. Colonial Documents, VI, 15–51; IX, 40–77.

[3] N. C. Colonial Records, III, 90–118; V, 1107–1144.

Would not find Justice, and the Value of said House and Glebe being small, an Appeale would not Lye from the Inferiour to your Majesty's Govr and Councill there.

The Society for the Propagation of the Gospel brought this matter to the attention of the Privy Council in a representation and petition, which on July 28, 1712, the Council referred to the Board of Trade for its report. In accordance with the report of the Board of Trade, an order in council was issued on February 6, 1713, that appeals should be admitted to the governor and council, and thence to the Privy Council, in all cases where the clergy were immediately concerned, regardless of the amount of money in question.[1] From the evidence at hand, this exemption from the general rule seems to have been little used, if at all.

Before the close of the seventeenth century, the question arose whether cases involving an infraction of the Acts of Trade could be appealed to the king in council. On May 27, 1697, the Privy Council issued orders for admitting appeals by customs officers to the crown in cases of seizure for illegal trading.[2] This class of cases came to form a fair proportion of those appealed.

In 1727, a practice that had been working much injury to appellants was remedied. Previous to that time, the instructions of the colonial governors had contained a proviso that the execution of the decree of a colonial court should not be suspended by reason of an appeal to the king in council, in any case where a judgment first given by an inferior court was afterwards confirmed by the governor and council. From this regulation, great inconveniences and injustice had resulted,

---

[1] Acts of the Privy Council, II, no. 1168; N. Y. Colonial Documents, V, 345–346, 352; Documentary History of N. Y., III, 164–165.

[2] Acts of the Privy Council, II, no. 480. The principle involved is indicated in Attorney-General Northey's opinion in a Nevis case; Chalmers, G., Opinions of Eminent Lawyers on Various Points of English Jurisprudence, 531–532; and in a representation of the Committee for Appeals to the Privy Council; Acts of the Privy Council, II, no. 635. When the colonial courts of admiralty were held by virtue of the royal commission, the appeals were reviewed by the Privy Council; if held by authority derived from the admiralty of England, they were adjudicated by the British Court of Admiralty.

because by the time the decision of the king in council was learned in the colonies, the appellee had often become insolvent or had removed himself and his effects from the province. In such a case, when the colonial judgment was reversed and the order in council arrived for making a restitution of estates or goods, it became ineffectual and the appellant was left without redress. The instruction to the governors of February 8, 1727, required them

to Suspend the Execution of any Judgment or Decree, in case of an appeale, till the same be Determined at home, unless good and Sufficient Security be given by the Appellee to make Ample Restitution of all that the Appellant shall have lost by means of such Judgment or Decree,

33

in case it should be reversed.[1] This regulation seems to have removed all cause for complaint on that score thereafter; and it was uniformly embodied in all later instructions to colonial executives.

In the instructions of February 4, 1746, the king in council formulated in a single comprehensive enactment the different practices that had been authorized in previous years, and, profiting by past experiences, introduced a few innovations.[2] According to these instructions: (1) the appeal must be made within fourteen days after sentence had been declared; (2) "good security" must be given by the appellant that he would effectually prosecute his appeal and would answer the condemnation, as well as pay such costs and damages as might be awarded, should the colonial judgment be affirmed; (3) execution of the sentence of the colonial court must not be suspended, unless the appellee give ample security to cover any possible damages suffered by the appellant in case his appeal should be sustained; and (4) the amount involved in the case must exceed £500. But cases "where the matter in question

[1] Acts of the Privy Council, III, no. 100; N. Y. Colonial Documents, V, 816–817; N. C. Colonial Records, II, 637.

[2] Burge, W., Commentaries on Colonial and Foreign Laws, I, Introduction, xlvii, xlviii. These instructions comprise the best single statement which is to be found in reference to appeals.

relates to the taking or demanding any duty payable to us,"
i. e. the crown, " or to any fee of office, or annual rent, or any
such like matter or thing, where the right in future may be
bound " were to be subject to appeal although the amount involved were less than £500.[1]

Any attempt to summarize, for the entire colonial period,
the development of the law regarding the minimum value
necessary for appeal, as set forth in the regulations of the king
in council, is unsatisfactory, because, as we have seen, the
practice varied. The prevailing practice, however, may be
stated as follows:

(1) Except in special classes of cases the minimum value
requisite for appeal was £300 sterling until 1746; after that
date, it was raised to £500 sterling.

(2) In a number of colonies, if not in all, cases involving
fines imposed for misdemeanors could be appealed at a much
lower amount, usually £200 sterling.

(3) From the second decade of the eighteenth century on,
New York cases in which the clergy were immediately concerned could be appealed, regardless of the sum of money in
question. Had occasion arisen, this rule would probably have
been applied to the other colonies.

(4) After 1746, any cases encroaching upon the crown's
prerogative in the matter of the taking of a duty or annual rent
or fee of office or the like could be appealed, regardless of the
money value involved.

(5) To all regulations requiring a minimum sum for appeal,
the Privy Council throughout the eighteenth century upon
occasion allowed exceptions. The restraints on appeals were
viewed as restraints upon the colonial authorities alone and not
upon the king in council. Exceptional cases were brought to

---

[1] The rules formulated in the general instructions of 1746 were restated in subse-
quent instructions to single colonial governors Of these only three sets are to be
found in print: those of Governor Dobbs, of North Carolina, in 1754, of Governor
Bernard, of New Jersey, in 1758, and of Governor Moore, of New York, in 1765.
All these specify the higher minimum of £500, together with the exceptions re-
cited in the general instructions of 1746. N. C. Colonial Records, V, 1107–1144:
N. J. Colonial Documents, IX, 40-77; N. Y. Colonial Documents, VII, 764–765.
Sir Henry Moore's instructions are given only in part.

34

the attention of the Privy Council by means of a petition for liberty to appeal, presented by the would-be appellant. An example of such an appeal is to be found in the action of the Privy Council of March 29, 1715, when two cases of Samuel Lillie, of Boston, were admitted for final adjudication, although the amounts involved were in each instance less than £300.[1] The general practice in such cases was stated in the opinion of Attorney-General Northey, in reference to a Jamaica case, December 19, 1717. The attorney-general said that, notwithstanding the fixing of a definite amount necessary for appeal in the instructions to the governor, " it is in his Majesty's power, upon a petition, to allow an appeal in cases of any value where he shall think fit, and such appeals have been often allowed by his Majesty." [2]

A final word remains to be said concerning the regulations of the Privy Council. On April 14, 1752, instructions were sent to the colonial governors that the various colonies should revise their laws, as Virginia had done in 1748–1749. One of the avowed purposes of this order for the framing of a body of well-digested laws was that the determination of appeals from the colonial courts " depends upon being duly informed of the Laws subsisting there." On this account also, instructions were sent to the chartered colonies, whose laws were not subject to disapproval by the crown, that they should transmit as soon as convenient " a true and Authentic Copy of all their Laws." These directions of the home government were not received with favor by the colonial legislatures; and the Privy Council waived its plan in 1761.[3]

Until the end of the seventeenth century, the provisions of colonial charters were of importance in the matter of appeals to the Privy Council. Throughout the greater part of that century there were frequent instances in which the authorities in the chartered colonies successfully refused to permit appeals,

[1] Acts of the Privy Council, II, no. 1150. *Cf.* the Massachusetts case of Leighton *v.* Frost in 1735; *ibid.* III, no. 345.

[2] Chalmers, G., Opinions, 489–491.

[3] Acts Privy Council, IV, nos. 167, 210, 444.

35

basing their denial on provisions, or on the lack of provisions, in the royal grants.[1]

An examination of the colonial charters[2] yields the following results. The grant of Maine to Ferdinando Gorges, in 1639, contained a provision that might be interpreted to refer to the appellate jurisdiction of the crown, but the word "appeal" did not appear. The Carolina charters of 1663 and 1665 contained references in terms almost as general. The grant to the Duke of York, in 1664, of New York, New Jersey and Maine was the first fundamental law that expressly reserved to the king, his heirs and successors the determination of appeals from judgments given in the colonial courts. The same provision was repeated in the grant of 1674 and in the exemplification of this grant by Queen Anne in 1712. The charter of Pennsylvania of 1681 followed very closely the form of statement in the New York grant in regard to appeals. All these patents reserved the determination of appeals to the king, but it cannot be doubted that the king in council was meant. The latest charter to mention the appeals was the charter of Massachusetts Bay of 1691. In this charter, the provisions of which were evidently modeled on the Andros commissions of 1686 and 1688, the king in council was expressly designated as the appellate tribunal, and the usual four rules governing appeals were laid down,[3] with the variation that only *personal* actions were named as being appealable. This clause created much controversy in the eighteenth century, as will be noted later. In the charters of Rhode Island, Connecticut, Maryland and Georgia there was no direct recognition of the appellate jurisdiction of the crown, but there were provisions from which the right of appeal was inferable, namely, that the inhabitants of the colonies and their children should be deemed British subjects and should be entitled to all the liberties and immunities thereof, and that no laws should be made by the colonial legislatures repugnant to the law of the realm.

[1] Cf. *infra*, p. 292.

[2] Thorpe, F. N., Federal and State Constitutions was used.

[3] Including the giving of security by the appellee for the privilege of a non-suspension of the colonial judgment; cf. *supra*, pp. 284, 285.

As the eighteenth century approached, the home government assumed and maintained the position that it was a matter of no consequence whether or not the colonial charters contained provisions authorizing appeals. This doctrine was plainly enunciated, in 1701, in the opinion of the law officers of the crown, elicited by the refusal of Connecticut to permit appeals;[1] it received its most vigorous and extreme expression in the famous Privy Council case of Christian *v.* Corren, appealed from the Isle of Man in 1716.[2] In this case, the counsel for the appellant argued:

> The subject cannot be deprived of his right to appeal by any words in the King's grant to that purpose, much less if the grant be silent in that particular. . . . It was the right of the subjects to appeal to the sovereign to redress a wrong done to them in any court of justice; nay, if there had been any express words in the grant to exclude appeals, they had been void; because the subjects had an inherent right, inseparable from them as subjects, to apply to the crown for justice.

Upon the weight of this argument, the Privy Council admitted the appeal in question. The extent to which this doctrine was applied in American cases is shown by the fact that the king in council received and decided a larger number of appeals from Rhode Island, whose charter did not authorize appeals, than from any other colony.

In case of a conflict between a colonial enactment and an order in council, the colonial enactment prevailed; provided always, of course, that it was not disallowed by the home government. Not only was the colonial law theoretically superior in the particular colony, but the colonial legislature could enforce its will through its control of the budget.

The importance of the legislation affecting appeals varied in the different colonies. An examination of statutes of five colonies, Virginia, Connecticut, Massachusetts, New York and Rhode Island, seems to indicate that most of the colonial legislatures

---

[1] *Cf. infra*, pp. 294-296.

[2] Macqueen, Appellate Jurisdiction, 740, 741, quoting from Peere Williams' Reports, I, 329.

either did not concern themselves with the matter of appeals, thus yielding to the orders in council unobstructed sway, or gave legal sanction to the orders and instructions of the home government, with some slight variations. Additional legislation was sometimes passed, defining for the particular colony what was meant by the term " good security."

Virginia passed no laws concerning appeals until 1710, when an act of the legislature expressly asserted the queen's right of determining appeals " in such cases where the same . . . may be allowable by the order or instruction of her majesty, her heirs or successors . . . ; and that all such appeals, commissions and instructions shall be allowed, held good, valid and available . . ." ' The legislature of Connecticut did not go so far as to deny or abridge the right of appeal by its enactments, but it refused to clothe it with its legal sanction. Three laws passed in Massachusetts (1692–1697), which sought to restrict the classes of appealable cases, were disallowed by the home government; and thereafter no further attempts were made to regulate appeals.' In any case, the process of appeals in that province was fully legalized and adequately provided for by the charter provisions. In New York, the first law touching appeals was enacted in 1683; the minimum amount involved necessary for appeal was fixed at £100, " anything to the Contrary hereof in any wise notwithstanding." ' This provision was contrary to the commissions of Governor Dongan and Governor Sloughter, of 1686 and 1690, which specified £300, and to the general instructions to the governors of 1689 which designated £500. However, no change was made in the law until 1691, when the appealable amount was raised to £300.' In this later law the provisions of the earlier law as to the security to be furnished by the appellant was retained. In order to carry a case to the king in council, the appellant was required: (1) to pay all costs of the colonial decree, and all debts and damages adjudged against him in any other suits

' Hening's Statutes, III, 489, 490.

' Acts and Resolves of Massachusetts, I, 72–76, 144, 145, 283–287, 367–375.

' Colonial Laws of New York, I, 128, 129.   ' *Ibid.* I, 226–231.

within the province; (2) to give " in two sufficient securetyes
by Recognizance" double the value of the debt or matter involved in the colonial court; and (3) to prosecute the appeal
with effect and make return thereof within twelve months, or
execution should issue against him or his securities.

Colonial legislation in general shows very little hostility to
the *principle* of the appellate jurisdiction of the king in council.
But there was a tendency, very slight in most colonies and best
expressed in the classic instance of Rhode Island, to shape the
process of appeals according to the needs of the particular
colony and regardless of the wishes of the home government.
Rhode Island was favorably situated to attain this end, because
its government was subjected only to the loosest supervision by
the home government, and under its charter it was largely
empowered to control its own destinies. The governor, probably, did not receive many of the periodical instructions from
the British administration regulating appeals, and thus, in a
sense, Rhode Island was given a free hand. The colony was
continually at odds with its neighbors over questions involving
boundary rights and consequently land titles. As a result, the
Rhode Island assembly was disposed to make appeals to England as expeditious and as easy as possible, for in this way it
might be possible to gain the sanction of the home government
for its claims.

Rhode Island legislation in regard to appeals began in 1706,
when no minimum value necessary for appeal was designated
and the only requirement fixed was the giving of bond by the
appellant as an earnest for prosecution.[1] Other evidence indicates that, in practice, a value of £20 was required before a
case was considered appealable.[2] As a result, many cases of
" very small moment " were appealed to the king in council, and
many persons of little means were compelled to lose their rights
through inability to defend them. The Act of 1719, accord-

39

---

[1] R. I. Colonial Records, III, 562. For a general discussion of the attitude of
Rhode Island, see H. O. Hazletine, "Appeals from Colonial Courts to the King in
Council with Especial Reference to Rhode Island," Annual Reports of the American
Historical Association, 1894, 299–350.

[2] R. I. Colonial Records, III, 548.

ingly, placed the minimum amount at £300 current money—a sum that, by the time the next law was passed, was equal to less than £30 sterling.[1]   Still finding that appeals were being carried to England in matters of too small value, the legislature in 1746 enacted that £150 sterling should be the limit below which no cases could be appealed.[2]   This new value was equal to £1650 current money.   This amount was found still to be too low, and an Act of 1764 increased it to £200 lawful money (*i. e.* gold and silver coins) and declared that suits whose foundation was " a bond conditioned for the payment of money only " should not be subject to appeal regardless of the amount involved.[3]   A later law of 1771 advanced the minimum value of appealable cases to £300 lawful money.[4]   Meantime various regulations had been passed by the legislature with the object of restricting the number of appeals and standardizing the process.   These provisions were summed up in the Act of 1764, which included a few features of an earlier law of 1750.

By the Act of 1764, three of the principles which distinguished the Privy Council enactments were incorporated in the laws of Rhode Island, but with certain marked variations: (1) the minimum value required for appeal was fixed, as noted above, at £200; (2) nothing was said about the fourteen days' limit for making appeals; (3) the appellant was required to give security for prosecution, but in the arbitrary amount of £250 lawful money; and (4) execution of the colonial judgment was to be suspended, unless the appellee gave bond in the sum of £250 to restore to the appellant whatever was lost by him in case the decision of the lower court was reversed.[5]

---

[1] Public Laws R. I., Digest 1730, 106. This ratio may be inferred from the circumstance that in 1747 Rhode Island received from Parliament £7800 sterling as her share of the colonial outlay for the Louisburg expedition. With this amount, the Rhode Island committee in charge of the matter redeemed £88,725 of bills of credit. It appears, accordingly, that £11 current money was deemed equal to about £1 sterling.   R. I. Historical Tracts, no. 8, p. 67.

[2] Public Laws R. I., Digest 1752, 30.

[3] Public Laws R. I., Digest 1767, 10.

[4] Public Laws R. I., Digest 1772, 38.

[5] Public Laws R. I., Digest 1767, 10. Supplementary acts of 1768 and 1769 made changes of no importance as regards the present study; *cf.* Public Laws R. I., Digest 1772, 8, 17.

This brief review has shown Rhode Island practically un-affected by the enactments of the home government. While the other colonies prior to 1746 had generally a minimum appealable value of £300, Rhode Island had none at all until 1719, when a £30 value was required; and after 1746 Rhode Island had the successive minimum amounts of £150, £200 and £300, while the other colonies apparently were restricted by a £500 proviso. Moreover, Rhode Island was left until 1764 without a code appeal at all comparable to that under which the other colonies had been acting since the beginning of the century. But attention should again be called to the fact that Rhode Island was not a typical instance.

41

II

From the fact that colonial legislation, as a rule, betrayed no opposition to the principle of appeal it is not to be inferred that there was no opposition in the colonies to the appellate system. There were, on the contrary, efforts to impede and even to prevent its operation; and, in the case of Massachusetts, there was obstructive legislation. These efforts may conveniently be described under four heads: (1) denial of the right of appeal; (2) hostile colonial legislation; (3) evasion by the colonial authorities; and (4) lax enforcement of the orders in council.

In the seventeenth century, when the home government had not yet begun to assert aggressively its prerogative to hear all appeal cases and the number of litigants seeking to appeal was comparatively small, numerous instances may be found of a denial of appeal successfully maintained by colonial authorities. These denials occurred almost exclusively in the chartered colonies. Thus, in November, 1637, the Massachusetts General Court refused an appeal to the Reverend John Wheelwright, declaring

an appeal did not lie in this case, for the King having given us authority by his grant under the great seal of England to hear and determine all causes without reservation, we are not to admit any such appeal . . . and if an appeal should lie in one case, it might be challenged in all, and then there would be no use of government amongst us.[1]

Throughout her existence as a corporate colony, Massachusetts stubbornly maintained her position of judicial independence.

In proprietary North Carolina, the court declared in some detail its reason for not granting an appeal to an aggrieved party.[2]   First, there was " no law, rule or custom for this court (whose authority, as appears by commission, is as full within this government as that of the King's Bench in Great Britain) to stop execution of their judgment, by appeal here made"; second, "this court cannot by law compel the parties to appear before the king and his council, nor ascertain any time for their so doing "; third, " nor is it certain that the king in council will take cognizance thereof."   Even as late as 1720, there may be found in the case of South Carolina a petition from the council and assembly to the king, declaring that no method of appeals existed " for the ease of Your Majesty's subjects to Your Majesty and Council, as is done in the rest of Your Majesty's colonies."[3]

The real struggle between the home government and the colonies over the appeal of cases to the king in council occurred in the closing years of the seventeenth century.   As before, the chartered colonies were most tenacious in their claims to the ultimate decision of causes arising within their boundaries; but suggestions of protest may be found in the royal province of New Hampshire,[4] and even in the Old Dominion itself, which had been subject to the appellate jurisdiction of the

[1] Osgood, American Colonies in the Seventeenth Century, I, 249.   For numerous other instances, see *ibid.* I, 285; III, 162, 184, 185, 190, 315, 318, 329, 330, 331, with references.   John Leverett, the Massachusetts agent, was reported to have declared in 1661 in London that, before they would admit of appeals, the colonists would deliver New England up to the Spaniard; Maverick to Clarendon, Collections N. Y. Historical Society, Fund Series, 1869, p. 30.

[2] Hawks, F. L., History of North Carolina, II, 209 (date of case is not indicated). Chalmers, G., Introduction to the History of the Revolt, I, 301, 302, alludes to other denials in Carolina.

[3] Osgood, *op. cit.*, II, 300, 301.

[4] New Hampshire Provincial Papers, II, 341, 342.

king in council almost from the beginning.[1] The attitude of the chartered colonies is indicated by a letter of the Board of Trade to the Earl of Bellomont of April 29, 1701, which speaks of " this declining to admit Appeals to his Maj'ty in Council " as " a humour that prevails so much in the Proprieties and Charter Colonies."[2] A representation of the Board of Trade to the king on March 26, 1701,[3] declared that " diverse of them [the chartered colonies] have denied appeals to your Majesty, . . . that benefit enjoyed in the Plantations under your majesties immediate Government." A representation of the Board of Trade of March 1, 1702, again averred that the chartered colonies " had refused . . . to allow appeals."[4] This position of judicial independence constituted one cause of the movement in progress at that time for the withdrawal of all colonial charters by an act of Parliament.

The case of Connecticut was the most conspicuous instance of the denial of appeals. Her charter made no mention of the appellate jurisdiction of the king in council, and she was not inclined to yield her privilege of settling finally any cases that arose within her limits. This attitude was in harmony with her determined purpose to maintain a politically self-sufficient commonwealth. As early as October, 1684, the Connecticut General Court grudgingly declared that, although they did not find anything in the charter " oblidging, requiring or comanding " them to grant the liberty of an appeal to His Majesty, they would not " in any wise put a barr upon the lawful liberty of the demandents, to impeed their appearance before his Matie or any of his courts."[5] This permission, however, was never acted upon by the parties who petitioned for the privilege. Before the end of the century, Connecticut had assumed a more

43

---

[1] Account of the Present State of the Government of Virginia (1696–98), in I Massachusetts Historical Society Collections, V, 139; Chalmers, Introduction *etc.*, I, 164.

[2] N. H. Provincial Papers, II, 341, 342.

[3] N. C. Colonial Records, I, 535–537, 540. This charge was repeated *verbatim* by the Board of Trade on January 10, 1705–06; *ibid.* I, 630–633.

[4] Palfrey, J. G., History of New England, IV, 200.

[5] Conn. Colonial Records, III, 167.

stiff-necked attitude.   In 1698, John and Nicholas Hallam, and
Edward Palmes and John Hallam, sought to appeal "two particular cases" to the king in council.[1]   Their petitions were
refused by the Connecticut court on the grounds that the colony
courts were the tribunals of last resort.   Thereupon the men
petitioned the Privy Council for liberty to appeal; and the
order in council of March 9, 1699, declared to the governor
and company of Connecticut that any persons, aggrieved by the
judgments of the Connecticut courts, should be allowed to appeal to the king in council, adding that it was "the inherent
right of His Majesty to receive and determine appeals from all
his Majesty's colonys in America; and that they do govern
themselves accordingly."   The colony, imagining that the
crown was taking away her charter rights, still refused to comply, the governor declaring, according to a representation of the
Hallams, that before an appeal should be allowed, "they would
dispute the point with your Majesty."   On October 22, 1699,
the governor and company of Connecticut presented their case
in a diplomatically-worded letter to the Board of Trade, justify-
ing their pretensions by their remoteness from England and by
the provisions of their charter.   Sir Henry Ashurst, the Connecticut agent, appeared in behalf of the colonial claims on
December 13.   The persistence of Connecticut in claiming that
appeals to England were illegal under her charter caused the
Board of Trade to turn to Attorney-General Trevor and
Solicitor-General Hawles for their opinion, both as to the
legality of appeals and as to the means of forcing Connecticut
to comply with the order of March 9.   On May 15, 1701, their
very important opinion was rendered to the effect that

though there is no reservation of Appeals to his Majesty in the Charter
granted to Connecticut, yet that an Appeal doth lye to H. M. in his
Council as a right inherent in the Crown, and in case they refuse to

---

[1] This account is based upon: America and West Indies Calendar, 1699, nos. 119,
120, 160, 161, 270, 290; 1700, nos. 385, 460, 477, 974, 1002, 1012, 1014, 1021;
1701, nos. 166, 442, 480, 533; and Macqueen, Appellate Jurisdiction, 805, 806;
Acts of the Privy Council, II, nos. 733, 734; Palfrey, New England, IV, 224; Caul-
kins, F. M., History of New London, 222–227.

allow the Appeal there, we think H. M. may proceed to hear the merits of the cause upon an Appeal made to him in Council, whether that Appeal be allowed or admitted there or not.[1]

In accordance with this opinion, an order in council on June 12 admitted John and Nicholas Hallam to appeal, these parties having given the proper security to prosecute their appeal and to abide by his majesty's determinations.

A representation of the Board of Trade to Queen Anne on January 10, 1706, declared that the authorities of Connecticut " have refused to allow appeals to Your Majesty in council, and give great discouragements and vexation to those that demand the same." [2]   Acts of the Connecticut government in 1704 and 1710 indeed acknowledged indirectly the legality of the appellate jurisdiction of the crown but refused to assist its operation.[3] So far as the published records of the Privy Council show, the colony consistently refused to permit appeals throughout her history.   On the other hand, the Privy Council invariably admitted cases from Connecticut upon petition.

The provisions of the Rhode Island charter were similar to those of the Connecticut instrument; but her views in regard to the desirability of appeals were very different, as has been noted.   As early as July, 1685, Edward Randolph charged Rhode Island with denying appeals to the king in council, but his evidence is not unimpeachable.[4]   In February, 1699, Francis Brinley, a merchant of Rhode Island, petitioned the Privy Council for leave to appeal, alleging that he had met with serious obstructions to justice in the local courts.[5]   The account of his case was admittedly vague and unsatisfactory; but the Board of Trade, still in the heat of the controversy with Connecticut, advised the Privy Council to assert its authority. The result was an order in council of April 27, 1699, directed

45

---

[1] America and West Indies Calendar, 1701, no. 442.

[2] R. I. Colonial Records, IV, 12–15.

[3] Conn. Colonial Records, IV, 480; V, 161.

[4] R. I. Colonial Records, III, 175.

[5] This account of the Brinley case is based upon: America and West Indies Calendar, 1699, nos. 122, 299, 315, 341; Acts of the Privy Council, II, no. 732.

to the governor and company of Rhode Island, which reiterated the declaration of the previous month to Connecticut, that it was " the inherent right of His Majesty to receive and determine appeals from all His Majesty's colonies in America and that they do govern themselves accordingly." Governor Cranston's letter to the Board of Trade in response to the order in council proves beyond question that Brinley's statements in his petition had been false. He was shown to have neglected all the legal requirements for rehearing of his case in the Rhode Island courts, and then Cranston continues:

> There was never any appeal desired by Brinley of this Government; neither was there any other person ever denied an appeal to His Majesty. But we believe in the case of small actions like this, which does not exceed £20, it will be a great prejudice to the poor subject to be liable to be appealed against. We beg you to state what value appeals shall be granted upon.[1]

However, Rhode Island, notable for her remissness in so many matters, did not succeed easily in clearing herself of the taint of denying appeals. The representation of the Privy Council against the colony on March 26, 1705, repeated the charge; and Governor Dudley, of Massachusetts, and Lord Cornbury, governor of New York, gave similar testimony in letters to the Board of Trade of November 2 and November 26, 1705.[2] But the Rhode Island officials stoutly denied the charges, saying they had not refused to allow appeals when duly applied for and when the value of the matter in controversy required the same.[3] In fact, as the eighteenth century progressed, Rhode Island showed herself very anxious to take advantage of the benefits of the appellate system; and the instances of appeals being denied by the courts of the colony were relatively few.

ARTHUR MEIER SCHLESINGER.

OHIO STATE UNIVERSITY.

[*To be continued.*]

[1] America and West Indies Calendar, 1699, no. 672.

[2] R. I. Colonial Records, 543, 545.   [3] *Ibid.* III, 548.

IN the preceding portion of this paper,[1] the rules governing appeals from the North American colonies to the king in council were stated, as set forth in orders in council, colonial charters and acts of colonial legislatures. Denials of the right of appeal were then examined. The following pages deal with obstruction of appeals by hostile legislation, by evasion and by disregard of decisions; procedure on appeal; and cases carried to the Privy Council in which the validity of colonial enactments was subjected to judicial determination.

47

In general, colonial statutes were not inimical to the principles of the appellate system, and they apparently never went to the extremity of denying the right of appeal. The nearest approach to an attempt at legislative obstruction is to be found in acts passed by the General Court of Massachusetts. The charter of 1691 provided that " personal actions " were appealable to the king in council and did not mention any other kinds. The fair presumption seemed to be that other classes of actions were not subject to appeal. Willingly assuming this interpretation, the General Court in November, 1692, passed an act for establishing judicatories, which repeated the charter phraseology of " personal actions " and added the words: "(and no others)." This act was thereupon disallowed by the Privy Council, on the ground that it perverted the meaning of the charter. Acts of 1693 and 1697, containing a similar wording, met a like fate; and finally the law of 1699 omitted all reference to appeals.[2] Apparently no further attempts were made by the General Court to give statutory force to their interpretation of the charter. However, agitation still continued, and the Massachusetts courts repeatedly denied appeals to the king in council, presumably on the ground that they were other than personal actions. As late as 1743, the

General Court presented a petition to the Privy Council, praying that judgments given in courts of the province upon any real or mixed actions might be final and that no appeals be allowed to the king in council therefrom ; but nothing came of the petition.[1]

Cases of evasion were not infrequent. According to a representation sent to the Board of Trade in 1715 by the king's orders, it was averred that " in many cases where . . . Governors ought to allow appeals, they frequently refuse them, pretending that the Land, Estate or Negro Slaves sued for are not of the value of £500, tho' they are worth much more." In such cases, the representation continued, appeals could be made to the king in council by petition, but this subjected the petitioners " to two or three long Voyages, with great hazard, expense and loss of time, before they can obtain Justice."[2] This statement was made in reference to the insular as well as to the continental colonies, but it was probably as true of the one set as of the other. Mr. H. D. Hazeltine finds, after studying the situation in Rhode Island, that

without doubt, the power assumed by the Assembly of chancerizing or mitigating the damages assessed by other colonial courts enabled that body to evade in some cases the necessity of allowing an appeal from its decision. If the Assembly anticipated that an appeal might be demanded from its decision, it could chancerize the damages to a point below the sum required for an appeal to the King in Council.[3]

But without an exhaustive study of abundant source material, it would be difficult to say how widespread this practice was.

Of neglect to give effect to the decisions of the King in Council, the published records of the Privy Council show very few examples. A conspicuous instance was the appeal of Leighton *v.* Frost from the superior and inferior courts of Massachusetts Bay in 1735.[4] The case involved a bitter con-

[1] Acts of the Privy Council, III, no. 581.

[2] N. C. Colonial Records, II, 161.

[3] Report of the American Historical Association, 1894, p. 336.

[4] Acts of the Privy Council, III, No. 345. For a fuller account, based on the

troversy between William Leighton, who was employed to fell trees upon public lands for use in the royal navy, and John Frost who charged that Leighton had cut down trees on land owned by him and had thus violated a law of the province. The Massachusetts courts declared against Leighton, awarded damages against him and refused him the right of appeal to the king in council. Leighton petitioned the Privy Council for the privilege; on July 9, 1735, his petition was granted; and on April 29 of the following year the king in council rendered a decision, reversing the judgments of the Massachusetts courts, and ordered that the money which the appellant had paid should be restored to him and directed a new trial, under certain specified circumstances, with the liberty of a second appeal to England.

In September, 1736, Leighton's attorney produced the order before the Superior Court of Massachusetts where it was publicly read and ordered to be recorded. After delaying for two years upon various pretexts, the court declared in June, 1738, that it had no authority to give an order for an execution against the appellee (Frost), for such would be contrary to the charter, the laws of the province and the constant usage of the court. Leighton thereupon applied to Governor Belcher for

49

court records of Massachusetts, see Davis, A. McF., "The Case of Frost *vs.* Leighton," *American Historical Review*, II, 229–240.

Another instance, which aroused considerable interest at the time, was the refusal of the superior court of Rhode Island to carry out the orders in council in the two appeals of J., T., and S. Freebody *v.* J. Brenton *et al.;* Acts of the Privy Council, V, no. 14; VI, nos. 871, 876. In these cases, the superior court in March, 1771, gave judgment against the orders in council of April 14, 1769. In spite of complaints made to the Privy Council, there is record as late as July 6, 1774, that the orders had not been executed. This defiant attitude of the Rhode Island courts in the pre-revolutionary period is also reflected in a letter of December 22, 1767, written by George Rome, of London, who was sojourning in the colony in order to collect numerous debts owing to British merchants. Referring to the Rhode Island courts, he laments: "We have appeal'd to his majesty in council for redress, got their verdicts reversed, and obtain'd the King's decrees for our money, but *that is all;* for altho' I have had them by me above twelve months, and employed two eminent lawyers to enforce them into execution conformable to the colony law, yet we have not been able to recover a single shilling, tho' we have danced after their courts and assembly's above thirty days, *in vain* to accomplish that purpose only;" *Boston Evening Post*, June 28, 1773.

enforcement of the order in council; but in September Belcher
declared, after conference with his council, that since the
superior court had refused to act and no application had been
made to him until after the decision of the superior court, it
was not proper for him to do anything in the matter. Leighton
now sought redress of the Privy Council. After due delibera-
tion in committee, the Privy Council on March 22, 1739,
directed that the order in council of April 29, 1739, be "forthwith and without delay carried into execution;" that Frost
should immediately restore the money paid to him, and that
the superior court should "take the necessary Steps to Com-
pell him thereto." The inferior court was also required to pay
"due Obedience" to the earlier order in council as well as the
present one; and the governor was ordered to support the
royal authority and "to cause every particular herein contained
to be without delay duly and punctually complyed with."

This peremptory order apparently afforded little opportunity
for evasion; yet the superior court in passing upon the matter
on June 26 felt no compunctions in declaring: "That they
have no authority by any Law of the province or usage of this
Court to order such an Execution. And the Provision made
in the Royal Charter respecting appeals to his Majesty in
Council does not, as they apprehend, warrant any such Execution." Here the matter is lost sight of until March, 1743,
when David Dunbar, surveyor-general of his majesty's woods
in America, presented to the Privy Council a memorial which
set forth that the order in behalf of Leighton had not yet been
executed. Dunbar apprehended that if an order in council
should be immediately sent to Governor Shirley, the present
executive, to enforce the former order it would "have so good
an effect as to deter others from attempts of the like kind." In
line with this suggestion, on June 21, 1743, the clerk of the
council addressed a letter to Shirley, inclosing copies of the
two former orders, with instructions that "in case the said
Orders have not been already carried into Execution, the same
to be Complyed with forthwith and without further delay."
He was further ordered to keep the king in council informed as
to the progress of affairs.

Therewith, the matter disappeared from the Privy Council records.   More than seven years had elapsed since the original order in council, and no efforts had been made by the Massachusetts authorities to execute the decree.   As a result of laxity in enforcement, the enactment of the king in council had been nullified and the judgment of the provincial courts made supreme. This case, however, is not to be regarded as typical. It was only in isolated instances that such disregard of decisions impaired the efficiency of the appellate system.

III

51

The general lines of the appellate system have been indicated ; its actual and intimate working remains to be considered.   In order to make the description complete, the features of many different appeals have been assembled.

A litigant, dissatisfied with the decision of the colonial court, might request of the court an appeal to the king in council.   If permission for an appeal were granted, the appellant was free to prosecute his appeal before the Privy Council, in the manner to be described later.   If such permission were denied by the colonial court, he petitioned the Privy Council that his appeal be admitted and heard.   The Privy Council, after reference to the Committee for Appeals (or " the Committee "), usually granted such a petition ; in some cases this was done even when the one-year period, allowed for making appeals, had elapsed [1] or when the necessary minimum value was not involved in the case.[2]   An appeal might also be provisionally admitted, if " the Governor and Council there have no other legal objection thereto." [3]   The Privy Council rejected the petition on such grounds as the following: the sum involved was less than £300 ; [4] the petitioners had not " applied for a review " in the colony ; [5] the proceedings in the colonial courts were erroneous and illegal.[6] After an appeal was admitted, the Privy Council referred it to the Committee for Appeals, who upon occasion directed the colonial court to transmit copies of all the proceedings [7] and, in

---

[1] Acts of the Privy Council, II, no. 1019.   [2] *Ibid.* III, no. 345.
[3] *Ibid.* II, no. 1019.   [4] *Ibid.* II, no. 990.   [5] *Ibid.* II, no. 1270.
[6] *Ibid.* II, no. 1298.   [7] *Ibid.* II, nos. 875, 1146, 1301.

some cases, their reasons for refusing to admit the appeal.[1]   In
addition (as in a Massachusetts case), the colonial governor
might be ordered to see that " all Persons be permitted without
Interruption to give Evidence, or discouragement to any to give
their Testimony in behalfe of the Appellant."[2]

When the proceedings had been duly transmitted, the appellant petitioned the Council for " a short day " for hearing
his appeal.   Upon receiving this petition, the Council referred
it to the Committee for Appeals, who fixed a date for examining the case.   Upon hearing the case, the Committee reported
back to the Council, who, any time within a month or five
weeks or less, invariably accepted the report and enacted it,
with the assent of the sovereign, in the form of an order in
council.   This order in council might affirm the colonial decision or reverse it or vary it, and was usually accompanied with
an award of costs against the unsuccessful litigant.   An order
in council might dismiss an appeal because the petitioner had
not appealed from the inferior court within the time limit,[3] or
because the counsel for the appellant refused to offer further
evidence when certain of his evidence was ruled out[4] or for
other reasons.   The orders, reversing or varying a colonial
decision, were frequently accompanied with permission or instructions for a retrial.[5]

If, after the Privy Council had admitted an appeal, such
appeal were not prosecuted within twelve months' time, it might
be, and frequently was, dismissed for non-prosecution.[6]   On
the other hand, if the appellee failed to enter an appearance
within a year after the appeal was in the hands of the Privy
Council, the appellant could secure a hearing *ex parte*.   A
warning, requiring all persons to attend, was first given by " a
summons sent upon the Exchange " or other suitable place,
such as, in one case, the Maryland Coffee House,[7] in another,
the abode of the appellee in Christchurch parish, South Caro-

[1] Acts of the Privy Council, II, nos. 913, 990.   [2] *Ibid.* II, nos. 480, 734.

[3] *Ibid.* II, no. 716.   [4] *Ibid.* III, nos. 414, 428.

[5] *Ibid.* III, nos. 390, 391, 487, 527; IV, nos. 190, 263.

[6] *Ibid.* III, nos. 27, 442.   [7] *Ibid.* II, no. 1339.

lina.¹ In either case, it was usual to mulct the unsuccessful litigant in a small sum as costs. Delays were frequently caused
by parties professing to be unprepared or by the failure of
counsel to appear; and in these cases, too, costs were sometimes
awarded, and in especially glaring instances, a date was "peremptorily" fixed for the postponed hearing.²

In the eighteenth century, the effective nucleus of the Privy
Council for the adjudication of appeals is spoken of by the
Privy Council records as "the Committee for Appeals" until
1734 or 1735, after which it is referred to simply as "the Committee."³ The first order regulating the make-up of this committee was that of December 10, 1696, which provided that all
appeals from the plantations should be heard, as formerly, by
a committee which should make a report thereon to the king in
council. Such committee should be composed of all the members of the Council or any three or more of them.⁴ Later
orders in council of 1727 and 1761 repeated substantially the
regulation of 1696.⁵ Evidently, then, the membership of the
committee was an unstable one, varying according to circumstances from a body of three to a committee of the whole.

An order in council of September 20, 1727, declared that in
prize cases a committee of a similar make-up should hear appeals either from the courts of admiralty of Great Britain or
from those of the American plantations.⁶ An order of November 23, 1761, however, specified that this committee should be
composed of "all the Lords and others of His Majestys most
Honourable Privy Council, The Chief Baron of His Majestys
Court of Exchequer, the Justices of His Majestys Courts of
King's Bench and Common Pleas, and the Barons of the Court
of Exchequer . . . or any three of them."⁷ It seems probable

53

---

¹ Acts of the Privy Council, IV, no. 150.   ² *Ibid.* II, no. 1256.

³ Previous to 1696, before the appellate function of the Privy Council became so
clearly differentiated, the organ of the Council for hearing colonial appeals may be
best followed in Professor C. M. Andrews's careful study, "British Committees, Commissions, and Councils of Trade and Plantations, 1622-75" (J. H. U. Studies,
XXVI, nos. 1-3); and in the Acts of the Privy Council, I and II, *passim.*

⁴ Acts of the Privy Council, II, no. 657.   ⁵ *Ibid.* III, no. 124; IV, no. 448.

⁶ *Ibid.* III, no. 124.   ⁷ *Ibid.* IV, no. 461.

that a committee of similar make-up heard appeals from the plantations, whether the appeals concerned prizes or not.

No description is at hand of the manner in which appeal cases were heard by the Privy Council committee; but the procedure was no doubt much the same as now prevails in England. Various regulations of the procedure may be found scattered through the Privy Council records; these were designed for the most part to make the hearing of cases as expeditious as possible.[1]

54

IV

Three of the cases which reached the king in council from the colonial courts involved the validity of colonial statutes.

The first case was that of Winthrop *v.* Lechmere.[2] In November, 1692, Massachusetts passed an act for the settlement and distribution of the estates of intestates. In 1699, Connecticut enacted a somewhat similar law, according to the provisions of which the real estate of an intestate was divided equally among his children, except that a double portion was given to the eldest son. These laws sanctioned a custom which had prevailed in New England from the earliest times, but they were at variance with the English common law, according to which the eldest son was the sole heir and was entitled to the whole estate exclusive of all the other children. In 1717, General Wait Winthrop, son of Governor John Winthrop of Connecticut, died intestate, leaving two children: John Winthrop, and Ann, the wife of Thomas Lechmere of Boston, the respondent in the appeal. The landed estates of the decedent in Connecticut were large; and on February 21, 1718, the administration of them was committed to John Winthrop. Winthrop claimed all the real estate as his own, holding that he was

[1] Macqueen, Appellate Jurisdiction, p. 804; Acts of the Privy Council, III, Nos. 142, 228; IV, No. 23; V, No. 297.

[2] Talcott Papers, in Conn. Historical Society Collections, IV and V, *passim;* Winthrop Papers, part vi, in 6 Mass. Historical Society Collections, V, 367-370, 423-428, 436-511; Conn. Colonial Records, VII, 20, 43, 122, 185, 191, 254, 571-579; 2 Mass. Historical Society Proceedings, VIII, 125-137; Acts of the Privy Council, III, No. 112; VI, nos. 367, 410, 431, 432; Chalmers, Opinions, pp. 341-42; C. M. Andrews, "The Connecticut Intestacy Law," *Yale Review,* III, 261-294.

General Winthrop's sole heir under the common law of England, and that the Connecticut statute of 1699, by which he would be entitled to two-thirds and his sister to one-third of the estate, was invalid because contrary to the law of the superior dominion.

Winthrop continued to hold the entire estate; and in July, 1724, Thomas Lechmere, the husband of Winthrop's sister, applied to the court of probate of Connecticut, claiming for his wife a proportion of the real estate left by General Winthrop. After nearly two years of litigation in the courts of the colony, the superior court on March 22, 1726, caused the letters of administration granted to Winthrop to be vacated and appointed Lechmere and his wife administrators of the estate. Winthrop prayed for an appeal to the king in council, but his petition was denied. At the next session of the General Assembly, he presented a memorial to that body and declared that he would appeal to the king in council. His petition being peremptorily dismissed by the Assembly, he entered a vigorous protest; and, in accordance with his threats, he presented his case to the king in council by petition, claiming that the Connecticut law was contrary to the common law of England and to the colonial charter. In February, 1727, his appeal was admitted, and in December the case was tried before the Committee for Appeals. On February 13, 1728, a decree, issued by the king in council, declared the Connecticut statute null and void because it was " contrary to the laws of England . . . and not warranted by the charter of that colony," and reversed the decisions of the Connecticut courts, thereby giving the whole of the real estate to John Winthrop.

Disrupting, as it did, the agrarian system which had prevailed in Connecticut from the beginning of its history, and thus affecting every person in the colony, the order caused great alarm.[1]

55

---

[1] On June 29, 1731, Governor Talcott, of Connecticut, wrote to Wilks, the new agent for the colony in London, that no intestate estate had been settled since the promulgation of the royal decree, " tho' many orphans and fatherless children groan under it, and the whole Government, with all possible submission and patience, have been waiting, as in hope of a gracious answer from the Crown." Conn. Hist. Soc. Colls., IV, 235.

But not alone in Connecticut was there consternation at this sudden unsettling of established conditions. Other New England colonies, with intestate laws and practices similar to those of Connecticut, did not know how soon their systems also would be subverted by the home government. The issues presented by this case were so important to all of the colonists that the government of Connecticut at once made active and determined efforts to secure a reversal of the decision.

While negotiations were yet pending for effecting this end, a Massachusetts case, similar to Winthrop *v.* Lechmere, was carried to the king in council. This was the case of Phillips *v.* Savage.[1] In 1729, Henry Phillips of Boston died intestate, survived by his mother, one brother, two sisters (one the wife of Habijah Savage and the other the wife of Arthur Savage), and the children of a deceased sister. Administration on his estate, appraised at £3950, was granted on July 17, 1730, to his brother, Gillam Phillips. On May 15, 1733, the judge of probate of Suffolk county confirmed in probate court the action of a board of referees in making a partition of the estate in five equal shares among the mother, brother, sisters and deceased sister's children, the latter taking their mother's share. On October 18, 1733, Gillam Phillips appealed to the governor and council from the decree of the probate court, which he insisted was wrong because he, as the only brother of the deceased, was sole heir according to the common law of England. On November 2, the case was heard before the governor and council, and this tribunal upheld the decree of the judge of probate. In the following November, Phillips petitioned the governor and council for leave to appeal to the king in council, but the petition was denied. However, an order in council of February 12, 1734, permitted him to appeal from the various judgments of the provincial courts; and the case was tried before the Committee for Appeals of the Privy Council on January 13 and 16, 1738. Although the appellant was represented by the distinguished Sir Dudley Rider (afterwards lord chief justice of Eng-

[1] Mass. Hist. Soc. Procs., 1860-62, pp. 64-80, 165-71; Acts of the Privy Council, III, no. 322; I Mass. Hist. Soc. Procs., XIII, 100-03.

land and the immediate predecessor of Lord Mansfield) and a lesser associate, John Brown, and although the case of Winthrop *v.* Lechmere was quoted as a precedent, the king in council on February 15, 1738, issued an order upholding the decrees of the Massachusetts courts and dismissing the appeal. The respondents had been ably represented by Sir John Strange, afterwards master of the rolls, and Jonathan Belcher, son of the governor of Massachusetts and a Harvard graduate.

The question at issue in both of these cases was identical—the validity of the colonial statute—and there can be no doubt that the laws respecting intestate estates in both Connecticut and Massachusetts were contrary to the common law of the realm. But the king in council decided differently in the two cases. The reason for this apparent change of front lay in the circumstance that the Massachusetts law in question, together with an amendment passed the same year, had been affirmed by an order in council of 1695; and this fact, which would have been sufficient in itself, was reinforced by the fact that several explanatory acts, of 1710, 1715 and 1719, had not been disallowed by the crown and that a supplementary act, passed as late as 1731, had received the royal confirmation. The charter of 1691 provided that a law, not disallowed within three years after passage, should continue in full force until its expiration or its withdrawal by the General Assembly. Thus, this provision of the charter placed the intestacy law out of reach of an order in council, which was of a legal value inferior to the royal charter. In the case of Connecticut, whose laws did not come before the crown for approval or disallowance, and whose charter expressly declared that no laws of the colony should be " contrary to the laws of . . . England," the Privy Council was unembarrassed by any previous confirmation of the law in question. This difference in the situation of the two colonies accounts for the difference in the decisions.

The decision of the king in council in the Massachusetts case greatly encouraged the people of Connecticut in their efforts to secure the reëstablishment of their intestacy law. Ever since the Winthrop *v.* Lechmere decision, strenuous efforts had been made by petition to the home government to secure the reëstab-

57

lishment of the law, or at least the confirmation of what had been done by the probate courts prior to Winthrop's appeal. The Connecticut case had been a private one and the colony had not been heard in the matter. There can be little doubt that the respondent, Lechmere, was inadequately defended, that his evidence was far from complete and his purse far from full. Winthrop, on the other hand, was ably represented by Attorney-General Yorke and Solicitor-General Talbot.

The opportunity of presenting the law to the king in council for a second judgment upon its validity came in another private appeal case, Clark *v.* Tousey.[1] In 1737, Samuel Clark of Milford appealed to the king in council for the recovery of certain lands in Connecticut, which he demanded as heir at law according to the English laws of descent but which, in accordance with the legal procedure of the colony, had been settled upon himself, together with Thomas Tousey, of Newtown, and Hannah, his wife, and four other defendants. The order in council of May 25, 1738, admitting the appeal, failed to reach Clark, and thus he did not prosecute his appeal within the time limit. Meanwhile he continued litigation in the Connecticut courts, but without success; and on May 17, 1742, a second petition for appeal to the king in council was granted by that tribunal. In the same month, the appellee, Tousey, appeared before the Connecticut General Assembly and stated that he was obliged to go to England to defend his suit. "Considering that almost all the inheritances in this Colony are dependent upon the settlement of intestate estates according to our ancient laws and customs, which, if they should be overruled and made void, would reduce the inhabitants to the utmost ruin and confusion," the Assembly voted that the sum of £500 should be loaned to Tousey to aid him in the suit.[2] In the following October, Eliakim Palmer, the colonial agent, was instructed to employ solicitors in Tousey's defense and to assist further in any way possible.

[1] Conn. Colonial Records, VIII, 283, 506–507; IX, 587–593; Conn. Historical Society Collections, IV and V, *passim ;* Acts of the Privy Council, III, no. 422; C. M. Andrews, "The Connecticut Intestacy Law," *Yale Review,* III, 261–294.

[2] Conn. Colonial Records, VIII, 463.

As a result of personal pressure and of a recognition of the
injustice of enforcing the customary law of one country on
another country, where the agrarian and economic life had
brought into existence a customary law very different, the king
in council was finally induced to render a decision which was
probably based more largely on political grounds than upon
purely legal considerations. One especially potent argument,
which was pressed from Connecticut again and again in correspondence with the home government, was the assurance
that, if so many people in the colony were dispossessed of
lands, the younger sons from sheer necessity would turn to
trade and manufacturing, or otherwise be obliged to leave the
country.[1] These combined efforts to secure a reversal of the
Privy Council's former decision were successful. Clark's appeal was dismissed by an order in council of July 18, 1745, and
the validity of the act of 1699 was finally established.

It should be noted that these cases were not considered of
great constitutional importance at the time. In the popular
mind, the power exercised by the king in council through the
medium of these private appeal cases was closely allied to the
power of that tribunal to disallow colonial statutes. The chief
solicitude of the colonists lay in the fact that the disallowance
of their land laws would entail " ruin and confusion." The attorneys for Savage, in Phillips *v.* Savage, impliedly conceded in
their argument that the king in council had the right to deny
judicially the validity of a provincial statute, but they argued
that the law in question had been placed beyond the crown's
reach by an earlier confirmation. Even in the Connecticut
cases, the constitutional question of interest to the present-day
student of law was obscured by two other constitutional questions; for Connecticut's opposition to the appellant, Winthrop,
was based principally upon her *general* disinclination to recognize the appellate jurisdiction of the king in council and upon
her unwillingness to have *any* of her laws acted upon by the
home government. Her acquiescence in the Winthrop *v.* Lechmere decision, though under protest, was an acknowledgement

_____
[1] Conn. Historical Society Collections, IV, 123, 147, 189; V, 245-248.

59

of the power of the king in council judicially to disallow her laws; and the colony did not regain her peace of mind until the same agency which had set aside her law, *i. e.*, an order in council in a private appeal case, had established its validity.

Besides the three cases mentioned, there may have been others of a similar character which the imperfect entries in the Privy Council records fail to disclose. Certain it is that the principle involved received a more or less general acceptance during colonial times; and as late as August 19, 1760, it was expressly enunciated by the law officers of the crown.[1] In an opinion rendered by Attorney-General Pratt (afterwards Lord Camden) and Solicitor-General York on the crown's power of disallowing laws, it was declared that there may be laws

in which particular provisions may be void *ab initio* though other parts of the law may be valid, as in clauses where any act of Parliament may be contraversed or any legal right of a private subject bound without his consent. These are cases the decision of which does not depend upon the exercise of a discretionary prerogative, but may arise judicially and must be determined by general rules of law and the constitution of England. And upon this ground it is, that in some instances whole acts of assemblies have been declared void in the courts of Westminster Hall and by His Majesty in Council upon appeals from the plantations.

An examination of the appeals mentioned in the Privy Council records and elsewhere brings to light some interesting facts, although the fragmentary character of the entries and the frequent neglect of the clerks to include important data leave open to question any conclusions based upon these facts. Between 1680 and 1780, the most significant period of the operation of the appellate system, 265 cases reached the Privy Council from the continental colonies of England.[2] This was an average of

---

[1] Statutes at Large of Pennsylvania, V, 735-737.

[2] Prior to 1680 it is often difficult to distinguish between an appeal in the technical sense of the term and an appeal in the sense of a petition. From early days, there was a close judicial connection between Virginia and the home government. Frequent petitions for justice were presented by aggrieved parties to the Privy Council, before all possible remedies had been sought in the colonial courts. Thereupon, an order in council would "will and require" the governor and council of Virginia to

five appeals for every two years. The greatest number of cases, 78, came from Rhode Island; Virginia was next, with 53; Massachusetts was third, with 44; and New York fourth, with 21. From Maryland 15 cases were appealed; from Pennsylvania, 13; from New Jersey and New Hampshire, 12 each; and from Connecticut, 9. North Carolina, South Carolina, Georgia and the Lower Counties were represented by only two appeals each. In the course of the eighteenth century there was a perceptible increase, year by year, in the number of appeals; but this increase was apparently not out of proportion to the growth of population. Of the total number of 265 appeals, 50 were admitted by the Privy Council upon petition. In other words, in nearly one-fifth of the total number of appeals, the colonial courts had refused the liberty of appeal to the aggrieved party.

An effort has been made to ascertain whether, as is commonly alleged, the value of the appellate system was seriously impaired by the length of time which was required to obtain from the king in council the determination of appealed cases. For this purpose 140 cases were selected at random, dismissals for non-prosecution not being included. The significant time measurement was deemed to be the interval between the first

direct their attention to the matter and to expedite justice as far as possible. There were also a number of cases carried to the king in council by persons whose property had been confiscated by arbitrary act of Governor Berkeley on charge of participation in Bacon's rebellion. Including this latter type of cases, there were, prior to 1680, apparently only fourteen appeals to the king in council: eleven from Virginia, three of which came before the Council as early as 1639; one from Maryland, 1668; one from Massachusetts Bay, 1678, and one from Rhode Island, 1679. After the year 1776, the only case appealed to the Privy Council was one from South Carolina in 1782.

As noted elsewhere, this study refers only to the colonies that later composed the original United States. From the other North American continental possessions of Great Britain, the first appeal was taken in 1708, from Newfoundland. In the years following, to the end of 1783, only twenty-six appeals reached the Privy Council, and these cases possessed no unusual features. Nine were appealed from Quebec; nine from Nova Scotia; four from Newfoundland; three from West Florida and one from East Florida. Fourteen of the cases originated in vice admiralty courts. Nine appeals received no recorded adjudication; two appeals were dismissed for non-prosecution; and one judgment was apparently never executed. Five appeals were heard *ex parte*.

appearance of an appeal upon the Council records and the issue
of an order disposing of the case. The average for the 140
appeals was twenty-two months, which compares favorably with
the record of the United States Supreme Court.[1] More than
one-third (49) of the cases were adjusted in a year or less;
three appeals required more than six years, one of them taking
almost twelve years. Dismissal of appeals for non-prosecution
was found to occur within three months after the petition for
such dismissal was filed.

A little less than one-half (126) of the total number of appeals resulted from litigation over real estate. This proportion
was to be expected in a new country where the titles to land
were not yet definitively settled. Approximately one-fifth (57)
of the appeals arose from suits for accounts, debts and the like.
One-seventh (38) of the appeals involved infractions of the
Acts of Navigation and Trade or arose from the adjudication of
prize cases. The rest of the appeals were of a miscellaneous
character. By far the greater proportion of the cases appealed
were cases of private law and involved nothing but private rights.

The king in council reversed the colonial courts 76 times and
affirmed their decisions 57 times. From these figures it would
seem that the king in council acted impartially and that the appellant could not rely upon any presumptive bias of that tribunal against colonial decisions. In 77 cases no decision is recorded; 45 cases were discharged for non-prosecution. Only
eleven appeals are noted in the records as having been heard
ex parte.

---

[1] Professor C. M. Andrews notes some conspicuous exceptions to the average
determined here. "The claim of Lord Fairfax to lands in Virginia was before the
council for twelve years, the delays seemed interminable, while the expenses were
correspondingly great. The Mac Sparran claim to lands in Rhode Island waited
nearly sixteen years before it was finally rejected, and for eleven years it lay pigeon-
holed in the Privy Council office. The case of Connecticut *versus* the Mohegan
Indians, which came before the council in 1704, was not finally settled in favor of the
colony till 1773. Most remarkable of all, though delayed by diplomatic negotiations,
was the claim of Jeronimy Clifford, whose estate in Surinam had been seized by the
Dutch after the exchange of that land for New Amsterdam in 1667, and whose legal
representatives were still petitioning the council in 1766, nearly a century later;"
Andrews, C. M., The Colonial Period, p. 180.

In conclusion, a few words should be said regarding the merits of the appellate system in general. The importance of the system should not be overemphasized. In the first place, the number of cases appealed was comparatively small; and the minimum amount that must be involved in order to make a case appealable tended to impair the usefulness of the system. Thus, a representation, presented in behalf of the king to the Board of Trade in 1715, declared, in reference to the English plantations in America, that the instructions of 1689 requiring a minimum value of £500

63

covered the Governors and Courts from an Inspection into their conduct in all cases of less value, thereby giving them the ultimate Jurisdiction in all other cases. And whereas most of the Suites amongst them concern Traffic, and not one in fifty [is] of so great a value, their power was made absolute in all the rest. This has subjected the people to many grievous wrongs . . . [1]

Secondly, some of the colonies were much more affected than others by the appellate jurisdiction. North Carolina, South Carolina, Georgia and Delaware escaped with practically no supervision whatever. Thirdly, as has been noted, 77 of the 265 appeals disappeared from the Privy Council records undetermined, which would seem to leave but 188 appeals that were of any effectiveness. Of these 45 were discharged for nonprosecution. A liberal estimate would leave about 150 cases determined on their merits, or three in every two years. And in a few of these cases the orders in council were laxly enforced. Fourthly, the expense of prosecuting an appeal in England was a serious drawback to the usefulness of the system.

Despite these shortcomings, the appellate jurisdiction of the king in council was a valuable institution and was far more efficiently exercised than is generally represented. Its performances were beyond a doubt regarded as satisfactory; there were relatively very few colonial complaints against the system, and, in at least one instance, that of South Carolina, the provincial council and assembly petitioned the king for the privilege of

[1] N. C. Colonial Records, II, 161.

appealing to him in council.[1]   Other evidence corroborates the conclusion that the king in council was in general an unbiased tribunal of justice.   The personnel of the Privy Council was strong and its procedure insured justice to both appellant and appellee.   The average time necessary for the determination of an appeal was comparatively short.   The frequency with which necessary documents were lost in transmission seems to be greatly overrated, for the Privy Council records note only three such instances in cases appealed from the continental colonies. On the whole, the king in council seems to have been a tribunal well adapted for the adjudication of colonial appeals.   Certainly no other existing institution in England could have exercised this function more satisfactorily.

ARTHUR MEIER SCHLESINGER.

OHIO STATE UNIVERSITY.

[1] Osgood, H. L., The American Colonies in the Seventeenth Century, II, 300–301.

COLONIAL COMMERCE[1]

As a rule trade and commerce in their various manifestations, as features of American colonial history, have been considered of minor importance by our historians and relegated to the obscurity of a few supplemental paragraphs. No writer has placed them in the same rank with government, administration, and social development, or has deemed their consideration essential to a proper understanding of the conditions under which our colonies were founded and grew up. Yet it is a well-recognized fact that during the greater part of our colonial period commerce and the colonies were correlative terms, unthinkable each without the other. As an underlying factor in colonial life commerce was of greater significance than it is to-day in the life of the United States, for some of the most vital aspects of our early history can be understood only when construed in terms of commercial relationship, either with England or with some of the other maritime powers of the period which were finding their strength and prosperity in colonial and commercial expansion.

In the domain of history a shift in the angle of observation will often bring into view new and important vistas and will create such new impressions of old scenes as to alter our ideas of the whole landscape. In the case of colonial history this statement is peculiarly true. Viewing the colonies as isolated units of government and life, detached in the main from the larger world of England and the Continent, leads us to ignore those connections that constituted the colonial relationship in which commerce played a most important rôle. The older view is natural because it is easily taken and satisfies local interest and pride; the newer point of observation is more remote, less obvious, and more difficult of attainment. Yet it is the only view that enables us to preserve the integrity of our subject and so to comprehend the meaning of our history. The thirteen colonies were not isolated units; they were dependencies of the British crown and parts of a colonial empire extending from America to India. They were not a detached group of communities; on the contrary they were a group among other groups of settlements and plantations belonging colonially to five of the European nations, Portugal, Spain, Holland, France, and England, and their history was influenced at

[1] A paper read in the conference on colonial commerce at the meeting of the American Historical Association in Charleston, December 30, 1913.

every point by the policies and rivalries of these maritime powers. The age in which they reached their maximum of strength as colonies was one in which the colonial relationship was highly developed and the feature of subordination to a higher authority an integral and dominant characteristic. Such an interpretation of colonial history is not a scholar's vagary, a matter of theory and hypothesis to be accepted or rejected as the writer on colonial history may please. It is historically sound, preserving the proper perspective, and preventing in no way the following out to the uttermost detail the local activities and interests of the colonists themselves.

66

The reason why this colonial relationship has been so persistently ignored in the past is not difficult to discover. The period of our history before 1783 has been construed as merely the ante-chamber to the great hall of our national development. In so doing writers have concerned themselves not with colonial history as such, but rather with the colonial antecedents of our national history. This form of treatment is common to all our histories, even the very best, because all limit their scope to the thirteen colonies, which formed but part of the colonial area and are segregated for no other reason than that they constituted the portion out of which the United States of America grew. In our text-books, not excepting the very latest, the colonial period is frankly presented as an era of beginnings, and stress is laid upon ideas and institutions that were destined to become dominant features of the nation's later career. With this mode of presenting the subject we may not quarrel, but it seems almost a pity, now that we are becoming such a nation of text-book writers, that the children of the country cannot be set upon the right way of understanding what the colonial period really means. Dealing with thirteen colonies, searching among them for the conditions under which were laid the foundations of the great republic, and treating those conditions as but preliminary to the history of the United States will never enable the writer to present an honest or complete picture of colonial life or to analyze successfully the causes that provoked revolution or rendered independence inevitable.

In one respect the colonial period is fundamentally different from that of our national history. For one hundred and seventy-five years, the people who inhabited the American seaboard were not members of an independent and sovereign state, free of all control except such as they exercised for themselves. Legally, they formed dependent and subordinate communities, subject to a will and authority higher than themselves and outside of themselves. This state of dependency was a reality and not a pretense. At least, the members

of the British Parliament deemed it so, when in 1733 they rejected a
petition from the assembly of Massachusetts as " frivolous and
groundless, an high insult upon his Majesty's government, and tending to shake off the dependency of the said colony upon this kingdom, to which by law and right they are and ought to be subject ".
At least the British executive and administrative authorities deemed
it so, when by a thousand acts and through hundreds of officials in
the colonies they endeavored to maintain the royal prerogative and
to carry out the British policy of making English subjects the sole
carriers of the whole British commerce and of appropriating and securing to England and her subjects " all the emoluments arising from
the trade of her own colonies ". The British merchants took this
view, when they could say, as Stephen Godin asserted in 1724, that
" it were better to have no colonies at all unless they be subservient
to their mother country ". Certainly the colonists deemed it so, when
by their very restlessness under restraint they betrayed the reality
of the ties that bound them. No act of the colonists, either individual or collective, can be traced to a conscious expectation of
future citizenship in an independent republic. No aspect of colonial resistance to the royal authority was ever due to any definite
belief that an independent nation was in the making. There is
nothing to show that a colonist ever allowed visions of such a future
to influence the course of his daily life. To the colonist there was
no United States of America in anticipation, and there should be
none to the student of colonial history to-day. The subject should
be dealt with for its own sake and not for its manifestations of
self-government and democracy; and the eye of the scholar should
look no further ahead than to its legitimate end, the close of a period
the era of revolution, war, and independence.

It may be stated as a general principle that studying a period of
history with its later manifestations before us is apt to lead to per-
versions of historical truth. With notions of the present in mind we
approach certain landmarks of our early history in much the same
spirit as that in which older writers approached Magna Carta. Most
of us make too few allowances for the differences of mental longitude
between the present and the past, and fail to realize that our thoughts
were not the thoughts of our forefathers and our institutions were
not the institutions they set up. The colonial period is our Middle
Ages, and he would be rash who interpreted the thoughts of that time
in the light of later views as to what democracy ought to be. There
are traces and important traces of radical notions in matters of government in our colonial period, for our colonies were settled during a
century of unrest in religion and politics; but these notions were not

the characteristic or the generally prevalent ideas that governed colonial action.. It is not profitable or scholarly to single out these manifestations, to study them apart from their surroundings, and to classify them as representative and typical of the period in which they appeared. I am afraid that the majority of the colonists listening to some modern comments upon the early institutions of New England and Virginia, would have replied in somewhat the same fashion as Maitland pictures William Lyndwood replying to questions on the "canon law of Rome":

> I do not quite understand what you mean by popular liberties and this thing that you call democracy. I am an Englishman and I know the liberties that I enjoyed in England. But these were class liberties, to be understood in the light of the law and of the rights of the crown and parliament; they are not what you mean when you talk about popular rights and liberties in a democratic republic. You mean equal liberties for all, including the mass of the people. But that is something we do not want, for that would admit all men of whatever station, property, or faith to equal privileges in society, church, and state, and such a philosophy of government is one in which only a dreamer would believe.

In truth, we have arrived at this idea of what our forefathers thought, by selecting certain documents and incidents, from the Mayflower Compact to the Declaration of Independence, and from Bacon's Rebellion to the various riotous acts of the pre-Revolutionary period; and, construing them more or less according to our wishes and prepossessions, have wrought therefrom an epic of patriotism satisfying to our self-esteem. We love to praise those who struggled, sometimes with high purposes, sometimes under the influence of purely selfish motives, against the authority of the British crown. But this, in an historical sense, is pure pragmatism. It is not history, because it treats only a part of the subject and treats it wrongly and with a manifest bias. It does not deal with what may be called the normal conditions of the colonial period. It ignores the prevailing sentiment of those who, however often they may have objected to the way in which the royal authority was exercised and to the men who exercised it, lived contented lives, satisfied in the main with the conditions surrounding them, and believing firmly in the system of government under which they had been born and brought up. It misunderstands and consequently exaggerates expressions of radical sentiment, and interprets such terms as "freedom", "liberty", and "independence" as if, in the mouths of those who used them, they had but a single meaning and that meaning the one commonly prevalent at the present time. It relegates to a place of secondary importance the royal prerogative and the relation with England, which beyond all other factors dominated the lives and actions of a majority of the colonists. Without an understanding of the relationship with England, colonial history can have no meaning. Before we can treat of colonial self-government, of the growth of democratic ideas, of the conflict between the colonies and the mother-country, and of the westward movement, we must know what England was doing, according to what principles she acted, and how these principles found application in the colonial world that stretched from Hudson Bay to Barbadoes. Only in this way can we deal with our own colonial problems, and only in this way can we answer those subordinate but important questions, why did not the West Indies and the Floridas revolt, and why did the Canadian colonies remain loyal to the mother-country.

69

This preliminary statement is necessary in order to explain the attitude that I shall take in regard to the subject under consideration here. One period of our history, that from 1690 to 1750, has long been recognized as a neglected period, and it will continue to be neglected as long as we treat colonial history merely as a time of incubation. Now just as an important period has suffered neglect from failure to make a radical change in our point of view, so an important phase of colonial history has suffered similar neglect from a similar cause. I refer to the subject of colonial commerce. The many divisions of this fundamentally important topic have lain hitherto strewn about over the pages of colonial history, veritable *disjecta membra*, without proper unity and co-ordination, and without that grouping of principal, subordinate, incidental, and extraordinary features, which taken together disclose the paramount significance of the whole.

Any study of colonial commerce should begin with a thorough grounding in the commercial policy of England from the beginning of the colonial period, and a thorough understanding of the place of the colonies, not only in England's commercial scheme, but also in the schemes of other maritime states of the European world. England's relations with the colonies were primarily commercial in character, not only because of the wide expanse of water that separated the mother-country from her outlying possessions, but much more because from the beginning to the end of the legal connection, England's interest in the colonies was a commercial interest. British merchants and statesmen valued the colonies just as far as they contributed to the commercial and industrial prosperity at home; and they actively promoted and upheld legislation that brought the colonies within the bonds of the commercial empire. Commerce was, therefore, the cornerstone of the British system. Naturally other interests, legal, political, institutional, religious, and military, assumed large proportions as the British colonial system was gradually worked out: but in the ultimate analysis it will be found that the building up of strong, self-governing communities in America and the West Indies was a contributory rather than a primary object, furthering the commercial aims of British merchants and statesmen through the establishment of vigorous but dependent groups of producers and consumers; for England was bound to protect and develop the sources of her wealth and power. England valued her colonies exactly as far as they were of commercial importance to her, and it was no accident that the terms "trade" and "plantations" were joined in the same phrase as the title of the British boards of control, or that in the same title "trade" took precedence over "plantations". The commercial history of every colony, without exception though not all in the same measure, was affected by this policy of the mother-country, who, possessing plenary authority, was able to enforce to no inconsiderable extent the policy that she laid down. A study of colonial commerce carries us at once, therefore, into the very heart of that most fundamental of all colonial questions, the relation of the colonies to the sovereign power across the sea.

If we limit our observation to a single colony or to the group of thirteen colonies, as we are more or less bound to do when dealing with colonial history as prefatory to that of the United States, we get an imperfect view of our subject, if, indeed, that can be called a view at all which is taken at such close range. Commerce thus seen appears to be an interesting, but not particularly conspicuous, feature of colonial life. Settlement, government, politics, religion, war, and social life generally have taken precedence of it in the narratives of our writers. If not ignored or treated as an issue of only local or minor consequence, it is used as a convenient text for moralizing on the unwarranted part which a government can take in interfering with the free and natural development of a high-spirited and liberty-loving people. As a rule such an attitude is due to the unprofitable habit of studying colonial history with our ideas warped and distorted by standards of judgment derived from the Revolutionary and national periods, a habit that is formed when colonial history is studied from the wrong end. Mr. Beer is showing us how to correct that habit, and his volumes are teaching us what can be done when the right vantage-point is sought for and attained. We are now beginning to learn that what we call colonial commerce was but part of that ocean-wide commercial activity of England and her merchants which stands as England's most vital possession of the

last two centuries, and thus was concerned with a larger world of
obligations and opportunities than that embraced by the thirteen
colonies. Construed in this way, colonial commerce grows in dignity
and rank and yields to no other phase of our history in the influence
it has exercised upon the life of the period to which it belongs.

In presenting our subject from this standpoint, we must in the
first place acquire a sound knowledge of the commercial ideas of the
period, of mercantilism and the self-sufficing empire in all aspects
of their development, and we must exhibit a sympathetic attitude toward views and opinions that had as legitimate a right to a place in
the commercial and political thought of the seventeenth and eighteenth centuries as have corresponding but different views and opinions a right to exist to-day. We must study understandingly the
conditions under which these commercial ideas came into being, and
must analyze thoroughly and carefully all orders, proclamations,
statutes, and instructions that represent official utterances upon these
points; the minutes of subordinate councils and boards; and the
letters, pamphlets, and memorials of private persons that contain
expressions of individual opinion. Furthermore, we must follow
in all their ramifications, in all the colonies dependent on the authority of the British crown, the attempts, whether successful or unsuccessful, to apply these regulations to the actual business of commerce.
The Navigation Acts were but the most conspicuous of hundreds of
official declarations, defining the limits within which colonial commerce could be carried on: yet even now we understand but im-
perfectly the influence of those acts upon our colonial history and
the extent to which they were obeyed.

In tracing the effect of the Acts of Trade and Navigation, we
shall meet with a series of institutions in the colonies that played
a continuous and active part in the every-day life of the colonists,
and we shall find that as yet scarcely one of these institutions has
been made the subject of any comprehensive treatment. The Navigation Acts gave rise to the plantation duty, the collectors and surveyors of customs, and the naval officers, and involved the intricate
question of salaries and fees; they brought into existence the courts
of vice-admiralty with their complements of officials, their procedure
under the civil law, their claims of jurisdiction, and their time-
honored antagonism to the courts of common law which had already
and everywhere been set up in America. We shall find that the
machinery for the control of colonial commerce, thus set in motion,
gave added duties, not only to existing departments and boards in
England—a subject of no little importance in itself for colonial history—but also to the governors of every colony without exception,

and to the admirals and commanders of ships of war engaged before 1713 (and even after that date on account of West African pirates and Spanish *guardacostas*, in the work of convoying fleets of merchant ships back and forth across the Atlantic) ; of looking after affairs in Newfoundland, where civil control was vested in an admiral-governor; and of interfering, long before the famous interferences of 1760 to 1765, to prevent illegal trade and the traffic in uncustomed goods. As we follow on in our study of colonial commerce, we meet with the attempts to set up ports of entry in Virginia, Maryland, and elsewhere for the discharge and lading of ships and the checking of illegal trade, and with the complicated problems of embargoes, chiefly in times of war, of the impressment of seamen from colonial vessels in England and from colonial ports in America for the manning of the royal ships, and of the issue of passes, provided by the Admiralty under special treaties between England and the Barbary States, great numbers of which were used in America by American-built ships to guard against capture by the Barbary cruisers, most dangerous of whom were the Algerine pirates. We are concerned with the question of privateering and the issue of letters of marque, and also with that of prizes, the establishment of special prize courts, and the disposition of ships captured in war. We are concerned also with the question of coast defense in America, the employment of frigates and smaller vessels for the guarding of individual colonies, and with the whole subject of piracy, including the efforts made through the navy, the colonial governors, and specially commissioned courts erected for the purpose, to suppress these marauders of the seas. Indirectly, we are concerned with England's attempt to persuade the colonies to produce naval stores for the use of the royal navy, an attempt which played an important part in the industrial history of the continental colonies, especially in New England; and we are also concerned with England's determination to control the supply of masts from the northern American forests, by means of special officials, notably the surveyor-general of the woods and his deputies, whose business was very obnoxious to the northern colonists.

Furthermore, the attempts of the colonists to evade the restrictions that England laid down for the control of navigation and commerce not only resulted in the seizure of scores of ships, their condemnation and sale, and the arousing of a great amount of ill-will and hostility, but they were also responsible, and often directly responsible, for events of political and constitutional importance, such as the loss of the Massachusetts charter, the consolidation of the northern colonies under Andros, the temporary control of Maryland and Pennsylvania by the king, and the unsuccessful efforts, lasting nearly half a century, to unite the proprietary and corporate colonies to the crown. These are important events in colonial history and can all be traced immediately or remotely to the demands of England's commercial policy.

Continuing this subject in its further ramifications, we find it leading us on into other aspects of the life of the colonies. Commerce influenced the passing of colonial laws; provoked the king in council to disallow colonial acts, because under the statute of 1696 the colonists were forbidden to have any "Laws, Bye-Laws, Usages or Customs" that were in any way repugnant to the terms of the act, and because the colonial governors were forbidden " to pass any laws by which the Trade or Navigation of the kingdom [might]in any ways be affected ";[2] brought about appeals to the High Court of Admiralty from the courts of vice-admiralty in America, and in a few cases at least from the common law courts in the colonies to the

73

[2] *House of Lords Manuscripts*, new series, II. 483–488, 494–499 (1696–1697); C. O. 5: 1364, pp. 474–476; *Acts of the Privy Council, Colonial*, vol. II., § 1271 (1717); C. O. 324: 10, pp. 443–454, 456–497 (1722); *Acts of the Privy Council, Colonial*, vol. III., § 58 (1724); C. O. 5: 1296, pp. 120–130; *Acts of the Privy Council, Colonial*, IV. 763–764 (1766).

Dr. O. M. Dickerson, in commenting on this paper at the Charleston meeting, expressed his belief that seventy-five per cent. of the " vetoes " of colonial laws must be explained on other than commercial grounds. Until the royal disallowances have been collected and their contents analyzed, we are hardly in a position to speak very positively about their numerical proportions, but after studying with considerable care those in print and in manuscript relating to all the colonies for the entire colonial period, I am convinced that Dr. Dickerson's percentage is too high. Dr. Dickerson must have failed to realize that scores of disallowances apparently concerned with other than commercial matters are found on closer inspection to have a trade motive somewhere lurking in them. This is particularly true of all that deal with financial legislation. But after all can we determine the place of trade and commerce in colonial history by simply counting the number of laws passed and disallowed that deal with this subject? I think not. The colonists had frequent warnings that legislation affecting trade or discriminating in any way against British merchants or British commodities would not be tolerated, and the governors were expressly instructed to veto such laws. It would be surprising, therefore, if any large number of such laws had been passed wittingly by the colonial legislatures. We can obtain a much more accurate estimate by studying the motives underlying British policy in this respect, as seen in the reports of the Board of Trade and of the Council Committee. Among the reasons for disallowance that stand out above all others are two: the impairment of trade and the infringement of the royal prerogative. Many of the other reasons are technical as having to do with the legal aspects of the case, and none of them to anything like the same degree represent the fundamental principles governing the relations of mother-country and colonies as do the two named above. In 1766 the Board of Trade itself summed up the leading motives controlling the disallowance, as " the Commerce and Manufactures of this country ", " Your Majesty's Royal Prerogative ", and " the Authority of the British Parliament ". It will be noticed that trade and commerce are mentioned first. *Acts of the Privy Council, Colonial*, V. 43.

Privy Council. It gave rise to the thousand and one complicated phases of international finance, involving mercantile dealings and transactions, currency, credit, and exchange, gold, silver, copper, and paper money, bills of exchange and rates of exchange, the drift of bullion from colony to colony, and above all that question, sometimes most difficult to answer in the case of individual colonies, of the balance of trade. It touched very closely the attitude of the Board of Trade, the Privy Council, and Parliament toward bills of credit and colonial banking, a phase of our early financial history that has nowhere been studied in its entirety. As we continue to the uttermost reaches of this subtle and penetrating force, we find ourselves in the very centre of colonial life, discovering unexpected traces of its influence upon other phases of colonial activity that seem at first sight far removed from the sphere of the Navigation Acts and all their works.

Thus we see how large is the field within which the commercial policy of England operated and how deep and far-reaching were the effects of this powerful agent in shaping the development of colonial history. In the aggregate, the results of this policy, which England by virtue of her sovereign authority was endeavoring to force upon the colonies, constitute an impressive picture, the details of which are so interwoven with the general life of the colonies as to be inseparable from it. From the historian they deserve and are capable of such treatment as will furnish an orderly and logical presentation of this neglected phase of our history.

Turning now to the second part of our general subject, we shall see that colonial commerce, quite apart from its connection with England's policy, was a dominant interest of the colonists themselves. There is danger lurking in the new point of view we are taking, the danger of giving exaggerated treatment to governmental policy and neglecting those parts of the story that represent colonial activity and private enterprise. We are right in taking our stand in the mother-country and in following thence the diverging lines of governmental influence in the colonies themselves. But when once these features of our subject have been outlined there still remains another and equally important group of subjects to be studied, the actual commercial and industrial conditions in the colonies and the extent to which these conditions reacted upon the policy at home. British governmental policy on one, side and colonial organization and development on the other are but the complementary parts of a common subject. Each is incomplete without the other, and neither can be fully understood unless the other has been adequately and impartially presented.

To the colonists in America a commercial and trading life was
the natural accompaniment of their geographical location. The
colonists did not confine their interests, as do most of our historians,
to the fringe of coast from Maine to Georgia. They ranged over a
larger world, the world of the North Atlantic, a great ocean-lake,
bounded on the east by the coast of two continents, Europe and
Africa, and on the west by the coast of a third continent, America.
On the northeast, the British Isles occupied a vantage-point of great
commercial and strategic importance, while within the ocean area
were scores of islands, massed chiefly along the southwestern border
or off the coast of Africa, from the Bahamas to Curaçao and from
the Azores to the Cape Verde Islands, which held positions of the
highest importance for purposes of trade and naval warfare. It is
an interesting fact that the British island colonies, and still more
those of France, Holland, and Denmark, have been mere names to
the students of our history; and it is equally significant that no atlas
of American history displays in full upon any of its maps the entire
field of colonial life. The American colonists were not landsmen
only, they were seafarers also. They faced wide stretches of water,
over which they looked, upon which hundreds of them spent their
lives, and from which came in largest part their wealth and their
profits. Though migration into the interior began early, nearly half
the eighteenth century had spent its course before the American colonists turned their faces in serious earnest toward the region of the
west. Though the lives of thousands were spent as frontiersmen
and pioneers, as many crossed the sea as penetrated the land, for
colonial interstate commérce was not by land but by water. In
the shaping of colonial careers and colonial governments, sea-faring
and trade were only second in importance to the physical conditions
of the land upon which the colonists dwelt. No one can write of
the history of Portsmouth, Salem, Boston, Newport, New Haven,
New York, Philadelphia, or Charleston, or of the tidewater regions
of Maryland, Virginia, and North Carolina, without realizing the
conspicuous part that commerce played in the lives of those communities and regions. Even within the narrower confines of their
own bays and rivers, the colonists of continental America, particularly of the northern part, spent much of their time upon the
water. They travelled but rarely by land, unless compelled to do so;
they engaged in coastwise trade that carried them from Newfoundland to South Carolina; they built, in all the colonies, but more
particularly in New England, hundreds of small craft, which penetrated every harbor, bay, estuary, and navigable river along a coast
remarkable for the natural advantages it offered for transit, trans-

75

port, and traffic by water; and they devoted no small part of their time and energies as governors, councillors, and assemblymen to the furthering of a business which directly or indirectly concerned every individual, and which became more exigent and effective as the numbers of the colonists increased and their economic resources expanded.

In elaborating this phase of our subject we are called upon to deal with certain aspects which, though inseparable from the larger theme, are more strictly colonial in their characteristics and connections. I refer to staple products, shipping, trade routes, and markets, and in close connection with these are the various aspects of commercial legislation in the colonies themselves. A study of staple products demands that we survey the entire agricultural and industrial history of the colonies from Hudson Bay to Surinam, and enter upon a discriminating analysis of the economic importance of their chief products from furs to sugar and from fish to lime-juice. A study of shipping for the purpose in hand demands that we find out where ships were built, what was their tonnage, and how they were manned, and acquire some knowledge of the fitness of certain types of vessels for ocean, island, and coastwise service, according to their size and rig. The study of trade routes, one of the most varied and tangled of problems, demands that we determine the customary routes with all their variations, examine the reasons why these routes came into being, analyze the conditions attending traffic by these routes, and follow each route from port to port, as far as descriptions, logs, and registers will allow, instead of being content to see the captains and masters sail out into the unknown and return from the unknown, with very indefinite ideas as to where they had been and what they had done there. A study of markets requires that we have some fairly exact knowledge of the staple demands of other countries and colonies than our own, of the conditions under which our colonial staples were distributed, and of the nature of the commodities that other countries could offer to the captains and supercargoes wherewith to lade their vessels, either for the return trip, for the next stage of a long voyage that might cover many countries, or for the kind of huckstering business that many masters engaged in, going from port to port as they saw opportunities for profit.

Having presented these general features of this phase of our subject, I should like to state somewhat more exactly what I have in mind, and to discuss at somewhat greater length topics which, though commonly classed as economic, are in no way the peculiar property of the student of so-called economic history. First of all as to staple products. In the far north, from Hudson Bay to Nova Scotia, Maine, and New Hampshire, furs, fish, and lumber predominated. These same staples were also of importance to central and southern New England, in addition to whale-fins and whale-oil, but the main products here were agricultural, including live-stock, naval stores, and also a great variety of provisions, many in their natural state and others dried, salted, and pickled, with some articles of wooden ware, among which were jocularly classed the wooden clocks and nutmegs of Connecticut. New England differed from her neighbor colonies to the immediate southward, not so much in the character of the staples exported as in the possession of large numbers of shipping ports through which she sent her surplus products to the world outside. New York, including within its area of supply Long Island, Westchester County, and the Hudson and Mohawk river valleys, exported a similar variety of domestic staples, with a greater amount of bread-stuffs and peltry, but lagged behind such towns as Salem, Boston, Newport, and Philadelphia in the extent of her export business. Though sharing with Albany and Perth Amboy the trade of the region, she surpassed all the others as an entrepôt for re-exported commodities from the tropical colonies. Philadelphia was wholly absorbed in commerce, and early became the main port, with Burlington and Salem as subsidiary, through which the farmers of Pennsylvania and West New Jersey and the tobacco raisers of Delaware sent their supplies. She specialized in wheat, beef, pork, and lumber, and during colonial times was the greatest mercantile city of the colonial world. She raised almost no staple suitable for export to England and did but a small re-exporting business. As she drew practically all manufactured commodities from England, the balance of trade in that direction was heavily against her. Thus we have in one group what are commonly known as the "bread colonies", possessed of diversified staples, similar in many cases to those that England produced for herself.

South of Mason and Dixon's line we enter the group of single staple colonies, in which the export was confined to a single commodity or to a small number of commodities. Maryland and Virginia raised very little except tobacco until after the middle of the eighteenth century, when the export of grain, largely to the West Indies, marked the beginnings of trade with the tropical colonies and laid the foundations of the prosperity of Baltimore and Norfolk. North Carolina in the seventeenth century was relatively unimportant as an exporting colony, supplying only tobacco to New England traders who shipped it to England; but afterward, particularly in the southern section, from the plantations along the Cape Fear

77

River, she developed a variety of staples, live-stock, naval stores, and provisions, and entered upon a considerable exporting activity. South Carolina was a long time in finding her staple industry, but the enumeration of rice in 1704 shows that out of the diversified commerce of the earlier era had come the one product that was to be the chief source of her wealth. In the eighteenth century rice, indigo, naval stores, furs, cypress, and cedar made up the bulk of her cargoes. Among the island colonies, Bermuda and the Bahamas, having no sugar and little tobacco, played but little part in the commercial life of the colonies. But with the West Indies—Jamaica, Barbadoes, and the Leeward Islands—we are face to face with that group known as the "sugar colonies" which formed till 1760 the leading factor in England's commercial scheme. Conspicuous among colonial staples were the products of these islands, sugar, molasses, and rum, with a small amount of indigo, cotton, ginger, allspice, and woods for cabinet work and dyeing purposes, some of which came from the mainland of Honduras. The contrast of the "bread colonies" and the "sugar colonies" forms one of the leading features of colonial history, and in their respective careers we have the operation of forces that explain many things in the course of colonial development.

With shipping we deal first of all with the actual extent of the ship-building industry, regarding which at present we have no very exact statistical information. Weeden has given us for New England an admirable, though rather miscellaneous, collection of facts that stand badly in need of organization. All the leading towns of the North had dock-yards and built ships, and many of the smaller towns on sea-coast and navigable rivers laid the keels of lesser craft. So rapidly did the business increase that New England after 1700 was not only doing a large carrying trade on her own account, but was selling vessels in all parts of the Atlantic world—in the southern colonies and in the West Indies, Spain, Portugal, and England. The golden age of New England ship-building was during the first third of the eighteenth century, and so rapid was the growth of the business that in 1724 English shipwrights of the port of London would have had a law passed forbidding the New Englanders to build ships or compelling them to sell their ships after their arrival in England. But here the colonists scored, for, as the counsellor of the Board of Trade said, the English ship-builders had no remedy, since by the Acts of Navigation the shipping of the plantations was in all respects to be considered as English-built. Later the business fell off, the centre of the ship-building activity moved north to north-eastern Massachusetts and New Hampshire, and the English builders ceased to be concerned. New York, too, had her ship-yards, as had northern New Jersey, that of Rip Van Dam occupying the water front on the North River in the rear of Trinity churchyard; and Philadelphia, the chief ship-building city in America, in the years between 1727 and 1766, built nearly half the entire number that were entered in the ship-registry of the port during those years. In the South ship-building was less of a negligible factor than has commonly been assumed. Maryland in 1700 had 161 ships, sloops, and shallops, built or building along the Chesapeake, and some of these were large enough to engage in the English trade. Virginia built chiefly, but not entirely, for river and bay traffic, and North Carolina, though hampered by the want of good ports and harbors, made ship-building one of the established industries of the colony. South Carolina carried on her great trade with Europe chiefly in British bottoms and during the eighteenth century had scarcely a dozen ships at any one time that belonged to the province. Among the island colonies only Bermuda and the Bahamas played any part as ship-builders; while the others, early denuded of available timber, remained entirely dependent on outside carriers.

79

In size, the New England built vessels were mainly under 100 tons, with a large proportion of vessels of less than 20 tons, in which, however, ocean voyages were sometimes made. Occasionally vessels were built of 250 and 300 tons, and a few, monster ships for those days, reached 700 and 800 tons. Gabriel Thomas tells us that ships of 200 tons were built in Philadelphia, but the largest ship entered in the register mentioned above was of 150 tons, with others ranging all the way down to 4 tons. The Maryland lists mention vessels of 300 and 400 tons built in that colony, but the number could not have been large. In 1767 a vessel of 256 tons was offered for sale before launching in Virginia.

Five varieties of vessels were in use: (1) ships and pinks, three-masters with square rig; (2) snows and barks, also three-masters, but with one mast rigged fore-and-aft; (3) ketches, brigs, and brigantines, with two masts but of different sizes, combining square rig with fore-and-aft, and schooners, a native American product, with fore-and-aft rig on both masts, though in its development the schooner often carried more masts than two, without change in the cut of the sails; (4) sloops, shallops, and smacks, single-masters carrying fore-and-aft sails; and (5) boats without masts—hog-boats, fly-boats, wherries, row-boats, and canoes. Bermuda boats were conspicuous among colonial vessels, because rigged with mutton-leg sails. No statement regarding relative numbers can be made until far more information has been gathered than exists at present, but the proportion of three-masters, two-masters, and single-masters was somewhat in the ratio of one, two, and three. Of the numbers of seamen we know as yet very little.

Turning now to the complicated question of routes, which criss-crossed so bewilderingly the waters of the Atlantic, we can, I think, group the courses without difficulty, if we keep in mind the nature of supply and demand and the requirements of the Navigation Acts.

The first determining factor was the requirement that all the enumerated commodities—tobacco, sugar, cotton, indigo, ginger, fustic and other dye woods, and later cocoa, molasses, rice, naval stores, copper, beaver and other skins—be carried directly to England, or from one British plantation to another for the supply of local wants, whence, if re-exported, they were to go to England. This requirement gives us our first set of trade routes. The chief staples of all the colonies from Maryland to Barbadoes were carried to England in fleets of vessels provided by English merchants that during the days of convoys went out in the early winter, about Christmas time, and returned to England in the spring. The providing of naval protection in times of war was a matter of constant concern to the Admiralty, while the gathering of vessels and the arranging of seasons was one of concern to the merchants. After 1713 when convoying became largely unnecessary except to the West Indies, individual ships sailed at varying times, frequently returning from Maryland or Virginia as late as the end of August. We may call this route back and forth across the ocean between England and her southern and West Indian colonies the great thoroughfare of our colonial commerce. It was regular, dignified, and substantial. Out of it grew two subsidiary routes, one from New York and New England with re-exported commodities to England, and one from South Carolina and Georgia to southern Europe under the privilege allowed after 1730 and 1735 of exporting rice directly to all points south of Cape Finisterre. Thus we have a series of direct routes from nearly all of the American colonies converging upon England and one route from South Carolina and Georgia diverging to any point south of France, but generally confined to the Iberian Peninsula and the Straits. Along these routes were carried a definite series of commodities, raised, with the exception of naval stores and beaver, entirely in colonies south of Pennsylvania. To this commercial activity must be added the traffic in these same commodities among the colonists themselves, a service chiefly in the hands of the northerners, who carried tobacco, rice, logwood, and sugar from the southern and West Indian colonies to their own ports and there either consumed them, re-exported them to England, or in the case of sugar and molasses worked them over into rum and shipped the latter where they pleased.

When we consider the export activities of the northern colonies, we find ourselves involved in a more varied and complicated series of voyages. First, all the colonies north of Maryland, except Pennsylvania, had a certain but not. very extensive trade directly with England. They carried in greater or less quantities an assortment of furs, fish, rawhides, lumber, whale-fins and whale-oil, naval stores, wheat, wheat flour, hops, and a little iron, though the largest amount of exported iron came from Maryland and Virginia. They also re-exported tobacco, sugar, molasses, rum, cocoa, hard woods, and dye woods. All these they carried in their own ships as a rule, and because their own products were not sufficient to balance what they wished to buy, they frequently sold their ships also to English merchants. Salem, Newport, and New York were the chief centres of the English trade. Secondly, the northern colonies carried on a very large trade in non-enumerated commodities with the countries of Europe. To various ports, from the Baltic to the Mediterranean, they sent quantities of "merchantable" fish, lumber, flour, train oil, and rice and naval stores before they were enumerated, chiefly to Spain, Portugal, southern French ports, and Leghorn, the mart of the Mediterranean. A few ships appear to have crept through the Sound into the Baltic; others, very rarely, went up the Adriatic to Venice; and in the case of a few enterprising merchants, notably John Ross of Philadelphia, vessels were sent to India and the East, though in 1715 New England reported no trade there, only a few privateers having occasionally "strol'd that way and [taken] some rich prizes".

The bulk of the northern trade, however, was not with Europe but with the West Indies and with the other continental colonies. The ramifications of this branch of colonial commerce were almost endless, the routes followed were most diverse, and the commodities exported included almost every staple, native or foreign, that was current in the colonial world. Philadelphia and New York traded chiefly with the West Indies and concerned themselves less than did New England with the coastwise traffic; but the New Englanders, in their hundreds of vessels of small tonnage, went to Newfoundland and Annapolis Royal with provisions, salt, and rum, to New York, the Jerseys, Pennsylvania, Maryland, Virginia, North Carolina, South Carolina, Bermuda, and the Caribbee Islands, peddling every known commodity that they could lay their hands on—meats, vegetables, fruits, flour, Indian meal, refuse fish, oil, candles, soap, butter, cider, beer, cranberries, horses, sheep, cows, and oxen, pipe-

81

staves, deal boards, hoops, and shingles, earthenware and woodenware, and other similar commodities of their own; and tobacco, sugar, rum, and molasses, salt, naval stores, wines, and various manufactured goods which they imported from England. They went to Monte Cristi, Cape François, Surinam, and Curaçao, to the islands off the coast of Africa, commonly known as the Wine Islands, and there they trafficked and bargained as only the New Englander knew how to traffic and bargain. It was a peddling and huckstering business, involving an enormous amount of petty detail, frequent exchanges, and a constant lading and unlading as the captains and masters moved from port to port. Sometimes great rafts of lumber were floated down from Maine, New Hampshire, and the Delaware, and not infrequently New England ships went directly to Honduras for logwood and to Tortuga and Turks Island for salt.

Let us consider the return routes. With the southern and West Indian colonies the problem was a simple one. The merchant ships from England went as a rule directly to the colonies, generally laden with English and Continental manufactured goods that according to the act of 1663 could be obtained by the colonists only through England. They followed usually the same route coming and going, though occasionally a ship-captain would go from England to Guinea where he would take on a few negroes for the colonies. Maryland seems to have obtained nearly all her negroes in that way.

But with the northern colonies, where the vessel started in the first instance from the colony, the routes were rarely the same. A vessel might go to England, huckstering from port to port until the cargo was disposed of, and then return to America with manufactured goods. It might go to England with lumber, flour, furs, and naval stores, then back to Newfoundland for fish, then to Lisbon or the Straits, then to England with Continental articles, and thence back to the starting point. It might go directly to Spain, Portugal, or Italy, trying one port after another, Cadiz, Bilbao, Alicante, Carthagena, Marseilles, Toulon, Leghorn, and Genoa, thence to England, and thence to America. It might go directly to the Wine Islands and return by the same route with the wines of Madeira and Fayal and the Canaries, though it was a debatable question whether Canary wines were not to be classed with Continental commodities and so to be carried to America by way of England only. It might go to Spain or Portugal, thence to the Wine Islands, thence to Senegambia or Goree or the Guinea coast for beeswax, gums, and ivory, thence back to Lisbon and home by way of England; or, if it were a slave ship, it might go to the Guinea coast, thence to Barbadoes, and home, or as was probably common, to

Barbadoes first, thence to Africa, thence back to the West Indies and home, with a mixed cargo of negroes, sugar, and cash. Frequently the captain sold his cargo and even his ship for cash, and if he did this in Europe, or in England to London or Bristol merchants, he would either return with the money or invest it in manufactured goods, which he would ship on some homeward-bound vessel, returning himself with his invoice. With the New Englander, and to a somewhat lesser degree with the New Yorker and Philadelphian, the variations were as great as were the opportunities for traffic.

In this brief statement, I have given but a bare outline of a difficult and unworked problem in colonial history. Did time allow I should like to consider certain supplemental phases of the general subject that are deserving of careful attention. These are, first, the methods of distributing colonial commodities in England and Wales and of sending them into the interior, into Scotland, and into Ireland; secondly, the character and extent of the plantation trade with Ireland and Scotland directly, a matter of some interest and a good deal of difficulty; and thirdly, the re-exportation of tobacco, sugar, and other tropical and semi-tropical products from England to the European Continent. But upon these subjects I can say nothing here. One topic must, however, be briefly discussed, the question of illicit trade and smuggling.

The nature of the smuggling that went on during our colonial period is very simple, though the extent of it and the relation of it to the total volume of colonial trade is very difficult to determine. It is doubtful if satisfactory conclusions can ever be reached on these points, owing both to the lack of evidence and to its unsatisfactory character. For the most part smuggling took three forms: first, direct trade in enumerated commodities between the colonies and European countries, and participated in by English, Irish, American, and West Indian ships, trafficking to Holland, Hamburg, Spain, Portugal, Marseilles, Toulon, and other Mediterranean ports; secondly, a direct return trade to America or the West Indies, without touching at England as the law required, and participated in by the same ships, carrying the dry goods, wines, and brandies of Europe. The latter traffic had many aspects, for it included the trade between American British colonies and American foreign colonies, in which enumerated commodities, or in many cases non-enumerated commodities, were exchanged for European goods, purchasable at St. Eustatius, St. Thomas, or Curaçao, or at Monte Cristi in Hispaniola. There can be little doubt that this trade attained considerable proportions and was one of the channels whereby brandies, cocoa, silks, linens, and the like came into the colonies. There was

83

much smuggled liquor drunk in the West Indies, and many were the damask gowns and silk stockings worn; and I fear that there were many things enjoyed in Newport, Boston, and Philadelphia that came either directly from France or by way of the foreign West Indies. Indeed, it seems to have been a common practice for ships of nearly every continental colony to go to Curaçao and return with European dry goods and cocoa.

Thirdly, there was a trade of the northern colonies with the foreign West Indies, in which a vessel would carry a general cargo to Jamaica or Barbadoes, sell all or a part of it for cash—gold or light silver—pass on to the French colonies of Guadeloupe, Martinique, or Santo Domingo, or to the Dutch colony of St. Eustatius, and there buy, more cheaply than at Jamaica, Barbadoes, or the Leeward Islands, their return cargo of sugar and molasses. There was nothing strictly illegal about this traffic, unless the northern trader laid out a part of his cash in European dry goods and smuggled them into the colonies by one or other of the many contrivances so well known to all West Indian traders; but it was injurious to the British sugar colonies in depriving them of a part of their market and draining them of much of their cash. It became illegal, however, when, after the passage of the Molasses Act, expressly designed to prevent this traffic, the Northerner evaded the duties imposed by this act on foreign sugar and molasses. Then if he brought in foreign sugar and molasses without paying the duty and on the same voyage stowed away hidden bales of Holland linens and French silks, casks of French brandies, and pipes of claret, he committed a double breach of the law. Lastly, if we were to go into the problem of illicit trade in all its phases, we should have to consider a certain amount of petty smuggling off Newfoundland, in Ireland, and at the Isle of Man, and by way of the Channel Islands; but upon these points our knowledge is at present very meagre.

A useful addition to this paper would be a statement regarding our sources of information, in manuscript in England and America, and in print in a great number of accessible works. There is an immense amount of available material in the form of correspondence, accounts, registers, lists, reports, returns, log-books, port books, statements of claims, letter-books, and the like, which, though often difficult to use, are all workable and illuminating to the student who has organized his plan of treatment in a logical and not a haphazard fashion. The subject is a fascinating one, and the more one studies it, the more important and suggestive it becomes. I cannot believe that the future will show such a disregard of its significance as the past has done, for when its place is once recognized and its influence determined, colonial history will become not only fuller and richer, but also more picturesque, and the life of the colonists will appear as broader and more varied. And just as the local field will be enlarged and extended, so will the place of the colonies in the British and European systems of commercial empire be given its proper setting, and the balance between things imperial and things colonial will be restored. Only when such balance has been sought for and attained will the way be prepared for a history of the colonial period that is comprehensive in scope, scientific in conception, and thoroughly scholarly in its mode of treatment.

CHARLES M. ANDREWS.

85

THE ORIGINS OF PAPER MONEY IN THE ENGLISH COLONIES [1]

ONE of the persistent conditions in the English colonies of North America was the scarcity of coined money. The American settlements were farming communities which had become indebted through buying foreign products in order to preserve their accustomed European standards of living. Most of the farmers, moreover, were engaged in raising similar crops. Since population increased rapidly (and more rapidly than economic pursuits were diversified), the colonists soon found that they had on hand an abundance of a few staple commodities—meat, tobacco, sugar, and grain. These products had to be used in order to pay debts and to purchase imported goods. It was therefore imperative that the highest possible prices for surplus produce should be realised in trade. Such prices, however, were determined by foreign market conditions over which the colonists had no control. The War of the Spanish Succession greatly disturbed foreign trade, and depressed the prices of many of the American staples. The colonists thereupon found themselves confronted with fixed debts that had to be paid out of shrunken income. One means of maintaining the prices of their produce which appealed to the colonists was that of enlarging their fund of currency. The more money a region had (so the colonial argument ran) the more the farmers would get for their crops, and the more easily they could pay their debts and buy supplies of manufactured goods.

England in the meantime did not provide the colonies with money. The English currency was not regulated with an eye to colonial needs; no coins designed especially for the colonies were issued at the Royal Mint in the Tower of London. The law of the land prohibited the exporting of English money, even to the American plantations. At the close of the seventeenth century, it had become England's settled policy not to allow the colonies to operate mints of their own. From the English point of view, the colonies should supply England with gold and silver;

---

[1] Material for this article was collected while the writer served as fellow of the Guggenheim Foundation. Manuscripts used in the Public Record Office, London, are the Colonial Office Papers, cited as C.O. Quotations have been modernised.

D 2

not England the colonies. The latter therefore were restrained
when they tried to stop the flow of specie from America to the
mother-country.[2]

What coin the colonies obtained soon found its way to England
in the course of ordinary trade. The settlers bought more in the
form of English goods and the services of English merchants and
shipowners than their native products would pay for. Shipments
of coin accordingly helped to redress the unfavourable balance of
trade. The colonies tried various schemes to keep a reasonable
supply of hard money. They passed laws against the exportation of silver and gold, and they endeavoured to draw in the coins
of Spain and her colonies by giving them a fictitious legal value
higher than their intrinsic worth. But these remedies failed,
and another currency device came into use, and what was then
a novel experiment—public bills of credit.[3]

Such paper was the outcome of financial practices long in
vogue. From the earliest times the colonists made use of private
credit. Men of property gave their promissory notes, and the
laws of the colonies generally safeguarded the transfer of such
notes : the signer was obliged to pay the full sum to the individual
to whom the note was finally endorsed. Hence, a note of a
respected person might pass from hand to hand in a locality
for several months, all the time serving as a substitute for money.[4]
Bills of exchange had the same effect. Most of the bills that
circulated in the colonies were simply cheques drawn on deposits
lodged with English agents. Endorsed from person to person,
such bills passed freely in public and private payments. In
Virginia, for instance, a duty of 2s. a hogshead on tobacco
exported was paid by shippers in bills of exchange. These were
then assigned by the receivers to the provincial officials in payment of their salaries. The latter used them to buy the tobacco
derived from the provincial quit-rents, endorsing the bills to the
Receiver-General, who thereupon sent them to the English
Exchequer or disposed of them otherwise as the Crown directed.[5]
The widespread use of personal notes and bills of exchange

[2] Curtis Nettels, " British Policy and Colonial Money Supply," *Economic
History Review*, Vol. III. (October 1931), 221, 228.

[3] *Ibid.*, 232–40, 244.

[4] For examples of this type of law see *Charter to William Penn and the Laws
of . . . Pennsylvania . . . 1682–1700* (Harrisburg, 1879), 210–11; *Records of
the Colony . . . of New Haven . . .* (edited by C. J. Hoadly, Hartford, 1858),
II. 574–5; *The Public Records of the Colony of Connecticut* (edited by J. H.
Trumbull and C. J. Hoadly, Hartford, 1850–90), I. 512.

[5] Hartwell, Chilton and Blair, " The Present State of Virginia," received
October 20, 1697 (C.O. 5 : 1309, No. 30 (i)).

accustomed the colonists to the practice of securing ready cash by anticipating future resources or by drawing on existing credit. The same thing happened in connection with public business. The Treasurers of different colonies issued promissory notes in order to pay debts in advance of tax collections. When the tax money came into the Treasury, the outstanding notes were redeemed. Likewise, the Treasurers issued orders directing the officers of the various towns to make public payments out of the colony's stock on hand in the town concerned. This obviated sending the tax money to the Treasury and back again to the locality. The orders thus given might pass among various people upon endorsement until payment was finally made.[6] At Nevis, Treasurer's notes caused some vexation. In 1686 the creditors of the colony protested against the use of the notes and requested payment in money or sugar. The prevalence of the notes is indicated by the Council's reply that the Treasurer "ought to have some time to consider of his affairs, and not to be surprised with so hasty a proposal." [7]

When the colonial Governments borrowed money directly, they again resorted to bills of credit. Massachusetts in 1676 borrowed from certain provincial merchants, offering Treasurer's receipts to the lenders. The security for the loan consisted of the public lands of the province. Such receipts might be transferred by the original owners to their creditors, and then circulate as a crude form of currency.[8] South Carolina prefaced its first paper issue with a loan secured from private individuals, probably covered by Treasurer's notes given in anticipation of taxes.[9]

The use of private and public credit in a small way naturally led to the suggestion of pooling resources and of issuing bills of credit through an organised body. One plan contemplated a private bank of property-owners who should pledge their property as security for bills to be issued. Ordinarily it was assumed that such bills would not bear interest, but would be redeemed at

---

[6] *Colonial Records of Connecticut*, I. 273; *Records of the Governor and Company of Massachusetts Bay* (edited by N. B. Shurtleff, Boston, 1853–54), V. 66.

[7] Proposal of Nevis Assembly, August 28, 1688; reply of Council (C.O. 155 : 1, 177–8). Rhode Island enacted March 23, 1697, "that all those bills for money due to the deputies for serving at assemblies, which are signed by the clerk of the House of Deputies, shall be good to all intents and purposes, as to demand and receive their salary by; and so to stand for the future." *Records of the Colony of Rhode Island . . .* (edited by J. R. Bartlett, Providence, 1856–65), III. 326.

[8] Act of February 21, 1676, *Massachusetts Colonial Records*, V. 71.

[9] *The Statutes at Large of South Carolina* (edited by Thomas Cooper and D. J. McCord, Columbia, 1836–41), II. 189, 810.

a specified time. Nor did the early plans call for a permanent
fund of coin or fluid capital for retiring the bills when due.
What was anticipated resembled a regulated company rather
than a joint stock. The members would pledge a certain amount
of either land or personal property as security for the bills, and
the company would determine the total amount to be issued.
The members would agree to accept the bills of fellow-members
in ordinary dealings, but apparently each member was to issue
his own bills and to have the responsibility for redeeming them.
From the scanty evidence remaining it appears that John Winthrop, Jr., suggested such a scheme for Connecticut in the 1660's.[10]
In Massachusetts the Rev. John Woodbridge championed a
similar proposal, publishing in 1682 his *Severals Relating to the
Fund*.[11] Perhaps a bank was actually in operation there for a
short period in 1681–82. In 1686 a new project was presented
by John Blackwell. The Council of Massachusetts gave its
sanction, and ordered that the bills of the new bank should be
esteemed current money in both public and private payments.
This bank, however, never actually got under way. It was
sponsored during the term of Governor Andros; it is likely that
the scheme became involved in his downfall.[12] Later, when
Blackwell was Governor of Pennsylvania, he recommended to
the merchants there that they might properly issue personal
bills to pass money among such people as would accept them.
Nicholson in 1695 reported that Pennsylvania had a bank of
£20,000, but he did not describe its features.[13]

The second plan suggested was an outgrowth of the notes of
provincial treasurers. Instead of allowing the Treasurer to
issue bills in anticipation of taxes, the Assembly assumed this
task itself. It provided for stamping bills of credit, which were
to be used at first to pay public debts and then to be retired
when certain designated tax money had been collected. The
colonial Treasury was pledged to the redemption of the bills
issued. This, of course, was the most common type of paper
money struck in colonial times.

[10] Curtis Nettels, "The Beginnings of Money in Connecticut," *Transactions
of the Wisconsin Academy of Sciences, Arts and Letters*, XXIII. (1927), 26–8.
[11] Reprinted in A. M. Davis, *Tracts relating to the Currency of Massachusetts-
Bay* . . . (Boston, 1902), 1–12.
[12] A. M. Davis, *Currency and Banking in the Province of Massachusetts-Bay*,
Publications of the American Economic Association, Third Series (New York,
1900–1), II. 75–81; J. B. Felt, *Historical Account of Massachusetts Currency*
(Boston, 1839), 46–7.
[13] Charles P. Keith, *The Chronicles of Pennsylvania* (Philadelphia, 1917),
I. 293.

A third plan combined certain of the features of the private bank and of public bills of credit. The colonial Government created a land bank by issuing bills of credit which were distributed among citizens in exchange for mortgages on their lands. The receiver of the bill paid to the colony an annual interest charge for the use of the money; likewise it was his duty to redeem the bills at a stated time. By this means public and private interests were bound together to make the land bank a going concern.

A Virginia Tobacco Act of 1713 provided for another use of credit. The planters were allowed to bring their tobacco to public warehouses, where it should be tested, weighed, and stored. The planter received in exchange certificates called tobacco notes. These stated the amount and quality of the tobacco deposited, and constituted the planter's title to the tobacco. The notes could then be used in all tobacco payments in the colony: they were freely transferable, so that the last holder acquired the right to remove and sell the tobacco which was covered by the note.[14]

By 1715 the colonial experiment with public bills of credit had made considerable progress. Massachusetts inaugurated the movement with its issue of 1690. South Carolina printed its first bills in 1703. Barbados made a fruitless attempt in 1706. The year 1709 brought forth the issues of Connecticut, New York, New Hampshire, and New Jersey. Rhode Island followed in 1710 and North Carolina in 1712. Thus before 1715 each of the mainland colonies except Virginia, Maryland, and Pennsylvania had established public paper in the form of bills of credit.

Many factors and conditions produced this innovation. It is difficult to determine to what extent the colonies were seeking consciously a remedy for their money troubles—to what extent they hoped, through bills of credit, to stimulate commerce. When considering the proposed bank in 1686 the Massachusetts Council had in mind particularly " the great decay of trade and obstructions to manufactures and commerce in this country, and multiplicity of debts and suits thereupon, principally occasioned by the present scarcity of coin." It did not appear " how the same may be remedied, unless some other secure medium be approved than a species of silver." [15] Later, William

---

[14] Spotswood to Board of Trade, December 29, 1713 (C.O. 5 : 1317, No. 20; Act of 1713, *Ibid.*, No. 44 (vii)).

[15] Report of Dudley and Council, September 27, 1686, quoted in Felt, 46, citing Massachusetts Archives, Usurpation, I.

Penn asserted that " the want of money to circulate trade . . .
has put Boston herself upon thinking of tickets to supply the
want of coin." [16] An Act of Massachusetts in 1690 mentioned
" the present poverty and calamities of the country, and through
a scarcity of money the want of an adequate measure of commerce." [17] The same view was reaffirmed by an Act of issue in
1702.[18] At the close of the war the Assembly declared that the
bills issued had greatly stimulated business, and that a trade
depression had occurred when most of them had been withdrawn.[19]
The movement after the war was borne along on the confidence
of the public that paper served effectively in place of coin.

It was undoubtedly a scarcity of coin that led the planters   *91*
of Barbados to issue their short-lived bills of 1706.   This scarcity
made the paying of money debts extremely difficult; it threw a
shadow of insecurity over the whole economic life of the island.[20]
Connecticut in 1709 justified its first issue by the claim of money
shortage, and South Carolina in 1712 sought to give " a further
encouragement to trade and commerce " by means of £52,000 of
new bills.[21]

An account of New York paper, written in 1720 by Sir H.
Macksworth, maintained that " the want of silver and gold was
the occasion of these bills and species, and that want was occasioned because they are confined in their trade, chiefly to Old
England, where the balance of trade being against them, they
have been forced to send almost all their silver and gold." [22]
The Assembly of Rhode Island stated its case in 1715 for reissuing
bills after the war.   The colony's money supply was exhausted,
" so that there is a sensible decay of trade, the farmers thereby
discouraged, husbandmen, and many others, reduced to great
want; and all sorts of business languishing, few having wherewith to pay their arrears; and many not wherewithal to sustain
their daily wants by reason that the silver and gold in the first
place to defray the incidental and occasional charges, have been

[16] W. T. Root, *The Relations of Pennsylvania with the British Government*
(New York, 1912), 182.
[17] W. B. Weeden, *Social and Economic History of New England* (Boston,
1890), I. 379.
[18] Act of November 21, 1702 (C.O. 5 : 771, 233–4).
[19] Act of November 4, 1714 (*Acts and Resolves of the Province of Massachusetts
Bay* (Boston, 1869–1909), I. 751).
[20] Messrs. Sharpe, Coxe, and Walker to Board of Trade, October 8, 1707
(C.O. 28 : 10, No. 40 (ii)).
[21] Connecticut Act of June 1709 (C.O. 5 : 538, 145); *South Carolina Statutes*,
II. 389.
[22] " Sir H. Macksworth's Proposal in Miniature . . ." (C.O. 5 : 1085, No. 30).

exhausted; and those few bills of public credit put forth by this
Government falling far short of discharging the colony's arrears,
has left us little or no medium of exchange." [23]

If coin shortage was an underlying cause, war provided the
immediate occasion for colonial paper. When Massachusetts
sent its expedition to Canada in 1690 under Phips it did not make
adequate financial arrangements. The leaders assumed that
success and enemy treasure would pay the necessary costs.
Failure, debts, unpaid soldiers, and threats of mutiny at Boston
were the actual results. This situation evoked the first paper
issues. Not a general shortage of money, but a shortage of cash
in the provincial treasury, observed Samuel Sewall at a later date,
gave birth to the first bills of credit.[24] When Joseph Dudley
became Governor in 1702, he found the supply of coin totally
insufficient for financing the French war. He was obliged to
maintain a thousand men at a yearly cost of £30,000. Without
public paper, he testified, he "could never have subsisted nor
clothed the forces, that have defended . . . these colonies . . .,
but must have left all to ruin and mischief." [25]

Frontier struggles also forced the Carolinas to act. Beginning with the South Carolina issue of 1703, caused by indebtedness arising from the St. Augustine expedition, the various acts
of the two provinces usually pleaded the exigencies of Indian
wars as the occasion for emitting additional bills.[26] The Canada
expeditions and the accompanying requisitions on the northern
colonies started New Hampshire, New York, Connecticut, New
Jersey, and Rhode Island on their paper careers in 1709–10, and
led to general reissues in 1711.

Once a colony had become accustomed to the bills, it quickly
added to the uses for which they were issued. Massachusetts in
1694 ordered that reissued bills should be paid out to meet the
general expenses of the province in anticipation of tax collections.[27] This practice continued, and later Acts enumerated
many purposes for the initial use of new bills: to pay public
debts, to provide for the support of the Government, and to
prosecute the war. Similar appropriations of newly issued bills
appeared in South Carolina in 1707,[28] in North Carolina in 1715,

[23] Act of July 5, 1715 (*Rhode Island Colonial Records*, IV. 189–90).
[24] Weeden, I. 379; Davis, *Currency and Banking*, I. 8.
[25] Dudley to Board of Trade, December 1, 1713 (C.O. 5 : 866, No. 153).
[26] South Carolina Act of May 8, 1703 (*South Carolina Statutes*, II. 210); C. J.
Bullock, *Essays on the Monetary History of the United States* (New York, 1900), 129.
[27] Act of June 22 (*Massachusetts Acts and Resolves*, I. 173).
[28] *South Carolina Statutes*, II. 302.

and in New Hampshire in 1712.[29]   Rhode Island in 1711 emitted
£300, which it lent to one of the public creditors.[30]   An important
issue in New York in 1714 was to be used to pay provincial debts
that had accumulated in the long struggle between the Assembly
and Governor Hunter.[31]   Ordinarily, after two or three years,
the individual colony abandoned the practice of designating newly
issued bills as for military service only, and ordered that they be
used in all sorts of public payments.

Only one colonial law suggests an open design of lessening
private indebtedness by means of public bills of credit.   This was
the Act of Barbados, the avowed purpose of which was to enable
debtors to pay their debts.[32]

93

The main interest in colonial paper centres in its relation to
other forms of currency.   How might a uniform value of paper
in terms of specie be preserved ?   What was the standard of
value to which public paper should conform ?   By 1690 every
colony had created a special currency of its own, called " current
lawful money of the province."   This currency consisted of
foreign coins (principally Spanish pieces of eight) which were
valued by provincial law in terms of shillings.   Thus a Massachusetts Act of 1692 defined pieces of eight, Mexico, pillar, or
Seville, of seventeen pennyweight, as worth 6s. each in the colony.
Such foreign coins were received and disbursed at their legal
rates in all public payments.   The persistent tendency of the
colonial legislatures was to give the silver in the piece of eight
a legal value higher than its intrinsic value when exchanged for
English coins.   Thus Massachusetts valued at 6s. a piece of eight
worth less than 4s. 6d. in English coin.   The piece of eight,
Mexico, pillar, or Seville, became the common measure of current
lawful money ; that is, an ounce of silver in colonial finance came
to mean an ounce of silver in pieces of eight, Mexico, pillar, or
Seville.   When bills of credit appeared, the colonial legislatures
intended that such paper should be equal to current lawful
money.   A certain number of shillings in bills of credit were
supposed to represent an ounce of silver, Mexico, pillar, or Seville,
as valued by law.   Although the earliest colonial Acts authorising
the issue of paper did not define bills of credit as current lawful
money, it was uniformly provided that such bills should pass as
current money in all public transactions—that they should be
receivable as such in all public payments.   When the bills were

[29] Bullock, 130.   [30] Act of October 15, 1711 (C.O. 5 : 951, 125).
[31] Act of July 1714 (C.O. 5 : 1144, 189).
[32] Act of 1706 (C.O. 389 : 19, 387).

made legal tender they became equivalent to current lawful money in private transactions.[33]

In the opinion of the colonists, the principal factor affecting the specie value of their paper was the provision made for redeeming it from tax revenues. When new issues of bills were voted, the legislatures levied taxes to create a fund for redemption.[34]

[33] *Economic History Review*, III. 234–40; Curtis Nettels, "British Payments in the American Colonies, 1685–1715," *English Historical Review*, XLVIII. April, 1933), 229–31.

[34] The first phase of the Massachusetts experiment extended from 1690 to 1702. The issues authorised in 1690 and 1691 amounted to £40,000. At first the people would not give current money in exchange for these bills at their face values. In October 1691, bills amounting to £10,000 that had found their way into the provincial treasury were destroyed. The next year an Act levied a tax of £30,000, presumably to retire the remaining £30,000 of bills in circulation—a tax to be collected in 1693 and 1694. After the latter year, Massachusetts paper travelled a smooth course. Ordinarily the total sum outstanding did not exceed £15,000. When reissues were made, only small amounts—£2,000 to £6,000 at a time—were returned to circulation. Moreover, the Assembly voted adequate taxes for redeeming newly issued bills. On the average the collection of such taxes came within eight months after the bills went into use. The sum of the bills outstanding in the single year between 1693 and 1702 was probably less than the total amount of taxes paid annually by the province. (Davis, *Currency and Banking*, I. 11–17.) The Acts relating to paper money for the period 1690–1702 are printed in *Massachusetts Acts and Resolves*, I. They are as follows: June 24, 1692, 29–30; July 2, 1692, 36; December 16, 1692, 93; December 11, 1693, 146; June 20, 1694, 165; June 22, 1694, 173; September 14, 1694, 177; October 27, 1694, 188; March 15, 1695, 201; June 27, 1695, 215; March 5, 1696, 228–30; June 17, 1696, 243; October 3, 1696, 250; December 18, 1696, 262; June 16, 1697, 278; October 29, 1697, 301; June 27, 1698, 337; December 9, 1698, 358–9; July 14, 1699, 356–7; March 23, 1700, 417; July 13, 1700, 438–41; April 19, 1701, 454; June 30, 1701, 483–6; June 25, 1702, 497. See also Weeden, I. 380–8.

In the early years of Queen Anne's War, Massachusetts paper continued to command full respect. The total amount placed in circulation was not excessive. The total sum of bills outstanding at the end of each year until 1710 was:

1702	· · ·	£5,000	1705	· · ·	£28,000	1708	· · ·	£43,000
1703	· · ·	10,000	1706	· · ·	28,000	1709	· · ·	64,000
1704	· · ·	22,000	1707	· · ·	28,000	1710	· · ·	89,000

During this period the province provided for the retirement of its bills. The issues of 1702–3 were redeemed by taxes within about a year, those of 1704–6 within about eighteen months, and those of 1707–8 within from two to three years. The issues of 1709, however, were to run four years, and by the time the bills of 1710 had been emitted the province had mortgaged its future income from direct property taxes for nearly five years to come. The taxes paid annually to redeem the bills amounted to about £22,000. However, when the bills were in the hands of the treasurer, the Assembly refused to destroy them; it merely issued them out again. Thus the special taxes did not lessen the total volume of paper outstanding: they only prevented an unmanageable increase.

For Acts of the period 1702–10, see C.O. 5: 771: Act of November 21, 1702, 234–5; March 27, 1703, 243; September 9, 1703, 152; March 24, 1704, 261; *Massachusetts Acts and Resolves*, I. Act of March 27, 1703, 515; July 27, 1703, 520–5; September 9, 1703, 533; November 23, December 2, 1703, 542; March 24, 1704, 540; June 24, 1704, 548–51; June 30, 1704, 561; August 17,

Taxpayers might pay their taxes in the outstanding paper, whereupon it would be destroyed. Or payment might be made in specie or produce, which could then be exchanged for the bills still in private hands. The security for the bills of Connecticut,[35]

1704, 561; November 18, 1704, 562; February 27, 1705, 562; June 30, 1705, 566–70, 580; December 3, 1705, 581; April 12, 1706, 581; July 9, 1706, 601; July 13, 1706, 589–93; December 7, 1706, 601; March 22, 1707, 602; June 13, 1707, 610; June 12, 1707, 617; July 1708, 624; July 3, 1708, 634–5; October 29, 1708, 635; February 26, 1709, 635; June 18, 1709, 645–6; November 8, 1709, 646; February 17, 1710, 647; June 20, 1710, 658–62; June 23, 1710, 658; November 11, 1710, 669.

After 1710 the situation changed. The time for paying taxes to redeem new bills was set farther into the future : postponements of six or seven years became the common rule. When the public resources were thus pledged so far ahead, the Assembly made use of private credit as a security for new bills. In 1711 an issue of £50,000 was lent to merchants of the province to be redeemed by them within two years. These merchants furnished the supplies for the Hill-Walker expedition, for which they were paid in the newly issued paper. The security they presented for redeeming the bills consisted of bills of exchange given them by British agents in payment for the supplies provided. As these bills of credit were like all other province bills, they added £50,000 to the total volume of paper, the merchants being allowed two years in which to redeem them. The Assembly next made use of private credit in 1714 and 1716, when it issued £50,000 and £100,000 respectively to be lent to private citizens on land security. Through these and other issues the total sum of the bills rose considerably— approximately to this extent :

Dec. 31, 1711 £145,000   Dec. 31, 1713 £152,000   Dec. 31, 1715 £170,000
Dec. 21, 1712 £160,000   Dec. 31, 1714 £184,000   Dec. 31, 1716 £202,500

In 1714 Paul Dudley referred to the " excessive price of every thing among us (and even the very necessaries of life)," and in 1717 Governor Shute complained of an " intolerable discount on the bills." Every one now noted the utter dearth of coin; paper served in all transactions. As measured by coin, sterling exchange, or prices of commodities, the bills of credit were falling steadily in value.

For Acts after 1710 see Massachusetts Acts and Resolves, I. June 13, 1711, 686; November 3, 1711, 687; March 19, 1712, 687; June 7, 1712, 693–5; June 13, 1712, 707; June 17, 1713, 711–15; June 16, 1713, 733; June 25, 1714, 741; June 22, 1714, 752; November 4, 1714, 750–2; August 25, 1715, Ibid., II. 34–5; December 20, 1715, 35; June 23, 1716, 70; December 3, 1716, 70. Order of Massachusetts Assembly, July 6, 1711, C.O. 5 : 898, No. 10 (x); Davis, Currency and Banking, I. 55–61; Act of November 4, 1714, Massachusetts Acts and Resolves, I. 750–51; Act of December 4, 1716, C.O. 5 : 774, 283; Massachusetts Acts and Resolves, II. 17–21, 33, 52–7; Dudley to Governor and Council of Massachusetts, August 17, 1714, C.O. 5 : 866, No. 159 (ii).

[36] The fact that Massachusetts paper maintained a parity with province money until about 1712 must have been instrumental in leading the other colonies to similar issues. Connecticut struck its first bills before the depreciation of Massachusetts currency. Those put into circulation between 1709 and 1716 represented £45,500. The aggregate of the bills outstanding at the end of each of these years was :

1709 · · · £19,000   1711 · · · £23,000   1714 · · · £26,350
1710 · · · 20,000   1712 · · · 24,500   1715 · · · 26,500
                     1713 · · · 25,200

Although each year showed an increase, it was normally very slight. When

New Hampshire, and New Jersey consisted only of general property taxes. Such taxes also secured part of the issues of every other colony, but in New York they were supplemented by revenues from an excise on strong liquors and from import and tonnage duties.[36] North Carolina used a poll tax, and South

---

new issues or reissues were voted, the Assembly always provided a tax—and one generally about 5 per cent. larger than the sum of the issue. But the collection of such taxes was placed far into the future. The tax to redeem the first issue became due half after one year, and half after two years. The tax for the second issue was postponed six years; for the third issue, eight; for the fourth, nine; and for the fifth, twelve. Then the Assembly became more cautious: issues of 1712 and 1713 were to be redeemed in from five to eight years. But the postponement increased again in 1714 and 1715 to ten years. The £26,500 in bills circulating in 1715 were covered by ten separate taxes, one of which was to be collected each year until 1725. By the close of the war the bills had become the common currency of the colony. *Colonial Records of Connecticut*, vol. 1706–16, Act of June 8, 1709, 111–12; in C.O. 5 : 538 : Acts of June 9–11, 1709, 145–8; October 1709, 148; May 1710, 152–5; October 1710, 155–6; May 1711, 157; June 1711, 171; May 1712, 175; October 1712, 183–4; May 1713, 185–6, October 1713, 189–90; May 1714, 193; October 1714, 199; May 1715, 201.

[36] Three separate issues of 1709 (£13,000 in all) initiated the paper policy of New York. The next emission (1711) created £10,000 in new bills. Then came a large issue for £27,680 in 1714, followed by a £6,000 addition in 1715. Rough estimates show the following amounts outstanding at the close of the years 1709–16 :

1709	· · · £11,000	1711	· · · £17,000	1714	· · · £33,365
1710	· · · 7,000	1712	· · · 13,000	1715	· · · 36,350
		1713	· · · 9,000		

The bills of 1709 (£13,000) were put out in advance of direct taxes previously granted amounting to £14,000. The Assembly arranged that these taxes should come in gradually, in seven instalments of £2,000 each, to be paid between November 1709 and November 1713. Of the total tax, £6,000 was to be paid within eighteen months, and the remaining £8,000 within thirty to forty-eight months. A further tax of £10,000 covered the issue of 1711—a tax consisting of ten semi-annual payments of £1,000 each beginning May 1714, and running through November 1718. However, the province now refused to pay interest on its outstanding bills, although it redeemed them promptly when the designated taxes came into the Treasury.

The issue of 1714 marks a change of tax policy. Instead of a direct tax, the Assembly provided that the income from an excise on strong liquors should secure the bills. For each of twenty-one years the excise revenue should be used to retire a part of the bills : the tax therefore would have to yield on the average £1,315 a year. Only bills of the 1714 issue could be tendered for the excise, and thereafter they were to be destroyed.

The issue of 1715 resorted to import and tonnage duties which were to cancel the new bills (£6,000) at the rate of £1,200 yearly in the period July 1716 to July 1720. By 1715 the future revenues of the province had been heavily mortgaged : approximately £4,500 was due in each of the years 1716, 1717, and 1718. For the next two years the taxes amounted to about £2,300, and for the period 1721 and 1734 the liquor excise was pledged to redeem a small annual quota of the remaining bills.

The province regularly valued its paper money at 8s. an ounce of silver. By

Carolina relied in part on duties on negroes and goods imported
and on furs and skins exported. Massachusetts, Rhode Island,[37]
and South Carolina each based a large issue on private land
securities.

Several practices of the colonies crossed their theory of redemption. First of all, the date of collecting taxes was postponed far
into the future. Massachusetts, Rhode Island, South Carolina,

---

1717 depreciation had set in. " The multiplying of paper money," wrote a
group of merchants trading to New York, " prevents the currency of silver and
gold, for whilst the former is in being, the other is kept up so that the traders
cannot remit in gold or silver as usual, neither is it to be got under 10 per cent.
more than usual whilst paper money is circulating." Act of June 9, 1709,
C.O. 5 : 1147, No. 26; July 26, 1711, *Ibid.*, Nos. 46, 47; Acts of November
1709, C.O. 5 : 1144, 102-3, 107-8; Act of July 1714, *Ibid.*, 191; memorial of
eight merchants trading to New York, C.O. 5 : 1051, No. 67; Acts of 1715,
C.O. 5 : 1051, No. 3; C.O. 5 : 1144, 208-9.

[37] The policy of Rhode Island differed materially from that of Connecticut.
The first issues of the former came in the year after July 1710—four separate
emissions amounting to £13,000. Instead of increasing gradually the amount of
its bills in circulation, the Assembly refrained for four years from further issues,
and then all of a sudden, in July and October 1715, flooded the colony with
£40,000 in new land bank-bills. In the meantime provision had been made for
supporting the first £13,000. The initial issue, for £5,000, was secured by a tax
to be collected in four annual £1,000 instalments beginning June 30, 1711. The
second issue, for £1,000, carried no tax at all, and the third issue, also for £1,000,
was protected by a £1,000 tax to be paid in June 1711. Thus on June 30, 1711,
two taxes were due—each for £1,000. It appears, however, that the colony
paid only £1,000 at that time. The bills thus received were not destroyed;
they were returned to circulation. Another issue of June 1711 added £6,000
more to the total volume of bills without an accompanying tax. In the summer
of 1711 therefore the paper circulating amounted to £13,000—for which only
£4,000 in taxes had been granted. Again in June 1712 the colony defaulted by
not retiring the £1,000 which was scheduled for cancellation then, and the tax
security shrank to £3,000. However, the Assembly voted a new tax of £8,000
in May 1713. But this tax did not become effective until June 1716; moreover,
it was to be paid in yearly instalments of £1,000, so that the security funds for
part of the bills did not come in until 1723. Once more the colony failed to
pay the £1,000 due in June 1713; this left £3,000 without security. A new tax
voted in February 1714 provided for sinking £2,000 of the delinquent bills in
April 1714. But when April came, the treasurer lacked the means, and of the
£3,000 in taxes due in 1714 only £1,100 could be found for retiring bills. Whether
the last instalment of the £5,000 tax, which should have been paid in June 1715,
was actually collected does not appear. The adding of £40,000 new bills made
the total in use somewhere near £51,000. The security for this sum consisted of
£40,000 in mortgages on individual estates and £8,000 in taxes due at the rate
of £1,000 yearly for eight years beginning June 5, 1716. The sudden expansion
of the paper currency caused an early depreciation. Although at first declared
to be equivalent to current New England money (then silver at 8*s.* an ounce),
by 1715 the Rhode Island bills had fallen to 12*s.* an ounce. (Rhode Island
Acts in *Rhode Island Colonial Records*, IV. 96; October 25, 1710, 102-3; November 27, 1710, 106; June 28, 1711, 123-4; November 14, 1711, 128; February 27,
1712, 137; June 30, 1712, 146; May 6, 1713, 150; February 24, 1714, 164-5;
May 5, 1714, 169-70; June 15, 1714, 176; July 5, 1715, 191; October 20, 1715,
July 5, and October 26, 1715, *Acts and Laws of Rhode Island* (1730), 79-81, 83.)

and New Hampshire [38] generally deferred such collections about four or five years. Connecticut and New Jersey each mortgaged part of their public revenues twelve years in advance, and New York secured one issue with taxes to be collected during a twenty-one-year term.[39] Such levies on future income meant that a large number of bills went into circulation for which there was no immediate possibility of public redemption at their face values.

In the second place, some of the Assemblies failed, at the time of issue, to provide adequate taxes for all the bills printed. Rhode Island, New Jersey, and South Carolina [40] each had paper

[38] In contrast to Rhode Island, New Hampshire held to a moderate course. Its first issues in 1709-10 placed only £5,500 in circulation. Small additions came later : £2,000 in 1711, £500 in 1712, and £1,200 in 1714. The close of the year 1715 found only £8,200 outstanding. More than adequate tax levies accompanied these issues. The initial bills of 1709, amounting to £3,000, were covered by a £5,000 tax to be paid £1,000 yearly, beginning December 1710. Afterwards, the Assembly provided that the securing taxes should be paid, on the average, about five years after the bills were emitted. However, when the first taxes were received into the Treasury the bills on hand were returned to circulation. From the £6,000 security fund collected before 1715, only £1,000 of the bills were redeemed. But the province, when reissuing old bills, granted new taxes to retire them. The £8,200 circulating in 1715 were secured by taxes previously voted amounting to £10,500. However, the mortgage on the province revenues for the period December 1715 to December 1719 was ten times larger than the sum actually redeemed in the years 1709-14. The bills still had good standing in 1715, when they brought silver at the rate of 9s. an ounce. (*Laws of New Hampshire* (edited by A. S. Batchellor, Manchester, N.H., 1904, 1913), II. : December 2, 1710, 102-4; May 14, 1711, 105; October 10, 1711, 112-13; October 15, 1712, 116; April 26, 1715, 186-7; see also Bullock, 207-8, 209, 211; see Act of May 15, 1714, C.O. 5 : 951, 189-90; December 6, 1709, 69-71. (Bullock, 210, 211.))

[39] New Jersey before 1715 created but a slight volume of paper. Only two issues appeared—one of £3,000 in 1709 and one of £5,000 in 1711. The taxes for the first fell due in June of 1710 and 1711. However, the colony defaulted in 1710, and that part of the tax was delayed until June 1712. The second issue (£5,000 of 1711) carried a tax of £5,440 to be paid in five yearly instalments, starting with 1712. An Act of March 1714 finally retired all the bills of the first issue, but it also put £2,000 of the new bills back into use—bills that had been paid as tax money in 1712-13. This sum of £2,000 went into circulation without any security to guard it. At the time the province was having great difficulty with tax collections : some of the unpaid taxes had been on the books of the province since 1708. At the close of 1714, the bills of credit outstanding must have amounted to about £4,700. Taxes amounting to £3,123 had been voted as security, leaving £1,677 unprovided for. Acts of June 30, 1709, February 10, 1711; July 16, 1711; March 11, 1714; C.O. 5 : 1006, Nos. 7, 30, 35, 42. See also Act for collecting taxes in arrear, March 16, 1714, *Ibid.*, No. 55.

[40] The first bills of South Carolina of 1703 (for £6,000) remained in use until 1707, although taxes were voted at the outset to redeem them. However, the province did not pay all these taxes, and moreover, as the money came into the Treasury, it was spent for other purposes. A new issue of £8,000 in 1707 retired the old bills then circulating. The security now provided consisted of duties on skins, furs, negroes, and goods imported and exported. For four years, until July 1711, these duties were to be used to retire the 1707 issue. Three additional emissions for £8,000 came in 1708 and 1711—one for £1,000, one for

outstanding at times which was not backed by any security at all. New Hampshire, on the other hand, usually provided a tax fund larger than the sum of the bills authorised.

Moreover, many of the colonies became delinquent in the payment of taxes provided as security. Rhode Island and New Jersey were serious offenders on this score, and South Carolina to a smaller extent. About 1715 Massachusetts showed signs of defaulting. All the colonies fell into the habit of reissuing the bills when they were received at the date scheduled for cancellation, although a new tax was generally voted to cover those put back into circulation.[41]

£5,000, and one for £2,000. The Assembly continued the duties until July 1716, and applied them to the gradual cancellation of these bills. Apparently it was expected that the duties would retire about £2,000 of the bills annually. In November 1711 another issue appeared—the so-called Tuscarora bills, amounting to £4,000. Accordingly, by the beginning of 1712, £16,000 in ordinary bills had been emitted in addition to the £4,000 of the Tuscarora issue. Had the special duties been used to redeem the earlier bills, a total of £8,000 should have been withdrawn by July 1711.

The issue of June 1712 tells what had happened. This Act created £52,000 in new bills. Of this sum £32,000 was to be lent on private security, and £4,000 to be put to public uses, although no security accompanied this particular £4,000. The remaining £16,000 was to be used to draw in old bills for their redemption, excepting the Tuscarora issue of 1711. This meant that none of the earlier bills struck between 1707 and November 1711 had been retired, for only £16,000 had been issued all together.

In 1716 it was estimated that there were bills in circulation issued before 1713 which amounted to £44,000. Apparently, only £8,000 of the issue of 1712 plus the Tuscarora bills (£12,000 in all) had been retired. The security for this £44,000 consisted principally of private mortgages and of the duties on imports and exports as extended to July 1716. In the meantime, the province added £30,000 of new bills in 1715, covering them by a property tax of that sum to be paid in 1717. Accordingly, in 1716 the paper currency amounted to about £74,000. Depreciation had not set in by 1710, when paper exchanged for silver at 8s. an ounce. In 1715, the rate was 10s. 2d. an ounce; in 1720, 27s. 6d. an ounce. (*South Carolina Statutes*, II.: May 8, 1702, 210; December 23, 1703, 231; November 4, 1704, 248; 257, 277; April 9, 1706, 277; July 5, 1707, 302–5; July 12, 1707, 308; February 14, 1708, 322; April 24, 1708, 326; March 1, 1711, 353–4; November 10, 1711, 366, 604; June 7, 1712, 604; an account of South Carolina paper in *South Carolina Statutes*, IX. 766, 769; " Demonstration of the Present State of South Carolina " presented to Board of Trade, June 23, 1716, by Richard Beresford, C.O. 5 : 1265, No. 30 (i)).

[41] North Carolina's initial issues of 1712 and 1713 created a paper currency of £12,000. Although tax security had been provided, it appears that these first bills remained current until 1715. An Act of that year authorised a new emission of £24,000, half of which was to discharge public debts : holders of the old bills had to exchange them for the new, thus retiring all bills save the new £24,000. In order to redeem the bills, an Act of 1715 granted an annual tax on polls and land amounting to £2,000. This tax should continue until the bills had been retired : it was not to be lowered or repealed, nor should any new bills be struck until all the 1715 issues had been withdrawn. The Assembly declared that £150 of the bills should be worth £100 sterling. This rated bills in silver at 7s. 9d. an ounce. In 1721 the paper currency amounted to £12,000, and its relation to sterling was still that of 150 to 100. (Bullock, 129–34.)

Besides providing taxes with which to redeem newly issued bills of credit, the colonies used other devices to uphold their intended values in specie. Acts of issue generally promised that the holders of the colony's bills might at any time exchange them for any stock in the colonial Treasury. But since the Treasuries ordinarily did not have any stock of either specie or goods of approved value, this promise probably had no effect in maintaining the specie value of the bills.

Some Acts went a bit further, and designated that certain taxes levied to redeem bills of credit could be paid only with such bills themselves or with silver coin. Connecticut, New Hampshire, and New Jersey used this device. New York at first provided that only the bills of a given issue could be used to pay the particular tax levied for sinking that issue.[42]

Since bills of credit seemed to entail borrowing from private citizens, the question· of an interest charge was considered. Massachusetts created a precedent in 1691 by agreeing to receive its own bills in all public payments at 5 per cent. advance. This premium remained in force until December 1693, when it was abolished by an Act of reissue. But it was revived in the following June, and was granted regularly during the next five years. The Assembly again abolished it in March 1700. Once more restored in 1702, it lasted without interruption during the next eighteen years.[43] Connecticut allowed a similar premium in the period 1709–14, and both Rhode Island and New Hampshire did so in their first Acts of issue. New Hampshire discontinued it in 1711, only to revive it in 1714. Rhode Island, on the other hand, allowed the 5 per cent. advance in public payments until 1715, when the Assembly abandoned it, alleging that experience had proved it "to be a damage to the colony, and no benefit to the inhabitants thereof."[44]

New York followed a slightly different plan at the start. Her first bills were to run for only short periods, and should be redeemed by taxes paid in the bills themselves. An allowance of 2½ per cent. was voted for every six months that the bills

[42] Connecticut Acts, 1710–15, C.O. 5 : 538, 156, 157, 171, 175, 183, 184, 186, 189, 193, 199, 201; New Hampshire Acts, 1709–14, C.O. 5 : 951, 69–71, 128, 189–90; New Jersey Acts, 1709, 1711, C.O. 5 : 1006, Nos. 7, 35; New York Acts, 1709–14, C.O. 5 : 1147, Nos. 26, 47; C.O. 5 : 1144, 103, 108, 191.

[43] Davis, *Currency and Banking*, I. 12; Act of December 11, 1693, *Massachusetts Acts and Resolves*, I. 146; Act of June 22, 1694, *Ibid.*, 173; Act of March 23, 1700, *Ibid.*, 417; Act of October 15, 1702, C.O. 5 : 771, 234; C.O. 5 : 866, No. 153.

[44] Bullock, 207, 210; *Rhode Island Colonial Records*, IV. 102, 189.

ECON. HIST.—NO. 9   E

remained in circulation before paid in for taxes. But the province
discarded the premium in 1711. Governor Hunter explained
that it induced holders of the bills to hoard them until the
interest became due, thereby destroying their effectiveness as
currency.[45]

South Carolina resorted to another arrangement. When its
initial bills were paid into the Treasury as tax money, the payer
received 12 per cent. interest computed from the time the bills
had been put into circulation by the colony. But this generous
allowance did not survive after 1707. It led to hoarding, and,
moreover, imposed an extra burden too heavy for the colony to
carry. The computing of interest on the bills, especially on those
paid into the Treasury and later reissued, added to the cost of
the experiment.[46] In 1715, Massachusetts, Connecticut, and
New Hampshire were allowing the 5 per cent. when the bills
were received in public payments. New York, New Jersey,
Rhode Island, and South Carolina, on the other hand, had
discarded the premium.

Many of the Assemblies attempted to force the acceptance of
their bills in private transactions. The first bills of Massachusetts
were not made legal tender. An Act of 1692, however, ordered
that they should pass current within the province "in all payments equivalent to money." This Act was confirmed by the
Crown in 1695. The Massachusetts bills issued between 1702
and 1712 were not declared legal tender, but the province in
1710 allowed debtors, by a deposit of sufficient bills, to escape
imprisonment until the bills could be converted into current
money.[47] Then in 1712 the bills were again made legal tender.
Rhode Island and Connecticut did not at the outset declare their
bills legal tender, although Connecticut acted in 1718.[48] New
York, New Jersey, and North Carolina regularly maintained
the legal tender principle. South Carolina applied it without
reservation to the first bills of 1703, but after 1707 confined it to
payments of 40s. or less arising under future contracts.[49] North

[45] New York Acts, 1709-11, C.O. 5 : 1147, Nos. 26, 39, C.O. 5 : 1144, 103,
107-8; Hunter to Board of Trade, May 7, 1711, C.O. 5 : 1050, No. 19.
[46] South Carolina Act, May 8, 1703, *South Carolina Statutes*, II. 211; Act of
July 5, 1707, *Ibid.*, 712.
[47] Act of 1692, *Massachusetts Acts and Resolves*, I. 36; Act of August 22,
1695, C.O. 5 : 906, 194-5; Act to prevent oppression of debtors, C.O. 5 : 866,
No. 153; Weeden, I. 380.
[48] Act of October 1718, quoted in Henry Bronson, "A Historical Account of
Connecticut Currency . . .," *Papers of the New Haven Colony Historical Society*
(New Haven), I. 39-40.
[49] *South Carolina Statutes*, II. 211, 304, 323, 326, 353.

Carolina in 1715 ordered that its paper should pass in all private transactions at the rate of £150 to £100 sterling.[50]

A simple declaration that bills of credit were legal tender did not compel creditors to receive them as such. Penalties had therefore to be imposed. South Carolina in 1703 prescribed that any person refusing bills tendered in payment of debts should forfeit twice the sum offered.[51] North Carolina in 1715 made the forfeiture one-half, and New Jersey in 1711 and New York in 1714 ordered that debts should be cancelled when creditors refused to accept payments in paper.[52]

Three of the colonies tried to enforce the currency of paper in daily buying and selling. Should any person in South Carolina (1716) refuse to take bills for goods offered for sale, he should pay three times the sum involved.[53] New Jersey (1711) and New York (1714) imposed a schedule of fines ranging from 40s. to £50, depending on the value of the property in question.[54] A curious Act of North Carolina in 1715 declared any member of the Assembly a public enemy who introduced a motion that was derogatory to the public credit, and ordered that he pay a fine of £20.[55]

Colonial bills of credit have occasioned widespread discussion of the reasons for the depreciation of paper currency. Both Adam Smith and Ricardo referred to the course of colonial paper in support of their monetary theories. This interest is easily understood. Paper currency issued under Government auspices originated in the thirteen colonies; and during the eighteenth century they were the laboratories in which many currency experiments were performed. The colonies provided the first instances of depreciation of public bills of credit; consequently the early explanation of this depreciation has been widely cited as the explanation of the commercial value of paper money in general.[56]

---

[50] Bullock, 129, says that North Carolina bills "seem to have been made a legal tender for all payments in which the rated commodities were receivable." For Act of 1715, see *Ibid.*, 130–31.

[51] Act of March 1711, *South Carolina Statutes*, II. 353.

[52] Bullock, 131; New York Act, July 1714, C.O. 5: 1144, 189–90; New Jersey Act, July 16, 1711, C.O. 5: 1906, No. 7.

[53] *South Carolina Statutes*, II. 665–6.

[54] C.O. 5: 1006, No. 35; C.O. 5: 1144, 189–90.   [55] Bullock, 131.

[56] American writers have generally explained the depreciation of colonial bills of credit by the weakness of the security behind them rather than by the quantities issued. For the views of two widely read authorities see R. T. Ely and others, *Outlines of Economics* (New York, 1917), 272; and J. Laurence Laughlin's comment in his edition of John Stuart Mill's *Principles of Political Economy* (New York, 1885), 356.

Adam Smith gives three reasons for the depreciation of colonial paper. The taxes voted to redeem it were postponed far into the future; interest was not provided to the holders of the bills in circulation; and the sum of the bills issued exceeded the sum paid in the colony each year in taxes. "The paper currencies of North America," he wrote, "consisted, not in bank-notes payable to the bearer on demand, but in a Government paper of which the payment was not exigible till several years after it was issued. . . ." Moreover, the colonies did not pay interest to the holders of this paper. "But allowing the colony security to be perfectly good, a hundred pounds payable fifteen years hence, for example, in a country where interest is at 6 per cent., is worth little more than forty pounds ready money." Continuing the argument, he admitted that the privilege of paying taxes in paper money gave it an enhanced value. "This additional value was greater or less, according as the quantity of paper issued was more or less above what could be employed in the payment of the taxes of the particular colony which issued it. It was in all the colonies very much above what could be employed in this manner." [57]

Ricardo offered another explanation. It is not necessary, he wrote, "that paper money should be payable in specie to secure its value; it is only necessary that its quantity should be regulated according to the value of the metal which is declared to be the standard. . . . Dr. Smith appears to have forgotten his own principle in his argument on colony currency. Instead of ascribing the depreciation of that paper to its too great abundance, he asks whether, allowing the colony security to be perfectly good, a hundred pounds, payable fifteen years hence, would be equally valuable with a hundred pounds paid immediately? I answer yes, if it be not too abundant." [58]

It is obvious that arguments drawn from colonial experience have not been based upon a detailed study of facts. The period of the beginnings of this paper brought out all the factors mentioned by Adam Smith, so that we have an opportunity to examine his views and those of Ricardo in the light of what actually happened.

Many writers agree that the paper of Massachusetts did not depreciate until after 1713. [59] Now, the bills issued in 1709 were

[57] *The Wealth of Nations* (Everyman edition, London, no date), I. 290–93.

[58] *The Principles of Political Economy and Taxation* (Everyman edition, London, no date), 239, 240–41.

[59] Dudley wrote to the Board of Trade, December 1, 1713: "The perfect want of money was such that the bills became current in all trade with merchants

not redeemable in taxes until four years after the date of issue; those struck in 1710–12 were not to be retired until six or seven years later. Between 1708 and 1712 the sums of paper outstanding varied from £43,000 to £89,000—amounts greatly in excess of the sums paid yearly in taxes. It is true that during this time Massachusetts allowed interest of 5 per cent. when the bills were paid into the Treasury as tax money. However, not all the bills in circulation were paid in during a given year; hence the holders of them did not realise the 5 per cent. premium on all the outstanding paper. The course of Massachusetts paper during these years exposed all the causes of depreciation enumerated by Adam Smith, and yet the bills did not depreciate. The paper money of the other New England colonies issued before 1713 was based on the same principles as that of Massachusetts—deferred payment of taxes, issues in excess of current yearly needs for tax money, and a premium of 5 per cent. paid on only that part of the bills which was used each year in public payments. Nor did the paper of the minor New England colonies depreciate, prior to 1713.

The other colonies shared this experience. That of New York is especially illuminating. Before 1711 the province allowed a full interest premium of 5 per cent. for every year a given bill remained in circulation. These bills apparently passed at a premium; at least Governor Hunter complained that they were hoarded. Since the normal rate of interest was 6 per cent. rather than 5 per cent., according to Adam Smith's view the bills should have been a little below par.[60]

Depreciation became serious in several colonies after 1713. There were two major differences between the issues before and after this year: the sum of bills emitted was considerably increased, and a new kind of security was provided. New issues in Massachusetts, Rhode Island, and South Carolina were secured by mortgages on privately owned lands. Unusually large emissions were: Massachusetts, £50,000 in 1714 and £100,000 in

104

and countrymen, with that honour that I never heard of any abatement in payment either in trade, or market, or any dealing whatsoever." C.O. 5 : 866, No. 153. See also Weeden, I. 381; Bronson, 28; and William Douglass, " A Discourse Concerning the Currencies of the British Plantations in America " (Boston, 1740), reprinted in *Colonial Currency Reprints* (edited by A. M. Davis, Boston, 1910–11), III. 315.

[60] Other evidences that colonial bills did not depreciate during this early period are the facts that conflicts between creditors and debtors over the paper question did not occur in the mainland colonies until after 1713, and that the rates of exchange between colonial paper and sterling had not altered in favour of sterling till the close of Queen Anne's War.

1716; New York, £27,680 in 1714; Rhode Island, £40,000 in 1715; and South Carolina, £52,000 in June 1712.

The evidence of the period before depreciation and of the years when depreciation set in seems to support the currency views of Ricardo rather than those of Adam Smith. The colonies whose paper had depreciated considerably by 1717 were the ones which had issued unusually large amounts—notably Massachusetts, Rhode Island, New York, and South Carolina. The quantities of paper printed, rather than the security behind it, apparently caused the depreciation. It is true, however, that there was a close relation between the security and the quantities of paper issued. When taxes for redemption were not collected until several years after the bills were authorised, this habit of deferred redemption speedily resulted in an increase in the supply of bills. Similarly, the use of private lands as security allowed the issues to expand almost indefinitely. It is difficult to perceive how depreciation of land-secured bills would have occurred had the total issues of a colony been restricted to the sum in circulation prior to 1712.

The trouble was that a new element entered the situation at the close of Queen Anne's War. During the war the several colonies had issued paper in moderate amounts, for definite military needs. The paper proved stable and convenient, and became the common medium of exchange. When the war ended, the original reason for the issues ceased to exist, and at the same time the bills in circulation were scheduled to be withdrawn. The result was a series of issues for general currency purposes. Having found that the bills afforded a satisfactory currency, many of the colonies now sought to enjoy this benefit in a larger way; hence the large emission at a single stroke. Because the needs of the colonial Governments for money shrank with the passing of war expenditures, a form of security other than taxes was introduced—mortgages on private lands. The basing of bills on such security opened the way for issues of unlimited sums. The resulting increased volume of paper rather than changes in the principles governing its emission apparently brought on the resulting depreciation.[61]

[61] Another factor affecting the supply of colonial bills was counterfeiting. The numerous laws of the period against counterfeits indicate that the practice was common. Thus the supply of the bills was actually greater than that authorised by the legislatures. See Connecticut Acts of May 1711 and May 1713, C.O. 5: 538, 169-70, 185; *South Carolina Statutes*, II. 303; 323, 326, 353, 666; New Jersey Act of July 16, 1711, C.O. 5: 1066, No. 35. A Massachusetts Act of June 24, 1714, provided the death penalty for counterfeiting. *Massachusetts Acts and Resolves*, I. 741.

Paper money issued in the United States under Government auspices has generally been based upon the main principle of colonial bills of credit. This principle—exchangeability of paper for specie—was derived originally from the experience of the colonists with private instruments of credit. The first public paper in America grew naturally out of the use of private credit at a time when paper money issued by Governments was unknown to the colonists. Accordingly, they applied to public bills the same principles to which they were accustomed in dealing with the notes and bills of individuals. They did not even give their issues the name of money; the term " bills of credit " signifies that such bills were regarded, not as issues of a sovereign creating money, but simply as devices for borrowing funds for public or private uses.

This practice harmonised with the legal theory of English colonisation. The charters of the colonies which issued paper money before 1715 did not confer the right of coinage. Massachusetts did erect a mint in 1652, and thereby became guilty of usurping the King's prerogative. Partly for this reason she lost her charter in 1684. English officials in 1686–88 definitely refused her the privilege of a mint.[62] Accordingly, when she issued bills of credit in 1690, they could not be regarded as money. Such colonial paper, legally, was similar to the notes or bills issued by a chartered company—not to currency established by the sovereign power. The British Government in all its regulations consistently treated these bills, not as money, but as promissory notes.

When the colonies emitted paper, their authority for the issues was not final; their Acts might be annulled by a superior. Over the assemblies of Carolinas stood the proprietors; over New York, New Hampshire, New Jersey, and Massachusetts stood the Privy Council, armed with the power of the royal disallowance; and over all the colonies stood the supreme authority of Parliament. And this superior power was exercised. The Privy Council disallowed a paper money Act passed in Barbados in 1706, and thereafter instructed all royal governors not to sign extraordinary Acts affecting trade without royal approval.[63] In considering the depreciation of colonial paper, it is well to remember that it was not issued by a sovereign authority with full powers of action.

It should be recalled also that public bills of credit appeared in America when the revenues and functions of the colonial Governments were extremely slight. Both Adam Smith and

[62] *Economic History Review*, III. 228–9.   [63] *Ibid.*, 241–3.

Ricardo assumed that the authority of Government behind money was a factor in determining its value—that the rule a certain currency should be received in all public and private payments at its stated value exerted an influence against depreciation. It is interesting to speculate on what might have been the course of colonial paper in different circumstances. As it was, the colonists did not have full authority for creating money. They had not been accustomed to regarding paper as money; its use previously had been restricted to private dealings. And they issued their original bills at a time when the functions and revenues of government were in their infancy. These facts indicate why the principles governing private credit instruments were applied to colonial bills of credit, and why the depreciation of those bills has been explained in the light of known experience with the value of private bills and notes.

For many years the paper of the colonies did not depreciate noticeably. Yet this paper was not uniformly legal tender; it was not actually redeemable from day to day in specie; the collection of taxes voted to secure it was deferred far into the future; the Governments which issued it did not have the final power of creating money; the supply of it exceeded the sum of taxes paid by a colony in a given year; a full interest premium at market rates was not provided annually to the holders of it; it was scarcely even regarded as money, but rather as a means of public borrowing, appearing as it did at a time when Government paper money was unknown; its authorised supply was exceeded by counterfeiting; and it was supported by Governments which occasioned but a slight demand for tax money. In view of these facts, it seems irrefutable that it maintained its value primarily because its supply was limited. This conclusion is strengthened by the fact that serious depreciation occurred when the quantity issued was greatly increased in several of the colonies after 1712.

CURTIS NETTELS

University of Wisconsin.

The Transatlantic Quaker Community in the Seventeenth Century

By FREDERICK B. TOLLES

I

THAT radical simplification and reorientation of Puritan piety which we call Quakerism is commonly regarded as a manifestation of extreme and anarchic individualism in religion. It is easy enough to see how this interpretation arose. George Fox and his disciples, in their search for a final source of authority in religious matters, turned away from the letter of the Scriptures whence the Protestant drew his warrant for religious truth, and away from an outward church to which the Catholic looked for the same assurance; casting off all reliance upon outward things, the Quaker turned inward and found his religious authority in the Divine Light shining in his own soul. Each man therefore had access to a private source of truth. What is this, one naturally asks, but sheer individualism, unrestrained, unmitigated, and unabashed? This is precisely what the orthodox Puritan or Anglican asked in the seventeenth century, and the answer he invariably gave to his own question was summed up in the title of an anti-Quaker tract of 1660: *Hell Broke Loose; or, An History of the Quakers.*

But actually, nothing is more striking in the faith and practice of the early Friends than their strong and binding sense of *community*. The Inward Light to which the Quaker appealed was not a different light for each individual, but the one true Divine Light "that lighteth every man that cometh into the world." The feeling of participation in a common religious experience with other "Children of the Light" worked powerfully to create a solidarity which gave the Quaker movement a capacity for survival when scores of cognate sects of the Commonwealth period disintegrated and disappeared. "When I came into the silent Assemblies of God's People," wrote Robert Barclay, the Scotch Quaker apologist, "I felt a secret power among them, which touched my heart, and as I gave way unto it . . . *I became . . . knit and united unto them. . . .*"[1]

[1] *An Apology for the True Christian Divinity, as the Same Is Held Forth, and Preached by the People, Called, In Scorn, Quakers*, Prop. XI, sec. vii (first English

108

The sense of spiritual community very early gave rise to a distinct and coherent group life, which was presently crystallized in a system of Monthly and Quarterly Meetings for discipline (note the word, which hardly connotes unrestrained individualism). In 1674 Robert Barclay provided an authoritative theoretical justification of the Quaker practice of submitting individual claims of divine leading to the corporate judgment or sense of the meeting in a treatise significantly entitled *The Anarchy of the Ranters and Other Libertines ... Refused and Refuted*. This group-consciousness effectually counterbalanced and controlled the individualistic and centrifugal elements in early Quakerism. And, what is important in the present connection, this sense of community was capable of extension over a wide geographical area.

109

In their first enthusiasm the early Quakers confidently expected the Society of Friends to be coterminous with the earth itself, and that right soon. Since the Divine Light lighted *every* man, so they conceived, it was only necessary to "publish the Truth" throughout the world by precept and example and all manner of men would forthwith embrace it. From his prison cell at Launceston Castle in 1655 George Fox wrote to his followers: "Let all nations hear the sound by word or writing. . . . Be patterns, be examples, in all countries, places, islands, nations . . . then you will come to walk cheerfully over the world, answering that of God in every one."[2] That Fox took seriously the universalistic implications of his own advice is shown by his dispatching epistles in 1661 to the Pope at Rome, the Emperor of Muscovy, the inhabitants of Jerusalem, the Great Cham of Tartary, the Great Mogul, the King of Surat in Bombay, and "all the Princes in Germany."[3] The fact that the ultimate boundaries of

edition, [London], 1678, p. 240). The italics are mine. A perceptive English writer has called attention to the frequency in early Quaker literature of the phrase "one another" in expressions like "mind that which is pure in one another, which joins you together," or "that all may be as one family, building up one another and helping one another" (A. Neave Brayshaw, *The Quakers: Their Story and Message* [New York, 1927], Chapter VIII).

[2] *The Journal of George Fox* (Bi-centenary edition, London, 1891), I, 315.

[3] *Annual Catalogue of George Fox's Papers*, ed. Henry J. Cadbury (Philadelphia, 1939), pp. 77-78. On the universalistic aspect of Fox's message see Henry J. Cadbury, "Answering That of God," *Journal of the Friends' Historical Society* (hereafter cited as *JFHS*), XXXIX (1947), 9-14.

the Society of Friends were to be somewhat less generous should not cause us to miss the hopeful grandeur of the early Quaker world-vision.

These two concepts—that of world conquest for the Truth and that of the holy community of the Children of the Light—were combined in an epistle which George Fox addressed in 1659 to "Friends in Barbadoes, Virginia, New England, and all the islands about": ". . . all my dear friends," he wrote, "be faithful . . . be obedient to the truth, and spread it abroad, which must go over all the world, to professors, Jews, christians, and heathen, to the answering the witness of God in them all. . . . And, friends, in the wisdom of God dwell, which preserveth in unity in the spirit and power."[4] To their vision of a world community of Friends the followers of George Fox were able to give a remarkable degree of reality between 1655 and 1700. In the end, to be sure, Quakerism was to take root only in those nations and their outlying provinces whose shores were washed by the Atlantic, and in none of those regions, save Pennsylvania and perhaps New Jersey, was there ever a majority who embraced the Quaker Truth. But even so, the Atlantic world of the early Friends was of vast extent and in it they achieved a genuine community.[5]

II

The successful effort to spread Quakerism "beyond the seas" can be likened to a large-scale military operation. The comparison may seem somewhat incongruous at first sight, but the warrant for it is found in the Quaker writings themselves, where the first missionaries are described as "spiritually weaponed and armed men" going forth "to fight and conquer all nations, and bring them to the nation of God."[6] Although the Quakers declined the use of carnal weapons, they had in their spiritual armory some potent instruments

[4]*A Collection of Many Select and Christian Epistles* (hereafter cited as Fox, *Epistles*), I, 169. The *Epistles* form Vols. VII and VIII of *The Works of George Fox* (Philadelphia, 1831).

[5]Here I must express my indebtedness to Professor Henry J. Cadbury of Harvard University for suggestions made both in correspondence and in his published writings, more particularly his "Intercolonial Solidarity of American Quakerism," *Pennsylvania Magazine of History and Biography* (hereafter cited as *PMHB*), LX (1936), 362-374.

[6]Quoted by Arnold Lloyd, *Quaker Social History* (London, 1950), p. 5.

of offense, not the least of which was their willingness to suffer for
the glory and spread of Truth. Their Supreme Commander was on
high with a direct line of communication to each of His soldiers, but
a secondary headquarters was maintained at Swarthmoor Hall in a
remote corner of Lancashire, where George Fox and Margaret Fell,
later his wife, received a constant stream of reports from the front.
Here in 1655 came a dispatch from Bristol: "Many are raised up and
moved for several parts; there are four from hereaway moved to go
for New England, two men and two women."[7] The invasion was on.

If one had an animated map of the Atlantic world, it would show   *111*
Quaker beachheads being established in rapid succession in every one
of the British provinces between 1655 and 1660. In some sectors,
notably the peripheral colonies of Surinam and Newfoundland, the
attack was apparently repulsed, or perhaps the objective did not
seem worth the expenditure of strength.[8] In the other areas from
Barbados on the south to the Piscataqua region on the north, the
invaders fanned out from their landing places and in an astonishingly
short time established viable Quaker communities in Barbados, the
Leeward Islands, Jamaica, the Bahamas, Bermuda, Virginia, Maryland, New York, Rhode Island, Massachusetts Bay, New Hampshire
and Maine.[9] The assault on the European continent, though part of

[7] John Audland to Margaret Fell, 1655, James Bowden, *The History of the
Society of Friends in America* (London, 1850), I, 42n.

[8] Our knowledge of the Quaker incursions into Surinam and Newfoundland is
fragmentary. One John Bowron traveled three or four hundred miles along the
lonely stretch of coast between the Amazon and the Orinoco *ca.* 1656, preaching
to the natives and attending their worship "which was performed by beating upon
Holly [hollow?] Trees, and making a great Noise with Skins, like a sort of Drums"
(*Piety Promoted, The Third Part. In a Collection of the Dying Sayings of Many of
the People Called Quakers* [Dublin, 1721], p. 248). Of Quaker activity in Newfoundland even less is known. George Fox records that in 1656 "Esther Beedle" (Hester
Biddle), a Quaker minister, went thither (*The Journal of George Fox*, ed. Norman
Penney [Cambridge, 1911], II, 334, hereafter cited as *Camb. Jnl.*). And there is a
reference to Quakers on the island three years later in a letter of John Davenport
to John Winthrop, September 28, 1659 (Leonard Bacon, *Thirteen Historical Discourses* [New Haven, 1839], p. 378).

[9] The planting of Quakerism in the North American colonies is well narrated in
Bowden and in Rufus M. Jones *et al.*, *The Quakers in the American Colonies* (Lon-
don, 1923). West Indian Quakerism still awaits its historian, although Henry J.
Cadbury has published some of the scanty source materials in the *Journal of the
Barbados Museum and Historical Society*; especially IX (Nov. 1941), 29-31; IX
(Aug. 1942), 195-97; XIV (Nov. 1946-Feb. 1947), 8-10.

the same grand strategy and prosecuted with equal determination, yielded only small pockets of Quakerism in Holland and remote outposts in Friedrichstadt and Danzig.[10] The longest and hardest battle was fought in Massachusetts, where by 1660 four Quakers had actually been put to death, but as early as 1658 a Friend writing "from a Lion's Den called Boston Prison" was able to report, using the military metaphor: "We have 2 strong places in this land, ye one at Newport in Road Iland & ye other at Sandwitch wch ye ennemie will never get dominion over. . . ."[11]

112   A second wave of invasion was launched in 1671, when George Fox himself led a task force of twelve Quakers to the West Indies. There they scattered, Fox sailing first to Jamaica and then to Maryland, whence he struck northward across what were to be Delaware and New Jersey to Long Island and Providence Plantation; turning southward again, he traveled across New Jersey and part of what was to be Pennsylvania to Maryland and then made his way by sea and land to Virginia and parts of the thinly settled Albemarle district of Carolina, covering in all some sixteen thousand miles.[12] In the wake of this momentous journey there occurred what, at the risk of running my metaphor into the ground, I may call the first Quaker landings in force—in West New Jersey after 1675 and in Pennsylvania after 1682.

In 1655 the Society of Friends had been an insignificant sect lurking, its enemies said, in the northern fells of England "like butterflies."[13] By the opening of the eighteenth century it had become a numerous and widely distributed religious body whose bounds were virtually identical with those of the Old British Empire itself. Although no estimate of population for the seventeenth century is better than a guess, it is likely that there were close to 50,000 Quak-

[10]William I. Hull, *The Rise of Quakerism in Amsterdam, 1655-1665* (Swarthmore, Penna., 1938); *idem, Benjamin Furly and Quakerism in Rotterdam* (Swarthmore, Penna., 1941); Anna Corder, "Quakerism in Friedrichstadt," *JFHS*, XXXIX (1947), 49-53.

[11]John Rous to Margaret Fell, September 3, 1658, Swarthmore MSS, Library of the Society of Friends, London (microfilm at Friends Historical Library of Swarthmore College), I, 82.

[12]*Camb. Jnl.*, II, 426.

[13]Fox, *Journal*, Bi-centenary ed., I, 413.

ers in the British Isles in 1700 and at least 40,000 in the Western Hemisphere.[14]

III

These were the human materials. To what extent and by what means were they shaped into a genuine community?

The most striking and effective instrumentality which the Society of Friends invented and perfected to this end was its itinerant ministry. It is necessary to grasp the theory of the Quaker ministry before one can understand and appreciate the manner in which it functioned. The early Friends bore a vigorous testimony against a learned "hireling" ministry such as the Anglicans, Presbyterians, and Independents maintained. According to the Quaker theory, anyone, man or woman, adult or child, learned or illiterate, might be divinely commissioned to prophesy, *i.e.*, to preach the word of the Lord; no university training was necessary, no outward ordination was effective, and above all, no one should make a "trade" of preaching. But in practice there were certain individuals to whom were vouchsafed special gifts of prophecy; these gifts were to be cherished and cultivated; and everything possible must be done to "liberate" such ministers to travel in the service of the Gospel by providing for their expenses and those of their families while they were away from their homes and regular callings.[15]

113

The first Quaker apostles to reach the American colonies in the 1650's had been ministers of this sort. Once the boundaries of the Quaker community were drawn, there continued to be scores of men and women who felt a "concern" to travel in both missionary and pastoral capacities, preaching in the already-established Quaker meetings and holding "appointed" meetings among the "world's people." Thus there was a constant circulation of "public Friends," as they were called, throughout the length and breadth of Quaker-

[14]For the British Isles see W. C. Braithwaite, *The Second Period of Quakerism* (London, 1921), p. 459; Isabel Grubb, *Quakers in Ireland, 1654-1900* (London, 1927), p. 89. For the American colonies see Jones *et al.*, pp. xv-xvi; Pierre Brodin, *Les Quakers en Amérique au dix-septième siècle et au début du dix-huitième* (Paris, 1935), p. 381.

[15]See Barclay, *Apology*, Props. X ("Concerning the Ministry") and XI ("Concerning Worship"); and, for a modern treatment, Howard H. Brinton, *Prophetic Ministry* (Wallingford, Penna., 1950).

dom, serving almost the same function as the circulation of the blood in the animal organism, giving Friends at the remotest extremities of the Atlantic world a sense of belonging to a single body.

The enemies of the Quakers were among the first to grant the effectiveness of this itinerant ministry. Read, for instance, the plaint of a harassed missionary of the Anglican Society for the Propagation of the Gospel just after the close of the century (and make allowances, if you will, for the understandable bitterness of a newcomer to the field who finds his territory already effectively "covered" by a competing organization):

114

> The Quakers compass sea and land to make proselytes; they send out yearly a parcel of vagabond Fellows that ought to be taken up and put in Bedlam. . . . Their preaching is of cursing and Lyes, poysoning the souls of the people with damnable errors and heresies, and not content with this in their own Territories of Pensylvania, but they travel with mischief over all parts as far as they can goe, over Virginia and Maryland, and again through Jersey and New York as far as New England....[16]

The typical manner in which a concern to travel in the ministry arose may be illustrated by the example of Elizabeth Webb of Gloucestershire, England, who traveled through virtually all the American colonies towards the end of the century:

> In the year 1697 [she wrote], in the sixth month, as I was sitting in the meeting in Gloucester, which was then the place of my abode, my mind was gathered into perfect stillness for some time, and my spirit was as if it had been carried away into America; and after it returned, my heart was as if it had been dissolved with the love of God, which flowed over the great ocean, and I was constrained to kneel down and pray for the seed of God in America. The concern never went out of my mind day nor night, until I went to travel there in the love of God, which is so universal that it reaches over sea and land.[17]

Once the concern had arisen, nothing was allowed to hinder its execution.[18] After arranging his or her worldly affairs and committing his or her family to the care of God and the home meeting, the

[16]Rev. John Talbot to the Secretary of the S.P.G., September 1, 1703, *Collections of the Protestant Episcopal Historical Society* (New York, 1851-53), I, xl-xli.

[17]Elizabeth Webb to A. W. Boehm, ca. 1711, *Friends' Library*, ed. William Evans and Thomas Evans (Philadelphia, 1837-50), XIII, 171.

[18]Occasionally a minister sought to resist or evade the call, as Joan Vokins did, but it persisted relentlessly until, in her case, "the Hand of the All-wise God was so heavy upon me, that I could no longer stay at home, although both sick and lame,

minister took shipping, usually with a companion, for some port in the colonies. In 1696 James Dickinson crossed to Virginia with the tobacco fleet and improved every opportunity to exercise his gifts *en route*. There were, he wrote, "above an hundred Sail in Company, the Masters of near twenty of them professed the Truth [*i.e.*, were Quakers] . . . we had several Meetings on board, and when the Weather was fair and calm, we went on board other Vessels, had Meetings, and warned the People *to repent*, directing them to *the Light of Christ, which made manifest their Sins. . . .*"[19]

Arriving in America, the minister set out on a long journey by land and water, on foot and horseback, that would carry him[20] thousands of miles, often over the roughest of trails or through trackless forests. Normally he required at least a year of traveling before he felt "clear" to return home; frequently the visits lasted two, three, or even more years. Shortly after the close of the century, one Friend calculated he had traveled 21,000 miles and visited 480 meetings in a little less than three years.[21]

There is little evidence that the itineraries were planned in advance: the ministers trusted to divine "leadings" and "drawings" to determine which localities they should visit.[22] The story of Joan

115

---

and much to undergo both inwardly and outwardly, yet did not dare to plead with the Lord any longer, or to make an Excuse. . .." (*God's Mighty Power Magnified: As Manifested and Revealed in His Faithful Handmaid Joan Vokins* [London, 1691], p. 31).

[19]*A Journal of the Life, Travels, and Labour of Love in the Work of the Ministry of . . . James Dickinson* (London, 1745), p. 83.

[20]I shall use the masculine pronoun henceforward, but it should be remembered that at least a third of the ministers who came to America were women.

[21]Bowden, II, 237.

[22]Friends along the less-traveled routes did request more visits, however, and some conscious effort was made to supply their needs. From Virginia, for example, came word that meetings were well attended when visiting Friends were present, "but few will com & sett & waight wth us when they are gon"; if the Lord would but send more visitors, the letter continued, Quakerism would wear a more prosperous face in those parts (Thomas Jordan to George Fox, November 18, 1687, *JFHS*, XXXIII [1936], 57). A similar wish was expressed by John Archdale, a Quaker Proprietor of Carolina (To George Fox, March 25, 1686, *ibid.*, XXXVII [1940], 18). In response to earlier such requests Fox had suggested that "public Friends" in Pennsylvania and New Jersey, where there was a superabundance of ministry, should "divide [themselves] to other meetings, and two and two to visit friends, both in New England, Maryland, Virginia, and Carolina. . .." (To ministering Friends, May 20, 1685, *PMHB*, XXIX [1905], 105-06).

Vokins is interesting in this connection. After traveling through Long Island, Rhode Island, East and West New Jersey, and along the west bank of the Delaware in 1681, she started back to New York, thinking to take ship for home. But before she reached New York, she recounts, "the Living God . . . laid it weightily upon me to go to *Barbadoes*, which was no little cross to my Mind. . . .'" So off to Barbados she started, but while she was on the high seas the Lord put it in her heart to visit Friends in the Leeward Islands, "so he carried the Vessel, let them that sail'd do what they could; and they could not steer their Course [to] *Barbadoes-Road* . . . and we laid by *Antego* a week." There she preached to the inhabitants until she was "clear"; whereupon she had a concern for Nevis, and willy-nilly the ship was carried thither by the power of the Lord, "the stormy wind fulfilling His word"—to the intense annoyance of the captain.[23]

A few representative itineraries will provide a notion of the range of the ministers' travels. I pass over the extraordinary voyagings of Mary Fisher, who was in Barbados in 1655, in Massachusetts Bay in the next year, back in England in 1657, on the island of Nevis in 1658, and at Constantinople in 1660, ending her days in Charleston, South Carolina.[24] A more nearly typical example from the earliest period would be Christopher Holder. This Gloucestershire Friend traveled through New England in 1656 and again in 1657; after his second visit to that inhosiptable region, he sailed for the West Indies, only to return in 1658 by way of Bermuda to Rhode Island and Massachusetts Bay. After a period of imprisonment in Boston jail, he carried the Quaker message to Virginia, returning in 1659 to Rhode Island and Massachusetts, before he went back to England in 1660. Thereafter he is said to have been in America "repeatedly"; there are references in Quaker documents to at least two later visits.[25]

The travels of Roger Longworth, a Lancashireman, took him through the most of the greater Atlantic world; he is described as having journeyed "six times . . . through Holland . . . also part of Germany and thereabout, several times as far as Dantzick. . . . Five times he passed through Ireland, visiting Friends. . . . Once he passed

116

[23] *God's Mighty Power Magnified*, pp. 38-43.

[24] Bowden, I, 39-41.

[25] *Ibid.*, I, 135-37.

through part of Scotland, twice at Barbados, once through New England and Virginia, twice in Maryland and the Jerseys, and twice at Pennsylvania; having travelled by land above 20,000 miles and by water not much less."[26] And all this between 1675 and 1687.

The doughty William Edmundson, called by some "the great hammer of Ireland" and by others a "Boanerges or son of thunder," traveled three times through the American colonies. His route in 1671 lay through Barbados, Antigua, Barbuda, Nevis, back to Antigua and Barbados, thence to Jamaica and to Maryland, Virginia, Carolina, back through Virginia and Maryland to New York, Rhode Island, and Massachusetts, where he sailed for Ireland. On his second visit, three years later, he landed again at Barbados, where he labored for five months, and then sailed north for Rhode Island and a tour of the continental colonies which was to take him into every one of the British provinces from "Piscattaway" on the northeast to Carolina at the south. His third trip in 1683 was confined to the West Indies, where he visited Barbados, Antigua, Nevis, Montserrat, Jamaica, and Bermuda.[27]

117

The influence of these visitors in uniting and solidifying the Quaker community, though impossible to measure, cannot but have been powerful. "They did not merely pay a flying visit to some annual conference," writes Professor Henry J. Cadbury. "They stayed weeks in each place visiting as it came along each of the Quarterly and Monthly Meetings and often spending months in household visits to the majority of the Quaker families before they returned home or went on into the next field of labor."[28] We cannot in the very nature of the case know what news and greetings they carried from family to family, from community to community, from colony to colony, and from the mother country to the provinces and back; their journals and letters ordinarily tell only of the religious messages they bore and the spiritual state of the meetings they

---

[26] *A Collection of Memorials Concerning Divers Deceased Ministers . . . in Pennsylvania, New-Jersey, and Parts Adjacent* (Philadelphia, 1787), pp. 4-5.

[27] *A Journal of the Life, Travels, Sufferings, and Labour of Love in the Work of the Ministry of . . . William Edmundson* (Dublin, 1715), pp. lvii, lviii, 52-67, 69-101, 108-12.

[28] "Intercolonial Solidarity of American Quakerism," *PMHB*, LX (1936), 366.

visited.[29] We can be sure, however, that besides the meetings for worship and the religious "opportunities" in Quaker households, there were less solemn times when the visiting Friend retailed all the news and perhaps some of the gossip he had picked up along his route or brought from England. Upon their return to England the traveling ministers normally made oral reports to the Yearly Meetings upon the state of Quakerism in the colonies, thus keeping America before the minds of those who stayed at home.

The number of Friends who crossed the Atlantic in the work of the ministry is as astonishing as the extent of their travels. I have compiled a list of a hundred and forty-eight British Friends who traveled in America between 1655 and 1700, and there is no reason to think that my list is definitive or exhaustive.[30] The number of travelers was greatest during the great missionary effort of the late 1650's; no fewer than forty-three came to the colonies before the end of 1660. There was a falling off in the late 1660's, related, no doubt, to the severity of persecution in England under the Clarendon Code. The number of visitors rose again in the early 1670's with the great journey of George Fox and his companions, and thereafter settled down to a fairly steady rate of from two to five transatlantic

[29]The correspondence of William Ellis is more revealing on this score than that which has survived from any other minister of the period. When he and a companion announced their intention of traveling to America in 1697, a friend asked them to seek out the family of a kinsman in West New Jersey and "take account from them of their welfare, both as to things of this life and to the Truth" (John Tomkins to William Ellis and Aaron Atkinson, December 1, 1697, James Backhouse, *The Life and Correspondence of William and Alice Ellis* [London, 1849], pp. 40-41). In Pennsylvania a Welsh Friend asked him, should he ever visit Dolgelly Meeting in Merionethshire, to inquire for his daughter "if she be then alive, and for her husband who is a priest." "If thou findest thyself free, and anything inclined thereunto," he went on, "knock at his door, and see whether she is quite dead, or slumbering among the dead" (Rowland Ellis to William Ellis, March 28, 1699, *ibid.*, pp. 121-22).

[30]Many meetings kept records of the visits of "public Friends." Professor Cadbury has collected references to approximately a hundred such records from British and American meetings. My list was compiled by collating and merging the few lists that were accessible to me and adding isolated references from other sources. It seems not unreasonable to suppose that an exhaustive listing would contain more than two hundred names. Michael Kraus, using one such list (printed in *JFHS*, X [1913], 117-33), reckoned approximately 150 transatlantic religious visitors before the end of the *eighteenth* century (*The Atlantic Civilization: Eighteenth-Century Origins* [Ithaca, N. Y., 1949], p. 59); actually, as we have seen, that many can be shown to have come to the colonies in the second half of the seventeenth alone. For other published lists see *Friends Intelligencer*, V (1848), 184 f; *PMHB*, XXXI (1907), 123-25; Jones *et al.*, pp. 540-42. (The latter list appears to be a composite.)

visitors every year to the end of the century. Bearing in mind that each visit normally lasted more than a year, one can say that there was scarcely a time during the second half of the seventeenth century when one or more Friends from the British Isles were not traveling in some part of the American colonial world.

It was a sign of the coming of age of American Quakerism when in the 1690's a current began flowing in the opposite direction. That decade saw at least ten American Friends traveling to England under a religious concern."[31] This reverse current was to become a steady stream in the next century, when notable Friends like John Woolman and John Pemberton were to be familiar and respected figures in English meetings.

IV

If the circulating ministry can be called the bloodstream of the transatlantic Society of Friends, perhaps its bony structure can, without forcing the metaphor, be identified with the system of Monthly, Quarterly, and Yearly Meetings, to whose creation and articulation George Fox devoted so much attention.

Even in its embryonic stages, the central organization in England was concerned with Quakerism overseas. Reminiscing towards the end of his life about the first General Meetings held in the 1650's in the north of England, Fox recalled that "there we had intelligence from all parts beyond the seas, how Truth prospered and spread, both in England, Wales, Ireland, Scotland, America, Holland, and Germany."[32] The greater part of this intelligence related to the sufferings of Friends under persecution, and Fox remembered that the meetings took action to relieve them by interceding with Parliament and the King, applying to ambassadors and "great persons" in the case of persecutions outside the realm, or writing to Governors in the colonies.[33] Later this function was assigned to the specially

---

[31]*Collection of Memorials*, pp. 21, 29, 35; Bowden, II, 52, 53; Ministering Friends Who Have Visited Foreign Parts on Truth's Service, MS in Charles Evans Collection, Haverford College Library.

[32]"Concerning Our Monthly and Quarterly and Yearly Meetings," *Letters, &c., of Early Friends*, ed. A. R. Barclay (London, 1841), p. 313.

[33]*Ibid.*, p. 314. See, for example, Fox's paper, written *ca.* 1660, to magistrates in New England, complaining against laws for the execution of Quakers (*The Swarthmore Documents in America*, ed. H. J. Cadbury, *JFHS*, Supplement 20 [London, 1940], pp. 42-46).

created Meeting for Sufferings which presently became a sort of standing executive committee for the whole Society. On this committee were representatives of all the English counties; in addition, a number of Londoners, with contacts or actual experience in the colonies, were named to correspond with Friends in the West Indies and North America.[34]

In the latter part of the 1660's, Fox established all over England a system of Monthly Meetings for discipline and business, which provided the real foundation for the structure of Quaker church government whose apex was the Yearly Meeting at London. In 1668 he wrote to Friends in America, encouraging them to do likewise, and three years later made his memorable journey through the colonies with the primary object of "[bringing] the transatlantic Quaker communities into line with the Society at home, both in practice and Church government."[35] A general Meeting was already in being in Rhode Island and by the end of the century a network of Monthly Meetings overspread the North American colonies, culminating in Yearly Meetings held in New England, New York, Philadelphia (for Pennsylvania and New Jersey), Maryland, Virginia, and North Carolina.

The creation and elaboration of this organizational structure provided regular channels for the flow of information and ideas between mother country and colonies. A few examples from the records of the Meeting for Sufferings in London will give us a glimpse of the machinery in action. Soon after that meeting was set up in 1676 there came reports that Friends in Bermuda were in difficulties over their conscientious refusal to pay tithes to the Church of England. The Meeting for Sufferings promptly went into action, directing its Clerk to secure copies of the latest letters patent to the Bermuda Company for study, deputing two members to wait upon the Company authorities in London, and writing back to the Bermuda Friends that intercession was being made on their behalf. At about the same time, word came from the Barbados Quakers of a recent law preventing Negroes from attending religious meetings, and a plea was promptly made to the Lords of Trade that the law should be set

---

[34]See *JFHS*, XXI (1924), 42-43, for the first list of representatives, dated June, 1676.
[35]Braithwaite, *Second Period*, p. 267; *Camb. Jnl.*, II, 126.

120

aside. Next year a deputation went before the agents of the New England colonies to seek relief from persecution for Friends there, and another group waited upon the newly appointed Governor of Jamaica on a similar errand.[36] Thus through official channels the concerns, preoccupations, and needs of American Quakers were registered in the consciousness of their brethren in England.

Mutual aid, one of the prime motives behind Quaker organization, did not flow in one direction only. The plight of Quakers held captive by Barbary pirates engaged the sympathies of American Friends. The Meeting for Sufferings had only to mention the needs of these unfortunate prisoners and American meetings responded with contributions towards their ransom.[37] In 1689, during the troubles in Ireland following the accession of William, the Barbados Friends, who were relatively wealthy, sent £100 to be spent for the relief of suffering Quakers.[38] By the end of the century enough wealth had accumulated in the hands of Edward Shippen, a Quaker merchant of Philadelphia, so that he was actually sending £50 in gold to England for the benefit of "poor Friends" there—another sign of the maturing of American Quakerism.[39] The extension of the Quaker humanitarian impulse into the wider Atlantic community beyond the Society of Friends was to come after 1700;[40] until then Friends were necessarily preoccupied with the sufferings in their own midst.

121

[36]MS Minutes of the Meeting for Sufferings, Library of the Society of Friends, London (microfilm at Friends Historical Library of Swarthmore College), 1, 2, 3, 5, 23, 39, 40. William Penn served on a number of these committees dealing with the sufferings of Friends in the American provinces in the late 1670's and it seems not unlikely that this activity may have tended to focus his attention upon America and the need for religious toleration there.

[37]Ibid., IV, 65, 71, 73, 74; *A Collection of the Epistles from the Yearly Meeting of Friends in London* (Baltimore, 1806), pp. 21-22, 25; [Samuel Tuke], *Account of the Slavery of Friends in the Barbary States* (London, 1848), pp. 17-22.

[38]JFHS, V (1908), 43.

[39]Shippen to William Ellis, September 27, 1699, Backhouse, *William Ellis*, p. 153. I have not stressed the business relations between Quaker merchants as a factor in strengthening the transatlantic Quaker community, since that was largely a development of the eighteenth century. See Frederick B. Tolles, *Meeting House and Counting House: The Quaker Merchants of Colonial Philadelphia* (Chapel Hill, 1948), pp. 89-91. But hostile critics were already charging that the Friends and their Society prospered "by keeping their Trade within themselves" (George Keith, et al., "An Account of the State of the Church in North America," *Coll. Prot. Epis. Hist. Soc.*, [New York, 1851-53], I, xix).

[40]Kraus, p. 126, and Chapter VI, *passim*.

V

The transoceanic Quaker organization existed not merely for mutual aid in the material sense, however, but also for mutual exhortation, edification, and comfort; and the spiritual community of Friends was no less real for subsisting on the plane of ideas and sentiments. What chiefly sustained this community of thought and feeling, apart from the work of the traveling ministers, was a systematic and constant transatlantic interchange of correspondence, modeled quite consciously upon the epistles which had helped shape and nourish the Christian community of the Mediterranean world in the first century.[41]

George Fox himself, nothing loath to assume the role of St. Paul, inaugurated the practice. In 1659 he composed an "Epistle General . . . to be sent abroad among the saints scattered in Old and New England, Germany, Holland, Ireland, Scotland, Barbadoes, and Virginia."[42] His general epistles were read in Monthly and Yearly Meetings all over the Atlantic world, and even those directed to specific meetings were widely circulated among other meetings, in whose record books copies may still be found.

Upon his return from his American journey in 1673 Fox suggested that Friends in Bristol undertake a regular correspondence with the American meetings, since there were frequent sailings for the colonies from that port.[43] Still later he sought to transfer the responsibility to the newly established Yearly Meeting held at London. But although a regular correspondence was set on foot by the Yearly Meeting in 1675, American Friends continued to seek Fox's advice and he to offer it until the end of his life, and after his death in 1691 the correspondence was kept up by his widow.[44] During his lifetime Fox wrote no less than eighty-eight epistles to organized groups of

[41]*Letters &c., of Early Friends*, pp. 316-17.

[42]*Epistles*, I, 159-64. As early as 1656 he had written "A paper to be scattered abroad all over the West Indies," but this was undoubtedly, if I may return to my earlier military metaphor, in the nature of a "propaganda barrage" designed to "soften up" the inhabitants for the missionary offensive which was just beginning. See *Annual Catalogue*, p. 59.

[43]Bowden, I, 355-57, 377-81.

[44]Jones *et al.*, pp. 313-14. Even before Fox's death, Maryland Friends were writing to his wife, addressing her as their "dear and tender nursing mother" (Isabel Ross, *Margaret Fell: Mother of Quakerism* [London, 1949], p. 289).

Friends in America,[45] not to mention the more general ones directed "to Friends everywhere," or those addressed to individuals but clearly intended to be shared with the recipient's meeting. Hardly a year went by, then, but Friends in the remote plantations received a communication direct from the founder and leading figure of the Quaker movement.

Read today, George Fox's epistles hardly seem like vibrant personal messages; indeed, they strike the modern reader as intolerably vague and repetitious. The burden of the more general letters is: "Mind the Light. Be faithful, be valiant for the Truth, and spread it abroad. Keep your meetings in the power of Truth, and live together in unity." But even these redundant exhortations doubtless came with a special force and unction to the distant meetings of Friends in America, for they were tangible evidence of the founder's continued affection for them and concern for their welfare. And many of the epistles contained specific and welcome advice on problems of church government or difficult cases of conscience. For example, in 1657 Fox addressed an epistle to "Friends beyond sea, that have Blacks and Indian Slaves," urging them to treat their bondservants as children of God—incidentally one of the very earliest pleas for the slave by a Quaker or anyone else.[46] To Friends holding public office in Charleston, South Carolina, he sent a cautionary reminder against swearing oaths; to the Jamaican Friends he suggested taking advantage of a change in administration to regain the lost privilege of affirmation; to the island of Nevis he wrote a long and important epistle of advice to Friends who had a scruple about serving with the local watch; to Maryland he wrote concerning the measures to be taken with a female member who was causing trouble to the meeting.[47] Thus Fox's powerful personality exerted itself even through the verbosity of his epistles to impress a measure of uniformity in faith and practice upon the far-flung Quaker community.[48]

123

[45]I arrive at this figure by adding to those reprinted in his *Works* (vols. VII-VIII) the ones listed in the *Annual Catalogue* of his writings but not reprinted.

[46]*Epistles*, I, 144-45; Thomas E. Drake, *Quakers and Slavery in America* (New Haven, 1950), p. 5.

[47]Bowden, I, 414; *Epistles*, II, 210-11, 86-92; *JFHS*, V (1908), 101.

[48]Not to be overlooked are the epistles written to American meetings by other prominent Quaker leaders. Josiah Coale, for example, wrote to Friends in Holland,

With the establishment of Yearly Meetings on both sides of the Atlantic, new channels of correspondence were opened up. At London, wrote the creator of the system, "Friends have an account once a year from all the Yearly Meetings in the world . . . and Friends at the Yearly Meeting write to them at their Yearly Meetings: so that once a year . . . God's people know the affairs of Truth . . . having a heavenly correspondence one with another in the heavenly society and fellowship."[49] One of the principal actions of the Yearly Meeting for Pennsylvania and New Jersey in 1683 was to appoint a committee to "take Care to write to the Yearly Meeting of Friends in England in order to give an Account of the Affairs of Truth here." In the next year's epistle was a passage which impressively voiced the feeling of oneness that united the scattered Quaker community: "Glad we are," runs this message, "to remember you and reach unto you in the bowels of tender love. . . . For we dearly love and embrace you though at this outward distance. Yea, oftentimes we confer with you and meet with you in our spirits, and have heavenly union with you in Christ Jesus to our great comfort, joy, and refreshment."[50] Epistles were exchanged between Yearly Meetings in the colonies as well as with London. The cumulative effect of this constant correspondence was not only to induce in individual Friends and meetings a feeling of emotional identification with the larger Quaker community but also in large measure to stereotype the thought and practice (and even the language) of that community.

This uniformity of thought was reinforced by the tendency of

Jamaica, New England, and Maryland, and requested that his epistles be "circulated among Friends in these places and read in their meetings" (*The Books and Divers Epistles of Josiah Coale* [(London), 1671], pp. 44-70). Moreover, there was much private correspondence between "public Friends" and members of meetings which they had visited. See the letters written to William Ellis by Pennsylvania Quakers after his return to England, Backhouse, pp. 112-68.

[49]*Letters &c., of Early Friends*, p. 315. In 1684, for instance, "account [was] given, by letters from Ireland, Scotland, Barbadoes, Bermudas, Carolina, and New England, Jamaica, and other plantations in America, that things are pretty well there, and truth spreads and increases; and that Friends generally are in love and unity" (London Yearly Meeting, *Epistles*, p. 23).

[50]MS Minutes of Philadelphia Yearly meeting, Department of Records, Philadelphia Yearly Meeting (microfilm at Friends Historical Library of Swarthmore College), I, 4, 6.

Friends everywhere to read the same books. The Quaker press in England was constantly busy turning out doctrinal and controversial literature which quickly found its way across the Atlantic.[51] After Fox's visit to the colonies, regular channels were set up for supplying the American Quakers with books; in 1689, for example, Philadelphia Yearly Meeting arranged with William Bradford, the printer and bookseller, to "take off" six copies of each new book published by the English Friends.[52] Bradford himself, before he fell out with his Quaker employers, reprinted a number of English Quaker publications.[53] By the end of the century the writings of American Quakers were being reprinted and presumably read in England—a further sign that Americans were moving towards something like equal partnership in the transatlantic Quaker community.[54]

125

VI

The unity of the seventeenth-century Society of Friends was temporarily shattered by three serious schisms. But even these incidents bore witness to the organic character of the transatlantic Quaker community.

Perhaps it is the leaven of individualism in the Society of Friends

[51]Despite the diligent attempts of the New England authorities to confiscate the "Erroneous Books and hellish Pamphlets" which the early Quaker missionaries brought with them, search of a house in Hampton in 1658 uncovered copies of books by William Dewsbury and John Lilburne, both Quakers (Joseph Besse, *A Collection of the Sufferings of the People Called Quakers* [London, 1753], II, 188). In the same year there is an item in the accounts of a fund collected at Kendal "for the service of Truth" indicating that books had been sent to Virginia (Bowden, I, 6on); and the Governor of Jamaica was reporting that Quaker tracts were being distributed in that island (Jones *et al.*, p. 43). For the reading of the early Philadelphia Quakers see Tolles, *Meeting House and Counting House*, pp. 157-60.

[52]Kirk Brown, "Friends' Libraries in Maryland," *JFHS*, II (1905), 130-31; MS Minutes of Philadelphia Yearly Meeting, I, 23-24.

[53]See Charles R. Hildeburn, *The Issues of the Press in Pennsylvania, 1685-1784* (Philadelphia, 1885), I, 5, 17, 19-20.

[54]George Keith's *Presbyterian and Independent Visible Churches in New England and Elsewhere, Brought to the Test*, written before its author's apostasy from Quakerism, and printed by Bradford in 1689, was reprinted in London in 1691. Jonathan Dickinson's *God's Protecting Providence*, first published in Philadelphia in 1699, was reprinted in London in 1700 and again in 1701; it was to go through at least six editions in England in the eighteenth century. See *Jonathan Dickinson's Journal*, ed. E. W. Andrews and C. M. Andrews (New Haven, 1945), Appendix B, pp. 177-87.

which has caused its history to be periodically marked by "separations." But what is more significant is the speed and completeness with which, in the seventeenth century at least, schisms were healed and the community restored to wholeness. And paradoxically, the very course of the major "separations" supplies the best evidence of the reality of the Atlantic Quaker community. Just as a virus introduced into the bloodstream will permeate and vitiate the entire organism until the body sets up resistance, so in the Society of Friends schismatic movements starting on one side of the Atlantic quickly spread to the other, revealing unmistakably the interrelatedness of its widely separated parts.

126

I shall refer briefly in conclusion to two of these schisms—that of John Perrot, which originated in England and spread to the colonies, and that of George Keith, which started in Pennsylvania and was carried to Great Britain.[55] There is no need to go into the theological bases of these movements. Suffice it to say that Perrot's heresy was an individualistic, almost solipsistic mysticism which denied all outward arrangements in worship, including even the custom of removing the hat as a mark of respect to the Deity when another Friend was praying; and that Keith's was an attack on the Quaker belief that men were saved by the inward Christ "without anything else," i.e., without need of faith in the historic Christ or the Scriptures.

The "hat" heresy, which sprang up in England in 1661, was carried by Perrot himself to the West Indies and thence to Virginia and Maryland; its effects were ultimately felt as far north as New York and on the other side of the Atlantic world at Rotterdam.[56] George Fox had to discharge several epistolary broadsides and visiting ministers like John Burnyeat had to labor mightily before the Perrot faction in America was quelled. But within a comparatively few years what Fox called the "spirit that run into the hat" was completely exorcised, and peace was restored to the church.[57]

[55]The third major schism—that of Wilkinson and Story—arose, like that of Perrot, in England, but was felt as far away as Barbados. See Braithwaite, *Second Period,* pp. 348-49.

[56]Bowden, I, 329, 348, 351-53, 371-72; Hull, *Benjamin Furly,* pp. 228-32.

[57]*Epistles,* I, 273-74, 306, 309-10; *The Truth Exalted in the Writings of . . . John Burnyeat* (London, 1691), pp. 32-35, 41-43.

The Keithian schism, which arose in the 1690's, showed that transatlantic currents of heretical thought could flow in the opposite direction.[58] Keith's followers, who called themselves "Christian Quakers," may well have included as many as a quarter of the Pennsylvania-New Jersey Friends. The heresiarch was duly censured and finally disowned by Philadelphia Yearly Meeting in 1692. This action was followed by judgments given against him by Friends in Barbados, Virginia, Maryland, New Jersey, Long Island, and Rhode Island—a striking instance in itself of the scope and effectiveness of the Quaker community.[59] Keith then carried his case to London where a group of "Christian Quakers" soon sprang into existence and where in 1695 he was again disowned. By the turn of the century Philadelphia Friends were able to report that "our old adversaries formerly Seduced and Headed by George Keith, are almost Mouldered to Nothing."[60] Community was restored.

"By the opening of the eighteenth century," observed the late Rufus M. Jones with characteristic insight, "the Friends were *one* people throughout the world, though there was absolutely no *bond* but love and fellowship. There was no visible head to the Society, no official creed, no ecclesiastical body which held sway and authority. But instead of being an aggregation of separated units, the Society was in an extraordinary sense *a living group.*"[61]

127

---

[58]A careful account of this movement is found in Ethyn W. Kirby, *George Keith* (New York, 1942), Chapters V-VII.

[59]Hugh Roberts to William Penn, *ca.* 1692, *PMHB*, XVIII (1894), 208.

[60]MS Minutes of Philadelphia Yearly Meeting, I, 78. The echoes, however, were slow in dying: in 1703 one Francis Bugg tried to revive Keith's attack on "Foxonian" Quakerism in a broadside with the suggestive title *A Bomb Thrown amongst the Quakers in Norwich, Which Will Reach Their Friends in Bristol, and Set Fire to the Combustible Matter thorow Their Whole Camp in England, Wales, and America.* This blast was promptly reprinted in New York, but so effective were the Quaker fire-prevention measures in America that it fizzled out and utterly failed to start a second conflagration.

[61]*Quakers in the American Colonies*, pp. 314-15.

THE JOURNAL OF ECONOMIC HISTORY

VOL. XII   SPRING 1952   NO. 2

British Mercantilism and the Economic Development of the Thirteen Colonies

128

MERCANTILISM is defined for this discussion as a policy of government that expressed in the economic sphere the spirit of nationalism that animated the growth of the national state in early modern times. The policy aimed to gain for the nation a high degree of security or self-sufficiency, especially as regards food supply, raw materials needed for essential industries, and the sinews of war. This end was to be achieved in large measure by means of an effective control over the external activities and resources upon which the nation was dependent. In turn, that urge impelled the mercantilists to prefer colonial dependencies to independent foreign countries in seeking sources of supply. If the state could not free itself completely from trade with foreign nations, it sought to control that trade in its own interest as much as possible. To realize such objectives, mercantilism embraced three subordinate and related policies. The Corn Laws fostered the nation's agriculture and aimed to realize the ideal of self-sufficiency as regards food supply. State aids to manufacturing industries, such as the protective tariff, sought to provide essential finished goods, including the sinews of war. The Navigation Acts were intended to assure that foreign trade would be carried on in such a way as to yield the maximum advantage to the state concerned.

Since the mercantilist states of Europe lacked the resources for complete self-sufficiency, they could not free themselves from dependence on foreign supplies. Economic growth therefore increased the importance of external trade, and the preference for colonies over foreign countries intensified the struggle for dependent possessions. The importance in mercantilism of a favorable balance of trade and of a large supply of the precious metals is a familiar theme. We need only to remind ourselves that the mercantilists considered it the duty of government to obtain and to retain for the nation both a favorable trade balance and an adequate stock of gold and silver. To this end the state should help to build up a national merchant marine and should foster domestic manufacturing industries. The chief means of procuring raw materials, a favorable trade balance, and an ample supply of the precious metals was that of exporting high-priced manufactured goods and shipping services.

Despite its emphasis on government action, mercantilism was not socialism. In England, the system invoked the initiative and enterprise of private citizens. It encouraged the merchants, shippers, and manu-facturers by conferring benefits upon them and by identifying their private interests with the highest needs of the state. So close was this identification that one may properly regard the theory of mercantilism as a rationalization of the special interests of dominant groups of the time. The mercantilist policy was an expression of an accord between landowners and merchant-capitalists in alliance with the Crown.

129

Is it possible to measure the influence of government on the economic development of an area? Whether such influence be large or small, it must necessarily be only one factor at work in the process of economic change. The range of influence of even the most powerful government is limited, whereas economic activity is world-wide in its scope and ramifications. Thus far no scheme of statecraft has succeeded in bending all the members of the perverse human family to its designs. To many students of economic affairs it may seem futile to attempt to isolate and to measure the effect of only one factor in the immensely intricate, varied, and shifting activities that are involved in the develop-ment of a large area, such as the thirteen colonies. But perhaps such an effort may serve a purpose. It at least stimulates thought, which is essential to intellectual growth, and growth—not final answers or ultimate solutions—is all that one can expect to attain in this world of perpetual change.

To begin with, we note that the thirteen colonies experienced a phenomenal development during the 150 years in which they were subject to the regulating policies of English mercantilism. Adam Smith said in 1776:

A nation may import to a greater value than it exports for half a century, perhaps, together; the gold and silver which comes into it during all this time may be all immediately sent out of it; its circulating coin may gradually decay, different sorts of paper money being substituted in its place, and even the debts, too, which it contracts with the principal nations with whom it deals, may be gradually increasing; and yet its real wealth, the exchangeable value of the annual produce of its lands and labor, may, during the same period, have been increasing in a much greater proportion. The state of our North American colonies, and of the trade which they carried on with Great Britain, before the commencement of the present disturbances, may serve as a proof that this is by no means an impossible supposition.

130

To what extent did English mercantilism contribute to this "real wealth"—this "exchangeable value of the annual produce of . . . lands and labor?" Lands and labor. Two of the most fundamental factors in the growth of the thirteen colonies were the character of the people and the nature of the land and resources to which they applied their labor. The connecting link between the two that gave the thirteen colonies their unique character was the system of small individual holdings that came into being, usually at the start of settlement. It provided a strong incentive to labor and was therefore a major factor in their development. Crèvecoeur spoke of "that restless industry which is the principal characteristic of these colonies," and observed: "Here the rewards of . . . [the farmer's] industry follow with equal steps the progress of his labor; his labor is founded on the basis of nature, self-interest, can it want a stronger allurement . . . ? As farmers they will be careful and anxious to get as much as they can, because what they get is their own."

Although the land system of the thirteen colonies has not usually been considered an element of mercantilism, yet it was not divorced from it. Why did the English Government grant to its colonies a benefit that was not commonly bestowed on settlers by the other colonizing powers? Small holdings inspired the colonists to work; their labor expanded production; and increased production enlarged English commerce. The resulting trade was more susceptible to control by the state than a comparable trade with foreign countries would have been. For this reason, the colonial land system may be regarded as an expression of mercantilist policy. Viewed in this light, mercantilism contributed directly to the growth of the settlements.

Such also was the effect of the policy of England with reference to the peopling of its part of America. The government opened the doors to immigrants of many nationalities and creeds. Its liberality in this respect was unique. It harmonized with the mercantilist doctrine. The Crown admitted dissenters and foreigners in order to expand colonial production and trade. Such immigrants were, to a large extent, industrious, progressive, and energetic. Their productivity was stimulated by the climate of freedom in which they lived—a climate that was made possible in good measure by the indulgence of the government. The resulting growth of English trade served the needs of the state as they were viewed by the mercantilists.

We shall next consider the effects of specific mercantilist laws and government actions on the economic development of the thirteen colonies. It appears at once that such laws and actions did not create or sustain any important industry or trade in Colonial America. The major economic pursuits of the colonies grew out of, and were shaped by, the nature of the resources of the land, the needs of the settlers, and the general state of world trade in the seventeenth century. No important colonial activity owed its birth or existence to English law. The statutes and policies of mercantilism, with an exception or two, sought to control, to regulate, to restrain, to stimulate, or to protect. In the great majority of instances it was not the role of the government to initiate, to originate, to create. All the important mercantilist laws were adopted in response to a development that had occurred. They undertook to encourage, or to regulate, or to suppress some industry, practice, or trade that had been initiated by private citizens and which they had proved to be profitable. When the origins of enterprise in America are considered, it appears that every important industry got its start by reason of the natural resources of an area, by virtue of the demand for a product, or because of such factors of trade as transportation or location. Ordinarily, the government did not subject a colonial activity to regulation by law until it had proved itself to be profitable. In Virginia, for instance, the government did not initiate the tobacco industry or attempt to stimulate its early development. Rather, the Crown sought to discourage it. After it had taken root under the influence of general economic conditions, the government stepped in to regulate it. The major Navigation Act was passed in response to the success of the Dutch in world commerce. The English Government did not legislate against certain industries in the colonies until they had grown of their own accord to the extent that they menaced their English counterparts. The currency policy which England applied to its colonies was worked out not in a vacuum but in answer to practices in which the colonists were engaging.

The effects of mercantilist laws naturally depended upon their

131

enforcement. Since they almost invariably sought to prevent something that the colonists had found to be profitable, the task of enforcement was difficult. It required the exercise of force and vigilance.

In a general way, the government attained a reasonable success in its efforts to enforce the policies that bore directly on the southern mainland colonies, whereas the principal acts which were designed for the Middle Colonies and New England could not be made effective.

The program for the plantation area embraced several policies. The Navigation Act of 1661 excluded from its trade all foreign merchants and foreign vessels. By the terms of the Staple Act of 1663 the planters must buy most of their manufactured goods from England. Slaves must be bought from English slave traders. The area must depend upon English sources for capital and credit, and the planters could not avail themselves of legal devices in order to ease their burdens of debt.

The government made a strenuous effort to enforce these policies. The decisive action centered in the three Dutch wars between 1652 and 1675. The defeat of the Dutch drove them from the southern trade and enabled the English merchants to hold it as in a vise. After 1665 the development of the plantation colonies proceeded in conformity with the tenets of mercantilism. The effect was to retard that development, since the planters were subjected to a virtual English monopoly and were denied the benefits of competitive bidding for their crops and the privilege of buying foreign goods and shipping services in the cheapest market.

Certain conditions of the period 1675 to 1775 favored the English mercantilists in their efforts to enforce the southern policy. The geography of the Chesapeake country made it easy to exclude foreign vessels, since the English navy had to control only the narrow entrance to the bay in order to keep foreign vessels from reaching the plantations. That the tobacco ships had to move slowly along the rivers made concealment impossible for interlopers. Secondly, there was the factor of debt. Once a planter had become indebted to an English merchant, he was obliged to market his crops through his creditor in order to obtain new supplies. Hence he lost the advantage of competitive bidding for his export produce. And finally, the four wars with France, 1689–1763, served to rivet the plantation area to Britain, as mercantilism intended. The British navy provided convoys for the tobacco ships, and the expenditures of the Crown in America for military purposes provided the planters with additional buying power for English goods, thereby increasing their dependence on British merchants, vessels, and supplies.

By reason of the acts of government, the economic development of the southern colonies exhibited after 1665 about as clear an example of effective political control of economic activity as one can find. The trade of the southern colonies was centered in Britain. They were obliged to employ British shipping, to depend on British merchants, and to look only to British sources for capital and credit. They were not permitted to interfere with the British slave trade. British investments enjoyed a sheltered market in that the Crown excluded the foreign investor from the area and prohibited the colonists from taking any legal steps that would impair the claims of British creditors. The resulting dependence of the plantation country gave it a strongly British character, retarded its development, fostered discontent, and goaded the planters to resistance and revolt.

133

The initial enforcement of the Navigation Acts in the 1660's reduced the profits of the tobacco planters and forced them to cut the costs of production. Slavery was the answer. Appropriately at this time the English Government undertook to furnish its colonies with an ample supply of slaves. The planters were obliged to buy them on credit—a main factor in reducing them to a state of commercial bondage. The English Government forbade the planters to curtail the nefarious traffic. American slavery was thus one of the outstanding legacies of English mercantilism. That resolute foe of English mercantilist policy, George Washington, subscribed to the following resolve in 1774: "We take this opportunity of declaring our most earnest wishes to see an entire stop forever put to such a wicked, cruel, and unnatural trade."

In another sense the Navigation Act of 1661 had a discernible effect on American development. It stimulated the shipbuilding and shipping industries in New England and the Middle Colonies. It did not, however, create those industries. But the English Government drove the Dutch from the trade of English America before English shipping could meet the full needs of the colonies. The Navigation Act gave to English colonial shipbuilders and shipowners the same privileges that were given to English shipbuilders and shipowners. Undoubtedly this favored treatment spurred on the shipping industries of New England. Shipbuilding flourished there, since the colonial builders were permitted to sell their product to English merchants, and New England shipowners could employ their American-built vessels in the trade of the whole empire. New England benefited directly from the expulsion of the Dutch from the trade of English America. After New England's shipbuilding industry had become fully established (and had proved itself more efficient than its English rival) the British Government refused to heed the pleas of British shipowners who wished to subject it to crippling restraints.

English policy for the plantation area was essentially negative. It did not originate enterprises. With one exception it did not attempt to direct economic development into new channels. The exception appears in the bounty granted for indigo—a form of aid that made the production of that commodity profitable and sustained it in the lower South until the time of the Revolution, when the industry expired with the cessation of the bounty.

134

The policies that affected the Middle Colonies and New England differed materially in character and effect from the policies that were applied to the South. The northern area received the privilege of exporting its chief surplus products—fish, meats, cereals, livestock, lumber—directly to foreign markets. As already noted, the northern maritime industries flourished under the benefits conferred upon them by the Navigation Acts. Freedom to export the staples of the area in company with vigorous shipbuilding and shipping industries induced the northerners to engage in a varied foreign trade. This outcome, however, was in part a result of certain restrictive measures of the English Government. It prohibited the importation into England of American meats and cereals, thereby forcing the colonists to seek foreign markets for their surplus.

The resulting trade of the northern area—with southern Europe, the Wine Islands, Africa, and the foreign West Indies—did not prove satisfactory to the English mercantilists. It built up in the colonies a mercantile interest that threatened to compete successfully with English traders and shipowners. It carried with it the danger that the northerners might nullify those features of the Navigation Acts which aimed to center most of the trade of English America in England. Nor did their reliance on foreign trade prove to be entirely satisfactory to the colonists. In time of war, their vessels were exposed to the depredations of the French. The English navy could not protect the diverse northern trades with convoys, as it protected the simpler, more concentrated commerce of the plantation area. The wartime disruption of the northern trade deprived the area of the foreign money and products that in peacetime its merchants carried to England for the purpose of buying English goods for the colonial market. The resulting decline of the exportation of English merchandise was then deplored by the English mercantilists. Unable to procure finished goods in England, the northerners were driven to manufacture for themselves. Thence arose what the mercantilists regarded as a fatal danger—the prospect that the colonies would manufacture for themselves, decrease their purchases in England, and produce a surplus of finished goods that would compete with English wares in the markets of the world.

To avoid this danger, the English mercantilists devised their major experiment in state planning of the early eighteenth century. They undertook to foster the production of naval stores in the Middle Colonies and New England. Such products would be sent directly to England as a means of paying for English goods. They would divert the colonists from domestic manufacturing and free them from their dependence on diverse foreign trades. They would transform the commerce of the northern area in such a way that it would resemble that of the plantation area—a simple, direct exchange of American raw products for English finished goods.

135

The naval-stores program was constructive in intent. The government sought to shape the development of the northern area, thereby solving a serious problem. But the policy failed. It did not stimulate the production of naval stores in the northern area sufficiently to provide it with adequate payments for English goods, or to divert the northerners from their foreign trades, or to halt the trend toward home manufacturing.

This failure led the mercantilists to embrace a purely negative policy. As the trade of the northern area with the foreign West Indies increased, the English Government undertook to stop it altogether. Such was its intent in imposing upon the colonies the Molasses Act of 1733. But that effort did not succeed. Again, a mercantilist policy failed to bear its expected fruit.

The early policies of mercantilism had a marked effect on the growth of the northern area. But the result turned out to be unpleasing to the English authorities. Their endeavors to give a new direction to the development of the area failed completely after 1700. A problem had arisen for which English mercantilism never found a solution.

The main element in this problem was the trend in the northern area toward domestic manufacturing. Since that trend menaced all the essentials of mercantilism, the English Government did its best to thwart it. Thus there was no more important ingredient in English policy than the determined effort to retard or prevent the growth in America of industries that would produce the sort of goods that England could export at the greatest profit. Such, chiefly, were cloth, ironware, hats, and leather goods. The effectiveness of the laws and orders against colonial manufacturing is a subject of dispute. It is difficult to prove why something did not happen. If the colonies were slow in developing manufacturing industries, was it the result of English policy or of other factors? The writer believes that English, policies had a strong retarding influence. The barriers erected were extensive and formidable. British statutes restrained the American woolen, iron, and hat industries. The colonies could not impose protective tariffs on imports from England. They could not operate mints, create manufacturing corporations, or establish commercial banks—institutions that are essential to the progress of manufacturing.

It was easier to enforce a policy against American fabricating industries than a policy that aimed to regulate maritime trade. A vessel could slip in and out of the northern ports. A manufacturing plant and its operations could not be concealed, unless, as in later times, it was engaged in mountain moonshining. The exposure of factories to the gaze of officials undoubtedly deterred investors from building them in defiance of the law.

New industries in an economically backward country commonly needed the positive encouragement and protection of government. It was the rule of mercantilism that handicaps to home manufacturing should be overcome by tariffs, bounties, and other forms of state aid. Such stimuli were denied to the colonies while they were subject to English mercantilism. Not only was the imperial government hostile; equally important, the colonial governments were not allowed to extend assistance to American promoters who wished to establish industries on the basis of efficient, large-scale operations.

An important aspect of the influence of state policy is its effect on the attitude of the people who are subjected to its benefits and restraints. The colonists as a whole were not seriously antagonized by the British imperium prior to 1763. Its most detrimental policy—that of the Molasses Act—was not enforced. In time of war (which meant thirty-five years of the period from 1689 to 1763) the military expenditures of the Crown in America helped to solve the most crucial problem of the colonies by supplying them with funds with which they could pay their debts and buy needed supplies in England. The shipbuilders and shipowners of the northern area shared in the national monopoly of imperial trade. Underlying all policy and legislation was the extremely liberal action of the English Government in making land available to settlers on easy terms and of admitting into the colonies immigrants of diverse nationalities and varied religious faiths.

After 1763 the story is different. The colonies no longer received the sort of easy money that they had obtained from military expenditures during the wars. Instead, they were called upon to support through British taxes the defense establishment that was to be maintained in America after the war. Britain now abandoned its old liberal practice regarding land and immigration and replaced it with restrictive measures suggestive of the colonial policies of France and Spain. The Crown proceeded to enforce with vigor all the restraints it had previously imposed on colonial enterprise. Most of the features of the imperial rule that had placated the colonists were to be done away with. Not only were the old restraints to be more strictly enforced, they were to be accompanied by a host of new ones. The policies of Britain after 1763 merely intensified the central difficulty of the trade of the colonies. How might they find the means of paying for the manufactured goods that they must buy from England? If they could not get adequate returns, they would have to manufacture for themselves.

In its total effect, British policy as it affected the colonies after 1763 was restrictive, injurious, negative. It offered no solutions of problems. In the meantime, the colonists, having lived so long under the rule of mercantilism, had become imbued with mercantilist ideas. If the British imperium would not allow them to grow and expand, if it would not provide a solution of the central problem of the American economy, the colonists would have to take to themselves the right and the power to guide their economic development. They would find it necessary to create a new authority that would foster American shipping and commerce, make possible the continued growth of settlement, and above all stimulate the growth of domestic manufacturing industries. Thus another result of English mercantilism was the American Revolution and the creation thereafter of a new mercantilist state on this side of the Atlantic.

137

CURTIS P. NETTELS, *Cornell University*

Communications and Trade:
The Atlantic in the Seventeenth Century

IN THE first half of the seventeenth century the northern mercantile nations of Europe followed Spain and Portugal in flinging their commercial frontiers westward to the New World. By the end of the century they had surpassed the Iberian nations in western trade and made of the Atlantic basin a single great trading area. Their economic enterprises created not only a crisscrossing web of transoceanic traffic but also a cultural community that came to form the western periphery of European civilization. The members of this community were widely separated, scattered across three thousand miles of ocean and up and down the coasts of two continents. But the structure of commerce furnished a communication system that brought these far-flung settlements together. The same structure proved to be a framework upon which certain important elements in colonial society took form. My purpose is to sketch certain characteristics of the Atlantic colonies in the seventeenth century which relate to these social consequences of commercial growth.

The formative period of northern Atlantic trade was the second third of the seventeenth century. In those years there were important commercial developments on the American continent by the English, the Dutch, and the French; but the swiftest advance took place in the Caribbean. "After 1625," A. P. Newton writes, "swarms of English and French colonists poured like flies upon the rotting carcase of Spain's empire in the Caribbean, and within ten years the West Indian scene was changed forever."[1] The Lesser Antilles became a battleground of the expanding European empires. The island of St. Christopher in the Leewards was jointly possessed by the French and English; Barbados, Nevis, Antigua, and Montserrat were indisputably English; Guadeloupe and Martinique were French; and Curaçao, St. Eustatius, and Tobago were in the hands of the Dutch.

The feverish activity that lay behind these developments resulted from the belief of numerous Europeans that wealth could be readily extracted from the places in the New World with which they were acquainted. But for every success there were a dozen failures. Hopes

[1] Arthur P. Newton, *The European Nations in the West Indies, 1493–1688* (London: A. and C. Black, 1933), p. 149.

378

were held for commercial designs that strike us now as ill-conceived, even stupid. Yet to contemporary merchants, cautious men who built fortunes on their ability to judge investments shrewdly, they were at least as promising as the schemes that succeeded.

Remarkable only for its subsequent fame but typical in its results was the Plymouth Company's colony at the mouth of the Sagadahoc River in New Hampshire. Behind the failure of this venture lay the belief that exploiters of North America, like those of Asia, had only to build coastal trading factories, to which throngs of natives would haul precious piles of goods to exchange for tinkling bells and snippets of bright cloth. English merchants invested approximately £15,000 in the Lynn Ironworks, which collapsed within two decades of its promising start in the early 1640's. At least three major fur companies foundered on the belief that the heartland of American pelts lay in the swampy margins of a mythical "Great Lake of the Iroquois," from which were supposed to flow all the main rivers emptying into the Atlantic. The Virginia settlements after the mid-twenties gradually gained a solid economic base, but only after a decade and a half of continuous failure. In the Caribbean islands, experimentation in all sorts of commodities preceded and accompanied the development of sugar as a staple crop.

Patterns of trade were established, of course, around the poles of successful economic ventures, and it was, therefore, only after the broad wave of failures had receded, leaving behind clear indications of natural possibilities, that the commercial system in its familiar form became evident.

The result was a network of trading routes woven by the enterprises of merchants, shipmasters, and colonists representing all the leading mercantile nations of western Europe. The character of each nation's involvement in the web of traffic was determined largely by the resources it controlled and its place in European affairs. Holland's concentration on the carriage of other nations' goods shaped its position; the commerce of France came to rest upon Canadian furs and West Indian sugar; England's position was determined by the very variety of her colonial products and of the interests of her merchants.

The form of England's commercial system was an interlocked group of irregular circles linking the fixed points of port towns in the British Isles, Newfoundland, the American mainland, the West Indies, the Wine Islands, and the continent of Europe. Outward from the larger ports in the British Isles flowed shipping, manufactures, and invest-

139

ments in colonial property, the enhanced value of which returned as colonial products to be sold at home or abroad. No important part of this flow was self-sufficient. Merchants in the colonies, who profited by injecting into the flow goods of their ownership which would be carried one or more stages closer to the ultimate resolution, became important agents in maintaining the efficiency of this mechanism. Their commerce was not independent, and if it appeared to be so to some of them that was because the efficiency of the system permitted them to operate successfully within a limited area. A breakdown in any major part of the mechanism affected all other parts. When, at the outbreak of the American Revolution, the link between England and her colonies was broken, the whole system, in so far as it affected the colonial merchants, was destroyed.

To contemporaries, the commercial system, which we may describe in abstract, geometrical terms, was not something impersonal existing above men's heads, outside their lives, to which they attached themselves for purpose of trade. Unconcerned with abstract economic forces, they knew that their trade was the creation of men and that the bonds that kept its parts together were the personal relationships existing among them.

Overseas commerce in the seventeenth century was capricious. Arrangements were interminably delayed by the accidents of sailing. Demand fluctuated almost incalculably, as one unforeseen crop failure could create a market which the arrival of a few ships could eliminate overnight. Reliable factors and correspondents were, therefore, of paramount importance, for the success of large enterprises rested on their judgment. In such a situation the initiation and continuance of commerce demanded deep personal commitments between people separated by hundreds of miles of ocean. How could such commitments be made? Not, in these early years, by impersonal correspondences between men brought into temporary contact by complementary business needs. The logic of the situation demanded that they follow pre-existent ties of blood or long acquaintance.

To a striking degree first commercial contacts were secured by the cement of kinship. Very frequently brothers, sons, and "in-laws" became the colonial agents of their European relatives. In the middle years of the seventeenth century a number of European—especially English and French—trading families spread out over the Atlantic world. Sons of Londoners seeking their fortunes entered trade in the West Indies and drew on their London connections who were them-

140

selves anxious to profit from the importation of colonial goods. Thus Richard Povey, brother of the famous London merchant-politician Thomas Povey, looked after the family interests in Jamaica, while another brother, William, attended to affairs in Barbados. Not infrequently the same family had other relatives on the American mainland who joined in the growing enterprise. The Winthrop family, starting with representatives in England and Massachusetts, ended with ties to Rhode Island, New London and Hartford, Connecticut, Teneriffe in the Canaries, and Antigua in the West Indies. Typical of the reports by young Samuel Winthrop of his progress in securing the last-named contacts are these sentences from a letter of 1648 to his father:

141

> Captain Clement everet a Justice of peace [in St. Christopher], who being our country man and hearing our name vsed me verry Courtiously, and assisted me much in my law suites which were there verry many. Justice Froth, who was of your acquantance in England (as he informes me), was his Granfather. I haue left in his handes my busines in St. Christpors.[2]

Jean Bailly of La Rochelle conducted his West Indian trade through two relatives in the Caribbean islands, especially Clerbaut Bergier in Martinique. But the most complete family commercial system of which we have any knowledge is that of the Hutchinsons; it is an almost ideal type of this sort of arrangement.

The Hutchinson family trading unit was based upon the continuous flow of manufactures exported from London by the affluent Richard Hutchinson to his brothers Samuel and Edward and his nephews Elisha and Eliakim in Boston, Massachusetts. They, together with Thomas Savage, who had married Richard's sister, retailed the goods in the Bay area and, through middlemen, sold also to the inland settlers. They conducted a large trade with the West Indies, sending provisions and cattle in exchange for cotton and sugar which they sold for credit on London. This West Indian trade of the Hutchinsons was largely handled for them by Peleg Sanford of Portsmouth, Rhode Island, whose mother was another sister of Richard and who was, hence, cousin and nephew of the Boston merchants of the family. Peleg, who had started his career as a commercial agent in the West Indies, exported their horses and provisions to Barbados where they were sold by his brothers, the Barbadian merchants William and Elisha Sanford.

The Hutchinsons with their Rhode Island and West Indian relations formed a self-conscious family group which considered it unfortunate

[2] Samuel Winthrop, Fayal, to John Winthrop, January 10, 1648, *Winthrop Papers* (Boston: Massachusetts Historical Society, 1929-47), V, 196.

but not unnatural that Edward Hutchinson should go to jail, as he did in 1667, as a consequence of his support of his nephew Peleg in a law suit.

Since commerce was so dependent upon personal relationships, the weaving of a network of correspondences was greatly facilitated by the migrations within the colonial area. Many mainland settlers transplanted themselves to the Caribbean islands and became factors in the West Indies for the merchant friends they had left behind. On the other hand, several merchants were involved in the movement of people among and out of the West Indies, and some of them became residents of the continental colonies. Thus, John Parris, a relative of the New Englander John Hull, moved from the West Indies to Boston where he engaged in large operations in an attempt to stock his Barbados plantation with slaves. Men who moved south to the Indies or north to the continent carried with them friendships and a knowledge of affairs in their old home towns which were used in broadening the foreign contacts of the colonial merchants.

A further consequence of the personal nature of commercial ties in this early period was the consistency, long before mercantilist legislation became effective, with which Frenchmen and Britishers dealt with their fellow nationals in trade. Correspondences with foreigners were difficult to establish and maintain. To British colonials in this period, it seemed that little reliance could be placed on the bonds of Frenchmen who desired nothing more than the collapse of the British settlements in the New World. In long-distance transactions Englishmen preferred to deal with their relatives and friends who, if necessary, could be brought to law in the British courts far more easily than could Frenchmen. Richard Wharton, one of the most enterprising colonial merchants of the seventeenth century, failed to extend his contacts into the French West Indies because of his inability to secure reliable French correspondents. The later enforcement of mercantilist legislation was greatly facilitated by this early tendency of overseas merchants to favor connections with, if not relatives or old friends, at least fellow countrymen.

Through channels of trade created by personal ties among Europeans scattered about the Atlantic world flowed not only physical commodities but the human communications that related the settlers to European life. The orbits of commerce formed by lines drawn between the fixed points of correspondents helped shape the character of urban development and the structure of society in the colonial settlements.

142

On the American continent, as certain trading centers became poles in the primary cycles of trade, others slipped back toward ruralism. In the passage of generations the communities involved in the major orbits came into closer cultural relations with Europe than they did with some of the neighboring backwoods villages. The Boston merchants' meeting place in their Townhouse Exchange was in every way, except geographically, closer to the "New-England walke" on the London Exchange than to the market places of most inland towns. Study of any of the continental trading regions reveals the varying degrees of provincialism that followed the solidification of the routes of commerce.

In New England, the most important commercial center in North America during the seventeenth century, Boston, with its excellent harbor and access to the provincial government and to flourishing agricultural markets, became the major terminus of traffic originating in Europe. With the exception of Salem and Charlestown, the other promising mercantile centers of the 1630's and 1640's fell back into secondary economic roles and relative seclusion from the cultural life of the Atlantic community. Plymouth, which had been the first trading center east of Manhattan, was described in 1660 as "a poor small Towne now, The People being removed into Farmes in the Country," and New Haven, whose optimistic merchant leaders had laid out "stately and costly houses," was "not so glorious as once it was," with its "Merchants either dead or come away, the rest gotten to their Farmes." [3] This is not to say that these essentially rural districts had no trade. On the contrary, there were men in the Connecticut River towns and along Long Island Sound who managed a considerable exchange of goods; but their dealings were different from those of the Bostonians. Engaged in secondary orbits of trade, they sent small but steady flows of local produce only to other American colonies or occasionally to the West Indies. The Connecticut River grandees were, like the younger Pynchon, primarily landed squires and only secondarily merchants. The few men in the small coastal villages who did devote themselves primarily to trade operated within a commercial sphere subordinate to that of the Bostonians and the Dutchmen.

Life in the inland areas and in the minor ports came to differ significantly from that in the commercial centers in direct contact with Europe. While Boston and New York assumed characteristics of British

143

[3] Samuel Maverick, *A Briefe Discription of New England and the Severall Townes therein, together with the Present Government thereof* ([ca. 1660]; reprinted in *Proceedings of the Massachusetts Historical Society*, Ser. 2, 1), pp. 243, 245.

provincial outports and while their leading residents groped for an understanding of their place as colonials in British society, towns like Scarborough, Maine, and Wethersfield, Connecticut, became models of new types of communities; and their inhabitants, restricted in experience to the colonial world, came to lack the standards by which to measure or even to perceive their provincialism. Fashion, patterns for styles of living, and the emulative spirit of provincialism followed the routes of trade, which, throughout the colonial world, became important social boundaries.

This fact became particularly evident in the last third of the century when national rivalries, both military and economic, required the presence of official representatives in the colonies from the home countries. These officers, civil and military, settled for the most part in the large trading centers, close to the main objects of their supervision. Their presence in what might be called the focuses of the primary trading orbits had a most important social consequence. These home country representatives were quickly surrounded by a number of Europeans new to the colonies: men seeking careers in the quickly expanding colonial administrations. Customs functionaries, lesser bureaucrats, fortune hunters in official positions—these newcomers, grouped around the chief European representatives, came to constitute colonial officialdom, which in all the main colonial ports became a major social magnet for the residents. For not only did it represent cosmopolitan fashion and political influence, but, in its access to those who controlled government contracts and who wielded the weapon of customs regulations, it offered great economic opportunities.

Toward these groups, therefore, moved every colonial with ambition and the slightest hope of success. The threshold of officialdom became a great divide in the society of the commercial towns. Next to this principle of association, "class," in the traditional European sense, was meaningless. In Europe the word "merchant" meant not only an occupation but a status and a way of life. In America, where, as Madam Knight discovered in her famous journey of 1704, they gave the title of merchant to every backwoods huckster,[4] trade was not so much a way of life as a way of making money, not a social condition but an economic activity. Similarly, how could the well-known American mariner, Captain Cyprian Southack, be prevented from describing himself, as he did on occasion, as "gent."?[5]

---

[4] *The Journal of Madam Knight* (New York: Peter Smith, 1935), p. 40.
[5] *Calendar of State Papers, Colonial Series, America and West Indies, 1712–1714,* ¶ 520.

The limits of officialdom, however, were palpable. No merchant would confuse failure with success in obtaining favors from customs officials or in gaining contracts for provisions and naval stores. It was well worth a merchant's noting, as Samuel Sewall did in his *Diary*, that he was not invited to the governor's dinner parties or to the extravagant funerals staged by the members of his group.[6]

It was as true in the seventeenth century as it is now that the introduction of an important new social barrier necessarily intrudes upon a variety of interests. The advent of officialdom was attended by upheavals throughout the Atlantic world. Wherever we turn in this period we find evidence of social dislocation as successful resident entrepreneurs came to terms with this important new force in the colonial world.

145

One of the first successful agricultural districts in Carolina was Albemarle County. Behind the barrier of shifting sand bars that blocked Albemarle Sound to all but the most shallow-draft ocean-going vessels lived, in the 1670's, approximately 3,000 settlers—farmers, coastal backwoodsmen, many of them tough, stubborn refugees from better-organized communities. Their one cash crop was tobacco, of which they prepared nearly one million pounds a year. This they disposed of to northerners on peddling voyages in exchange for the commodities they needed. The Navigation Law of 1673 levied duties on tobacco at the port of lading, and Albemarle, like all other commercial centers, was soon visited by a customs collector. The settlers resisted, fearing an increase in the price of goods if their tobacco was taxed, and they forced the governor to remit to the traders three farthings in every penny taken. In 1677 the appointment of an imperious collector of customs determined to enforce the law led to a rebellion of the settlers headed by one John Culpeper. Until the legal authorities could regain control, Culpeper acted as collector, formed a temporary government, and barred the royal comptroller and surveyor of the customs at Albemarle from the exercise of his office.

Culpeper's rebellion, though it was soon quelled and finds little mention in American history, was a significant event. It is a simplified example of what was taking place throughout the colonies. We do not yet have a full account of Leisler's rebellion which kept New York in turmoil for two years. But when we do, it will be found that it was in great part the culmination of resentments that accompanied the intro-

---

[6] *Diary of Samuel Sewall,* April 13, 1686; June 15, 19, and October 3, 1688; December 8, 1690 (*Collections of the Massachusetts Historical Society,* Ser. 5, V, 132, 217, 228, 338).

duction of English officialdom into that province. Leisler's career, in fact, can only be understood against the background of family rivalries that grew up around this pre-eminent principle of association.[7] Edmund Andros, famous for his difficulties as the governor of the Dominion of New England, had a less notorious but equally important reign as the Duke of York's governor in New York. In this position he precipitated social differences among the merchants who resisted when they could not take advantage of his influence. He was finally recalled on charges of excessive fee-taking and profiteering.

The rebellion of 1689, which overthrew his administration of the Dominion of New England, divided the northern merchants on lines not of ideology but of interests defined by the degree of proximity to officialdom. No ideology, no religious belief, no abstract political principle or party loyalty separated the Boston merchants Richard Wharton and Charles Lidget, but in 1689 they were on opposite sides of the political fence. Lidget ended up in the Boston jail with Andros because his connections, inherited from his father who had built the family fortune on the timber he sold to the Navy mast contractors, linked him to the leaders of the official group. Wharton died in the midst of his fight for the removal of Andros whose favor he had been denied. The fact that Lidget was one of the founders of the first Anglican Church in New England does not indicate a religious or ideological orientation different from Wharton's. The latter, if he was not an active Anglican, certainly was not a dissenter. Both men married heiress daughters of nonconformist New Englanders.

In the West Indies the same principle was at work during most of the seventeenth century. But toward the end of the century controversies touched off by the intrusion of officialdom diminished in the islands as a consequence of the consolidation of large plantations and the growth of absenteeism. The resident nonofficial population became less active politically as the large planters returned to the home country, leaving their estates in the hands of managers and agents. But battles over the economic benefits of political and social advantage were not ended; they were merely transferred to London where they punctuated the history of the West India interest.

By the end of the century this principle of association in the commercial centers was deeply woven into the fabric of American society.

[7] Jerome R. Reich's *Leisler's Rebellion: A Study of Democracy in New York, 1664–1720* (Chicago: University of Chicago Press, 1953) came to my attention after the writing of this paper. The information it contains bears out the above interpretation. See especially pp. 37–40, 44, 50–51, 58–59, 70, 71–73, 87, 98, 126, 138–41, 143, 160–66.

Its importance did not diminish thereafter. Recently, Oliver Dickerson in his book *The Navigation Acts and the American Revolution* [8] destroyed a number of myths by pointing out the importance of what he called "customs racketeering." From his researches it appears that the merchant group was as deeply divided on the eve of the Revolution as it was in 1689. Both John Hancock and Thomas Hutchinson were leading Boston merchants, but the former was clearly victimized by the strategy of the Hutchinson-Bernard clique which controlled the channels of prerogative. And in South Carolina, Henry Laurens, probably the richest merchant in the southern colonies, whose mercantile connections were with the opponents of the King's Friends, suffered equally from the rapacity of the official group.

Further study of the merchants as a social group may reveal that this principle of association, which emerged as an important social force when the nations of Europe undertook to draw together the threads of trade spun by seventeenth-century entrepreneurs, was a major determinant of the movement that led to Revolution.

BERNARD BAILYN, *Harvard University*

[8] Philadelphia: University of Pennsylvania Press, 1951.

England's Cultural Provinces: Scotland and America

John Clive and Bernard Bailyn*

THE question of the origin of the "Scottish Renaissance"—that remarkable efflorescence of the mid-eighteenth century, with its roll call of great names: Hume, Smith, Robertson, Kames, and Ferguson—is one of those historical problems which have hitherto stubbornly resisted a definite solution. This may be due to its very nature; for, as the greatest of recent historians of Scotland has remarked, "We recognize as inadequate all attempts to explain the appearance of galaxies of genius at particular epochs in different countries."[1] This is not to imply that attempted explanations have failed to be forthcoming. On the contrary, ever since a learned Italian named Carlo Deanina applied himself to the problem in *An Essay on the Progress of Learning among the Scots* (1763), historians have suggested different reasons for that striking and apparently sudden outburst of creative energy. Macaulay saw the principal cause for what he considered "this wonderful change" from the barren wastes of seventeenth-century theology in the act passed by the Estates of Scotland in 1696, setting up a school in every parish. Buckle, sounding a suitably Darwinian note, observed the energies displayed in the Scottish political and religious struggles of the seventeenth century surviving those struggles and finding another field in which they could exert themselves.

There is something to be said for both these points of view. The national system of education, though in practice never quite as ideal as in conception, enabled many a poor farmer's boy to go on to one of the universities as well prepared as his socially superior classmates. Nor can it be denied that in spite of the Fifteen and the Forty-five the general atmosphere of eighteenth-century Scotland was more conducive to peaceful pursuits than that of the strife-torn decades of the seventeenth century. But it requires no more than a little reflection on cultural history to perceive that neither peace nor public education, nor their conjunction, guarantees the intellectual achievements suggested by the word "renaissance."

* Mr. Clive and Mr. Bailyn are Instructors at Harvard University.
[1] P. Hume Brown, *Surveys of Scottish History* (Glasgow, 1919), 131.

Similar objections may be advanced concerning some of the other so-called "causes" of Scotland's golden age. Thus it is certainly true that the eighteenth century, in contrast to the seventeenth, was for Scotland a period of increasing economic prosperity. However, the disastrous Darien scheme of the 1690's ate up that capital fuel without which even the most rigorous Protestant ethic could not become economically efficacious. The immediate effect of the Union of 1707 was not the expected sudden prosperity, but increased taxation and loss of French trade. Nor, until much later, was there a compensating expansion of commerce with England and the colonies. Real economic advancement did not come until the latter half of the century, too late to serve as a satisfactory reason for the first stages of Scotland's great creative period. As for the influence of "New Light" Hutcheson, his Glasgow lectures—effusions on the marvelous powers of the "moral sense" by an enthusiastic disciple of Shaftesbury—no doubt "contributed very powerfully to diffuse, in Scotland, that taste for analytical discussion, and that spirit of liberal inquiry, to which the world is indebted for some of the most valuable productions of the eighteenth century."[2] But holding them solely responsible for the Scottish enlightenment is surely expecting a little too much even from the most lucid philosopher. Furthermore, it is worth noting that, after Hutcheson's first year at Glasgow, at least one contemporary observer singled him out for praise because he was maintaining the cause of orthodox Christianity in a university shot through with free thought.[3] The fact is that, by the time Hutcheson began his lectures, considerable breaches had been made in the dam of orthodox austerity so laboriously constructed during the embattled decades of the previous century.

Adequate explanation of the origins of the Scottish renaissance, therefore, must take account not only of a variety of social factors at the moment of fullest flowering, but also of the conditions of growth in the preceding period.[4] Thus broadened, the problem seems to involve the

[2] Dugald Stewart, "Account of the Life and Writings of Adam Smith, LL.D.," in William Hamilton, ed., *The Collected Works of Dugald Stewart, Esq., F.R.S.E.* (Edinburgh, 1854-1860), X, 82.
[3] Robert Wodrow, *Analecta* (Edinburgh, 1842-1843), IV, 185.
[4] A re-evaluation of Scottish cultural history in the two or three decades just before the Union of 1707 is especially desirable. Henry W. Meikle, *Some Aspects of Later Seventeenth Century Scotland* (Glasgow, 1947) was a step in the right direction. Detailed study of the Church, the Bar, and the University of Edinburgh around the turn of the century shows that a spirit of increasing tolerance and ever-broadening

entire history of Scotland for the better part of a century. The numerous elements that entered into the renaissance must be brought together. But the interpretation of broad historical movements of this kind is not simply a matter of listing factors. A knowledge of their configuration is equally important. Comprehension of Scotland's renaissance must rest on an appreciation of the essential spirit of the time and place, as well as on the accumulation of cultural data.

The underlying unity of this renaissance, the profound impulses that elevated the life of a nation, require deeper study and thought than they have yet received. We do not propose to solve such problems in these few pages. We seek, merely, possible perspectives in which to perceive them, and we find an approach suggested by the subject of the present symposium. For the American colonies, too, enjoyed a flowering in the eighteenth century—not a renaissance, but yet a blossoming worthy of the designation "golden age." British North America produced no Hume or Adam Smith, but in Edwards and Franklin, Jefferson, Madison, and Adams, Rittenhouse, Rush, Copley, West, Wythe, and Hutchinson it boasted men of impressive accomplishment. Its finest fruit, the literature of the American Revolution, has justly been called "the most magnificent irruption of the American genius into print."[5]

The society in which the achievements of these men were rooted, though obviously different from that of Scotland in many ways, was yet significantly related to it. Elements of this relationship struck contemporaries much as they have later scholars. "Boston," writes one critic, "has often been called the most English of American cities, but in the eighteenth and early nineteenth centuries it was a good deal more like Edinburgh than like London. . . . The people, like those of Edinburgh, were independent, not easily controlled, assertive of their rights. . . ."[6] In Boston, New York, and Philadelphia, as in Edinburgh and Glasgow, private clubs, where pompous, often ridiculously elaborate ritual threw into bold relief the fervor of cultural uplift, were vital social institutions. Similar to the quality of social mobility that led Dr. Alexander Hamilton to berate New York's "aggrandized upstarts" for lacking "the capacity to observe the different ranks of men in polite nations or to know what it is that

---

intellectual and cultural interests had by then invaded all three of these institutions to a considerable degree.

[5] George S. Gordon, *Anglo-American Literary Relations* (Oxford, 1942), 27.
[6] Henry W. Foote, *John Smibert, Painter* (Cambridge, 1950), 60, 61.

150

really constitutes that difference of degrees" was the spirit of "shocking familiarity" in Scotland of which Boswell, on his continental tour, took care to warn Rousseau.[7]

Such remarks tell much and suggest more. They lead one to pursue the question of the social similarities bearing on intellectual life into richer, if more remote regions. They suggest the value of a comparison of the cultural developments in Scotland and America from the standpoint of the English observer in London. Certain common social characteristics of these flowerings, thus isolated, might throw new light on the basic impulses of the Scottish renaissance and prove of interest to historians of both regions.

We find, first, a striking similarity in the social location of the groups that led the cultural developments in the two areas.

Whatever else may remain obscure about the social history of colonial America, it cannot be doubted that advance in letters and in the arts was involved with social ascent by groups whose status in Europe would unquestionably have been considered inferior or middling. Despite the familial piety that has so often claimed nobility for *arrivé* forbears, and with it a leisured, graceful intimacy with the muses, there were few cultivated aristocrats in the colonies to lead intellectual and artistic advances. Throughout the North, the middle-class origins of the literati were unmistakable.

Who led the cultural advance in the northern towns? Ministers, of course, like William Smith, Provost of the College of Philadelphia, who carried with him from Aberdeen not only a headful of learning but frustrated ambitions that developed into a common type of cultural snobbery; like Samuel Johnson, President of King's College, who grew up in Connecticut where, he wrote in his poignant *Autobiography*, "the condition of learning (as well as everything else) was very low," and whose "thirst after knowledge and truth" alone saved him from a hopeless provincialism; or like the supercilious Mather Byles, scion of a local intellectual dynasty, who snapped the whip of sarcasm over a mulish populace while proudly displaying a note from Alexander Pope elicited by fawning letters and gifts of hackneyed verse.[8]

[7] Carl Bridenbaugh, ed., *Gentleman's Progress: The Itinerarium of Dr. Alexander Hamilton 1744* (Chapel Hill, 1948), 186; Frederick A. Pottle, ed., *Boswell on the Grand Tour: Germany and Switzerland, 1764* (New York, 1953), 259.

[8] Albert F. Gegenheimer, *William Smith* (Philadelphia, 1943), chapters I-IV; Herbert and Carol Schneider, eds., *Samuel Johnson* (New York, 1929), I, 57; Arthur W. H. Eaton, *The Famous Mather Byles* (Boston, 1914), 101-103, 232-233.

Equally important were lawyers like John Adams, William Livingston, and James DeLancey, whose cultural even more than political ascendancy was assured "in a Country," Cadwallader Colden wrote in 1765, "where few men except in the profession of the Law, have any kind of literature, where the most opulent families in our own memory, have arisen from the lowest rank of people. . . ."[9] Along with these two professional groups, there were a few of the leading merchants, or, more frequently, their more leisured heirs, like the versifier Peter Oliver or his politician-historian cousin, Thomas Hutchinson. These men, potentates on the local scene, were no more than colonial businessmen in the wider world of British society. Even the brilliant classicist and scientist, James Logan of Philadelphia—"aristocrat" by common historical designation—would have been but a cultivated Quaker burgher to the patrons of arts and letters in London.

If such were the leaders in the northern port towns, who followed? The numerous cultural associations, the clubs, were recruited from the professional middle and tradesman lower-middle classes. Franklin's famous Junto was a self-improvement society of autodidacts. Its original membership included a glazier, a surveyor, a shoemaker, a joiner, a merchant, three printers, and a clerk. And though Philadelphia's merchants derided the Junto as the "Leather Apron Club," they themselves, in their own societies, like their fellows in Annapolis's Tuesday Club, or Newport's Literary and Philosophical Society, could not help finding relaxation in most un-aristocratic self-improvement.

But it is, of course, in the South where the brightest image of the aristocrat, the landed gentleman as the man of letters, has appeared. Wealth in land and slaves, we have been told again and again, combined to create a class of leisured aristocrats—the Byrds, the Carters, the Lees—whose lives glowed with vitality in letters as in politics. But careful study has shown this to be a myth. "The most significant feature of the Chesapeake aristocracy," writes Carl Bridenbaugh,

was its middle-class origin. . . . Leisure was a myth; endless work was a reality quite as much for successful planter-gentlemen as for their lesser confreres—and the same held for their womenfolk as well. . . . Those who have appointed themselves custodians of the historical reputation of this fascinating region have generally insisted that it produced that which, by its very nature,

[9] Cadwallader Colden to the Earl of Halifax, February 22, 1765, quoted in Paul M. Hamlin, *Legal Education in Colonial New York* (New York, 1939), 37.

it could not produce—a developed intellectual and artistic culture rivaling that of any other part of the colonies. . . . They led a gracious but not a cultured life. . . . The Chesapeake society produced a unique bourgeois aristocracy with more than its share of great and noble men; they were, however, men of intellect, not intellectuals.[10]

What of the deeper South—the society of colonial Carolina? "Families of actual gentle birth were even fewer [here] than in the Chesapeake country; the bourgeois grown rich and seeking gentility set the style. . . . The striking aspects of colonial Charles Town were the absence of cultural discipline and the passiveness of the city's intellectual and artistic life." If Carolina's rising merchant-planter families produced "the only leisure-class society of colonial America" where alone "enjoyment, charm, refinement—became the *summum bonum*," they yet failed to furnish even a few recruits to the arts and sciences.[11]   *153*

How sharp is the contrast to Scotland, with its ancient landed families and tighter social organization?

It would be wrong to ignore the share of the aristocracy in the cultural life of eighteenth-century Edinburgh; but, due to special circumstances, its role remained contributory rather than decisive. The Scottish nobility and gentry had largely remained Jacobite and Episcopalian, even after the re-establishment of the Church of Scotland. This meant that they were unencumbered by those ascetic proclivities against which even moderate Presbyterians still had to struggle. Too poor to travel abroad, they spent their winters in what was no longer the political but still the legal and ecclesiastical capital, where they wrote and sang ballads, sponsored assemblies and diverse entertainments—fostered, in short, an atmosphere of ease and social grace. But if they were masters of the revels, they were masters of little else. While Jacobitism kept conscientious younger sons out of professions requiring an oath to the House of Hanover, poverty forced many of them to earn their living as tradesmen. "Silversmiths, clothiers, woollen drapers were frequently men of high birth and social position."[12] Economic necessity of this sort helped to create in the Old Town of Edinburgh a society in which social demarcations were far from sharply drawn,

[10] Carl Bridenbaugh, *Myths and Realities: Societies of the Colonial South* (Baton Rouge, 1952), 12, 17, 51, 52, 53.

[11] *Ibid.*, 65, 99, 117.

[12] Henry Grey Graham, *The Social Life of Scotland in the Eighteenth Century*, 4th ed. (London, 1937), 33.

in which status was as much a function of professional achievement as of birth. Thus Peter Williamson's first *Edinburgh Directory* (1773-1774), listing citizens in order of rank, was headed by the Lords of Session, Advocates, Writers to the Signet, and Lords' and Advocates' Clerks. The category of "noblemen and gentlemen" followed after.[13]

This order of precedence was symptomatic of the fact that in the course of the century, social and cultural leadership had fallen to the professional classes, and especially to the legal profession. A good example of the close connection between Law and Letters is provided by an analysis of the membership of the Select Society, founded in 1754 for the dual purpose of philosophical inquiry and improvement in public speaking. By 1759, this society (then numbering 133 members) had come to include all the Edinburgh literati; and out of 119 who can be readily identified by profession, at least forty-eight were associated with the law in one way or the other.[14] Along with university professors and members of the Moderate party among the clergy, it was the lawyers who played the principal role both in the mid-eighteenth and early nineteenth-century stages of the Scottish enlightenment; one need only mention the names of Kames, Mackenzie, Monboddo, Scott, Jeffrey, and Brougham. That Scotland retained its own legal system after the Union, that the law thus became the main ladder for public advancement, and that there prevailed a great interest in legal studies had other less direct though no less important consequences. The traditionally close involvement of Scottish and Roman law, as well as the liberal influences brought home from Holland by generations of Scottish law students at Utrecht and Leyden, proved to be forces conducive to fresh currents of philosophical and historical thought. In his Glasgow lectures on moral philosophy, Francis Hutcheson presented "the most complete view of legal philosophy of the time."[15] And those early public lectures Adam Smith delivered in Edinburgh after his return from Oxford (1748-1751) in which he first enunciated the principle of the division of labor had as their actual subject matter "jurisprudence," or

[13] See Harold W. Thompson, *A Scottish Man of Feeling* (New York, 1931), 34-35.

[14] The list, dated October 17, 1759, is printed in Dugald Stewart, "Account of the Life and Writings of William Robertson, D.D.," *Works*, X, 205-207. The Reverend Alexander Carlyle, who supplied Stewart with it, notes in his *Autobiography* (Edinburgh, 1910), 311-312, that it is incomplete. But he lists only two additional members, one of them a lawyer.

[15] S. G. Kermack, "Natural Jurisprudence and Philosophy of Law," in *An Introductory Survey of the Sources and Literature of Scots Law* (Edinburgh, 1936), 441.

the philosophy of law.[16] To these lectures, the first part of Robertson's *History of Charles V* owed a great deal. A considerable part of the intellectual history of Scotland in the eighteenth century might be written in terms of direct and indirect legal influences. There was no doubt about the fact that, as one traveler commented late in the century, it was the lawyers who "indeed, in some measure give the tone to the manners of the Scotch Metropolis," that they, "in short, are the principal people in that city."[17]

The similarity in social origins between the Scottish and American literati became evident at a time when another more complicated relationship between the two societies was being formed. Trade, migration, and cultural exchanges mark one phase of this relationship. But these direct transfers of goods, persons, books, and ideas reflect the profound fact that Scotland and America were provinces, cultural as well as political and economic, of the English-speaking world whose center was London. From this common orientation flowed essential elements of cultural growth.

English sovereignty over the American colonies meant not only regulations and fees, but also the presence of a particular group of men who dominated the stage of colonial affairs. They had first appeared in large numbers in the seventies of the previous century, when, after the settlement of the Restoration government, England had attempted to lace together the scattered segments of its Atlantic empire. To accomplish this, she had dispatched to the centers of settlement royal officials—governors, admirals, customs officials, inspectors of forests, collectors general and particular, minor functionaries of all sorts—empowered to assert the prerogatives of sovereignty. In the course of a half-century, the more highly placed of these men, together representing officialdom, became focuses of society in the port towns. Their influence was immense. Not only did they represent political power and economic advantage, but, in most urban centers, they were models of fashion. More than links between governments, they brought England with them into the heart of colonial America. As the brightest social luminaries in the provincial capitals, they both repelled and attracted. Social groups as well as political factions formed around them.

[16] William R. Scott, *Adam Smith as Student and Professor* (Glasgow, 1937), 55-61.
[17] Thomas Newte, *Prospects and Observations on a Tour in England and Scotland* (London, 1791), 364.

155

Officialdom, usually considered a political influence, was in fact a most important shaping force on the formation of colonial society. These agents of imperialism could not help but influence the growth of the arts in the colonies. Arbiters of taste, they attracted, patronized, helped to justify those who devoted themselves to letters, arts, and the graces of life.

In Scotland, too, the political connection with England led public men to become cultural go-betweens. Here, though, it was not an enforced officialdom that mattered; only the hated excisemen correspond in position, and Boswell was unusual in wanting more official Englishmen in Scotland to make the Union more complete. The situation, in fact, was reversed; but the effects were similar. The sixteen peers and forty-five members of Parliament who represented Scotland at Westminster (and who had such a hard time making ends meet in London) brought back English books and English fashions. They were catalysts in the process that gave Edinburgh its own *Tatler,* as well as its coffee-houses and wits, and, later in the century, its gambling clubs and masquerades.

Officialdom in the colonies, Scottish Members of Parliament, the Union of 1707—political relationships between England and her dependencies thus brought about cultural links as well. The existence of imperial agents and local representatives to the cosmopolitan center served also to emphasize the provincial character of life in both regions. Scotsmen and Americans alike were constantly aware that they lived on the periphery of a greater world. The image they held of this world and of their place in it was perhaps the most important, though the subtlest, element common to the cultural growth of America and Scotland in the eighteenth century.

Life in both regions was similarly affected by the mere fact of physical removal from the cosmopolitan center. For, though the Scottish border lay less than three hundred miles from London, as late as 1763 only one regular stagecoach traveled between Edinburgh and the British capital. The trip took about two weeks, or fully half the traveling time of the express packet from New York to Falmouth, and those few who could afford to make it considered it so serious an expedition that they frequently made their wills before setting out. As far as the English were concerned, Smollett's Mrs. Tabitha, who thought one could get to Scotland only by sea, represented no great advance over those of her countrymen earlier in the century to whom "many parts of Africa and the Indies . . . are better known than a Region which is contiguous to our own,

156

and which we have always had so great a concern for."[18] Even toward the middle of the century, there were occasions when the London mailbag for Edinburgh was found to contain only a single letter.

But isolation, as Perry Miller has pointed out, "is not a matter of distance or the slowness of communication: it is a question of what a dispatch from distant quarters means to the recipient."[19] News, literature, and personal messages from London did not merely convey information; they carried with them standards by which men and events were judged. In them, as in the personal envoys from the greater European world, was involved a definition of sophistication. *Tatlers* and *Spectators* were eagerly devoured in Edinburgh as in Philadelphia. Scottish ladies, like their American counterparts, ordered all sorts of finery, from dresses to wallpaper, from England. There were Americans who echoed the Scottish minister's complaint that "all the villainous, profane, and obscene books and plays, as printed in London, are got down by Allan Ramsay, and lent out, for an easy price, to young boys, servant weemen of the better sort, and gentlemen."[20] Franklin's excitement at first reading the *Spectator* and his grim determination to fashion his own literary style on it is only the most famous example of the passion with which Americans strove to imitate English ways. "I am almost inclined to believe," wrote William Eddis, "that a new fashion is adopted earlier by the polished and affluent Americans, than by many opulent persons in the great metropolis. . . ."[21]

Communications from England exerted such authority because they fell upon minds conscious of limited awareness. A sense of inferiority pervaded the culture of the two regions, affecting the great no less than the common. It lay behind David Hume's lament (in 1756) that "we people in the country (for such you Londoners esteem our city) are apt to be troublesome to you people in town; we are vastly glad to receive letters which convey intelligence to us of things we should otherwise have been

---

[18] John Chamberlayne, *Magnae Britanniae Notitia: or, the Present State of Great Britain* (London, 1708), iii.

[19] Perry Miller, *The New England Mind: From Colony to Province* (Cambridge, 1953), 6.

[20] Wodrow, *Analecta*, III, 515.

[21] William Eddis, *Letters from America . . . 1769, to 1777, inclusive* (London, 1792), quoted in Michael Kraus, *The Atlantic Civilization: Eighteenth-Century Origins* (Ithaca, 1949), 37. Cf. Mr. Bramble's comment in *Humphry Clinker*, "A burgher of Edinburgh, not content to vie with a citizen of London, who has ten times his fortune, must excel him in the expence as well as elegance of his entertainments."

ignorant of, and can pay them back with nothing but provincial stories which are in no way interesting." And it led Adam Smith to admit that "this country is so barren of all sorts of transactions that can interest anybody that lives at a distance from it that little intertainment is to be expected from any correspondent on this side of the Tweed."[22] It rankled deeply in those like the seventeenth-century cosmopolite John Winthrop, Junior, who longingly recalled in "such a wilde place" as Hartford, Connecticut, the excitement of life in the European centers. The young Copley felt it profoundly when he wrote from Boston to Benjamin West in London, "I think myself peculiarly unlucky in Liveing in a place into which there has not been one portrait brought that is worthy to be call'd a Picture within my memory, which leaves me at a great loss to gess the stil that You, Mr. Renolds, and the other Artists pracktice."[23] The young Scot returning to Edinburgh after a journey to the continent and London felt he had to "labour to tone myself down like an overstrained instrument to the low pitch of the rest about me."[24]

158

The manners and idioms that labeled the provincial in England were stigmas that Scotsmen and Americans tried to avoid when they could not turn them, like Franklin in Paris, into the accents of nature's own philosopher. There was no subject about which Scotsmen were more sensitive than their speech. Lieutenant Lismahago may have proved to his own satisfaction that "what we generally called the Scottish dialect was, in fact, true, genuine old English," but Dr. Johnson laughed at Hamilton of Bangour's rhyming "wishes" and "bushes," and when, in 1761, Thomas Sheridan, the playwright's father, lectured in Edinburgh (and in Irish brogue) on the art of rhetoric, he had an attentive audience of three hundred nobles, judges, divines, advocates, and men of fashion. Hume kept constantly by his side a list of Scots idioms to be avoided, and was said by Mcnboddo to have confessed on his deathbed not his sins but his Scotticisms.

[22] David Hume to John Clephane, April 20, 1756, J. Y. T. Greig, ed., *The Letters of David Hume* (Oxford, 1932), I, 229; Adam Smith to Lord Fitzmaurice, February 21, 1759, quoted in Scott, *Adam Smith as Student and Professor*, 241.

[23] John Winthrop, Jr., to Henry Oldenburg, November 12, 1668, *Winthrop Papers*, Part IV, in Massachusetts Historical Society, *Collections*, 5th ser., VIII (1882), 131; J. S. Copley to Benjamin West, November 12, 1766, *Letters and Papers of John Singleton Copley and Henry Pelham, 1739-1776*, in Massachusetts Historical Society, *Collections*, LXXI (1914), 51.

[24] George Dempster to Adam Fergusson, December 5, 1756, James Fergusson, ed., *Letters of George Dempster to Sir Adam Fergusson, 1756-1813* (London, 1934), 15.

By 1754, the emergence of American English, adversely commented on as early as 1735, was so far advanced that the suggestion was made, facetiously, that a glossary of American terms be compiled. The scorn shown by Englishmen for Scots dialect was not heaped upon American speech until after the Revolution. But well before Lexington, Scottish and American peculiarities in language were grouped together as provincial in the English mind, a fact understood by John Witherspoon when he wrote in 1781, "The word Americanism, which I have coined . . . is exactly similar in its formation and signification to the word Scotticism." The same equation of verbal provincialisms underlay Boswell's recounting of an anecdote told him "with great good humour" by the Scottish Earl of Marchmont:

. . . the master of a shop in London, where he was not known, said to him, "I suppose, Sir, you are an American." "Why so, Sir?" (said his Lordship.) "Because, Sir (replied the shopkeeper,) you speak neither English nor Scotch, but something different from both, which I conclude is the language of America." [25]

The sense of inferiority that expressed itself in imitation of English ways, and a sense of guilt regarding local mannerisms was, however, only one aspect of the complex meaning of provincialism. Many Scotsmen and Americans followed the Reverend John Oxenbridge in castigating those who sought to "fashion your selves to the flaunting mode of *England* in worship or walking." [26] In the manner of Ramsay of Ochtertyre's strictures on eighteenth-century Scottish authors, they inveighed against the slavish imitation of English models, such "a confession of inferiority as one would hardly have expected from a proud manly people, long famous for common-sense and veneration for the ancient classics." [27] Awareness of regional limitations frequently led to a compensatory local pride, evolving into a patriotism which was politically effective in the one area, and, after the Forty-five, mainly sentimental in the other, due to the diametrically opposed political history of the two—America moving from subordination to independence, Scotland from independence to subordination. It

[25] John Witherspoon, "The Druid, No. V [1781]," reprinted in M. M. Mathews, ed., *The Beginnings of American English* (Chicago, 1931), 17; G. Birkbeck Hill, ed., *Boswell's Life of Johnson* (New York, 1891), II, 184.
[26] John Oxenbridge, *New-England Freemen Warned and Warmed* . . . ([Cambridge], 1673), 19.
[27] John Ramsay, *Scotland and Scotsmen in the Eighteenth Century*, edited by Alexander Allardyce (Edinburgh, 1888), I, 5.

159

was the conviction that life in the provinces was not merely worthy of toleration by cosmopolites but unique in natural blessings that led Jefferson, in his *Notes on Virginia,* to read the Count de Buffon a lesson in natural history. It was a kindred conviction that, in spite of its "familiarity," life in Edinburgh had a congeniality and vigor all its own, that made Robertson refuse all invitations to settle in London. Hume, too, in the midst of his Parisian triumphs, longed for the "plain roughness" of the Poker Club and the sharpness of Dr. Jardine to correct and qualify the "lusciousness" of French society.[28] Hume's complex attitude toward his homeland is significant; it is typical of a psychology which rarely failed to combat prejudice with pride.

For Scotsmen, this pride was reinforced by the treatment they received in England, where their very considerable successes remained in inverse proportion to their popularity. One day, Ossian, Burns, and Highland tours might help to wipe out even memories of Bute. Meanwhile, in spite of their own "Breetish" Coffee House, life in London was not always easy for visitors from north of the Tweed. "Get home to your crowdie, and be d—d to you! Ha'ye got your parritch yet? When will you get a sheeps-head or a haggis, you ill-far'd lown? Did you ever see meat in Scotland, saving oatmeal hasty pudding? Keep out of his way, Thomas, or you'll get the itch!"[29] The young Scotsman thus recounting his London reception added that there was little real malice behind such common jibes. But Boswell's blood boiled with indignation when he heard shouts of "No Scots, No Scots! Out with them!" at Covent Garden. Yet only a few months later, he may be found addressing a memorandum to himself to "be *retenu* to avoid Scotch sarcasting jocularity," and describing a fellow countryman as "a hearty, honest fellow, knowing and active, but Scotch to the very backbone."[30]

The deepest result of this complicated involvement in British society was that the provincial's view of the world was discontinuous. Two forces, two magnets, affected his efforts to find adequate standards and styles:

[28] William Robertson to Baron Mure, November, 1761, Dugald Stewart, "Life of Robertson," 136; David Hume to Adam Ferguson, November 9, 1763, Greig, *Letters of David Hume,* I, 410-411.

[29] William Tod to William Smellie, November 29, 1759, in Robert Kerr, *Memoirs of the Life, Writings, and Correspondence of William Smellie* (Edinburgh, 1811), I, 46.

[30] Frederick A. Pottle, ed., *Boswell's London Journal, 1762-1763* (New York, 1950), 71; Frederick A. Pottle, ed., *Boswell in Holland, 1763-1764* (New York, 1952), 137, 260.

the values associated with the simplicity and purity (real or imagined) of nativism, and those to be found in cosmopolitan sophistication. Those who could take entire satisfaction in either could maintain a consistent position. But for provincials, exposed to both, an exclusive, singular conception of either kind was too narrow. It meant a rootlessness, an alienation either from the higher sources of culture or from the familiar local environment that had formed the personality. Few whose perceptions surpassed local boundaries rested content with a simple, consistent image of themselves or of the world. Provincial culture, in eighteenth-century Scotland as in colonial America, was formed in the mingling of these visions.

161

The effect of this situation on cultural growth in the two regions cannot, of course, be measured. Undoubtedly, provincialism sometimes served to inhibit creative effort. But we suggest that there existed important factors which more than balanced the deleterious effects. The complexity of the provincial's image of the world and of himself made demands upon him unlike those felt by the equivalent Englishman. It tended to shake the mind from the roots of habit and tradition. It led men to the interstices of common thought where were found new views and new approaches to the old. It cannot account for the existence of men of genius, but to take it into consideration may help us understand the conditions which fostered in such men the originality and creative imagination that we associate with the highest achievements of the enlightenment in Scotland and America.

THE ORIGINS OF AMERICAN MILITARY POLICY

By Louis Morton*

All too often, those who write about the American military tradition start with the Revolution, or with the beginning of the Federal government. They would have us believe that the founders of our nation created and formulated out of thin air a military policy at once complete and perfect.

162 To represent the origins of American military policy in this way is of course a distortion. The roots of our military policy, like the beginnings of our representative government and political democracy, are to be found in the early settlements at Jamestown, Plymouth, and elsewhere—in the arrangements the settlers made for their defense. The seeds of our policy go back even further in time—to the experience of the English people.

In this 350th anniversary year of the founding of Jamestown, it is perhaps not out of place to review some of the origins of our national defense establishment. Not only will we understand better why certain things are as they are today. We will also be struck by the fact that many of the problems and solutions of those earlier days are still with us in different form.

Before the new world settlers left their homes in the old world, they provided for their defense on the unknown continent of America. The businessmen who financed the colonizing ventures had invested too much money to risk the destruction of their property. The religious leaders were practical men, not visionaries, and their hope of attaining freedom from persecution was too strong to allow them to be negligent of their military strength. The British crown, which authorized the expeditions and granted lands, but which took no risks, empowered the colonists to take whatever measures were required (in the words of the Massachusetts Charter of 1628) "to incounter, expulse, repell and resist by force of armes, as well by sea as by lands" any effort to destroy or invade the settlement.

Weapons and military stores were therefore included in the cargo of the ships that came to Virginia and Massachusetts. Among the settlers were experienced soldiers, men specifically engaged to train the colonists in the use of arms, organize them into military formations, and direct them in battle if necessary. Such a man was Captain John Smith, an adventurer and veteran of the religious

*Dr. Louis Morton is in the Office of the Chief of Military History, Department of the Army.

[1] Although there is an extensive bibliography containing material bearing on colonial military institutions, there is no single work on the subject. The records of the colonial legislatures constitute the basic primary source, a portion of which has been reproduced in Arthur Vollmer, *Background of Selective Service*, Mon. No. 1, Vol. II; *Military Obligations: The American Tradition* (1947). The best general treatment is in Herbert L. Osgood, *American Colonies in the Seventeenth Century*, I, Chap. XIII, II, Chap. XV. Works dealing with conditions in specific colonies or areas include: P. A. Bruce, *Institutional History of Virginia in the Seventeenth Century*, Vol. II, Part 4; W. P. Clarke, *Official History of Militia and National Guard in Pennsylvania*, (Phila. 1909), 3 vols; David W. Cole, "Organization and Administration of the South Carolina Militia System" (M.A. Thesis, University of South Carolina); Wesley Frank Craven, *Southern Colonies in the Seventeenth Century* (Louisiana State U. Press, 1949); Allen

French, "Arms and Military Training of our Colonizing Ancestors," *Massachusetts Historical Society Proceeding*, LXVII; A. Hanna, "New England Military Institutions of the Seventeenth Century," (Ph.D. Dissertation, Yale); Dallas Irvine, "First British Regulars in North America," *Military Affairs*, IX, 1945; Douglas E. Leach, "The Military System of Plymouth Colony," *The New England Quarterly*, XXIV (September 1951); H. Telfer Mook, "Training Days in New England," *The New England Quarterly*, XI (December 1938); S. P. Mead, "The First American Soldiers," *Journal of American History*, I (1907); H. L. Peterson, "Military Equipment of Plymouth and Massachusetts Bay," *New England Quarterly*, XX; J. S. Radabaugh, "The Militia of Colonial Massachusetts," *Military Affairs*, Spring 1954; L. D. Scisco, "Evolution of Militia in Maryland," *Maryland Historical Society*, XXXV (1940); Morison Sharp, "Leadership and Democracy in Early New England Defense," *American Historical Review*, XL (January 1945).

wars on the Continent. Such a man was Captain Myles Standish, hired by the Pilgrims to accompany them to Plymouth.

Not even a John Smith or a Myles Standish could fight off an Indian attack by himself. The settlers had to do that together, and every able-bodied man became in times of military emergency a front-line soldier. There was never any question about this. The obligation of every male who could carry arms to perform military service in the defense of his community was an ancient English tradition dating back to Saxon times. Such documents as the Assize of Arms (1181), the Statute of Westminster (1285), and the Instructions for General Musters (1572) rooted the obligation of military service firmly in English law. As late as 1588, when the Grand Armada threatened invasion, "the rugged miners poured to war from Mendip's sunless caves . . . and the broad streams of pikes and flags rushed down each roaring street" of London to defend the nation against the approaching Spanish fleet.

According to this tradition, which became organized into the militia system, every able-bodied man was considered a potential soldier. He had to train and drill in military formation at stated intervals. By law, he was required to possess arms and equipment and to have them ready for immediate use.

The system was local in character and organized on a geographical basis. It was administered by county and town officials who had full authority to impose punishment and collect fines. Yet English law also restricted the use of the militia to inhibit the crown from using it as an instrument of despotism and from employing it outside the kingdom. The militia, thus, was a military system for emergencies of short duration in defensive situations.

Since this was the military tradition of the colonists, this was the basis of the military system they employed in the New World. It was admirably suited to their needs. But there was an important difference. In England there had been but a single militia organization; in America there were as many militias as there were colonies. No man would serve in any but his own. "Let the New Yorkers defend themselves," said a North Carolinian of a later day. "Why should I fight the Indians for them?"

Arrived in the New World, the colonists were as much concerned with preparations for defense as with food and shelter. Acting in accordance with instructions from home, the original settlers of Jamestown—100 men and 4 boys—split into three groups upon landing. One group provided fortifications for defense, another furnished a guard and planted a crop, the third explored the nearby area. Within a month after their arrival, they had built a primitive fort, a triangular stockade of "Planckes and strong Posts, foure foot deepe in the ground."

The Puritans, similarly instructed in England, were also militant in defense of their property. As one of their number remarked, "they knew right well" that their church "was surrounded with walls and bulworks, and the people of God, in re-edifying the same did prepare to resist their enemies with weapons of war, even while they continued building."

Probably the first military legislation in the English colonies was the code of laws proclaimed in Jamestown by Sir Thomas Dale in 1612. On military leave from his post in the Netherlands, Dale assumed the governorship of Virginia at a time when the colony was in danger of extinction, its inhabitants on the verge of starvation. The strict regime he imposed, based on existing military regulations and on "the laws governing the Armye in the Low Countreys," was even more severe than the English laws of the period. But it accomplished its purpose.

163

Order was restored, crops were planted, and peace was made with the Indians. "Our people," wrote John Rolfe, "yearly plant and reape quietly, and travell in the woods a-fowling and a-hunting as freely and securely from danger or treacherie as in England."

Martial law soon outlived its usefulness. As soon as the colony ceased to be a military outpost, the Virginians wrote into civil law the requirements for military service. The Massacre of 1622, which almost destroyed the colony, was still fresh in mind when the General Assembly in 1623 required all inhabitants "to go under arms." Three years later, Governor Yeardley specified that all males between 17 and 60 years of age were to serve when necessary and perform military duty when required. Changes were afterwards made in the law, but the obligation of universal service was never abandoned. Failure to comply subjected the offender to punishment and fine, as one John Bickley discovered when, for refusing to take up arms, he was sentenced to be "laid neck and heels" for 12 hours and pay a fine of 100 pounds of tobacco.

A local official known as the Commander controlled the militia in each district. He was charged with responsibility for seeing that his men were properly armed and supplied with powder and shot. Later, as the population grew and his duties increased, a lieutenant commander was appointed to assist him. The commander's duties were so varied and extensive as to make him the most important person in the community, its chief civilian as well as military official. Not only did he supervise the construction of defenses, drill his units, and have custody of the public gunpowder, but he also saw to it that everyone attended church services and observed the laws relating to the tobacco trade. Though the commissioning of officers remained in the hands of the governor, the commander appointed his own subordinates.

Once a man acquired a military title he retained it. So numerous were the officers produced by this system and so fond were the Virginians of their titles that a visitor in a later period, struck by the abundance of military rank, remarked that the colony seemed to be "a retreat of heroes."

The Pilgrims too lost no time in organizing their defenses. Captain Standish was designated military commander of the colony. Under him were formed four companies, each with its own commander and designated area of responsibility. A visitor at Plymouth in 1627 noted approvingly the defensive works and the careful preparations to meet an attack. "They assemble by beat of drum," he explained, "each with his musket or firelock in front of the captain's door; they have their cloakes on and place themselves in order, three abreast, and are led by a sergeant without beat of drum. Behind comes the governor in a long robe; beside him, on the right hand, comes the preacher with his cloak on, and on the left hand the captain with his side-arms and cloak, and with a small cane in his hand; and so they march in good order, and each sets his arms down near him. Thus they are constantly on their guard night and day."

By the middle of the seventeenth century Plymouth had established a military system based on universal service. Each colonist was required to own and maintain his own weapons, and the governor was authorized by law to prescribe military training. As new towns grew up along the frontier, they were brought into the defensive organization by the requirement to maintain their own companies under the central control of the government at Plymouth. The local companies elected their own officers, subject to approval of the government, and the officers appointed subordinates, selected training days, and drilled their units. Regulations were enforced by fines, collected by the clerk of the com-

164

pany or the local constable, and these fines often supported the military activities of the community. If the General Court (the legislature) required it, each town provided a quota of men for military expeditions.

The military system of the Puritans was much like that of Plymouth and Jamestown. According to a law of 1631, all males between 16 and 60, whether freemen or servants, were to provide themselves with weapons and to form into units for training. A council was established for the specific purpose of supervising military matters, for, declared the General Court, "the well ordering of the militia is a matter of great concernment to the safety and welfare of this commonwealth." Additional regulations were issued from time to time and in 1643, after the Pequot War, the entire militia system was overhauled. One of the results was the selection of 30 soldiers within each company "who shall be ready at halfe an hour's warning upon any service they shall be put upon." Here in essence are the Minutemen of the Revolution, more than a century later.

As in the other colonies, provision was made in the law to excuse from military service those with "natural or personal impediment" such as "defect of mind, failing of sences, or impotence of Limbes." Certain professions were also exempted—public officials, clergymen, school teachers, and doctors —as were those who practiced critical trades.

The companies established in Massachusetts numbered from 65 to 200 men, two-thirds of whom were musketeers and one-third pikemen. When the number exceeded 200, a new unit was formed; when it was less than 65, several towns combined to form a single unit. The officers elected by the men consisted of the captain, a lieutenant as his principal assistant, an ensign, sergeants, and corporals. The company clerk kept the roster of men liable for military service, checked attendance at drills, and collected the fines.

At an earlier date than any other colony, Massachusetts formed the militia into regiments. The Act of 1636 divided the military companies then in existence into three regiments and required regimental training at first once a year and then every three years. Commanded by a sergeant major, who was assisted by a muster master, the regiment came ultimately to comprise all the units in a county and its strength consequently varied. Plymouth adopted the regimental organization in 1658 when Josiah Winslow was given the rank of major and designated "chief officer over the military companies of this jurisdiction," "All Captains, inferior officers and soldiers," read his orders, "are hereby required to be in ready subjection to you during your continuance in the said office."

Training was the primary activity of the militia, and regular training periods were an integral part of the system. The first drills at Jamestown were held shortly after the colony was founded. Captain Smith, when he became President of the Council, held drills and target practice on a level stretch of ground within plain view of the Indians, who could see for themselves the effect of cannon shot on the trunk of a tree.

Training exercises in Virginia were initially held, by custom, on holy days. In 1639, when a muster master-general was appointed to enforce the militia regulations, even though the captain remained immediately responsible for training their men, no specific time was set by law for drills. In some districts they were held monthly, in others every three months. Failure to attend brought a fine, but absence was apparently so common that the the General Assembly finally set a stiff penalty of 100 pounds of tobacco, declaring that the offenders were bringing about the "ruin of all military discipline." By the end of the seventeenth century the militia regulations in Virginia required an annual drill for the

165

entire regiment and quarterly exercises for companies and troops.

Training in New England was put on a regular basis earlier than in Virginia. In Plymouth drills were held six times a year to assure, in the words of the General Court, "that all postures of pike and muskett, motions, ranks and files . . . skirmishes, sieges, batteries, watches, sentinells, bee always performed according to true military discipline." The first military law of the Puritans called for weekly training periods, held every Saturday. In 1637, when conditions had become more settled, the number of training days per year was fixed at eight, and this number remained in effect for the next forty years.

From the weekly training of the first settlers to the monthly sessions a few decades later can be measured the decreasing threat of Indian attack. Before the century was out, the number of drills per year had dropped to four, with provisions for two extra days if the unit commander thought them necessary. Regimental drills, when held, were deductible from the total. But during times of emergency, interest in military matters revived phenomenally; during King Philip's War drills were held as often as twice a week.

The military code of the day enforced a strict discipline. A militiaman in Virginia guilty of three offenses of drunkenness had to ride the "wooden horse," an ingeniously uncomfortable and ignominious seat; if drunk on post he was liable to the death sentence. Drunk or sober, if he lifted his hand against an officer, he lost the hand; if he raised a weapon, the penalty was death. Should he express discontent with his lot during a march, complain about the ration, or sell his gun, he was treated as a mutineer.

Imposed freely, fines provided one of the sources for defraying militia expenses. All the colonies had laws fining those who failed to supply themselves with arms or to maintain them properly. Failure to attend drill as

well as quarreling, and drunkenness during the drill were also punishable by fines.

The drill was usually held in a public place, such as the commons in Boston, and began early in the day. After roll call and prayer, the men practiced close order drill, the manual of arms, and other formations to the accompaniment of drums. Then followed a review and inspection by higher officers and public officials. After that, the units might form into smaller groups for target practice and extended order drill. Training closed with a sham battle and final prayers. By now it was early in the afternoon and the militiamen retired for food and other refreshment. The rest of the day was spent in visits, games, and social events.

The manuals provided for a remarkably complicated series of motions for forming troops, marching, fixing the pike, and firing the musket. These were standard in European armies, where the perfection of mechanical motions governed warfare, but they bore no relation to Indian fighting in the forests of North America. Nevertheless, the militiamen in the New World had to go solemnly through the prescribed movements on each training day. Fifty-six separate motions were required to load and fire the matchlock musket; only eleven for the pike, a fact which may account in part for its retention as a weapon and its popularity among troops. It was also a case, not altogether unusual in a more recent day, of the failure of training to keep pace with changing conditions.

The militia was not limited to foot soldiers; horsemen too were included. From the start, cavalry was the favored arm, and cavalrymen acquired special privileges that gave them higher status. Few men could afford to supply the horse and equipment required, a fact that limited membership to the well-to-do. Massachusetts, for example, restricted service in the cavalry to those with property valued at 100 pounds sterling.

Many advantages accrued to members of a horse unit. The trooper was exempted from training with the foot companies and from guard duty. He enjoyed special tax privileges; he could not be impressed into another service; he did not have to pay the customary fees for pasturage on common grounds.

The number as well as the quality of militia units varied widely in different periods and among the various colonies. Governor Berkeley of Virginia estimated in 1671 that he could put 8,000 horse in the field if needed, and the following year the militia of the colony consisted of 20 foot regiments and 20 horse, a proportion marking clearly the southerner's preference for cavalry.

Second only to Virginia was Massachusetts, which in 1680 had about the same number of foot companies but fewer companies of horse. Since the number of men in the companies varied so widely, exact comparisons are impossible. For Connecticut exact figures appear in the report made by the governor in 1650. "For the present," he wrote, "we have but one troope settled, which consist of about sixty horse, yet we are upon raysing three troopes more. . . . Our other forces are Trained Bands. . . . The whole amount to 2,507."

Though the militia was organized into units, it rarely fought that way. It was not intended to. The system was designed to arm and train men, not to produce military units for combat. Thus, it provided a trained and equipped citizen-soldiery in time of crisis. In this sense it was a local training center and a replacement pool, a county selective service system and a law enforcing agency, an induction camp and a primitive supply depot.

The forces required for active operations against the Indians came usually from the militia. The legislature assigned quotas to the local districts. Volunteers usually filled them. But if they did not, local authorities had the power to impress or draft men, together with their arms and equipment (including horses), into service. The law on this point was specific. The Virginia Assembly in 1629 gave the commanders power to levy parties of men and employ them against the Indians. In Plymouth during the Pequot War, when each town was required to furnish a quota, some of the men volunteered only on the understanding that if they did not, they would be conscripted.

Service was usually limited to expeditions within the colony, but there were numerous occasions when militiamen were employed outside. This right was specifically recognized in the law. Thus, in 1645, the Massachusetts General Court empowered the governor and council "to raise and transport such part of the militia as they shall find needful" outside the Commonwealth "without their free and voluntary consent" for a period of six months. When the term of service was over, the forces thus raised were dissolved and the men returned to their homes where they resumed their place in the militia.

There was no central command for the militia of all the colonies; each had its own organization and its own commander. Supreme authority within each colony rested usually with the legislative body and was based on the charter. In practice, however, the legislature left the administration of the militia system to other groups, sometimes the Upper House and at other times to various committees or commissions on military affairs or martial discipline.

The utmost care was exercised to maintain civilian supremacy. The General Court of Massachusetts repeatedly asserted its authority over military officials and representatives of the crown. The establishment of the Artillery Company of Boston in 1638 caused some suspicious officials to liken it to the Praetorian Guard in Roman times and to the Knights Templar; care was taken to make certain that the Artillery Company would not become "a standing authority of military men, which might easily in time overthrow the civil power."

The actual management of war was delegated to the governor and a small group of advisers usually, but the legislature in almost every case retained control of the funds and watched expenditures with a suspicious eye. When an expedition was formed, it was the legislature that gave approval, furnished the money—and later appointed a committee to look carefully into the conduct of operations.

The principal officer of the militia and the only single individual who could be considered to exercise supreme command was, in Massachusetts, the sergeant major-general; in Virginia, the governor. When New Hampshire, New York, and Massachusets came under royal authority late in the century, command of the militia there passed to the governor also.

The office of sergeant major-general—later shortened to major general—was an elective post and carried with it extensive powers and excellent opportunities for personal profit. In addition to general supervision of the militia, the sergeant major-general mobilized the militia, moved units to threatened areas, and procured arms and supplies. He commanded one of the regiments and had the unique privilege of training his own family. In wartime he commanded the colonial forces in the field, which, on occasion, he himself had raised and equipped.

To overcome the absence of a single unifying military authority in the New World, the colonies of New England formed a confederation in 1643. Representatives of Massachusetts, Connecticut, New Haven, and Plymouth came together in Boston and agreed that "inasmuch as the Natives have formerly committed sundry insolencies and outrages upon several Plantations of the English, and have of late combined themselves against us . . . we therefore doe con-

ceive it our bounden duty to enter into a present Confederation among ourselves, for mutuall help and strength." Two commissioners from each colony met as a body, which had authority to declare war, call on the member colonies for funds and troops, select commanders, and unify in other ways the military efforts of the colonies in time of emergency.

Though it lasted 42 years, the Confederation ran into trouble immediately and foundered finally on the rocks of jealousy and conflicting interest. From the outset, Massachusetts contested the right of the Confederation to declare war or draft Massachusetts troops. The dispute came to a head in 1653 when Massachusetts refused to obey a Confederation ruling. There was considerable feeling also about the choice of commander, for no colony was agreeable to placing its troops under an outsider. Like sovereign powers of a later day, each colony was jealous of its prerogatives and quick to object to seeming encroachment on its authority.

In no colony was there a group that resembled a military staff. The need did not exist. In peacetime the various officials of the militia system sufficed; in war the Assembly and the Council of War exercised control over military operations and procured the equipment and supplies needed by the troops. The commander was always adjured to take counsel of his assistants, and he was expected to abide by their advice. In this sense the various councils were policy-making bodies rather than staffs.

Supplying the military forces of the colonies was a comparatively simple matter. The first procurement agencies were the joint stock companies that had financed the original settlements, but by the middle of the century responsibility had devolved upon the colonists. The procurement of individual arms and equipment was, in general, the responsibility of each militiaman. Every colony required each householder to provide for himself and his family weapons and equipment, and specified the type and condition of both. The community itself provided for the poor who served out the cost of their arms in labor. In addition, most colonies required the local authorities to keep on hand a supply of weapons and powder for emergencies, to be paid for by the town or county. Normally there was no need for commissary or quartermaster in Indian warfare. Operations were of brief duration and the militiaman provided his own weapons, ammunition, clothing, and provisions, for which he was usually recompensed.

Extended operations, though uncommon, could hardly be supported in so informal a manner and there were in each colony various regulations and officials to provide the materials of war. In Massachusetts there was from earliest time an officer — variously known as surveyor of ordnance, overseer of the arms, or surveyor general — who had charge of weapons and ammunition. The officer was responsible for making certain that the towns had a supply of powder and ammunition; he also kept records and made purchases for the colony. Commissaries were appointed when required and were given authority to collect provisions. Two such officers designated for a force numbering 200 men sent against the Indians in 1645 were directed to procure bread, salted beef, fish, flour, butter, oil, cereals, sugar, rum, and beer. Only occasionally were such officials required to purchase arms.

When the colony needed funds for an expedition, it could fix quotas for the counties, borrow from private individuals, or impose special taxes. All methods were followed. The General Assembly in Virginia customarily set levies on the counties and imposed taxes payable in tobacco. In 1645 the expense of an expedition of 80 men to Roanoke was met by a levy of 38,000 pounds

of tobacco to pay for the hire of boats, the purchase of provisions, powder, and shot, and the payment of surgeons' salaries. The pay of the men alone amounted to 8,000 pounds of tobacco. Those suffering injuries received special compensation. The levy was made against three counties, each tithable person paying about 30 pounds of tobacco.

Even in that era war was a costly business and a fearful drain on the economy. In the greatest Indian war of the century — against King Philip — Massachusetts spent 100,000 pounds sterling, an enormous sum for that day. And though the legislature fixed prices and dealt harshly with profiteers, the war debt at the close of hostilities was larger than the aggregate value of all the personal property in the colony.

By the end of the seventeenth century, the militia system was firmly established in the American colonies. Though the training it afforded was less than adequate and the number of training days had steadily declined as the frontier moved westward, the system had become deeply imbedded in the traditions and laws of the colonists. Under this system they had defended their settlements, driven back the Indians, and preempted the most desirable lands along the Atlantic seaboard. A century of military experience had made little impression on the method of instruction, but it had demonstrated to the colonists that a military system based upon the obligation of every able-bodied citizen to bear arms provided a practical solution to their defense needs. Other problems would arise later that could not be solved by this method alone, but the militia system, in one form or another, remained an integral part of the nation's military policy for almost two more centuries. The obligation of universal service on which it was based, though often ignored, has never been abandoned. It constitutes yet today the basis of our military organization.

The Tempo of Mercantile Life In Colonial America

❡ *This study of the working habits of early American businessmen focuses on long-forgotten details that help clarify methods of the day and suggest that business in colonial times had not yet become an end in itself nor a dominant means for self-expression.*

by Arthur H. Cole

**PROFESSOR EMERITUS
AT HARVARD UNIVERSITY**

A dimension of entrepreneurial life for which we possess few data is that of the pace or pressure of activities. The modern businessman, especially the American specimen, is supposed to be subject to nervous strains and frequently the victim of certain occupational diseases; but we know little about the conditions encountered or endured by his predecessors, let alone those sustained or enjoyed by entrepreneurial figures of previous periods in countries other than our own. Was the merchant of our colonial ports more, or less, "driven" by his occupation than the American industrialist of the mid-nineteenth century, the banker of 1900, or the chain-store executive of the present day? Was our colonial merchant or his counterpart in London more, or less, active than contemporary traders in Amsterdam, merchants of sleepy Moscow, or the shopkeepers of never-changing Baghdad? If variant, how greatly different? Such questions could be answered only with much research and only with rough estimates. However, I do believe pace or tempo constitutes an important feature of business life, and I propose here to present data upon the time scales of merchants in the decades around 1750 in our port towns. Perhaps other scholars will find it possible and interesting to assemble and arrange corresponding information relative to other times and other climes.[1]

For the early American case, there is, of course, little direct evidence. Especially unfortunate is the circumstance that the merchants of that era and location seem rarely to have posted their experiences in diaries; at least few such diaries have survived for our use. Most of my data will be "circumstantial," indirect, tangential; but the aggregate appears to yield a fairly clear picture.

Perhaps I should first specify what I mean by "merchant" in this context. I do not need to repeat what is broadly understood: that he was located in the larger coastal towns; that he was concerned primarily in foreign commerce; that he often dealt in a considerable miscellany of goods, from laces to rum; and that his business was largely of a wholesale character. He did deal in small retail quantities, but already there were retail "country" stores established by the middle of the eighteenth century in the villages of the region, and there were specialized retail shops in the larger towns. I am here ignoring the smaller traders.

Organizationally the "merchant" was still a pretty simple phenomenon. Typically he operated alone, that is, in single proprietorship, although not infrequently he joined one or more other mer-

[1] The ensuing article may well be viewed as an extension of the excellent article entitled "Success and Failure Factors: American Merchants in Foreign Trade in the Eighteenth and Early Nineteenth Centuries," by Professor Stuart Bruchey, published in the *Business History Review*, Vol. XXXII (Autumn, 1958), pp. 272–292. It was cast in its present form before I read Professor Bruchey's argument. I should also note that this present article owes much to the affection for statistical measurement that my research assistant, Miss Ruth Crandall, has carried these many years. In connection with an inquiry on a related subject which she undertook a decade ago, she put together several of the series which I have only recently gotten around to examining, and which encouraged me to seek additional ones — and so to prepare this article.

chants in a short-run joint venture of ship ownership or mercantile transaction. And his staff hardly rivaled that of John Wanamaker or Richard Sears. He would probably have a clerk who "kept the books," copied letters into a letter book for permanent recording, and waited upon customers when the proprietor was out at the coffee house. Sometimes the merchant might have both a clerk and a bookkeeper-scrivener, and he might be blessed with young relatives on whom he would call, perhaps at little cost. Henry Lloyd of Boston had a couple of nephews whom he sent off on errands.

In general, the establishment operated by the colonial merchants seems to have been less like a country store, as Baxter characterized the Hancock emporium, than like a warehouse. Goods arrived in sizable, variegated quantities, and were sold off gradually over a period of months or years. The Browns of Providence Plantations did much of their foreign business in the form of "ventures"; the records of their enterprise still contain scores of bundles of documents arranged in this manner; and these records indicate that "ventures" — even after 1790 — were not wound up for appreciable periods after the return of the pertinent vessel: the goods brought back were not yet sold in sufficient volume to permit a reasonably close calculation of profit or loss. In the meantime the goods lay in the "warehouse," as I have called the central shop. (To be sure, ventures would be held open also by the slowness of obtaining returns from the goods shipped abroad.)

However, there was a dimension to the work of the export-import merchant which should not be overlooked. While he did have help from his London or other foreign correspondents, he had few, if any, local ancillary institutions on which to lean: banks, insurance companies, labor exchanges, etc.

* * *

The actual amount of work done in such establishments can be estimated but rarely. In some cases the appropriate books of account have not survived, while authors of company histories or businessmen's biographies have not thought the significance of the figures upon sales to be worth the labor of counting up the transactions as they appear individually in the day books or ledgers of the enterprise. Even in the uncommonly rich Hancock materials, there were a couple of defects in the series of account books, which prevented Baxter from presenting a continuous picture.

Baxter does give summations by years — even by months — of the quantities of "credit sales," that is, sales that were charged to customers. (Baxter seems to have counted all entries in the "journals" except payments of debts and those relating to goods put into the hands of "manufacturers.") At all events, data are offered of these credit sales for the years 1755–1757, 1759–1762, and 1764–1775. The last three years — 1773–1775 — manifest rather rapidly declining business, and the figures for these years should surely be ignored if one is seeking to cover normal activities only. For the remaining 16 years, the credit sales averaged 778 per annum or 15 per week. It is somewhat difficult to imagine Thomas Hancock and his clerk being very busy while they were carrying through two or three transactions each weekday, even if some of the sales were sizable.

In the Brown collection at Providence the day books are more satisfactory for the years after the French and Indian War than for those earlier; and actually the evidence for the years 1767–1772 was examined. By use of sampling technique, it was estimated that the average daily transactions were as follows:

1767	. . . 31	1770	. . . 40
1768	. . . 28	1771	. . . 33
1769	. . . 38	1772	. . . 31

The mean for the whole period is 32 and, even with allowance for the fact that three brothers were engaged in the mercantile operations, obviously the shop of the Browns was a busier place than that of Thomas Hancock appears to have been. However, the transactions at Providence were very largely retail, and even 40 such actions per day would not keep a single clerk in a heavy perspiration.

*   *   *

Another element in merchants' activities that is susceptible of quantification, at least of a rough sort of measurement, is their correspondence. This element has two or three aspects: how many letters did the men write? how many did they receive? how promptly did they attend to their incoming messages? how rapid was the course of communication between important centers? The amount of information on these several points varies in bulk, and is not altogether self-consistent. However, one can, I believe, grasp the general nature of the processes.

Outgoing correspondence can be appraised with modest accuracy from the letter books that have come down to us, volumes into which such outgoing messages were transcribed laboriously for centuries, until finally the letter press was devised in the early part of the nineteenth century. The letter books of our colonial merchants, to be sure, are not simon-pure mercantile materials. To some extent they contain letters which their owners wrote in other capacities or activities, e.g., as politicians or public figures in the affairs of the colonies. Also some of the letters contain a mixture of business and other matters. At all events, I have included all letters in my counts of the several series on the theory that if a man, primarily a merchant, had to write a certain number of letters as a member of the governor's council or in any similar capacity, that activity did result in his being more pressed in his mercantile role.

I have utilized seven series of manuscript or printed letters. They are as follows:

The letter books of Thomas Hancock of Boston, which cover ten months of 1736 and the whole years of 1737–1739 and 1746–1754.

The letter book of John Rowe of Boston, which gives one a record for the full years 1760 and 1761 only, although extending somewhat into neighboring years.

The printed letters of John Watts of New York, which cover the four years, 1762–1765.

The manuscript volume of Henry Lloyd of Boston from which we can secure data only for the two calendar years 1765 and 1766.

The letters preserved in the Brown collection at Providence.

The printed letters of James Beekman of New York, 1767–1771.

The printed materials of John Norton & Sons, who had their American station in "York Town," Virginia.

The data from these various sources are given in Table I.

I am not able adequately to account for the substantial divergences among these series. Differences in the length of the individual letters do not seem a satisfactory answer, although it is true that Henry Lloyd's letter book contains a higher proportion of brief messages than the letter books of the other merchants, even occasionally as brief as a couple of lines. Again, Thomas Hancock apparently meant to have only those letters bound for foreign parts copied into his correspondence volumes. James Beekman followed almost the same practice; and some of the other merchants may have ignored some domestic letters. But did not foreign letters comprise the greater bulk of their writing? In general, Lloyd seems furthest out of line. He is reported to have been a man of exceptional energy (although this characteristic may have been derived merely from the number of letters that he wrote or that he had put into his letter book — and then we haven't made much of an advance!); he may have been a fastidious man, and so caused a larger proportion of his letters to be preserved in his letter book; and surely he was tied in with a number of correspondents in other American ports as well as men in the West Indies and in England. He functioned more as a factor or agent of these other merchants than as a self-sufficient merchant himself.

TABLE I

Number of Letters Sent Out by Specific Colonial Merchants
(Annual Averages)

	Hancock	Rowe	Watts	Lloyd	Brown	Beekman	Norton
1707–09	25						
1746–49	93						
1751–54	68						
1760		211					
1761		197					
1762			130				
1763			109				
1764			104				
1765			104	577	209		
1766				658	284		
1767					368	31	7
1768					411	30	28
1769					376	29	23
1770						43	21
1771						37	18
Annual Average	62	204	112	618	330	34	19

Leastways, I am disposed to put the typical number of outgoing letters as perhaps 200–300 a year, or roughly four to six a week. Again, this quantity of work would not appear to have placed a heavy burden on an able-bodied merchant, even if letter-writing was a more laborious process than in recent days of stenographers, dictating machines, and the like. Even the highest figure, that of Henry Lloyd in 1766, would yield in average of only 13 outgoing letters a week.

An appraisal of the volume of incoming correspondence is subject to the hazard that some proportion of the original receipt was subsequently lost or destroyed. No filing system was evolved in the business world beyond the bundling up of each year's letters — and that practice was employed infrequently. Pasting of letters into scrapbooks had to await the middle decades of the nineteenth century, and the filing cabinet the last decades of the same period.

Accordingly, one may well be skeptical of the record of the Norton Company of Virginia already introduced. To be sure, their outgoing correspondence did not rise to great numbers of messages, an average of only 20 per year in the period 1768–1771; but the incoming stream was a mere trickle, less than four letters per annum over the same interval.

James Beekman of New York did much better — as many as 37 incoming letters per annum in the 1766–1771 period — while the Hancock enterprise received a still greater number of letters, or preserved more. Here I have secured a breakdown by origin:

TABLE II

NUMBER OF LETTERS RECEIVED BY THOMAS HANCOCK

(Per Annum by Decade)

	1730's	1740's	1750's	1760's
Domestic	3	6	39	49
Canadian	1	28	91	89
Foreign	11	35	44	86
Total	15	69	174	224

Again it is obvious that the quantum of correspondence was not heavy.

The volume of incoming letters ranged higher at the Browns' establishment, at least by the latter 1760's. In the years 1765–1769, the number per annum averaged 336. Conceivably this is a minimum figure; this many have been preserved.

Data on the promptness with which merchants attended to their correspondence are yet less abundant. Frequently, to be sure, merchants do commence their letters by reference to the message to which they were responding, but only rarely do they indicate likewise the date on which this incoming message had arrived; and, as will be established shortly, the period of ocean transit for letters was quite too varied to allow for good estimation. Again, our colonial merchants quite rationally spaced their letter-writing to some degree in relation to the prospects of the messages being started on the way to their destinations. They waited until a vessel was almost due to leave their port. Thus John Smith, in one of the diaries quoted below, makes an entry for March 12, 1748: "Busy in writing letters per Burk who sailed this day for London. I wrote but one letter of friendship." [2]

The Norton materials, however, do provide more precise information. The head of the establishment at Yorktown, or his clerk,

[2] *Hannah Logan's Courtship*, edited by Albert Cook Myers (Philadelphia, 1904), p. 182.

was meticulous enough to record on the backs of the individual letters — probably letters folded preparatory to being put into bundles — the date when the letter was written, that when it was received, and that when it was answered. At least he did so on a goodly proportion of the letters that survived and were published 20 years ago under the editorship of Frances Norton Mason; and the editor was meticulous enough to reproduce these "endorsements" in the printed volume. These data show, with respect to 24 letters, that ten were answered during the same month, ten during the succeeding month, two the second succeeding month, and two still more tardily. Their London correspondents were still less prompt — and of course delay on that end must have slowed up activities at the Virginia post. Pertinent information is provided with regard to 86 letters from Yorktown to England. Of these messages, 21 were answered the same month, 24 the succeeding month, 12 the second succeeding month, and as many as 29 three to six months after their arrival in London!

*　*　*

In strict logic, perhaps it should have made no great amount of difference whether the cycle of correspondence between an American port and any given foreign one was lengthy or rapid. To be sure, there was bound to be a little more uncertainty wrapped up in a correspondence period of six or eight months than in one of six or eight weeks, given the basic constitution of the world and the nature of human beings. There might well have been a psychological "side effect." With no cable facilities, regularized mail services, or even clipper ships, the zeal of merchants must have been much damped down by an appreciation of all that could well have happened in the distant market, between the time of the dispatch of the last letter from foreign correspondents and the time when, prompted by that letter, a ship from America could be fitted out, loaded, and sailed to the particular foreign mart. And, of course, the vessels with letters or goods *might* be at the bottom of the sea.

Secondly, there was the element of irregularity. Baxter reports the typical length of time required for the exchange of letters between London and Boston — a prime route in the colonial days — to have been four months. This seems to be correct; but that is at best a modal figure. There was a spread in the possibilities which such a merchant would surely have taken into account. It is obvious from Table III that, while such a merchant might be fortunate enough to obtain a letter in five weeks in the east-bound leg of the journey alone, he might also have to wait more than twelve. And the same was true of letters between Yorktown, Virginia, and London, except that the modal figure would seem to be nearer eight weeks than ten. Here the Boston-London data pertain to all the letters in the Hancock files which carry not merely the date of composition but also that of receipt in Boston; and the Virginia-London record is that of the Norton correspondence with the "endorsements" already mentioned. Even the institution of "packet" boats did not correct the difficulties. A half-dozen letters in the Hancock collection are labeled to have come in that manner, and the divergence is still considerable — from eight to thirteen weeks. And it seems probable that, with the longer period of transit necessary in the communication between Boston and Leghorn or Providence and Surinam, the variation would also become greater.

The transmission of letters by land was subject to many delays, especially prior to the time when, under Franklin, the posts were ridden at night. At best it was not swift.

TABLE III

Length of Time Required for the Transmission of Letters between Boston and London and between Yorktown, Virginia, and London

No. of weeks	No. of letters Boston to London	No. of letters Yorktown to London
5	1	1
6	1	5
7	2	12
8	6	28
9	4	11
10	7	10
11	2	8
12	4	8
Over 12	5	6
Total Number	32	89

Thus, the Browns at Providence received a letter from Williamsburg, Virginia, only after the elapse of 20 days. But, as I have said, mere slowness need not have caused a sluggish tempo of commercial life; theoretically compensatory measures could have been taken in consequence of which the actors on their parts might have been as pushed and strained as men of more recent decades.

As in the case of ocean-borne communication, the major disturbing element seems likely to have been the uncertainty or irregularity of transmission; but it appears that the vagaries of land transmission were not as great as those of movement by water. Anyway, the movement of letters — and goods — across the ocean was, generally speaking, much more important to the colonial merchant than that by land.

* * *

Uncertainty of another variety seems to have operated in the same direction as that of ocean communication, the uncertainty of commercial arrangements. There was the common uncertainty of trading ventures, which can be illustrated by a program that Henry Lloyd outlined in an inquiry to Hugh Hall Wentworth for a "good double deck't Vessell of 140 to 160 Tons" which he might charter for a voyage:

> [She would] proceed to Baltimore & there load Corn & Flour for Spain and Italy as Markets bear. She will probably [be] ⅔ or ¾ Laden in ye Hold with Wheat in Bulk (perhaps wholly) & with Flour in Casks to fill up. But Indian Corn, Beans or Bread may also be Ship't, . . . Cadiz to be the first port, there the place of her discharge will be settled, perhaps there or at Lisbon, Malage, Alicant, Carthagina, Barcelona, Seville, Genoa, Leghorn, or Naples.

Then there was the case of Lloyd trying to send goods from Boston to Aaron Lopez at Newport:

> Am sorry I could not ship [the goods] sooner, but no Vessell has offer'd except Capt. Taylor & his Vessell was clear'd out & I thought gone long before [the goods] were ready & I did not know to the contrary till the night he sail'd or I should have ship't them by him.

But perhaps the difficulties can best be illustrated by the series of letters which Lloyd dispatched in connection with a single piece of business. Action began when on October 24, 1765, one Charles Murray, a member of the firm of Scott, Pringle, Cheap & Company of Madeira, wrote Lloyd from Philadelphia asking the latter to purchase a shipload of fish and send it to Madeira. Lloyd wrote to Timothy Rogers in Gloucester that he was relying upon him as to the quality of the fish and for information as to when the vessel would be ready to sail "that I may not be behindhand with the necessary papers."

> Lloyd to Murray: I have purchased a cargo of fish in Gloucester and agreed for a fishing schooner, equipped to carry 1100 to 1200 quintals, freight at 2/9 per quintal, the best terms I could make and the only vessel cleared out with fish before November first and ready to take in or get to sea by the last of the month. It will probably sail in 10 or 12 days. I will forward your letters to Scott & Pringle in London by two vessels going this

BUSINESS HISTORY REVIEW

week and shall write them myself to advise that I will draw on them and to ask them to procure insurance on the cargo. The owner of the schooner expects your house to procure a return freight.

Nov. 11, Lloyd writes to Scott & Pringle in London: I have purchased a cargo of fish for your house in Madeira which I shall dispatch from Gloucester this month, weather permitting, in Schooner Sea Horse, 70 tons, Samuel Robinson, Master, with cost here with all charges on board not to exceed 12/3 sterling per quintal. I shall draw on you for the whole amount at 30 days sight, the freight to be 2/9 sterling per qtl. Request that you make insurance to the value of the cargo.

Nov. 23, Lloyd to Allen: Mr. Rogers tells me that the fish will be on board, if weather holds good, by next Monday. I shall go myself or send my nephew to give the necessary dispatches next Monday or Tuesday.

Nov. 25. Lloyd to Allen: My nephew Henry Smith will be with you this evening to dispatch Capt. with all possible speed.

Nov. 25. Lloyd to Murray: Have received yours of the 15th. I expect that the vessel will be filled up this day, after which nothing on my part will retard her sailing by or before the last of the month. Am sorry that I could not prevail upon owner to take the freight in wines, or that I was obliged to give so high a freight. Not having the chance for any other vessel put me in his power. There is no prospect of your market being overdone from this quarter. By next post or the post after you will receive a copy of the invoice. Exchange being at par here it will be to your interest to draw on London rather than to make use of the proceeds of the oil to pay for the fish.

Nov. 28. Lloyd to Scott, Pringle, Cheap & Co., Madeira: I enclose bill of lading for 1097 quintals of fish which I expect will sail from Gloucester in a day or two. Amounts to £902-8-0 lawful money. Shall draw on Scott & Pringle in London by Mr. Murray's order, agreeable to show order.

Copy of this letter sent by way of Philadelphia.

Dec. 2. Lloyd to Murray: Enclosed bill of lading. Sailing held up by necessity of sending to Portsmouth for a Mediterranean pass.

Dec. 9. Lloyd to Willing & Morris, Philadelphia. Tell Murray his vessel sailed last Friday morning soon after a severe North East storm.

Thus, at the end of six weeks and after the expenditure of no little trouble, with presumably the insurance arranged for in distant London and hopefully a return cargo to be secured, a shipload of fish had been dispatched to Madeira — to arrive perhaps a month later, if no accident befell.

These and other data of colonial mercantile life point to the looseness of existent business relationships; a vessel would sail to Cadiz in the hope that by the time of its arrival there, someone would have information by aid of which she could be sent forward to one of a half-dozen possible destinations; a merchant might be informed of a ship's imminent departure and he might not; and a businessman by dint of a sheaf of letters and a special visitation by his emissary might induce a ship's captain to load up his vessel and depart for the agreed destination. Here, as in the case of correspondence, there was much uncertainty; and while uncertainty might on theory be expected to produce, as it were, no more than a spate of nervous twitchings in efforts to stimulate action, it seems to have succeeded in delaying action itself.

The foregoing episode may well be considered an instance in what must have been a persistent problem, at least of merchants located north of Philadelphia, the problem of assembling an export cargo. I say "must have been," because unhappily we know precious little about the process. Apparently, the staves and the salt fish, the flour and the pit iron walked themselves to the ports. Miss Hanna, in her *Trade of the Delaware District before the Revolution,* speaks of "traders" being engaged in the operation; but that is all I have found in secondary sources, and Hedges mentions the enhancement of the difficulties in securing certain supplies as the colonial decades rolled by.[3] However, the nature of the mercantile organization remains obscure. Perhaps producers of the several commodities brought their goods to the main ports by the best means available to them, perhaps country stores took the commodities in and then sent them on by boat or cart, and possibly, indeed, there were "traders" along the coasts who, with small ships or other means, acted as intermediaries between producers and port merchants, perhaps even having their own warehouses for the storage of the goods. In any case, it would appear that the trade was poorly organized and might well have been in the hands of a number of small men. (Possibly the port merchants reached out themselves, by small coasting vessels or otherwise, to assemble materials from the hinterlands — indeed, this may have been a prime duty of "outside" clerks; but there is little evidence to this effect. It is not atypical that Baxter in his *House of Hancock* fails to mention the whole matter.) At all events, even if the available diaries make no specific mention of the subject, it seems reasonable to suppose that the process of getting together a shipload, especially of the mixed character common to northern mercantile transactions, could have been the source of considerable concern and no little effort on the part of the aforesaid port merchants.

181

*   *   *

[3] Mary Alice Hanna, *The Trade of the Delaware District before the Revolution* (Northampton, 1917), p. 243; James B. Hedges, *The Browns of Providence Plantations* (Cambridge, 1952), p. 23.

The delay in getting Captain Robinson started for the Madeiras is not atypical for this era of commercial life. Slowness was expected. In Lloyd's letter about chartering a vessel for the trip to Cadiz, he specified the detail that the captain should "have 30 days to Load & 25 to Discharge" cargo. This was in 1766.

A decade earlier, the French writer, Butel-Dumont, in his *Histoire et Commerce des Colonies Anglaises*, states, with respect to the tobacco ships that plied the area of Chesapeake Bay, that they were "ordinarily three to four months, often six months, in the country collecting a cargo," and that a merchant who thought to save money by utilizing an unusually large vessel found that "it had had sometimes to spend the winter in Maryland in order to make up a load."

From his study of the Brown papers, Professor James B. Hedges has estimated that a vessel coming into Providence would require three months to get ready to start out again on a long voyage, although this time might be shortened somewhat if the ship's captain had been able to send a message by another ship coming more directly or leaving the foreign port somewhat earlier, a message carrying news of the conditions in that foreign mart.

Turn-around time was increased no doubt by the necessity of overhauling vessels, scraping their bottoms, and so on, work that could best be done in the vessel's home port. The layover there may have been lengthened by the practice of discharging the ship's crew as soon as the vessel arrived in port. In the light of the long voyages of the period and perhaps of the discipline on shipboard, one can understand the practice, but, even so, it is difficult to understand, given the size of the vessels of the period, why loading or discharging cargo should have required each a month's time. As to the slowness of loading in the tobacco trade, Butel-Dumont himself stated that the task could be accomplished in a fortnight if the tobacco were assembled previously at one place on the coast; one might add that this stratagem was adopted in these very pre-Revolutionary decades by the merchants of Glasgow, who were enabled thereby to cut severely into the tobacco trade of London and other British ports.[4] On the whole, however, it seems evident that turn-around time was considerable in the colonial era and that this feature of mercantile life was not well organized, at least for speed of operations.

•   •   •

[4] Jacob M. Price, "The rise of Glasgow in the Chesapeake Tobacco Trade, 1707–1775," *William and Mary Quarterly*, 3d series, Vol. 11 (1954), pp. 179–200.

What, then, did the typical merchant do with his time? Was he busy? Or did he follow a pretty modest pace in the performance of his role? Unfortunately for all of us, as already suggested, few contemporary sources have come down to us, by aid of which we can attempt to reconstruct the daily lives of typical merchants. In particular, there are very few diaries of colonial merchants on which to lean.

Baxter expresses a belief that the Town House in Boston played an important role in Boston business of the later colonial period. Its ground floor provided a covered area where merchants could meet conveniently, talk, and transact business, and Baxter quotes from Sears' *John Hancock* the assertion that it was "the custom of Boston" for the merchants "to shut up their warehouses at one o'clock, and go on 'change, and return about four o'clock in the afternoon." One is tempted to comment that, though business in Boston in the 1750's and 1760's was brisk and although the processes of that business were awkward, three hours daily seems a lengthy period for the disposition of business alone.

183

Something of the real flavor of mercantile life, at least among the established merchants of the era, is to be gained, I think, from the diary of John Rowe, also of Boston. Here are the entries that he made in April, 1765, and I would comment that this passage contains more references to business matters than other portions of his record and would call attention to the fact that his zeal to put down his business activities did not lead him even to make entries for each successive day: [5]

> April 10. The Charitable Society met this day at Mrs. Cordis', and dined, as usual, had a Genteel dinner and twenty three dined there, made choice of officers for the Year ensuing. . . .
> Wind N. E. it has continued in this quarter 21 days, all but one half day.
> April 20. Agreed with Mr. Eben Lewis to build me a Schooner forty four foot Keel, seventeen foot Beam & seven foot and ½ in the Hold @ £19.10 p ton to have a long quarter deck. Went after dinner round by Jamaica Pond came back to Greatons & spent an hour with James Otis, Nath Bethune, Solo. Davis, Colo Richd Gridley, Saml Hughes & Thos. Gray.
> April 22. This morning Mr. Longley & Parket began to pull down my House in Pond Lane. Went to Fanewill Hall and met the Committee about the Town affairs. . . .
> Sold the Schooners Cargo this forenoon at Publick Vendue & I think very well.
> Apr. 30. Mr. Pickering sent me a dozen fine large Trout. Set out after

[5] *Letters and Diary of John Rowe, Boston Merchant . . .* edited by Anne Rowe Cunningham, 1903, pp. 80–81.

dinner from Boston for Plymouth in company with the Rev. Walter, Mr. Sam Calef, Major Vassall, Joshua Loring junr & Edwd. Winslow Jr. Stopt at Bracketts, Braintree. reached Cushing' & spent the eve'ing & slept there.

May 1. Set out early this morning, reached Pembroke went fishing had bad luck, began to Rain, which was much wanted.

Entries in a diary of Robert Pringle, merchant of Charleston, South Carolina, are no more enlightening.[6] At the time when he began to keep his record, Pringle was 44 years old, and apparently already well advanced on his mercantile career. The first note in the document gives the situation, and the first few entries are representative of the whole sequence:

May 3, 1746. This day gave up to Wm. Hare the key to the store on Elliotts wharf having given up the store there & moved some Loaf Sugar &c to the Inglis Store.

Bott of Isaac Holmes 70 lb. of Bacon at 2/ per lb for house use.

May 6th. Sold Charles Hill 6 Walnut Tree Chairs with Chintz Bottoms £45.

Gave Charles Hill our English Goose & Gander for a Breed.

Lent Charles Hill in Cash — £40.

May 9th. Bot: at Vendue 2 Groce Botles for £10 & recd only 7 doz & 3 Botles.

And so it goes on, typically not more than one entry per day, and frequently none; while often the single note refers to such personal purchases as the above. There *are* entries of a clearly business character, the arrival of a given vessel or the sale of an item or two, accepting bills of exchange, and the like, but these entries are a distinct minority in the whole record.

The third diary of which I have knowledge is even more disconcerting. It is the diary of a young man, one in his middle twenties, and the son of a well-to-do merchant. The son, one John Smith, was supposedly in business in Philadelphia and, according to the editor of the diary, doing famously. The young man does record purchasing and furnishing a house in town and of setting up a "plantation" in the country. The diary was published under the title, *Hannah Logan's Courtship*, and it does contain much of the love affair of John Smith. However, the difficulty from our point of view is finding any references to business matters. The following section is representative: [7]

[6] "Journal of Robert Pringle, 1746–1747," *South Carolina Historical and Genealogical Magazine*, Vol. 26 (1923), pp. 21–30, 93–112.

[7] *Hannah Logan's Courtship*, edited by Albert Cook Myers (Philadelphia, 1904), pp. 158–159.

S. E. Morison in his *Maritime History of Massachusetts* (Boston, 1921), pp. 30–32, gives a picture of leisurely life in Boston in the post-Revolutionary period.

1st (4th day) Was at our meeting. Sam¹ Pennock spoke. The Shoemaker Lad prayd. . . . I. P. junʳ, Wᵐ Logan, R. Pleasants, R. Langley, Jemmy Pemberton, & I rode, after dining at I. P.'s, to Germantown to see it, and after going through it we came in to Stenton & drank Tea. Found G. Tennent there. We conversed freely. We met my dear Hannah at the Gate, having rode over with Chelly Pemberton, who is there to Endeavor the recovery of his health. I spent the evening at Wᵐ Logan's.

2d (4th day) Waited upon R. Pleasants & R. Langley to see the State House, Library &c., and dined with them at I. Pemberton's, junʳ. Then waited upon them to Skuylkill on their way home. . . . In the afternoon, met at James's Coffeehouse with the Auditor's appointed by the Court upon the Affair between Carpenter & Shute. Gave them our reasons for awarding as we did — withdrew to Wᵐ Logan's, where I drank Tea, & spent part of the Eveng at J. Armitt's. Gave a poor widow £20 that has several small children.

4th (6th day) My partner & I spent some part of it [the day] in Examining our Books. Had the visits of several friends.

5th (7th day) W. Callendar, E. Catherall, W. Logan, Jemmy Pemberton, A. James, J. Foulk & myself rode to the Point, and had an agreeable Jaunt.

6th (1st day) Was morning & afternoon at our own meeting.

7th (2d day) Employed in Examining our Compʸ Books. Samuel Mickle's wife died to-day.

8th (3d day) Was at meeting. . . . Saw dear Hannah going home alone in the Chaise, and as I knew her fears of being talked of, I did not venture to wait upon her.

CONCLUSION

The evidence relative to the pace of commercial life in our colonial era is neither abundant nor conclusive, but it seems to point rather clearly in the direction of a situation markedly different from that of recent times.

1. The tempo was slow insofar as the number of transactions per man per time-period, letters written or received per week or month, and the like are concerned.

2. In some measure, this restricted pace was the consequence of prevailing uncertainties. An extreme possibility in the case of an international trader was the loss of vessels, conceivably all of his ships, as a result of the hazards of the ocean; and it would indeed be somewhat unreasonable to expect merchants to become or remain excited in planning the future activities of vessels that might very well be at the bottom of the sea. In a lesser degree it seems improbable that the merchant should become full of anticipations relative to shipments of wheat or lumber or fish when he had no recent information on the state of markets in the ports where he possessed correspondents.

3. The pace was also slowed in all probability by reason of the awkwardness of transacting business within the existing business system. There were scarcely any specializing institutions or individuals; arrangements in business were dependent upon negotiations with other parties who might very well be preoccupied with quite variant activities or problems. Likewise there appears to have been little that was standardized in the system — documents as well as procedures. And business information flowed by the somewhat hazardous channels of word of mouth — and even in a port no larger than Boston of the period, a vessel could sail without one of the leading merchants having advance knowledge. The processes of domestic trade whereby goods were assembled for export seem to have been still relatively primitive.

4. The pace was likewise slowed by the nonbusiness activities of the existing merchants. As John Rowe was involved in the Charitable Society and the "Town Affairs," so John Watts was on the Governor's Council, etc. They were also undoubtedly active in their respective churches. In brief, they were members of their several communities. Consequently, they could be well occupied throughout their days and yet sustain only a moderate pace within their shops or "warehouses." As yet, perhaps, business had not become so much an end in itself, and success in business did not become so adequately a basis for self-satisfaction, as was to become the case in the next centuries.

5. Yet, even if the eighteenth-century merchants in our coastal towns cannot be said to have been busy in the sense of being constantly active in the affairs of their enterprises or persistently driven from pillar to post by the exigencies of their engagements, one need not conclude that they were lazy, though this may seem paradoxical. It seems quite possible that no small portion of the colonial merchant's time might be taken up with the weighing of the alternatives that lay before him as he considered the launching of each new venture, as he tried to calculate the risks and appraise the chances of gain. In a sense, such traders were playing with high stakes at hazard. They had typically only a few ships in their command; these vessels could make but a voyage or two a year; there were the dangers of the sea to consider; and there were the characteristics of the ship's captain or supercargo and foreign correspondents to take into account; and there were the problems of what commodities to send and what to ask for in return, how best to provide the captain with funds either to allow him to seize a specially favorable commercial opportunity or even just to cover the costs of emergency repairs on

his vessel; there were, indeed, many things to think upon. Many years later, Walter Bagehot remarked in his *Lombard Street* of the merchants of London that they *ought* not to be "busy." Correspondingly, perhaps the minds of the American colonial merchants were quite well occupied, even if their fingers and legs were not!

POSTSCRIPT

At the start of this article, I suggested the desirability of obtaining measurements of the pace or tempo of business in "other times and other climes"; and in an effort to promote such measurements for the United States in periods later than the colonial era, I append the ensuing comments upon pertinent and probably available data. *187*

Certain information relating to speed of operations becomes relatively abundant in decades of the nineteenth century. With the establishment of newspapers in all the principal ports, and specializing commercial papers in the most important ones, it is easy to acquire data on the arrival and departure of specific vessels. Identification of the ships, their size, customary routes, etc. could be made largely from advertisements in the same journals — advertisements for cargo. To be sure, this particular feature of American enterprise grows less significant for the whole economy as the decades roll by, but there seems no reason to doubt the sensitivity of cargo vessels to the forces making for increased tempo in other sections of the country and in other lines of business. Such a measurement would help to indicate the rapidity of change toward an accelerated tempo.

A larger amount of data on the speed of mails within the country is to be found in the files of the United States Post Office; and actually one variety of summary is already compiled in a series of maps presented by the American Geographical Society in its *Atlas of the Historical Geography of the United States* of 1932. Data upon overseas mails are also procurable with relative ease, e.g., through the use of date lines in the dispatches printed in domestic newspapers relative to the news from abroad.

The flow of correspondence into and out of individual enterprises appears to be a somewhat dubious measure over the decades of the pressure or pace of business. The problem of homogeneity raises its bothersome head, especially when burgeoning hierarchies may properly be assumed, and yet one has no basis for determining whether, or in what degree, assistants wrote routine letters. With the introduction of manufacturing industry, this phase of correspondence would seem to have increased in volume as the business system grew in complexity with letters to insurance companies, to selling agents, to railroad officials, etc. If it were not for the increase at an indeterminable rate of the volume of letters "prepared for the signature" of the top executive officers of enterprises, it might be possible to construct a series reflecting more or less well the enhancing speed of business operations by counts (on a sound sampling basis) of the "front" or "head" office correspondence of successive typical business leaders, e.g., the treasurer of a New England cotton mill, the president of a railroad, or the head of an investment banking enterprise. When correspondence is preserved with company records, it is that of the top office that has most likely been retained. And for a while technological change worked in favor of those coming on later and wishing to count the number of letters, at least outgoing ones. From the 1840's onward, the letter press came into vogue; letters were written with a special type of ink, and were overlaid each with a tissue sheet of paper (which formed pages in a sort of scrapbook), moistened and pressed in a hand-screw press. In this manner a copy of the original was made upon the tissue paper; and the present-day inspector of the concern's books finds a sequence of outgoing letters neatly arranged (if sometimes indecipherably preserved!) in chronological order in a set of folio volumes. This practice persisted for a period after typewriters came into use.

To be sure, this sort of series might be viewed as running upon adverse technological changes when one has proceeded into the latter decade of the last century. First there was the invention of the typewriter, followed soon by the evolution of the stenographer; and it is a question whether a businessman by himself and a businessman with a secretary are homogeneous letter-writing units! There is doubtless a modicum of truth in the sort of contention that President Eliot of Harvard is alleged to have employed when some of his faculty members asked for typewriters and secretaries, namely, "All you'll do is write more letters!" Secondly, there was the introduction in the 1880's of the telephone. Thereafter the quantity of correspondence into or out from the enterprise would have much less significance as a measure of aggregate activity.

Thirdly, the formation of an index of change in the form of the number of major officers in corporations becomes possible, to a degree, after company reports began to be enlarged, and after specialized business directories began to be published. However, the coverage varies considerably among industries, manufacturing enterprises being poorly represented until the present century, while neither type of printed document carried the listing of officers down very far or very consistently as between industries. One would not be at all sure what his data were really measuring. In addition, there is the logical question whether the number of subordinate officers varied directly or inversely with the rate of pressure upon the top officers of enterprises. Professor Cochran has contended that industrial executives in the latter nineteenth century didn't allow themselves enough officers of junior rank; they tried to keep too many decisions in their own hands.

The increase in the number of junior officers may be related to the pressure upon top executives in yet another way, or subject to interpretation in the light of another business element, that of internal organization. In recent years a good deal has been written in the literature of business upon the "span of control." Such a concept would have gained slight attention in the nineteenth century; executives were still inclined to think in terms of the small enterprise and with the proprietor accessible to all persons connected with the concern. Wherefore it would appear feasible, at least over several decades, to think of the pressures upon a given top executive in terms of the number of persons who reported to him directly.

Unhappily, data on internal company organization and practice are scanty until relatively recent decades. Few organization plans, if any, have survived that date back to the nineteenth century, and, of course, we know now that the informal organization may have functioned considerably at variance to the formal one. The administrative setup of certain railroads and banks at certain times might be deduced from contemporary materials. On the whole, however, information in this area appears likely never to be adequate enough to give much help in measuring the increase in the pace of American business life.

My friend, Professor Andrew B. Jack, has suggested to me another variety of company-internal evidence — the increase in the number of control accounts in company accounting procedures ("fictional" accounts such as "materials," "labor," and the like) — which might be looked upon as ultimately leading to the establishment of the office of controller and the elaboration of statistical measurements. Tied in also with cost accounting, these control accounts — their establishment and their proliferation — seem to Professor Jack to imply greater anxiety on the part of officers over the actions of their enterprises, a desire to plug up leaks of unnecessary expenditures, the wish to have more frequent and more nearly current reports of operating results, etc.

In favor of the use of this index is the availability of enough sets of company records to establish approximate timing of change even as among several industries. However, one could argue adversely that the phenomena are merely "outward and visible signs" of what earlier was "internalized" by businessmen: the latter carried the same anxieties and suffered the same strains but the lack of knowledge of certain accounting and statistical techniques prevented them from manifesting their worries and perplexities in these particular ways. There is something to be said for this latter argument; and yet I am disposed to find merit in this variety of measurement. Perhaps anxiety was "the mother of invention" here. Surely the notion of control accounts was as old as double-entry bookkeeping, and the timing of their introduction or expanded use in specific situations was in part a function of anxiety seeking relief out of a literature that had been more or less available previously.

Still another sort of measurement — one in the nature of estimating results of strain — may lie in the differentials in the life spans of businessmen relative to adult males as a whole in the relevant populations. Unhappily I doubt if adequate data are available for more than the past fifty or seventy-five years.

The only further measuring rod that has risen in my imagination is one that at first blush may seem too trivial for serious note. I do suggest it as worthy of consideration. It is the number of meals, and especially dinners, that the executive was required by the exigencies of his activities to take away from his home. To be sure, sundry factors other than the pressures of business played important parts, e.g., the growth of urban centers, changes in local transportation facilities, the increased formalization of social life, etc. However, I believe it possible to substantiate the following course of development.

In our predominantly mercantile era, a young man aspiring to a mercantile career was under the necessity after a period of apprenticeship of absenting himself from home for months, if not years on end, but thereafter he expected to return to his native town, settle down with a family, and have all his meals in the bosom of his family, except as he (or they) might go for a social meal at the homes of relatives or friends. As the married man of our earlier decades took satisfaction in "never having passed a night apart from his wife," so typically the businessman expected to dine and sup at his own board.

On the other hand, I would surmise that the cotton-mill treasurer of the 1830's, with mills at some distance from Boston and with selling agents in New York and perhaps Philadelphia, would anticipate being away from home — for some meals and probably overnight — several times a year.

Even more frequent excursions around the country and more frequent business dinners away from his family seem likely to have been the fate of the industrialist, investment banker, or railroad executive — at least, those of the top echelons of their respective enterprises — in the latter nineteenth century. Now there were meetings of trade associations, inspection of the sources of raw materials, attendance upon sessions of congressional tariff committees, dinners of the local chambers of commerce, etc. And the twentieth century added such meetings as the Council on Foreign Relations, the Boston Conference on Distribution, of the trustees at some school of business, of local charities, and so forth. 191

Possibly the diaries of businessmen in the nineteenth century are sufficiently numerous to give an investigator some notion of the multiplicity of such combined business-social engagements among representative groups of businessmen at selected intervals within the hundred years, e.g., the period of the 1850's and that of the 1890's. I suspect that the typical business executive of the twentieth century, however, kept — and does keep — no diary; and I fear that this is also true of the typical secretary of a typical businessman. Even executives' "calendars" are thrown away after the engagements have been kept (or forgotten!). It appears to me likely that the investigator would have to jump from the 1890's to the present day. But perhaps the lack of stopping place at some intermediate date is not too important. I have the impression that conditions have not altered much in the past few decades; perhaps the saturation point was reached by the 1920's or 1930's — or should we view this as an equilibrium point between business obligations and marital peace?

The index that I here propose may sound a trifle quixotic on initial consideration, as I have intimated; but I have a few scraps of data to lend support. A story came to me rather directly about a wealthy man of New York City who, after a luncheon with an old college friend, remarked that it had been the first such meal in months where he had not been asked for money. Again, Mr. Oswald Knauth, erstwhile president of Federated Department Stores, once related to me some of his personal experiences. And the Standard Oil Company of New Jersey maintains a bureau in its secretary's office to which invitations of professional and charitable institutions are referred, and where decisions are made as to what invitations should be accepted and what officers should, if possible, be induced to represent the company.

I should be glad to hear of alternative and better means of measuring the enhanced tempo or pressures of business life over the decades.

Colonial and Revolutionary Origins of the American Law of Treason

Bradley Chapin *

THE constitutional definition of treason against the United States, a substantial example of eighteenth-century liberal statesmanship,[1] is cast in the words of a fourteenth-century English statute. By what process did the medieval become modern, the monarchical, republican?

193

The roots of our substantive law are in a statute enacted in the twenty-fifth year of the reign of Edward III.[2] Of the seven heads of action made treasonable by that ancient law, the more significant were compassing or imagining the death of the king, adhering to the king's enemies, giving them aid and comfort, and levying war against the king. Through two subsequent centuries Parliament protected the sovereign by modifying the statute until the urgent pressures of the Reformation and the later crises of the seventeenth century demanded a more flexible weapon. Then, facile judges construed the acts of speaking or writing words tending to subvert government and of conspiracy to levy war as acts compassing the king's death; further, resistance to the execution of a general law came by construction to be a levying of war.[3] The Glorious Revolution, with its constitutional theories of legal resistance, brought no change to this sovereign-protecting law.[4] In substance what had been treason to Judge

---

* Mr. Chapin is Assistant Vice-Chancellor and a member of the Department of History at the University of Buffalo. This paper in an abbreviated form was read at the 1956 meeting of the American Historical Association.

[1] James Madison, "Federalist 43," *The Federalist and Other Constitutional Papers* . . . , ed. E. H. Scott (Chicago, 1894), I, 240; Baron de Montesquieu, *The Spirit of Laws* (Worcester, 1802), I, 223.

[2] 25 Edward III, st. 5, c. 2.

[3] Queen *v.* Bradshaw et al.; King *v.* John Twyn; Algernon Sidney's Case (for full citations of cases referred to in this paper, see TABLE OF CASES below, pages 17-21.); William S. Holdsworth, *A History of English Law* (London, 1931), VIII, 309-321.

[4] See particularly the significance of Dammaree's Case in Bradley Chapin, "The American Revolution as Lese Majesty," *The Pennsylvania Magazine of History and Biography*, LXXIX (1955), 312.

George Jeffreys of the Bloody Assizes remained treason to the Chief Justice, Baron Mansfield, a century later.[5] However, the revolution settlement did bring reform to the procedural law. A pioneering statute, the Trial of Treasons Act, gave the accused traitor the right to a copy of the indictment, a list of witnesses, the names of the panel of jurors, the right to counsel, the right to compel witnesses in his behalf to attend, and the guarantee that his guilt could be established only by two witnesses to an overt act.[6] From these substantive and procedural roots an American law of treason grew.

The remoteness of the colonial subject from the person of the sovereign eliminated several substantive heads of the old law, most important, the concept of compassing the death of the king.[7] The colonial wars made possible the crime of adhering to the enemy, but the common law prescribed no clear rule as to whether or not trading with the enemy amounted to treason. In making such trade illicit, the colonial assemblies defined the crime by statute, its nature varying with the jurisdiction, being sometimes regarded as a misdemeanor, sometimes as treason.[8]

The great colonial treason, levying war against the king's government, took many forms: actual armed insurrection; war by construction (that is, aggravated resistance to the execution of law); and novel treasons which translated some act of political opposition into the high crime. The best examples of outright insurrection are Nathaniel Bacon's armed challenge of Governor Sir William Berkeley[9] and the North Carolina Regulators' resistance to Governor William Tryon at the Alamance.[10] Jacob

---

[5] Case of Lord George Gordon; King *v.* Thomas Hardy.

[6] 7 & 8 William III, c. 3.

[7] See a possible exception in King *v.* John Gunter and nine others (Va.); the indictment alleges what amounts to a conspiracy to levy war, which was, by construction, a compassing of the king's death.

[8] Richard Pares, *War and Trade in the West Indies, 1739-1763* (Oxford, 1936), pp. 420-422; *The Colonial Laws of New York,* ed. Robert C. Cumming (Albany, 1894), III, 1050, 1077, 1121; Julius Goebel and T. Raymond Naughton, *Law Enforcement in Colonial New York, a Study in Criminal Procedure (1664-1776)* (New York, 1944), pp. 85*n*, 241-245.

[9] By court-martial, King *v.* Thomas Young and eleven others (Va.); by civil trial, King *v.* Giles Bland and eight others (Va.); though there has been great difference of opinion over Berkeley's policy ever since the event, particularly in relation to method, the English commissioners were in perfect accord that there had been a *treasonable* levying of war, *Calendar of State Papers, Colonial Series, America and West Indies, 1677-1680,* ed. W. Noel Sainsbury and J. W. Fortescue (London, 1899-1939), pp. 37, 42.

[10] King *v.* Benjamin Merrill et al. (N. C.); though in the *Virginia Gazette*

Leisler's armed defense of Fort James in the face of royal troops and his refusal to surrender to Governor Henry Sloughter of New York amounted to levying war.[11] The attempt of the "Long Finn" to detach the Delaware settlement from the Du'te of York's jurisdiction in 1669 probably belongs in the category of bona fide insurrection.[12] The best example of a constructive levying of war is the Virginia plant-cutters' rebellion in 1681. Governor and Council debated the question whether this misguided effort to control tobacco prices amounted to riot or treason. Governor Thomas Culpeper, arguing that the forcible and general effort to destroy the plants came within the rule of Queen *v.* Bradshaw, forced a treason prosecution.[13] A later example, the New York antirent riots of the 1760's, ended in brief, futile resistance to the Twenty-Eighth Regiment. Though William Prendergast directly levied war, in this case the attorney general preferred to base the prosecution on the law of constructed war because the evidence relative to the antirent riots was much fuller.[14] The novel colonial treasons were used for various purposes. Sometimes such a charge facilitated the destruction of a defeated faction. New York brought Nicholas Bayard near the shadow of the gallows in an action based on a provincial statute that made any act of opposition to government an act of levying war. The act alleged was the circulation of petitions critical of government.[15] In some cases, charges of treason were made to dramatize local grievances. A seventeenth-century grand jury indicted two men for high treason, alleging in one instance denial of trial by jury,[16] in the other, collecting customs without proper authority.[17]

Colonial differences in procedural law with regard to treason were fewer than those in substantive law. The record reveals a fair duplication of English practice as established in the reported cases and the Treason Act of 1696.[18] In America as in England, only the high courts—either the

---

(Purdie and Dixon), Nov. 7, 1771, the accusation is made that the indictments came under a provincial statute modifying the local riot act.

[11] King *v.* Jacob Leisler (N. Y.); King *v.* Jacob Milborne (N. Y.); but some of his adherents were tried for riot, implying constructed war.

[12] King *v.* John Binckson (Long Finn) (N. Y.).

[13] King *v.* Sommersett Davies et al. (Va.).

[14] King *v.* William Prendergast (N. Y.); King *v.* Elisha Cole (N. Y.).

[15] King *v.* Nicholas Bayard (N. Y.).

[16] King *v.* Francis Rumbouts (N. Y.).

[17] King *v.* William Dyer (N. Y.).

[18] Robert L. Stevens to B. Chapin, Jan. 17, 1949; the English barrister was impressed by the fact that the procedures in King *v.* Jacob Leisler (N. Y.) were "just the same as those employed in Old Bailey . . . ."

superior court or the circuit judge armed with the commissions of general gaol delivery and of oyer and terminer—heard and determined cases of treason.[19] Special commissions of oyer and terminer, under which the executive could choose his justices and act quickly, were much used.[20] Of arrest and commitment little is known. Indictments show a reasonably accurate imitation of English forms.[21] The plea on indictment was regular, and in one celebrated case the accused felt the *peine fort et dure* before being condemned irregularly as a mute.[22] An accused traitor normally had the advantages guaranteed by the Trial of Treasons Act even though the statute was not in force in the colonies. He had a list of the panel of jurors, a copy of the indictment, and the right to counsel.[23] Judges accepted the statutory rules of evidence requiring more than one witness to an overt act.[24] Judgment of guilt usually brought a motion to arrest, and, once given, carried the same inevitable consequences as judgment at King's Bench, attainder working a corruption of the blood and forfeiture of property.[25] In sentencing, the judge read the barbarous old formula which called for hanging, disembowlment, and quartering.[26] Normally,

---

[19] King *v.* Sommersett Davies et al. (Va.); King *v.* Francis Rumbouts (N. Y.); King *v.* Elisha Cole (N. Y.); King *v.* William Dyer (N. Y.), transfer of the case from the Mayor's Court on the grounds of inadequate jurisdiction. *The Statutes at Large of Pennsylvania* . . . , ed. James T. Mitchell et al. (Harrisburg, 1896-1915), II, 134, 149.

[20] King *v.* Benjamin Merrill et al. (N. C.); King *v.* William Prendergast (N. Y.); King *v.* Jacob Leisler (N. Y.); King *v.* Nicholas Bayard (N. Y.); King *v.* Giles Bland and eight others (Va.).

[21] King *v.* Nicholas Bayard (N. Y.); the outline in King *v.* William Prendergast (N. Y.); King *v.* John Gunter and nine others (Va.).

[22] King *v.* Jacob Leisler (N. Y.). At English law a special jury was impanelled to determine whether the accused stood mute from malice or act of God.

[23] At least three colonies re-enacted its provisions; Mitchell, *Pennsylvania Statutes at Large*, III, 200; *The Statutes at Large of South Carolina*, ed. Thomas Cooper and David J. McCord (Columbia, 1836-41), II, 539, 717, 747; *The State Records of North Carolina*, ed. Walter Clark (Winston and Goldsboro, 1895-1905), XXIII, 319-325; In re Beverly (Va.); King *v.* Nicholas Bayard (N. Y.).

[24] *Ibid.*; King *v.* William Prendergast (N. Y.); King *v.* Elisha Cole (N. Y.); *The Perpetual Laws of the Commonwealth of Massachusetts, from the Establishment of Its Constitution to the First Session of the General Court in A.D. 1788* (Worcester, 1788).

[25] King *v.* Nicholas Bayard (N. Y.); King *v.* Sommersett Davies et al. (Va.); Tryon recommended that Benjamin Merrill's heirs have his estate, King *v.* Benjamin Merrill (N. C.); King *v.* Jacob Leisler (N. Y.); King *v.* Richard Lawrence (Va.); King *v.* Jacob Milborne (N. Y.).

[26] *Ibid.*; King *v.* Benjamin Merrill et al. (N. C.); King *v.* William Prendergast (N. Y.); King *v.* Jacob Leisler (N. Y.).

however, the governor stayed execution, and often an appeal to English authorities brought reversal of the judgment.[27]

The colonial record of both substantive and procedural law with regard to treason in several jurisdictions indicates that the colonial magistrates used established English law on an *ad hoc* basis, selecting the substantive and procedural rules necessary to meet local emergencies. No native body of American precedent emerged; instead, the intermittent experience of a century resulted in a bench and bar increasingly familiar with English case and statute. No frontier thesis depicting a crude jurisprudence based largely on Coke's *Institutes* will explain the first formative era in relation to this head of law.[28] In using the English law of treason, the colonists made small innovations, largely in relation to the substantive law. Such experimentation came either when the old law prescribed no clear rule or when temporary, local circumstances seemed to demand some extension of the law. The eighteenth-century criminal law cried for reform, but he who seeks a process of rational clarification in the colonial jurisdictions returns disappointed. In 1775, the American law of treason was the law of England transferred to a new home. What was old far outweighed what was new.

[27] Tryon reprieved six condemned regulators during the king's pleasure; in the cases of Leisler and Milborne, a petition to Privy Council was referred to the Lords of Trade where permission was granted to apply to Parliament for reversal of attainder; Privy Council removed the sentence of Nicholas Bayard.

[28] For example, James Emmot in King *v.* Nicholas Bayard (N. Y.) argued that the evidence did not meet the requirements of the statute of 1696 and that 1 Henry IV, c. 10 limited treason to the categories established by 25 Edward III, c. 2, and further that king's counsel may not challenge jurors without cause. Benjamin Kissam, summing up for the Crown in King *v.* William Prendergast (N. Y.), cited Michael Foster, *A Report of Some Proceedings on the Commission for the Trial of the Rebels in the Year 1746 . . . and of Other Crown Cases: To Which Are Added Discourses upon a Few Branches of the Crown Law* (Dublin, 1791), hereafter cited as *Crown Law*; William Hawkins, *A Treatise of the Pleas of the Crown . . .*, 2 vols. (London, 1716-21); Mathew Hale, *Historia Placitorum Coronae: The History of the Pleas of the Crown*, 2 vols. (London, 1736), hereafter cited as *Pleas of the Crown*; and John Kelyng, *A Report of Divers Cases in Pleas of the Crown . . . in the Reign of the Late King Charles II . . .* (London, 1708). See also the opinion of the attorney general relative to the degree of criminality of the regulators, *Colonial Records of North Carolina*, ed. William L. Saunders (Raleigh, 1886-90), VIII, 251-253. The Revolutionary cases also give evidence of extensive familiarity with English precedent. See Pennsylvania *v.* Abraham Carlisle where James Wilson cited Foster, *Crown Law*; Hale, *Pleas of the Crown*; Vaughan's Case. The attorney general drew heavily on Foster, *Crown Law*; William Blackstone, *Commentaries on the Laws of England*, 4 vols. (Oxford, 1765-69), was cited, as were statutes from Edward I to Anne.

The shaping of an American treason law harmonious with republican
government began with the Revolution. The problems were to construct
a law that could protect the state from disloyal acts involving a betrayal
of allegiance, to limit that law so precisely that it could not be used to
destroy normal political opposition, and to protect the rights of the individual accused in times of high political excitement. In its origins, the
law was a product of the nation, developing from the experience of the
Continental army between June 1775 and June 1776.

Military and civilian disloyalty faced Washington from the beginning
of the crisis. The original articles of war, establishing the crimes of mutiny
and sedition—the military equivalents of treason—provided an inadequate
punishment for the first convicted American traitor, Benjamin Church,
who in October 1775 was found guilty by a court-martial of criminal correspondence with the enemy.[29] Congress, prodded by Washington,
amended the articles of war to provide the death penalty.[30] The Commander in Chief first used the reinforced articles to break the Tory plot
at New York in June of 1776. Authorizing the execution of Thomas
Hickey, who had enlisted in the plot, he took a step as permanent as the
grave. By making death the penalty for action in behalf of the king,
Washington stood irrevocably committed as the representative of a
sovereign state. The involvement of civilians in the plot had brought increased army pressure on Congress for a general definition of the crime
of treason.[31] On June 24, 1776, Congress passed resolves claiming a new
allegiance and defining treason as levying war and adhering to the enemy,
giving him aid and comfort.[32] This first public act to declare George III

[29] *Journals of the Continental Congress*, ed. Worthington C. Ford (Washington,
1904-37), II, 113, 116, 119, 265-267, hereafter cited as *Journals*; *The Writings of
George Washington*, ed. John C. Fitzpatrick (Washington, 1931-44), III, 327, 505-
513; Allen French, *General Gage's Informers* (Ann Arbor, 1932), pp. 155-157, 187;
American Archives, ed. Peter Force, 4th Ser. (Washington, 1837-46), III, 1479-1486;
Massachusetts Historical Society, *Collections*, LXXII (Boston, 1917), 137-138, 152-153,
180.

[30] Oct. 2, 22, 1775, Washington Papers, XVIII, Library of Congress; Ford, *Journals*, III, 331, V, 789-790; Force, *American Archives*, 4th Ser., III, 1158.

[31] *Journals of the Provincial Congress, Provincial Committee of Safety, and Council of Safety of the State of New York, 1775-1777* (Albany, 1842), I, 495, 497, hereafter cited as *Journals of the New York Provincial Council*; Fitzpatrick, *Writings
of Washington*, V, 182; Curtis P. Nettels, "A Link in the Chain of Events Leading
to American Independence," *William and Mary Quarterly*, 3d Ser., III (1946), 36-47.

[32] Ford, *Journals*, V, 475-476.

the enemy explicitly defied the old sovereignty and was a *de facto* declaration of independence.

The states, relieved of the original responsibility of assuming sovereign powers, declared levying war and adherence to the enemy to be acts of treason.[33] The question necessarily arose, what did the ancient words mean in the new jurisdictions? Some legislatures began the process of definition by reciting specific acts constituting levying of war or adherence to the enemy; for example, taking the king's commission, joining his army, furnishing the enemy with arms, and committing conspiracy to levy war.[34] With the exception of a New Hampshire law making the maintenance of certain opinions treason,[35] the statutes authorized punishment only of direct, positive aid to the king. Several states, by constitution and statute, opened the door to the common law.[36] The old law was to be a source of definition, but whether or not the constructive treasons were to be law in America was a question to be answered by the judges who put the law into action.

A second group of statutes established a pattern for American legislation. Stringent wartime laws were enacted defining and punishing as less than treasonable many acts interfering with the war effort. Covering generally the law of treasonable words and seditious libel, they made criminal the acts of disloyal persuasion and verbal resistance.[37] These

199

[33] Mitchell, *Pennsylvania Statutes at Large*, IX, 18-19, 45-47; *Acts of the Council and General Assembly of the State of New Jersey* . . . , comp. Peter Wilson (Trenton, 1784), pp. 4-5; *Laws of Massachusetts*, pp. 357-362; *Laws of Maryland Made Since M, DCC, LXIII* . . . , comp. A. C. Hanson (Annapolis, 1787), Feb. 1777, c. 20; *The Public Records of the State of Connecticut*, ed. Charles J. Hoadly, I (Hartford, 1894), 4; *Laws of the State of North Carolina*, ed. James Iredell (Edenton, 1799), pp. 284-286; *The Statutes at Large; Being a Collection of All the Laws of Virginia* . . . , ed. William W. Hening (Richmond, 1809-23), IX, 168; Cooper and McCord, *South Carolina Statutes at Large*, I, 150, IV, 479; *Journals of the New York Provincial Congress*, I, 527; *Laws of New Hampshire* . . . , ed. Albert S. Batchellor et al. (Manchester, N. H., 1904-22), IV, 71-74.
[34] Pennsylvania, South Carolina, New Jersey, Massachusetts, Maryland, Connecticut, New Hampshire in the statutes cited in note 33.
[35] Batchellor, *Laws of New Hampshire*, IV, 75-76, 384-385.
[36] Constitutions of New Jersey, New York, Delaware in *The Federal and State Constitutions, Colonial Charters, and Other Organic Laws of the United States*, ed. Benjamin P. Poore, 2d ed. (Washington, 1878), pp. 277, 1313, 1337-1338; Hanson, *Laws of Maryland*, Feb. 1777, c. 20.
[37] *Ibid.*; Mitchell, *Pennsylvania Statutes at Large*, IX, 19-20, 45-47; Wilson, *Acts of the New Jersey Council and General Assembly*, pp. 4-5, appendices 8-11; Iredell, *Laws of North Carolina*, pp. 284-286; Batchellor, *Laws of New Hampshire*, IV, 75-76; Cooper and McCord, *South Carolina Statutes at Large*, IV, 345; Hoadly,

statutes limited the concept of treason by closing the door to judicially
constructed treasons. While such laws may seriously abridge principles
of civil liberties as they are understood in time of peace, they at least
produce no "bloody assize," and did not do so during the Revolution.

The state governments began at the same time to purge the procedural
law of its barbarities. The Congressional resolve of June 1776 recommended adoption of that part of the Trial of Treasons Act which established rules of evidence. The states followed the advice relative to counsel,
panel, indictment, and process;[38] and several states, moving ahead, made
substantial procedural reforms. New York barred the barbarous *peine fort
et dure.*[39] Forfeiture of property followed judgment in all states, though
further consequences affecting relatives were modified. Virginia saved the
widow's dower,[40] Pennsylvania and North Carolina made public provision for dependents,[41] and three states barred any corruption of the
blood.[42] The hideous punishment awaiting the condemned traitor at
common law was replaced with hanging.[43]

State executive and judicial officials extended the process, begun by the
legislatures, of adapting the old law. The first questions, intensely practical
for those involved, were: Who owed allegiance to the United States and
at what point should the treason laws be enforced? In general, it came to
be held that anyone, alien or citizen, permanent resident or temporary
visitor, who enjoyed the protection of government owed allegiance.[44]

Public Records of Connecticut, I, 227-228; *Laws of the State of New York* (Albany,
1886-88), I, 370-371; cf. Willard Hurst, "Appendices to the Brief for the United
States on Reargument," Anthony Cramer *v.* United States, 325 United States, Report 1, and Hurst, "Treason in the United States, I: Treason down to the Constitution," *Harvard Law Review,* LVIII (1944), 226-272.

[38] See the statutes cited above in note 33.

[39] *Laws of New York,* I, 43-44.

[40] Hening, *Virginia Statutes at Large,* IX, 168.

[41] Mitchell, *Pennsylvania Statutes at Large,* IX, 18-19, 45-47; Iredell, *Laws of
North Carolina,* pp. 284-286.

[42] Hening, *Virginia Statutes at Large,* IX, 168; Wilson, *Acts of the New Jersey
Council and General Assembly,* p. 4; *Laws of Massachusetts,* pp. 357-362.

[43] *Ibid.;* Wilson, *Acts of the New Jersey Council and General Assembly,* pp.
23-24; Hanson, *Laws of Maryland,* Apr. 1782, c. 42; Mitchell, *Pennsylvania Statutes
at Large,* IX, 45-47; Batchellor, *Laws of New Hampshire,* IV, 71-74; *Laws of New
York,* I, 43-44; three states provided for the death penalty without describing the
method, Hening, *Virginia Statutes at Large,* IX, 168; Hoadly, *Public Records of
Connecticut,* I, 4; Iredell, *Laws of North Carolina,* pp. 284-286.

[44] *Pennsylvania Archives,* ed. Samuel Hazard et al. (Philadelphia and Harrisburg,
1852—), 1st Ser., VII, 645; Opinion of Thomas W. McKean on the law of treason,

Some men, particularly those of considerable property, tried to claim a neutral position. They hesitated to take positive action because "it is very uncertain who will Rule yet for the matter is not Determined."[45] State officials rejected the fiction of neutrality and refused to protect the lives and property of men who shunned the risk of war in the hope of guaranteeing identification with the victor. They drove men to a decision. John Jay answered one New Yorker seeking recognition as a neutral, saying, "Sir we have pass'd the Rubicon and it is now necessary [that] every man Take his part, Cast of[f] all alliegiance to the King of Great Britain and take an Oath of Aliegiance to the States of America or Go over to the Enemy for we have Declared our Selves Independent."[46] The passing of the Rubicon, the Declaration of Independence, made allegiance to American authority an essential prerequisite to residence in the states. Yet it would have been harsh policy to require that residents owed allegiance on July 4, 1776. Justice demanded that persons be given a reasonable time to decide whether they would become American citizens or remain subjects of George III. The pattern of treason prosecutions indicates that the states permitted a period of election between the publication of the Declaration of Independence and the passage of the treason statutes.[47]

201

From the standpoint of the commission of the great crime, the question of loyalty became real only when the armies were in action. The New England statutes, passed after that area had ceased to be a military theater, were all but dead letters.[48] The first large-scale trials came in

---

June 23, 1777, Miscellaneous Manuscripts, New York Public Library, New York City; the states were following the long established English rule, Edward Coke, *The Third Part of the Institutes of the Laws of England* . . . , 4th ed. (London, 1669), pp. 4-5; Hale, *Pleas of the Crown*, I, 58-61; Foster, *Crown Law*, pp. 183-186.

[45] *Minutes of the Committee and of the First Commission for Detecting Conspiracies in the State of New York*, ed. Dorothy C. Barck, 2 vols. (New-York Historical Society, *Collections*, LVII-LVIII [New York, 1924-25]), I, 149, hereafter cited as *Minutes of the New York Committee*; see *Calendar of Virginia State Papers*, ed. William P. Palmer et al. (Richmond, 1875-93), II, 183.

[46] Barck, *Minutes of the New York Committee*, I, 149.

[47] The evidence is largely negative, that is, there were no treason prosecutions in the period mentioned; see also *Maryland Gazette* (Annapolis), Feb. 18, 1780; *Minutes of the Provincial Congress and the Council of Safety of New Jersey* (Trenton, 1879), p. 167; *Colonial Records of Pennsylvania* (Philadelphia, 1852-53), XII, 71; Hazard, *Pennsylvania Archives*, 1st Ser., VII, 644-646; Pennsylvania v. Samuel Chapman.

[48] For exceptions, see Connecticut v. Moses Dunbar et al.; Connecticut v. Elisha Wadsworth; Connecticut v. Gurdon Whitman; The Case of Asa Porter; Massachusetts v. Smith alias Williamson; Massachusetts v. Samuel Stearns.

New Jersey, a consequence of Washington's retreat and counterattack. As the British moved ponderously across the state, men came in to accept General Sir William Howe's pardon, to enlist in his army, or to sell supplies and information. The New Jersey government, having dissolved under pressure, reorganized after the battles of Trenton and Princeton. Thereafter, a council of safety moved about the state holding preliminary hearings. Only flagrant acts of disaffection—direct aid to the enemy army—ended in charges of treason. Armed with special commissions, the justices rode the circuits, held court, and delivered the jails.[49] Governor William Livingston pushed the prosecutions until the early months of 1779.[50] Then the pace of proceedings slackened as the British eased the pressure of war in the North.

The strategic importance of New York made that state a real or potential battleground throughout the war. The problem of disloyalty came in early with the armies, and military activity became treason's barometer. Washington's retreat from the state in late 1776 caused a wholesale deportation of suspected traitors to New England, but the state never brought these persons to trial.[51] All during 1777 the threat of a two-pronged invasion quickened legal proceedings. British-sponsored agents infiltrated the extreme northern and southern counties, offering protection and enlisting men; and groups of Tories broke through the Patriot lines to go over to Howe in the city. Despite this exodus, Patriot jails were crammed with persons of dubious loyalty, and county committees clamored for a general jail delivery. In response, the New York legislature empowered courts-martial—in lieu of the nonexistent civil courts—to try spies and traitors.[52] First action came from Alexander McDougall, commanding on the edge of the tension-ridden "neutral ground" north of Manhattan. His court-martial tried and condemned three agents who had enlisted men in Howe's service.[53] Across the Hudson, General George Clinton sentenced thirty men to hang for attempting to get

202

---

[49] See all of the New Jersey cases cited in the TABLE OF CASES.

[50] MS. speech of Livingston at Haddonfield, Feb. 25, 1777, State Library, Trenton, N. J.

[51] Barck, *Minutes of the New York Committee*, I, 1-9, 11-12, 16, 26, 78; a few were sent to Pennsylvania, Hazard, *Pennsylvania Archives*, 1st Ser., V, 40.

[52] *Journals of the New York Provincial Congress*, I, 856-857.

[53] New York *v.* Simon Mabee; New York *v.* John Williams; New York *v.* Job Babcock.

through to the city by force.[54] In the northern counties fear of Indian
attack aggravated the fear of invasion. British agents circulated with en-
listment papers. In a desperate game of self-interest, men tried to pick
the winning side. At Albany thirty-one men stood their trial. Two were
hanged.[55]

In Pennsylvania, General Howe's occupation of Philadelphia in
1777-78 set the stage for a series of treason trials in that state. From Lan-
caster, the council of safety, a provisional body with sweeping powers of
trial and punishment in cases of disloyalty, sporadically moved against
persons suspected of treasonable action.[56] During the period of exile from
Philadelphia, no case was brought to the conclusion of a conviction, but
immediately after the American reoccupation of Philadelphia in the summer of 1778 an urgent demand for vengeance expressed itself. Action
against those who had betrayed their allegiance took every form, from
mob violence to trials before the highest courts of the commonwealth.[57]
The focal point of the drive against disloyalists, however, was the long-
anticipated session of the court of oyer and terminer for Philadelphia in
September 1778. While the court was in session, the city rocked with a
political controversy intimately connected with the whole question of
disaffection. The grand jury considered forty-five bills and indicted twenty-
three persons. The trials of the two men found guilty, Abraham Carlisle
and John Roberts, are *causes célèbres* of the Revolution. Both Quakers,
they had entered British service during the occupation. Carlisle acted as
a gatekeeper and issued passes to those entering or leaving the city.
Roberts recruited men and furnished supplies. The court sentenced both
men to hang.[58] Though great pressure was brought to bear for pardon,

203

---

[54] New York *v.* Jacobus Rosa, Jacob Middagh et al.; apparently only Rosa and
his lieutenant, Middagh, were hanged; *Journals of the New York Provincial Congress*, I, 937.

[55] New York *v.* James Huetson, Arnout Viele, et al.

[56] Hazard, *Pennsylvania Archives*, 1st Ser., V, 665-666, VI, 25, 36-38, 45, 53, 445-
458, 460, 487-488, 507, 542-543; *Colonial Records of Pennsylvania*, XI, 343, 352, 386,
406, 557, XII, 778.

[57] Pennsylvania *v.* Peter Deshong; also courts-martial by the Pennsylvania navy
(Pennsylvania *v.* Samuel Lyons et al.), and by the Continental army (United States
v. George Spangler, United States *v.* Frederick Verner).

[58] Pennsylvania *v.* Abraham Carlisle; Pennsylvania *v.* John Roberts; Pennsyl-
vania *v.* Joshua Molder; Pennsylvania *v.* John Taylor; Pennsylvania *v.* Joseph
Malin; Pennsylvania *v.* William Hamilton; Pennsylvania *v.* George Cook, Jr.;
Pennsylvania *v.* Jacob Meng; Pennsylvania *v.* Joseph Turner.

the council of safety remained adamant, and the men were executed in November 1778.

Their trial had come in the wake of the British army. In that summer of 1778 the situation was ripe for a bloody repression. The Patriot party had suffered stinging defeat and endured rigorous exile while Tory Philadelphians had lived in comfort, some even in luxury, during the winter of Valley Forge. The desire for revenge had been so strong among the extreme Whigs that, impatient with the slowness of regular justice, they attempted to take the law into their own hands. In the face of such pressure, the state tried the men at a solemn assize where learned lawyers searched the ancient books to find precedents of common and statute law to protect the accused. The trials were examples of criminal justice, not political reprisal.[59]

The climax of the Revolution brought treason to Virginia. Benedict Arnold's raids, the activities of British privateers, and the arrival of Lord Cornwallis, convinced many that expediency dictated betrayal of allegiance to the state. With a major British army on Virginia soil, the state could do little to bring its traitors to justice. Furtively, on an emergency basis, the Executive Council struck back with courts-martial and with special commissions of oyer and terminer.[60] After Yorktown, cases of treason clogged court calendars. Through 1782 the worst offenders were brought to Richmond for trial.[61] Though the state won many convictions, the legislature consistently exercised its pardoning power,[62] and not a single traitor was hanged in Virginia during the Revolution.[63]

Treason, then, was an incident of battle and an act, not a state of mind. The vast majority of cases came under the head of adhering to the enemy, giving him aid and comfort. The common acts of treason were joining

---

[59] There are scattered examples of later trials, for example, Pennsylvania *v*. John Elwood; Pennsylvania *v*. George Hardy; Pennsylvania *v*. James Stevens; Pennsylvania *v*. William Cassedy alias Thompson; Pennsylvania *v*. Ralph Morden; Pennsylvania *v*. Isaac Green the younger.

[60] Virginia *v*. John Lyon; Virginia *v*. Will, a mulatto slave; Virginia *v*. Fauntleroy Dye.

[61] Palmer, *Calendar of Virginia State Papers,* III, 120, 194, 361. The records of the general court were destroyed by fire in April 1865, William J. van Schreeven to B. Chapin, Dec. 16, 1950.

[62] Hening, *Virginia Statutes at Large,* XI, 21-22, 129, 152, 253.

[63] See the Case of Josiah Phillips who, though attainted as a traitor, suffered death under a court sentence for felony and murder.

the British army,[64] serving as a recruiting agent,[65] or giving substantial aid to the King's forces.[66] Trading with the enemy was not generally regarded as treason.[67] Not a disloyal intent, but an overt, substantial adherence amounted to treason.[68] The legislatures cut away part of the English law, and executive and judicial officials, rejecting theories of constructive treason,[69] restricted the crime to an even narrower range. The law moved in the direction of Article III, section 3 of the Constitution of the United States.

The historians of loyalism, implying persecution, have left a false impression concerning procedural rights during the Revolution.[70] They have generalized too much on statutory evidence. Faced with overwhelming problems of governmental organization, many legislatures modified procedure, particularly in relation to jurisdiction, by authorizing inferior courts or special tribunals to hear and determine cases of treason.[71] Reading the statutes alone, one might conclude that most traitors were accused by special committees acting under the motivation of the witch-hunter and were given either drumhead justice by courts-martial or prejudged trials

205

[64] For example, Pennsylvania v. John Roberts; New York v. Job Babcock; Virginia v. John Gammon et al.; New Jersey v. Lieut. Jacob Boskirk et al.; Maryland v. Daniel Daly; Maryland v. James Chalmers; Maryland v. James Frisby; Maryland v. John Sterling.

[65] For example, New York v. Simon Mabee; New York v. John Williams; New York v. Anthony Hill; New York v. James Huetson, Arnout Viele, et al.; New Jersey v. Iliff; New Jersey v. Ezekiel Beech; New Jersey v. Harbert Henry; New Jersey v. Cornelius Clawson et al.; Maryland v. John Caspar Frietschie.

[66] For example, Pennsylvania v. Abraham Carlisle; Pennsylvania v. John Elwood; New Jersey v. Anthony Woodward alias Little Anthony.

[67] Hazard, Pennsylvania Archives, 1st Ser., V, 665-666. For possible exceptions see New York v. John Likely; New York v. Anthony Umans; New Jersey v. Esther Morse.

[68] Pennsylvania v. Joseph Malin.

[69] The Virginia draft riot cases were exceptions. See Palmer, Calendar of Virginia State Papers, II, 40, 56, 57, 107, 134, 144, 164-165, 177, 213, 215-216, 285, 470, 496-497, 509-511, 682-683.

[70] Claude H. Van Tyne, The Loyalists in the American Revolution (New York, 1902), pp. xi, xii, chaps. 9, 10, 12. Note the choice of chapter titles. Alexander C. Flick, Loyalism in New York during the American Revolution (New York, 1901), p. 127; James W. Thompson, "Anti-Loyalist Legislation during the American Revolution," Illinois Law Review, III (1908), 81-90, 147-171.

[71] Hening, Virginia Statutes at Large, X, 309-315, 381, 413-416; Clark, State Records of North Carolina, XXIV, 348-349; Wilson, Acts of the New Jersey Council and General Assembly, pp. 14, 42; Colonial Records of Pennsylvania, XI, 326; Journals of the New York Provincial Congress, I, 911.

by special commissions of oyer and terminer. The record leads to contrary conclusions.

Though the legislatures had tampered with jurisdiction, the vast majority of cases were tried before supreme courts or at the regular circuit. There is evidence of great reluctance to use the special commission of oyer and terminer.[72] The one great block of cases tried by court-martial came in New York when civil courts were nonexistent and invasion imminent. The officers of these courts showed a marked distaste for this duty. The legislature maintained a strict surveillance of the trials, reading the record verbatim and reviewing every sentence.[73] This is hardly a picture of summary military justice.

The cumulative procedural record exhibits a similar process in every jurisdiction. Many agents made arrests: military officers, executive and judicial officials, local committees, special commissions.[74] Commitments were normally made by a justice of the peace, though special commissions sometimes exercised that authority.[75] The writ of habeas corpus was available.[76] Jurors showed a real reticence to expose men to trial for treason. Neither aroused public opinion nor persuasive attorneys general could stampede them into finding large numbers of true bills.[77] The ac-

---

[72] *Archives of Maryland,* ed. William Hand Browne et al. (Baltimore, 1883—), XVI, 488; Hazard, *Pennsylvania Archives,* 1st Ser., VI, 7, 44, 750, 769-770; Palmer, *Calendar of Virginia State Papers,* II, 215-216, III, 101; *Selections from the Correspondence of the Executive of New Jersey* (Newark, 1848), pp. 63-67.

[73] *Calendar of Historical Manuscripts Relating to the War of the Revolution in the Office of the Secretary of State, Albany, N. Y.* (Albany, 1868), II, 182, 258-260; *Journals of the New York Provincial Congress,* I, 902-905, 916, 926, 928, 965, 974.

[74] Hazard, *Pennsylvania Archives,* 1st Ser., VI, 53, 446-447; *Calendar of New York Historical Manuscripts,* II, 83-85, 113-115; Palmer, *Calendar of Virginia State Papers,* II, 163-164; Browne, *Archives of Maryland,* XLV, 467, 469, 482; *Minutes of the Council of Safety of the State of New Jersey* (Jersey City, 1872), pp. 14, 18, 186; *Journals of the New York Provincial Congress,* I, 591, 1056, II, 272; Barck, *Minutes of the New York Committee,* I, 25, 30, 31; *Calendar of Maryland State Papers, the Black Books* (Annapolis, 1943), p. 224.

[75] *Ibid.,* p. 222; Browne, *Archives of Maryland,* XXI, 160; *Minutes of the Council of Safety of the State of New Jersey* (Jersey City, 1872), pp. 12, 24, 25, 26, 31, 41, 53, 55, 64, 65, 82, 113, 128, 146, 167, 169, 189, 204, 269, 272, 277, 285; *Journals of the New York Provincial Congress,* I, 1056, II, 272; *Colonial Records of Pennsylvania,* XI, 43, XII, 553; Palmer, *Calendar of Virginia State Papers,* II, 207, 406, III, 419; *Correspondence of the New Jersey Executive,* pp. 107-108; Barck, *Minutes of the New York Committee,* I, 25, 57, 78, 139-140, 160-161, 179, 198, 209.

[76] *Pennsylvania v.* Joseph Griswold.

[77] *Pennsylvania Evening Post* (Philadelphia), Oct. 21, 1778; circumstances sur-

cused traitor had a copy of the indictment.[78] Process on indictment was regular. The defendant had counsel, often brilliant. Judges required multiple witnesses to the overt act specified in the indictment as evidence sufficient to convict.[79] At judgment the condemned traitor was reminded of the heinous nature of his crime.[80] Motions to arrest seldom succeeded.[81] In every case, sentences called for execution by simple hanging.[82] The pardoning power was used widely and took every form from blanket amnesty to "shadow of the gallows" pardons. Only a tiny minority of those charged with treason ever experienced the terror of the gallows and the hangman's noose. Drastic purges and violent assizes were not a part of the Revolution. There was no reign of terror. The record is one of substantial justice done.

207

The American Revolution was a transitional era in the development of constitutional law. In the growth of an American law of treason, the Revolutionary experience served as a link between the law of England and the Federal Constitution. The English and colonial law, designed for the protection of a king, existed in an extended and ill-defined state. During the Revolution, Congress and the states roughhewed a new law by modifying the old. The definition of treason written into the Federal Constitution was a refinement and restatement of a trend clearly discernible in the Revolution. It was a clear case of making new constitutional quilts out of old legal rags.

TABLE OF CASES

ENGLISH CASES

---

rounding New Jersey v. John Eddy; Virginia v. Andrew Wayles et al.
[78] Pennsylvania v. Joshua Molder et al.
[79] Pennsylvania v. Abraham Carlisle; Pennsylvania v. John Roberts.
[80] Pennsylvania v. John Roberts.
[81] See an exception in Virginia v. Thomas Davis.
[82] According to local legend, John Caspar Frietschie and his associates suffered death under the horrible common-law sentence. The governor commuted the sentence to hanging. Dorothy M. Quynn, "The Loyalist Plot in Frederick," *Maryland Historical Magazine*, XL (1945), 201-210.

Case of Lord George Gordon (1781), *ibid.*, XXI, 486.
King *v.* Thomas Hardy (1794), *ibid.*, XXIV, 199.
Peter Messenger et al. (1668), *ibid.*, VI, 879.
John Twyn (1663), *ibid.*, VI, 513.
Algernon Sidney's Case (1683), *ibid.*, IX, 952.
Vaughan's Case (1696), *ibid.*, XIII, 525.

NEW JERSEY CASES

New Jersey *v.* Joseph Alward (1777), *Minutes of the Council of Safety of the State of New Jersey* (Jersey City, 1872), p. 82.
Ezekiel Beech (1777), *ibid.*, p. 128.
Lieutenant Jacob Boskirk et al. (1777), *ibid.*, p. 167; *New Jersey Gazette* (Burlington), Jan. 14, 1778.
Jacob Bogart et al. (1777), *Minutes of the New Jersey Council of Safety*, pp. 65, 171; *Selections from the Correspondence of the Executive of New Jersey* (Newark, 1848), pp. 107-108.
Cornelius Clawson et al. (1777), *Correspondence of the New Jersey Executive*, pp. 107-108.
Jacob Dancer (1777), *ibid.*, p. 57; *Minutes of the New Jersey Council of Safety*, p. 41.
John Eddy (1777), *Minutes of the New Jersey Council of Safety*, p. 81; *Correspondence of the New Jersey Executive*, pp. 63-67.
Ezekiel Forman (1778), *New Jersey Gazette* (Burlington), Feb. 25, 1778 (Trenton), July 20, 1778.
Thomas Fowler (1777), *Minutes of the New Jersey Council of Safety*, p. 25; *Correspondence of the New Jersey Executive*, p. 51.
Edmund Harris (1777), *Minutes of the New Jersey Council of Safety*, p. 31.
Peter Helme (1779), *New Jersey Gazette* (Trenton), Oct. 27, 1779.
Harbert Henry (1778), *Minutes of the New Jersey Council of Safety*, p. 272.
John Hinchman (n.d.), Affirmation of Samuel Hugg, New Jersey State Library, Trenton, N. J.
Iliff (1778), *New Jersey Gazette* (Burlington), Jan. 14, 1778.
John Kirby et al. (1778), *Minutes of the New Jersey Council of Safety*, pp. 204-245, 249-250, 269.
John Lawrence (1777), *ibid.*, p. 17.
James Morris (1777), *Correspondence of the New Jersey Executive*, p. 77.
Esther Morse (1778), *Minutes of the New Jersey Council of Safety*, pp. 186-189.
Isaac Ogden et al. (1777), *ibid.*, p. 74; *Correspondence of the New Jersey Executive*, pp. 78-80.
Jacobus Outwater et al. (1778), *Minutes of the New Jersey Council of Safety*, pp. 277, 284, 285.
John Polhemus (1778), *New Jersey Gazette* (Trenton), July 20, 1778.
Richard Robins (1777), *Minutes of the New Jersey Council of Safety*, p. 26.
William Smith (1778), *ibid.*, p. 270.
Jacob Thorn (1777), *ibid.*, p. 146.
Wells and 16 others (1778), *Pennsylvania Packet* (Philadelphia), Dec. 10, 1778.

Anthony Woodward alias Little Anthony (1778), *Minutes of the New Jersey Council of Safety*, p. 268; *Correspondence of the New Jersey Executive*, pp. 51-52.

NEW YORK CASES

King *v.* Nicholas Bayard (1702), *Calendar of State Papers, Colonial Series, American and West Indies, 1702*, ed. W. Noel Sainsbury and J. W. Fortescue (London, 1889-1939), pp. 230-231, 235; *Calendar of Council Minutes, 1668-1783*, ed. Melvil Dewey (Albany, 1902), p. 163; "The Case of William Atwood," New-York Historical Society, *Collections*, XIII (New York, 1881), 11; Howell *State Trials*, XIV, 477.

John Binckson (Long Finn) (1669), *Minutes of the Executive Council of the Province of New York*, ed. Victor H. Paltsits (Albany, 1910), I, 311-322.

Elisha Cole (1767), John Tabor Kempe Lawsuits, New-York Historical Society, New York City.

William Dyer (1682), *Documents Relative to the Colonial History of the State of New York*, ed. John R. Brodhead and Edmund B. O'Callaghan (Albany, 1853-87), III, 289, 302-308; "Proceedings of the General Court of Assize," New-York Hist. Soc., *Collections*, XLV (New York, 1913), 3-38.

Jacob Leisler (1691), *Documentary History of the State of New York*, ed. Edmund B. O'Callaghan (Albany, 1849-51), II, 205-208, 211-212; *Calendar of Council Minutes*, p. 63; "Documents Relative to the Administration of Leisler," New-York Hist. Soc., *Collections*, I (New York, 1869), 311-314, 317, 333, 336-365; Colonial Entry Book, Series 5, Vol. MXXXVII, foll. 7, 11, 13, 14, Colonial Office Papers, Public Record Office, London; *Calendar of State Papers, American and West Indies, 1689-1692*, pp. 433, 671, 695, *1693-1696*, pp. 148, 231, 267, 470-471, 671; *Documents Relative to the Colonial History of New York*, III, passim.

Jacob Milborne (1691), same sources as Leisler's Case.

William Prendergast (1765), Notes on the July Assize, New-York Hist. Soc.; New York Council Minutes, pp. 49-57, New York State Library, Albany, N. Y.; *New York Gazette; or, the Weekly Post-Boy* (Holt), Sept. 1, 1766.

Francis Rumbouts (1682), "Proceedings of the General Court of Assize," pp. 3-38.

New York *v.* Job Babcock (1777), *Calendar of Historical Manuscripts Relating to the War of the Revolution in the Office of the Secretary of State, Albany, N. Y.* (Albany, 1868), II, 86-88.

James Huetson, Arnout Viele, et al. (1777), *ibid.*, pp. 196-231.

Anthony Hill (1777), *ibid.*, pp. 86-88.

John Likely (1777), *ibid.*, pp. 179-182.

Simon Mabee (1777), *ibid.*, pp. 83-85.

Jacobus Rosa, Jacob Middagh, et al. (1777), *ibid.*, pp. 113-115, 123-129; *Journals of the New York Provincial Congress* (Albany, 1842), I, 889.

Anthony Umans (1777), *Calendar of Historical Manuscripts*, II, 179-182.

John Williams (1777), *ibid.*, pp. 85-86.

209

PENNSYLVANIA CASES

Pennsylvania *v.* Abraham Carlisle (1778), 1 Dallas 40; *Pennsylvania Archives,* ed. Samuel Hazard et al. (Phila. and Harrisburg, 1852—), 1st Ser., VII, 44-52; *Colonial Records of Pennsylvania* (Phila., 1852-53), XI, 606-607, 613, 614.

Samuel Chapman (1781), 1 Dallas 53.

William Cassedy alias Thompson (1779), *Colonial Records of Pennsylvania,* XII, 222-223, 309.

George Cook, Jr. (1778), *Pennsylvania Evening Post* (Philadelphia), Oct. 9, 1778.

Peter DeShong (1778), *ibid.; Pennsylvania Archives,* 1st Ser., VI, 641.

John Elwood (1778), *Pennsylvania Archives,* 1st Ser., VII, 59-61; *Pennsylvania Evening Post,* Nov. 6, 1778; *Colonial Records of Pennsylvania,* XI, 624, XII, 48.

Isaac Green the Younger (1781), *Colonial Records of Pennsylvania,* XII, 778.

Joseph Griswold (1780), *ibid.,* pp. 7, 85, 566; *Pennsylvania Archives,* 1st Ser., VIII, 649-652.

William Hamilton (1778), *Pennsylvania Evening Post,* Oct. 16, 1778.

George Hardy (1779), *Colonial Records of Pennsylvania,* XI, 753-754, 761, 764; *Pennsylvania Archives,* 1st Ser., VII, 326-327; *Pennsylvania Packet,* May 4, 1779.

Samuel Lyons et al. (1778), *Pennsylvania Evening Post,* Aug. 28, 1778; *Colonial Records of Pennsylvania,* XI, 566, 579; *Pennsylvania Archives,* 1st Ser., VI, 697-699.

Joseph Malin (1778), 1 Dallas 33.

Jacob Meng (1778), *Pennsylvania Evening Post,* Oct. 9, 1778.

Joshua Molder et al. (1778), 1 Dallas 33.

Ralph Morden (1780), *Colonial Records of Pennsylvania,* XII, 535, 549; John M. Coleman, "The Treason of Ralph Morden and Robert Land," *Pennsylvania Magazine of History and Biography,* LXXIX (1955), 439-451.

John Roberts (1778), 1 Dallas 39; *Pennsylvania Evening Post,* Nov. 6, 1778.

James Stevens (1779), Docket Book of Edward Shippen, Historical Society of Pennsylvania, Philadelphia, Pa.

John Taylor (1778), 1 Dallas 33.

Joseph Turner (1778), *Pennsylvania Evening Post,* Oct. 21, 1778.

Case of Frederick Verner (1778), *Pennsylvania Archives,* 1st Ser., VI, 697-699, 704, 713, VII, 246; *Journals of the Continental Congress,* ed. Worthington C. Ford (Washington, 1904-37), XI, 797-798; *Colonial Records of Pennsylvania,* XI, 561.

VIRGINIA CASES

In re Beverly (1682), *The Statutes at Large; Being a Collection of All the Laws of Virginia . . . ,* ed. William Hening (Richmond, 1809-23), III, 541.

King *v.* Sommersett Davies et al. (1683), *Virginia Magazine of History and Biography,* III (1896), 225-238, XVIII (1910), 253, 254.

John Gunter and nine others (1663), *ibid.,* XV (1907-08), 38-43.

Richard Lawrence (1685), *ibid.,* XI (1903-04), 63-64.

Thomas Young and 11 others (1676-77), *Virginia Statutes at Large*, II, 545-548.

Giles Bland and eight others (1676-77), *ibid.*, pp. 549-553; *Calendar of State Papers, America and West Indies, 1675-1676*, pp. 448, 493, 515, 1677-1680, pp. 37, 40-42.

Virginia *v.* James Caton et al. (1782), *Calendar of Virginia State Papers*, ed. William P. Palmer et al. (Richmond, 1875-83), III, 194.

Thomas Davis (1777), *Virginia Gazette* (Purdie), Aug. 8, 1777.

Fauntleroy Dye (1781), *Calendar of Virginia State Papers*, II, 145-146, 169-170, 190.

John Gammon et al. (1781), *ibid.*, p. 626.

Albridgton Holland et al. (1782), *ibid.*, III, 361.

James Hughes (1782), *ibid.*, p. 120.

John Lyon (1781), *ibid.*, II, 305-306, 340, 350.

Robert Smith (1782), *ibid.*, pp. 624-625, III, 120.

Andrew Wayles et al. (1777), *Virginia Gazette* (Purdie), Aug. 8, 1777.

Will, a mulatto slave (1781), *Calendar of Virginia State Papers*, III, 90, 93.

MISCELLANEOUS CASES

Connecticut *v.* Moses Dunbar et al. (1777), *The Independent Chronicle and Universal Advertiser* (Boston), Mar. 20, 1777.

Elisha Wadsworth (1777), *ibid.*

Gurdon Whitman (1777), *ibid.*

King *v.* Benjamin Merrill et al. (N. C., 1771), *The State Records of North Carolina*, ed. Walter Clark (Winston and Goldsboro, 1895-1905), VIII, 490, 495, 531-532, 635-636, 639, 643, 649-651.

Maryland *v.* James Chalmers (1778, 1780), Eastern Shore Criminal Prosecutions, Hall of Records, Annapolis, Md.

Daniel Daly (1778), *ibid.*

John Caspar Frietschie (1781), *Archives of Maryland*, ed. William Hand Browne et al. (Baltimore, 1883—), XLV, 467, 469, XLVII, 328-330.

James Frisby (1780), Eastern Shore Criminal Prosecutions.

John Sterling (1779), *ibid.*

Massachusetts *v.* Smith alias Williamson (1777), *Virginia Gazette* (Purdie), June 6, 1777; Samuel Stearns and John G. L. Clark, "The Famous Doctor Stearns," American Antiquarian Society, *Proceedings*, N.S., XLV (Worcester, 1936), 317-424.

The Case of Asa Porter (N. H., 1776), *Documents and Records Relating to the State of New Hampshire . . .*, ed. Nathaniel Bouton, VIII (Concord, 1874), 324-331, 413-416, 436, 568, 577, 578, 585.

The Case of Josiah Phillips (1778), W. P. Trent, "The Case of Josiah Phillips," *American Historical Review*, I (1896), 444-454.

Anthony Cramer *v.* United States (1944), 325 United States Reports 1.

United States *v.* George Spangler (1778), *Pennsylvania Magazine of History and Biography*, LV (1931), 49.

Frederick Verner (1778-79), *Colonial Records of Pennsylvania*, XI, 561; *Pennsylvania Archives*, 1st Ser., VI, 704, 713; Ford, *Journals*, XI, 797-798.

William Penn, Parliament, and Proprietary Government

Alison Gilbert Olson*

FROM the first establishment of a Parliamentary committee on trade in 1643 (replacing the previous royal commission) to the last American pamphlet claiming allegiance to George III while repudiating his Parliament, politicians on both sides of the Atlantic were aware that the issues of imperial administration were inseparable from those of British domestic politics—and particularly the struggle between Crown and Commons. A politician drafting imperial legislation was likely to bear in mind the problems of Westminster before those of the Atlantic seaboard. And when he debated bills concerning the American colonies, he could scarcely forget his "connections," his patrons, and even his constituents. As a consequence, the imperial policies of the embryonic political parties in England reflected party stands on domestic issues.[1]

In domestic politics Toryism was roughly synonymous with defense of the royal prerogative, and Whiggism with the supremacy of Parliament. The Tories were the party of landed gentry, stolid Church of England men, while the Whigs looked for support to chartered trading companies and were more sympathetic to dissent. These conventional differences between parties on domestic issues can be verified within broad limits by reference to Parliamentary biographies, debates, and division lists. But for the study of imperial policies, debates and division lists are no help. Down to the eve of the American Revolution almost no votes on imperial issues have survived. In their absence historians have tried to guess what the imperial policies of Whigs and Tories must have been, on the basis of

* Mrs. Olson is a member of the Department of History, Douglass College, Rutgers University, New Brunswick, New Jersey. She holds a Fellowship from the American Council of Learned Societies, to whom she wishes to express her thanks.

[1] By the terms "Whig" and "Tory" I mean to designate political groups somewhere in-between the rather-too-extensive "parties" of Sir Keith Feiling, *A History of the Tory Party, 1640-1714* (Oxford, 1924) and C. B. Roylance Kent, *The Early History of the Tories* (London, 1908), and the rather-too-limited family "connections" of Robert Walcott, *English Politics in the Early Eighteenth Century* (Cambridge, Mass., 1956). The idea of a party united mainly on principle and appealing for popu-

their known domestic stands. Linking the Tories with Crown and Church, historians have agreed that the Tories must have favored tight imperial control by the King, especially over colonies peopled by dissenters, while the Whigs, as the party of chartered rights and freedom for dissent, must have favored far looser imperial control directed by Parliament.

The trouble is, of course, that although colonial policies were linked with domestic issues, the connection was not always simple or direct. The principles behind the domestic policies of each party were often at cross-purposes with one another when applied to colonial government. As a case in point, consider the attempts to bring the semi-independent proprietary colonies of North America under direct control of the Crown.

213

In 1701 the enemies of American proprietary government brought before Parliament a bill to achieve exactly such a result. It declared void all clauses relating to government in the charters of the proprietary and corporate colonies, and provided for the resuming of these governments by the Crown.[2] During the next five years this bill was brought up repeatedly. It was delayed to death in the House of Lords in 1701, but in 1702 the Lords threatened to bring it up again. After several weeks they decided not to, but in 1703, 1704, and 1705 committees of the Privy Council or the House of Lords considered it again, and in 1706 the House of Commons debated a similar bill for two months before defeating it by a close vote on the second reading. For five dangerous years the proprietors demonstrated sufficient political support to wear down and finally defeat the attacks upon their governments.

---

lar support sounds more like the 20th than the 18th century. The idea that politics were determined almost solely by connections is relevant to the era of Whig supremacy under the Hanoverians rather than the age of William and Mary and Anne, when genuine differences of principle existed among the political factions. With one or two exceptions I have accepted Walcott's family connections as he gives them, but I have then gone further and loosely labeled the connections as Whig or Tory by their voting records on strategic issues. For the records of significant votes see Robert R. Walcott, "Division Lists of the House of Commons, 1689-1715," *Bulletin of the Institute of Historical Research,* XIV (1936), 40, 25-36; Thorold Rogers, *Protests of the House of Lords,* I (Oxford, 1875); Feiling, *Tory Party,* appendix 1; and Richard Chandler, *The History and Proceedings of the House of Commons from the Restoration* . . . (London, 1742-44), II, III, passim.

[2] Thus the proprietors of American colonies might keep their lands in America but would have to forfeit their peculiar political privileges and turn over the administration of their colonies to royal governors. For the course of the bill in 1701 see Louise Phelps Kellogg, "The American Colonial Charter," *American Historical Association, Annual Report* . . . *1903,* I (Washington, 1904), 287-289.

On and off for five years, then, members of Parliament debated the pros and cons of an issue which was ostensibly clear-cut: should the government permit partially autonomous units to exist within the empire? If the Tories favored stronger imperial control they should have supported the bills; by the same logic the Whigs should have come to the defense of the proprietors and "colonial liberty." As the party of chartered rights, dissent, and Parliamentary supremacy, they would have had all the more reason to do so. Considered superficially, the alignment of issues involved in the proprietary bills reinforces the traditional view of party stands on colonial policies.

On second look, however, the picture is not nearly so simple. Most of the proprietors were former royal favorites, and their colonies were gifts from the later Stuarts. To protect their charters was also to respect an outdated use of royal prerogative. To a Whig, which was more important: the inviolability of charters or the supremacy of Parliament? Most of the proprietary colonies were havens for dissenters. They were also havens for smugglers. To protect the one was to overlook the other. To a Whig merchant whose fortunes derived from monopolies under a mercantilist system, which was more important—religious freedom or mercantile regulation? In effect the bills to abolish the proprietorships amounted to Parliament's rescinding a royal decree. To strengthen Parliament's legislative authority over the colonies was automatically to weaken the monarchy vis-à-vis Parliament; but if Parliament used its legislative power to enforce colonial obedience to the Crown alone, its effect would ultimately be to weaken the ties of empire.

All of these arguments confronted the British political leader as he considered the proprietary bills. How did he vote? Customarily historians have assumed that the Whigs supported the proprietors and the Tories opposed them.[3] In the absence of voting records we must turn to the correspondence of the politicians and proprietors themselves to see if this was true. The most active of the proprietors was William Penn.

At the time the first of the bills was brought up Penn had already sur-

---

[3] See, for example, the interpretations of such reliable historians as Gertrude Ann Jacobsen—"The weight of Whig opinion in Parliament, however, was on the side of the colonies . . . ."—in her biography, *William Blathwayt* . . . (New Haven, 1932), 336, and Louise Kellogg—"The Whig and dissenting interests in England regained power in time to serve their brethren on the farther side of the Atlantic"—"American Colonial Charter," 305.

vived several attempts to take the proprietary colonies away from their owners. Charles II had granted him the charter for Pennsylvania in 1681; in that very year the Merry Monarch was also having writs of quo warranto prepared against the established proprietary colonies.[4] James II opened his reign with another series of quo warrantos on the colonies in 1685; Penn was able to have the proceedings against his own colony dropped within a year. From London Penn wrote to one of his friends in Philadelphia that "my being here . . . 'has prevented a Storm as to us, that is falling upon other Colonys, and secured my point in great measure with the King who is very particulerly kinde to me . . . ."[5]

When the Dominion of New England was created by James, Penn succeeded in having Pennsylvania left out of it. In 1697 the newly created Board of Trade recommended that proprietary charters be vacated. Penn was called before a committee of the House of Lords to testify about alleged abuses in the administration of his colony. He was warned that his deputy governors must take an oath to carry out all orders from the King. But no bill against proprietary colonies was presented.[6]

In the two decades since he had received his charter, then, Penn had saved his colony by one narrow escape after another.[7] Time and again he took refuge in his friendship with the Stuarts and his connections with their close advisers. The ambitious Robert Spencer, Earl of Sunderland,

215

[4] For this see Hampton L. Carson, "The Genesis of the Charter of Pennsylvania," *Pennsylvania Magazine of History and Biography*, XLIII (1919), 289-331; Philip S. Haffenden, "The Crown and the Colonial Charters, 1675-1688," *William and Mary Quarterly*, 3d Ser., XV (1958), 297-311, 452-466; Fulmer Mood, "William Penn and English Politics in 1680-81," *Journal of the Friends' Historical Society*, XXXII (1935), passim.

[5] To T. Lloyd, Sept. 21, 1686, Frederick B. Tolles, ed., "William Penn on Public and Private Affairs, 1686," *Pa. Mag. of Hist. and Biog.*, LXXX (1956), 241. See also Haffenden, "Crown and Colonial Charters," 452-466. To the already unmanageable Council of Pennsylvania, Penn described the same achievement: ". . . I will tell you that no interest of my own could have prevaled with me so painfully to have stemed the tyde of Quo warranto's & had not yours done it some busy bodys would have had their mouths stopped for good and all." Sept. 25, 1686, "Letters of William Penn," *Pa. Mag. of Hist. and Biog.*, XXXIII (1909), 305.

[6] See Leo F. Stock, *Proceedings and Debates of the British Parliaments Respecting North America* (Washington, 1924-41), II, 192-202.

[7] Only once between 1681 and 1701 had Penn lost the government of his colony; but this was in 1692 when the circumstances were exceptional. In America, the French war created a military emergency calling for the maximum co-operation and obedience to the home government on the part of the colonies; in England, Penn was in hiding because his complicity in Jacobite plots had been exposed. Even then,

who was Secretary of State for the Northern Department almost continuously from 1679 until the Revolution, was a college companion of Penn's. When Penn was in America he exchanged gifts with Sunderland; in England the two friends shared country visits or dinners spent reminiscing about Oxford.[8] With Edward, Viscount Conway, another Secretary of State, the Proprietor had an advocate in the Viscountess, a Quaker convert devoted to Penn.[9] With the Marquis of Halifax and the Earl of Rochester, two ministers who alternated as Lord Privy Seal and Lord President of the Council,[10] and with Lord Keeper Francis North, Penn worked at developing cordial friendships which, if hardly intimate, were still useful.[11] A generation's worth of Stuart ministers knew Penn well. Many of them kept their offices or at least their influence under William; as long as their courtly power continued, Penn's colony was safe.

But closer than his connection with any of the courtiers was Penn's friendship with James II himself, first as Duke of York and later as King. Penn's father had been a notable Cavalier admiral; the memory of this service combined with his own loquacious affability, naïve optimism, and unintimidated support for the principles of dissent won him James's indestructible respect. Penn saw the King when he liked, talked without

---

the proprietary government was restored in two years. See George Hilton Jones, *The Main Stream of Jacobitism* (Cambridge, Mass., 1954), 17, 20; Samuel M. Janney, *The Life of William Penn* ... , 2d ed. (Philadelphia, 1852), 360-387; Bishop Gilbert Burnet, *History of His Own Time* (London, 1823), IV, 119-122.

[8] Penn to Henry Sydney, July 24, 1683, Penn to Sunderland, Aug. 8, 1684, Historical Society of Pennsylvania, *Memoirs*, IV, Pt. i (Philadelphia, 1840), 174-177, 183-186; Penn to Sunderland, May 28, 1683, *ibid.*, II, Pt. i (Philadelphia, 1827), 243-247; John P. Kenyon, *Robert Spencer, Earl of Sunderland, 1641-1702* (New York, 1958), passim. Henry Sydney, Sunderland's uncle, thought Sunderland very sympathetic to the Quakers on Penn's account; R. W. Blencowe, ed., *Diary of the Times of Charles the Second by the Honourable Henry Sidney afterwards Earl of Romney* ... (London, 1843), I, xxxviii-xxxix. See also, n. 32, below.

[9] Marjorie Hope Nicolson, ed., *The Conway Letters: Correspondence of Anne, Viscountess Conway, Henry More, and Their Friends, 1642-84* (New Haven, 1930), passim.

[10] For George Savile, Marquis of Halifax (1633-95), see Thomas Seccombe in *DNB* s.v. "Savile, George"; Helen Charlotte Foxcroft, *A Character of the Trimmer* ... (Cambridge, Eng., 1946), passim. For Laurence Hyde, first Earl of Rochester (1641-1711), see A. W. Ward in *DNB* s.v. "Hyde, Laurence."

[11] Penn to Hyde, Mar. 5, 1682/3, Hist. Soc. of Pa., *Memoirs*, IV, Pt. i, 173-174; Penn to Lord North, July 24, 1683, Penn to Halifax, Mar. 9, 1683/4, *ibid.*, I, 2d ed. (Philadelphia, 1864), 439-441, 446-449.

restraint, and intervened successfully on behalf of unpopular political prisoners. He was messenger, negotiator, adviser, and confidant. So close was Penn reputed to be to James that when he and Charles, Lord Baltimore, quarreled over the boundary between their respective colonies, Penn was accused of persuading the King to start quo warranto proceedings against Maryland.[12]

The situation which confronted Penn in 1701, however, did not promise the success he had enjoyed in the past. Heretofore he had counted on his influence at court. But the warm hearts and erratic emotions of the Stuarts could no longer help him. Instead of a royal writ of quo warranto, he now faced an act of Parliament. And against Parliament he could not even count on the support of the King. Penn's repeated association with Jacobite plots and, indeed, his brief self-imposed exile in France, were probably too much even for the intentionally nearsighted William III to overlook. Penn did not know which way William would throw his influence but he half expected it would be against the proprietaries.

Moreover, Penn could not expect support from other American proprietors or even from the people of his own colony. Strong anti-proprietary parties were growing in all the North American provinces still owned by private individuals, and Pennsylvania was no exception. In the face of growing provincial hostility some of the proprietors of the Carolinas and the Jerseys were losing interest in their undertakings.[13] The proprietor of Maryland, embittered by his boundary dispute with Penn, was almost as interested in seeing Penn lose his colony as in saving his own. Penn's opposition in Pennsylvania was so strong that his own secretary could not see why he wanted to keep the colony.[14]

---

[12] Clayton C. Hall, *The Lords Baltimore and the Maryland Palatinate* (Baltimore, 1902), 117.

[13] Edward McCrady, *South Carolina under the Proprietary Government, 1670-1719* (New York, 1897), 291; William A. Whitehead, *East Jersey under the Proprietary Governments* (Newark, 1875), 218-226; Edwin P. Tanner, *The Province of New Jersey, 1665-1738* (*Columbia University Studies in History, Economics, and Public Law*, XXX [New York, 1908]), chap. 8; John E. Pomfret, "The Proprietors of East New Jersey," *Pa. Mag. of Hist. and Biog.*, LXXVII (1953), 251-293; John E. Pomfret, *The Province of West New Jersey, 1609-1702* (Princeton, 1956). Penn was a proprietor of both Jerseys, and one of the few who opposed surrendering the government.

[14] James Logan to Penn, Dec. 1, 1702, *Correspondence of William Penn and James Logan* (Hist. Soc. of Pa., *Memoirs*, IX-X [Philadelphia, 1870-72]), I, 147; hereafter cited as *Penn-Logan Correspondence*.

The proprietors' problems played directly into the hands of a group of government investigators, chief among them the famous Edward Randolph, Robert Quarry, and Penn's own ex-governor in East Jersey, Jeremiah Basse.[15] Together they took every opportunity to accuse the American proprietors of mismanagement. In part their complaints were based on personal grievances,[16] but they also pointed out genuine administrative shortcomings in the proprietaries—connivances, not to say corruption, on the part of underpaid proprietary deputies dealing with easy-handed local officials and recalcitrant provincial assemblies.

Specifically they criticized the proprietary colonies for failing to provide their share of money and troops for intercolonial defense, condoning piracy, inflating their currencies, forbidding appeals to English courts, and trading with the Scots. But since no one would have claimed that these abuses were confined only to the proprietary colonies, Quarry, Randolph, and Basse went on to suggest that the chartered colonies exerted a bad influence on the others. Their very lawlessness set an example which inhabitants of the royal colonies emulated. They refused to co-operate on intercolonial projects like defense and left an intolerable burden of men and money on the other colonies. Therefore, since taxes were lighter and regulation more lax in the proprietaries, people emigrated to them from the royal colonies, making the burden even greater on the people who remained behind. Finally, their "spirit of independence" from England was encouraging similar thought of freedom from the mother country in other colonies.[17]

In their own way, Quarry, Randolph, and Basse were part of an embryonic colonial service; what they wanted was a more tightly administered empire. They did not particularly care whether the bonds of

[15] Penn to Charlwood Lawton, Dec. 21, 1700, July 2, 1701, Penn Letter Book, 1699-1701, 74-81, 106-107, Historical Society of Pennsylvania, Philadelphia. Penn thought that Quarry had been summoned to report against him by "the party"— William Blathwayt (a member of the Board of Trade), and the Bishop of London. Penn to Logan, Feb. 4, 1701/2, *Penn-Logan Correspondence*, I, 71; Penn to Logan, July 25, 1702, *Pa. Mag. of Hist. and Biog.*, XXXVI (1912), 303-308; Penn to Harley, c. 1701, *The Manuscripts of His Grace the Duke of Portland* . . . (Historical Manuscripts Commission, *Fifteenth Report*, Appendix, Pt. IV [London, 1897]), IV, 30; hereafter cited as *Portland MSS*.

[16] Basse, for instance, had been notably unsuccessful as governor of East Jersey and he attributed his failure to lukewarm support on the part of Penn and several other proprietors.

[17] The specific charges are listed, among other places, in Stock, *Proceedings*, II,

empire were knit by King or Parliament, as long as the knitting was done; they were not particularly interested in the economics of mercantilism, so long as the regulation was efficient. Ironically, their complaints appealed most to peers and commoners interested in transferring power from Crown to Parliament and in creating an empire more noted for the principles of its mercantile regulation than for its efficient administration.

The investigators, then, formed one group interested in terminating the proprietary charters; and members of Parliament interested in developing a stronger Parliament-directed mercantile empire formed another. Together they were powerful enough to bring the question of proprietary rights before Parliament or the Privy Council every year between 1701 and 1706. Against them Penn could not count on the support of the King, his own colonists, or the other proprietors. Clearly he must have gone directly to members of Parliament. Which ones?

At first glance the logic of Penn's situation points overwhelmingly to his soliciting the Whigs. For one reason, the Whigs emphasized chartered rights, while the Tories were more concerned with prerogative. The Tories' indifference to James's flagrant disregard of chartered rights—borough, university, or colonial—was well known. The later Stuarts, no matter how marked their personal charity to Pennsylvania, had been anxious to apply quo warrantos to all the other proprietary or corporate colonies, and their Tory supporters were not prepared to stop them.

Equally well known was the Tory affiliation with the Church of England, which was particularly marked after the accession of Queen Anne in 1702. All the proprietary colonies except the Carolinas were owned by dissenters, and even South Carolina had one Quaker proprietor.[18] Penn, of course, was a Quaker; the other Jersey proprietors were largely Quaker or Presbyterian. The Bahamas were owned by Puritans, Maryland by a Catholic. The two corporate colonies—Rhode Island and Connecticut—were Baptist and Puritan respectively. The Bishop of London, Henry

---

385-386. The grander claims of deleterious influence on royal colonies are indicated in Robert N. Toppan, *Edward Randolph* (Boston, 1898-1909), VII, 533, 535-543, 636-639; Gov. Francis Nicholson to the Board of Trade, Aug. 1, 1700, Dec. 2, 1701, William L. Saunders, ed., *The Colonial Records of North Carolina*, I (Raleigh, 1886), 527-528, 542-543; Quarry to the Board of Trade, Mar. 31, 1702, Herman V. Ames, ed., "Pennsylvania and the English Government, 1699-1704," *Pa. Mag. of Hist. and Biog.*, XXIV (1900-01), 61-80.

[18] John Archdale.

Compton, nominal head of the Anglican Church in America and arch-enemy of the dissenting colonies, was a Tory supporter in 1701.[19]

For reasons of principle—their identification with chartered rights and the toleration of dissent—Penn might logically have sought support for his cause from the Whigs. Reasons of friendship would have made it even more likely. In the last years of Charles II, Penn himself had been a Whig, even going so far as to write a Whig election pamphlet in 1679, and to campaign in Surrey for the radical Whig, Algernon Sydney.[20] Penn's personal friendships outlasted the Revolution, and he was still a welcome dinner guest of respectable supporters of the Whig "junto" which dominated government councils between 1694 and 1698. The Duke of Devonshire, the Earl of Bellomont, Algernon Sydney's brother Henry, Earl of Romney—all the old friends were surely willing to help.[21]

Did Penn therefore expect all his Whig associates to defend his proprietary rights? The interpretation is appealing, but it raises several problems. How could Penn have counted on Whig support when the Board of Trade members instrumental in pressing for the resumption bills were largely Whig? Oliver Dickerson, the closest student of the Board of Trade at the time the proprietors were under attack, wrote of the Board, "in politics . . . the Whigs were the only party represented."[22] This is not quite true, for William Blathwayt was on the Board, but he and Dartmouth were the only two members actively concerned with the proprietary bills who were Tories in the years 1701-06.[23]

[19] For Compton's political career see Edward Carpenter, *The Protestant Bishop* (London, 1956); Arthur L. Cross, *The Anglican Episcopate and the American Colonies* (New York, 1902); Charles P. Keith, "The Bishop of London and Penn's Indian Policy," *Pa. Mag. of Hist. and Biog.*, XXXI (1907), 385-392. Both Cross and Keith try to show that Penn's relations with the Bishop were cordial. There is no doubt, however, that the Bishop and the Quaker disliked each other intensely. Compton blamed Penn's influence for James's failure to appoint him Archbishop of Canterbury, and Penn thought that Compton was at the bottom of the attempts to destroy the proprietary and corporation charters. See, for example, Penn to Lawton, Aug. 27, 1701, Penn Letter Book, 1699-1701, 114-117; Penn to Logan, Apr. 8, 1704, *Penn-Logan Correspondence*, I, 278.

[20] Penn, *England's Great Interest in the Choice of This New Parliament* . . . , in Catherine Owens Peare, *William Penn: A Biography* (Philadelphia, 1957), 203, 204-207.

[21] For William Cavendish, Duke of Devonshire, Richard Coote, Earl of Bellomont, and Lord Romney, see below, nn. 27, 29, 30.

[22] Dickerson, *American Colonial Government, 1696-1765* . . . (Cleveland, 1912), 30.

[23] For William Legge, first Earl of Dartmouth (1672-1750), see G. F. Russell Barker in *DNB* s.v. "Legge, William."

Moreover, one of the Board's purposes was to consider the interests of English merchants—mainly Whigs—trading in America. It was the merchants who were pressing for resumption of the proprietaries. In 1706 the Whig merchants trading to Carolina presented to the House of Lords a memorial against the proprietors.[24] In 1710 Penn wrote retrospectively of the attempts to vacate the proprietorships: "For what with the Impracticable Designs of the Malignant & those not far from You a Resolution was taken here among both Merch[an]ts & the great men of the government of putting a period to your assemblies & to leave your legislation to the Parlmt of England whch I hope now to p[re]vent."[25] If Penn appealed to Whig principles and friendships so could a number of his enemies.

221

And who, in fact, were Penn's well-known Whig supporters? It is true that a number of his associates had backed the junto at the height of its power, 1694-98—Lords Sunderland, Romney, Bellomont, Peterborough, Dorset,[26] and Devonshire. All of these were friends of long standing; most of them had known Penn as long before as the days of Charles II and some, like Sunderland, had known him since college in the earliest years of the Restoration. There is no question of their personal devotion to Penn. But they could scarcely be called strong Whig supporters of his proprietary rights in 1701, for two reasons: first, because most of them were deserting the Whigs for the Tories at this time; and second, because none of them had any real power left anyway.

The old Duke of Devonshire,[27] outspoken advocate for the dissenters, had known Penn at least since the time they had worked together in a Jacobite plot in 1690. Devonshire had been one of the signers of the invitation to William of Orange in 1688; his duplicity two years later was characteristic of Revolution politics in general. He had supported the junto in office until 1696; but voted against them on one of the critical bills of that year—the attainder of Sir John Fenwick for his complicity in a plot

[24] McCrady, *South Carolina*, 428-432.
[25] Penn to Friends, Feb. 10, 1710/1, Penn Manuscripts, Private Correspondence, I, 37, Hist. Soc. of Pa., Phila.
[26] For Charles Mordaunt, Earl of Peterborough, and Charles Sackville, Earl of Dorset, see below, nn. 31, 36.
[27] William Cavendish, first Duke of Devonshire (1640-1707), K.G. 1689, Lord High Steward at the coronation of William and Mary, never held a major office but was always a regent during William's absences on the Continent; see Frances Bickley, *The Cavendish Family* (London, 1911), chap. 6. For an interesting discussion of the gradual defection from the junto of many of Penn's supporters, see Andrew Browning, *Thomas, Earl of Danby*, 3 vols. (Glasgow, 1951).

to murder the King. In the junto ministry Devonshire was Lord Chamberlain; he continued in this position after the junto fell. As a sure sign of his final desertion of the Whigs, he opposed the partition treaty of 1701, drafted by the King himself but approved by the Whigs in his cabinet. That year Devonshire was seventy, his political power spent, and his political allegiance tending to the Tories.

The same was true of Peterborough, Romney, Sunderland, and Bellomont, a quartet of mutual friends who listened sympathetically to Penn's dinner-table laments about Quaker persecutions, and read with patience his transatlantic complaints about the burdens of proprietors. These were the intellectual companions who first discussed with Penn his scheme for uniting the European states in one government,[28] and the personal friends to whom Penn freely described America as a haven from the injustices of England. They had all been Whigs, once.

The Earl of Bellomont[29] was governor of New York, a position of no political influence in England; moreover, he had less than a year to live when the proprietary bill first came up. Lord Romney[30] was a good friend of William's, but he had proved incompetent in major office. In 1701 he held the minor post of Groom of the Stole and had no power outside his ability to extract personal favors from the King. In 1702 he was appointed to Anne's Privy Council under a Tory ministry.

The eccentric Earl of Peterborough,[31] a loyal friend of Penn and Sunderland, had once supported the junto. But at Sir John Fenwick's trial he had been disgraced for sending indiscreet advice to the defendant and was struck off the Privy Council. Bitterly he turned to the Tories;

---

[28] Peterborough to Penn, 1710, Penn-Forbes Letters, II, 77, Hist. Soc. of Pa., Phila.

[29] For Richard Coote, first Earl of Bellomont (1636-1701), see H. M. Stephens in DNB s.v. "Coote, Richard." For letters of Penn and Bellomont, see Penn-Forbes Letters, II, passim.

[30] Henry Sydney, first Earl of Romney (1641-1704), was one of the seven signers of the invitation to William of Orange, was Secretary of State briefly after the Revolution (1690-92), Lord Lieutenant of Ireland (1692-93), and was appointed Master General of the Ordnance in 1693. He was created Viscount Sydney in 1689 and Earl of Romney in 1694, largely as a reward for his services to William in Holland before the Revolution. See his Diary of the Times of Charles the Second, ed. Blencowe; and Penn to Romney, Sept. 6, 1701, Penn Letter Book, 1699-1701, 144-147.

[31] Charles Mordaunt, third Earl of Peterborough (1658-1735), was with Sydney and William in Holland before 1688, and was First Lord of the Treasury, 1689-90. After Fenwick's trial he was voted to the Tower and for several years was out of favor. On Anne's accession he was restored to favor through the influence of the

when his reputation was finally restored by appointment to the Spanish naval command in 1702, it was under Queen Anne and a Tory ministry.

Sunderland,[32] Romney's nephew, old and suffering from a heart ailment, was in virtual retirement at Althorp, his country home. He did not come to Parliament during the 1701 session and died at Althorp before the next session got under way. Moreover he, too, had deserted the junto in 1701 and was using what little power he had left to ally his friend Shrewsbury[33] with the young Tories Robert Harley and Sidney Godolphin.[34] He was even trying, though with embarrassingly little success, to tone down the radical republicanism of his son, Lord Charles Spencer, by marrying him to Marlborough's daughter.[35] Two other erratic Whigs were friends of Penn through the Sunderland circle: the rakish Duke of Dorset,[36] Lord Chamberlain under the junto but generally bored with politics, and Dorset's friend Anthony Henley, M. P. for Andover and Weymouth.[37]

223

Duchess of Marlborough, and later went on to win fame in the Spanish campaigns of the War of the Spanish Succession. Peterborough was later ambassador to Vienna, 1710-11, and Naples, 1711-13, K. G. 1713. After 1715 he was suspected of Jacobite leanings and never held another major office. For him, see Frank S. Russell, *The Earl of Peterborough and Monmouth* . . . , 2 vols. (London, 1887).

[32] Robert Spencer, second Earl of Sunderland (1640-1702), held no office after the Revolution except that of Lord Chamberlain briefly in 1697, but was an archintriguer influential behind the scenes; see Kenyon, *Sunderland*.

[33] For Charles Talbot, 12th Earl and only Duke of Shrewsbury (1660-1718), see A. W. Ward in *DNB* s.v. "Talbot, Charles."

[34] For Harley and Godolphin, see below, nn. 43, 60.

[35] Charles Spencer, third Earl of Sunderland (1674-1722), M. P. for Tiverton, 1695-1703, married Lady Anne Churchill in Jan. 1700. Spencer was later Secretary of State for the Southern Department (1706-10), Lord Lieutenant of Ireland (1714), Lord Privy Seal (1715), Secretary of State for the Northern Department (1717), and Lord President of the Council and First Lord of the Treasury (1718-21) until forced to resign in 1721 because of scandals connected with the South Sea Bubble; Kenyon, *Sunderland*, 307-317.

[36] Charles Sackville, sixth Earl of Dorset (1637/8-1706), was Lord Lieutenant of Sussex, dismissed by James in 1687 but restored by William and Mary in 1689, Lord Chamberlain, 1689-97, K. G. 1691, and one of the regents during the King's absence on the Continent, 1695-98.

[37] Anthony Henley (d. 1711), a student at Oxford sometime during the Protectorate, was M. P. for Andover, 1698-1700, and subsequently for Weymouth and Melcombe Regis, 1702-11. Although commonly considered a Whig, he was more likely a follower of Sunderland and disaffected from the junto in 1701. In 1702 he was returned from Weymouth as a government member, another indication that he was probably not supporting the Whigs at this time.

These were Penn's close friends among the supposed Whigs: Sunderland ailing at Althorp, Bellomont living out his last days in New York, Peterborough in disrepute, Romney and Dorset out of all office, Devonshire an aging figurehead. Penn asked Devonshire, Dorset, Henley, and Lord Charles Spencer to help him in the proprietary crises; the others he left alone.

Inevitably, he turned to the Tories, both the older branch, led by the Earl of Nottingham and his brother Heneage Finch, and more especially the younger branch led by the fast-rising Robert Harley.[38]

Penn first heard about the threat to the proprietaries in the autumn of 1700. Since he could not leave Philadelphia at once, he anxiously wrote to his London agent, Charlwood Lawton, to round up help immediately from "R. Har., Sir E.S., Sir C.M., Sir J. Low. of the Adml's son." By R. Har. Penn meant Robert Harley, Sir E.S. was Sir Edward Seymour, Sir C.M. was Sir Christopher Musgrave, and Sir J. Low, Sir John Lowther of Whitehaven (whose father was at the Admiralty). Lawton was not merely to solicit their votes; he was to ask them for help in writing a pamphlet and otherwise preparing Penn's public defense.[39]

Seymour,[40] Musgrave,[41] and Lowther[42] were sturdy representatives of West Country squiredom. They were arrogant and not above an occasional bribe, yet their political conduct was probably more principled than that of most of their contemporaries. When James fled the throne, their consciences forbade recognizing William and Mary as anything more than

224

[38] For Daniel Finch, second Earl of Nottingham (1647-1730), see T. E. Kebbel in DNB s.v. "Finch, Daniel." For Heneage Finch and Harley, see below, nn. 51, 43.

[39] Dec. 21, 1700, Penn Letter Book, 1699-1701, 74-81.

[40] Sir Edward Seymour (1633-1708) was M. P. from 1661 to 1708 for a variety of constituencies including Gloucester, Devonshire, Exeter, and Totnes. He was a Lord of the Treasury 1691-94, and at Anne's accession he was made Comptroller of the Royal Household and Ranger of Windsor Forest, an appointment he held until 1704. For him see A. Audrey Locke, *The Seymour Family, History and Romance* (London, 1911), chap. 8. For Seymour, Lowther, and Musgrave see also Feiling, *Tory Party;* Walcott, *English Politics;* Browning, *Danby.*

[41] Sir Christopher Musgrave (1632-1704), M. P. for Carlisle, Westmoreland, Appleby, Totnes, and Oxford University in various sessions between 1661 and 1704, was Lt. General of the Ordnance, 1681-87. Like Seymour, he supported the impeachment of the junto lords in 1701. Under Anne he was one of the tellers of the Exchequer until his death.

[42] Sir John Lowther (1643-1705/6), was M. P. for Cumberland, 1665-1700; see Walcott, *English Politics*, 25. Penn's daughter Margaret married Anthony Lowther, a relative of Sir John's.

regents for the exiled King, but they nevertheless tried to find some ground for *rapprochement* with the new sovereigns, even to the extent of supporting their attempts to create a Tory ministry in 1692. After all, Mary was James's daughter. But Mary's death two years later, and William's assumption of the crown in his own right brought the paradox of the Tory position into bold relief; the "old Tories" went into opposition for the rest of William's reign. They opposed the attainder of Sir John Fenwick and refused to join voluntarily an association to protect William in 1696. They opposed the partition treaties negotiated by the King and approved by his junto ministry. Only with William's death and the accession of Anne, daughter of James and niece of their patron saint the Earl of Clarendon, did the "old Tories" accept the Revolution settlement.

225

Robert Harley,[43] on the other hand, represented the younger, moderate Tories not born until after the first revolution of the century and not active in politics until after the second. For fifteen years after 1688, Harley worked and voted with Seymour, Musgrave, and Lowther. But while he opposed Fenwick's attainder he counseled the Tories not to boycott the association to protect William. He did not approve the partition treaties negotiated with the junto's consent, but he saw no point in impeaching the junto for assenting to them. He came into office with the conservative Tories at Anne's accession but broke with them three years later because of their opposition to a vigorous prosecution of the Continental war and their support of the Occasional Conformity Bill. His disagreements with the "old Tories," then, were largely over tactics in William's reign and war and religion in Anne's; conspicuously they did not occur on questions of royal prerogative.

Harley knew Penn far better than Seymour, Musgrave, or Lowther did, and was more sympathetic to his case. Harley's own background was Presbyterian; moreover, he was aware of Penn's immense influence over dissenters' votes.[44] In 1698 Penn asked Harley to be on guard lest a bill

---

[43] Robert Harley, first Earl of Oxford (1661-1724), M. P. for New Radnor from 1690 until his elevation to the peerage in 1712, was speaker of the House of Commons (1701-05), Secretary of State for the Northern Department and privy councilor (1704-08), commissioner for negotiating the Treaty of Union with Scotland (1706), Chancellor of the Exchequer (1710-11), and Lord High Treasurer (1711-14). He was impeached in 1715 but acquitted two years later. For him see Edward S. Roscoe, *Robert Harley, Earl of Oxford* . . . (London, 1902) and O. B. Miller, *Robert Harley, Earl of Oxford, Prime Minister, 1710-1714* (Oxford, 1925).

[44] Charles Cholmondeley to Harley, July 22, 1710, *Portland MSS.*, IV, 551.

for resuming the proprietaries come before Parliament,[45] and after that, as he rose to be Secretary of State and ultimately Lord High Treasurer, Harley was constantly at Penn's service. The two men corresponded regularly during the proprietors' crisis of 1701 when Penn was away in America, and the following year when the proprietary bill was threatened again Penn, then back in England, went straight to Harley to get his advice in person.[46] Overwhelmed with debts, rebellion in his colony, and self-pity, Penn finally decided to sell Pennsylvania to the government; it was Harley who tactfully negotiated a settlement acceptable to both sides.[47] Gratefully—and cleverly—Penn named the Lord Treasurer a trustee of the Pennsylvania government in his will of 1712.[48] Of all Penn's supporters the amiable Robert Harley, a moderate Tory, was the most loyal and most effective. Penn himself sized up Harley's ability: "to moderate one sort and to excite t'other to help us."[49]

Harley, Seymour, Lowther, and Musgrave were to be the nucleus of Penn's defense, but in the letter suggesting their names, Penn also mentioned four other members of the House of Commons—"Sir H. Finch, Ld Spencer, Henly, the Frd. Harcourt," with the remark, "Set all hands to work." Spencer was the radical son of Penn's friend Sunderland; Henly, an erstwhile Whig, also knew Penn through Sunderland and Dorset.[50] Finch[51] was an arch-Tory inseparably allied with Seymour, Musgrave, and Lowther, and Sir Simon Harcourt[52] was a lifelong friend and ally of Harley's.

In the House of Commons, Penn expected predominantly Tory support; he was not disappointed. The proprietary bill was presented to the Lords instead of the Commons in 1701; but in 1706 the same bill was presented in the Commons, and this time the Tories had a chance to

[45] Jan. 30, 1698/9, *ibid.*, III, 601-602.
[46] Penn to Harley, Mar. 28, 1702, *ibid.*, II, 36.
[47] Culver H. Smith, "Why Pennsylvania Never Became a Royal Province," *Pa. Mag. of Hist. and Biog.*, LIII (1929), 141-158.
[48] Penn MSS., Private Corr., I, 63.
[49] To Harley, Jan. 30, 1698/9, *Portland MSS.* (Hist. MSS. Com., *Fourteenth Report*, Appendix, Pt. II [London, 1894]), III, 602.
[50] See nn. 35, 37, above.
[51] Sir Heneage Finch, first Earl of Aylesford (1647?-1719), M. P. for Oxford 1679-85, Guilford 1685, and Oxford 1689-1703, when he was elevated to the peerage. He had been solicitor general 1679-86, but held no subsequent office.
[52] First Viscount Harcourt (1661-1727), knighted in 1702, was M. P. for Abingdon (1690-1705), Bossiney (1705-09), and Abingdon (1710-11), before he was raised to

demonstrate their support. On March 2, 1706, the bill for resuming proprietary colonies was defeated on the second reading in the Commons by
a vote of fifty to thirty-four. The tellers for the minority (favoring the bill)
were T. Owen, an independent member on his own interest at Bramber,
and Lord William Powlett, M. P. for Winchester on the family interest of
his brother, the Duke of Bolton, a supporter of the former junto members.[53] Against the bill, tellers were Arthur Annesley and Richard
Shakerly, both followers of the Tory Earl of Nottingham. Over the five
years, therefore, Tory support for the proprietaries remained steady,
despite the fact that the Tories were in office when the bill came up the
first time and out of office on the second occasion.

227

Penn had concentrated his appeals on the House of Commons' members in 1701, and he was clearly surprised to learn that the bill had gone to
the Lords instead. By the time he found out, it was too late to do more
than send thanks and prayers for continued help via "a small cargoe of
letters to be deliv'd to those Lords who I am Inform'd have been very
kind in my affair. To those great men (as I said before) that have been
kind for the continuance of their favor and justice viz the D. of Somerset,
D. Devonshire, Marq. Normanby, Earl of Dorset, Ld Jeffery & Ld.
Powlett."[54] Later he wrote to Lord Godolphin on the same matter.[55]

Together these peers represented every shade of Toryism. They ranged
from the moderation of Dorset and Devonshire to the conservatism of John
Jeffreys,[56] so Jacobite in sympathy that not even the "old Tories" were
willing to claim him. In-between were Somerset[57] and Normanby,[58] both

the peerage in 1711. He was solicitor general (1702-07), attorney general (1707-08
and 1710), Lord Chancellor (1713-14), and privy councilor (1710-14, 1722-27). Harcourt was a noted lawyer and though a close friend of Harley's, he refused to join
voluntarily the association to protect William.

[53] For Charles Powlett, second Duke of Bolton (1661-1722), see Thomas Seccombe
in *DNB* s.v. "Powlett, Charles."

[54] Penn to C. Lawton, Aug. 27, 1701, Penn Letter Book, 1699-1701, 114-117.

[55] Mar. 3, 1702/3, *ibid.*, 151-152. Penn had also written Godolphin on Mar. 27,
1701; Penn MSS., Three Lower Counties, 73.

[56] John, second Baron Jeffreys (1670?-1702), son of the infamous George, Lord
Jeffreys, of the Bloody Assizes, never held an office.

[57] Charles Seymour, sixth Duke of Somerset (1662-1748), was "one of those in
arms" to support William of Orange in 1688, was Master of the Horse and privy
councilor under Anne, 1702-11, managing to stay in office through numerous minis-
terial upheavals before being dismissed as the result of a quarrel with Henry St.
John. For him, see Locke, *Seymour Family*, chap. 7.

[58] John Sheffield, first Duke of Buckingham and Normanby (1648-1721), Lord

cousins of Sir Edward Seymour and sporadically allied with his conservative Tories, Lord John Powlett,[59] cousin and follower of Robert Harley, and Lord Godolphin,[60] who claimed to be a Tory but managed by phenomenal flexibility to stay at the Treasury through virtually every administration, Whig or Tory, from 1679 to 1710. He was the leading Tory in office with the junto, and was best known as a member of the triumvirate (with Marlborough and Harley) which dominated the government from 1702 to 1708.

Despite their varied careers and connections, all these members of the House of Lords could be identified as Tories during the years when Penn solicited their help. All of them voted against the junto in 1696 by opposing the attainder of Sir John Fenwick. All except Dorset and Devonshire supported the impeachment of the former junto lords in 1701, and everyone except Jeffreys (who died in 1702) and Dorset (who was no longer interested in politics) held office in Anne's first Tory ministry, 1702-06.

Jeffreys was one of the tellers in favor of a motion to delay the proprietary bill to certain death in June 1701. John Powlett became such a close friend of Penn that he, along with Harley, was appointed trustee of

Chamberlain and privy councilor, 1685-88, had supported James to the last. In 1694 he was created Marquis of Normanby and restored to the Privy Council, but two years later he was dismissed for failing to join the association to protect William. He was created Duke of Buckingham and Normanby (1702/3), was Lord Privy Seal (1702-05), commissioner for the treaty with Scotland (1706), privy councilor (1710-14). Normanby was also known as a poet and historian.

[59] John Powlett (1668-1743), created first Earl Powlett in 1706, was Lord Lieutenant of Devon (1702-05, 1711-14), First Lord of the Treasury (1710-11), Lord Steward of the Household (1711-14), K.G. 1712, privy councilor (1702-14). Prince Eugene described him as a "true patriot in the opinion of the Tory party"; quoted in G. E. Cokayne, *The Complete Peerage*, X (London, 1945), 620.

[60] Sidney Godolphin, first Baron Godolphin (1645-1712), was M. P. for Helston, 1668-79, and St. Mawes, 1679-81, before being raised to the peerage in 1684. From 1672 to 1689 he was constantly in the service of the Stuarts, first as a Groom of the Bedchamber, 1672-78, and then as a Lord of the Treasury, 1679-84, 1687-89, and Secretary of State, 1684. Though he remained with James to the last, he was immediately appointed First Lord of the Treasury by William and held the office nearly always between 1689-98, again 1700-01, and again 1702-10. From 1702 to 1706 Marlborough and Godolphin worked closely with Harley in a cabinet dominated by moderate Tories. They broke with Harley beginning in 1706-08 when Harley began drifting back to the conservative Tories. In 1708 they forced Harley out of office; when he returned two years later they were forced to resign. For him see Hugh F. H. Elliot, *The Life of Sidney, Earl of Godolphin* ... (London, 1888).

the government of Pennsylvania in Penn's will of 1712.[61] Normanby and Somerset defended Penn in colonial matters even to the extent of taking his side in an internecine quarrel among the proprietors of East and West Jersey in 1702.[62]

But above all it was Godolphin who helped Penn most in the House of Lords. Godolphin had been on respectable terms with Penn at least since the reign of James II, when they were thrown together as two of the last adherents of the old King. Both men corresponded with James in exile; when Penn's correspondence was discovered and he was driven into hiding, Godolphin visited him in seclusion and worked to have the charges against him dropped.[63] When Penn returned to London from America in 1701, Godolphin was the first person he saw about "his business." Like Somerset and Normanby, he put in a word with the Queen on behalf of Penn's candidate for governor of the Jerseys.[64] Most important of all, Godolphin was apparently instrumental in preventing a revival of the proprietary bill before the Lords in 1703.[65] Godolphin was not a political crusader, but he was a fairly capable administrator and what he could comfortably effect for Penn behind the scenes he was more than willing to do.

Godolphin, Harley, Seymour, Finch, Lowther, Musgrave—these men, all Tories, carried Penn's defense. But Penn was not the only representative of proprietary or charter colonies who called upon Tories for help. John Granville, Lord Bath,[66] most conscientious and most influential of the heterogeneous Carolina proprietors, was a Tory himself, related by

229

[61] Penn MSS., Private Corr., I, 63.

[62] Penn to Logan, July 28, 1702, *Pa. Mag. of Hist. and Biog.*, XXXVI (1912), 303-308.

[63] See Burnet, *History of His Own Time*, III, 132, VI, 8, for Penn's earlier connection with Godolphin.

[64] Penn to Logan, July 28, 1702, *Pa. Mag. of Hist. and Biog.*, XXXVI (1912), 303-308.

[65] Penn to the Lord Treasurer (Godolphin), Mar. 3, 1702/3, Penn Letter Book, 1699-1701, 151-152.

[66] John Granville, first Earl of Bath (1628-1701), loyal defender of Charles I and II, was granted several minor offices at the Restoration and raised to the peerage in 1661. In 1687/8 he was one of James's representatives to gauge the temper of the southwestern counties on the repeal of the Test and Penal laws. He was appointed privy councilor in 1689, and was Lord Lieutenant of Devonshire and Cornwall, 1689-96, but held no other major offices. He died in August 1701 and was succeeded by his son, the second Earl, who died two weeks after his father. His other son, John, was created Baron Granville in 1702.

marriage and politics to Edward Seymour, Heneage Finch, and the Duke of Somerset.

Of the known supporters of the proprietary and corporate colonies, only one—Lord Charles Spencer—was a Whig, and he supported the proprietors only because his father was a special friend of Penn's. Three others—Dorset, Devonshire, and Anthony Henley—had supported the junto, but by 1701 they were lacking either political power or sustained loyalty to the Whigs. Somerset was an unconnected magnate generally voting Tory. The rest of the proprietary supporters—the most numerous and the most influential—were Tories.

There is no single explanation for Penn's Tory support; the reasons were in part personal, in part political.[67] Penn's father had served Charles I and Charles II, and the son inherited not only the royal debt which was converted into the American colony, but also the friendship of a number of strong royalists. At James's court the younger Penn was notoriously powerful, and he remained loyal to James long after 1688. He was one of the dissenters who unrealistically hoped to bring James back—"with terms," including a guarantee of toleration for Protestant dissenters. In attempting to negotiate with the exiled King, Penn was associated with the Jacobite wing of the Tory party[68] and with other Tories like Godolphin, who clandestinely gave information to James's agents but would never publicly avow the slightest enthusiasm for the Jacobite cause. Significantly, the single issue on which the greatest number of Penn's supporters voted alike was Fenwick's attainder. For some peers and commoners, opposing the proprietary bills may have been a way of openly expressing continued sympathy for an old Cavalier family.

For more of them it was the safest way of obtaining electoral support from the foremost dissenting leader in England. So great was Penn's command of dissenters' votes that in 1688, when Sunderland had tried to work out some concessions which would quell the opposition to James, he had sought out Penn alone to speak for the political views of Protestant dissenters. Throughout his exile and seclusion in the 1690's his position among Quakers remained fairly steady. During the years when his pro-

---

[67] Bribes were certainly not one of the reasons: for gentlemen accustomed to four-figure bribes the few hundred pounds Penn had to offer would not have been worth considering.

[68] Though Seymour, Musgrave, Lowther, and Finch did not correspond with James, their patron Clarendon was involved in the same plot for which Penn had to go into hiding.

prietorship was in danger the Tories solicited Penn's help with Quaker votes in the county elections of Suffolk, Somerset, Worcester, Chester, and Sussex.[69] With the exceptions of Suffolk and of Sussex, where Penn had lived for several years, these counties are grouped in or near Wales, making them conspicuous as Robert Harley's home grounds.[70] While the Tories were known as the Church of England party, they were not above soliciting dissenters' votes as ardently as the Whigs. Moderate Tories like Harley actually favored a policy of generous toleration. But even conservatives like Seymour did not hesitate to support the Occasional Conformity Bill and solicit Penn's electoral help at the same time.

Some of the Tory opposition to the proprietary bills was therefore traded for Penn's help in county elections. But in making the trade and supporting proprietary rights the Tories were also reflecting their fundamental party attitudes—aversion to excessive governmental interference in the regulation of trade and desire to protect the prerogative.

Traditionally the Whigs have been given credit for saving the proprietary and corporate colonies, but William Penn's experience in opposing the proprietary bills shows that the reputation of the Whigs is largely undeserved. It also shows that constitutional changes in the British Empire cannot be understood without a knowledge of contemporary domestic politics. Mainly because of Tory opposition—from the friends of Penn, his father, or the other American proprietors, from politicians who needed Penn's help with dissenters at the polls, from statesmen genuinely concerned to protect the prerogative—the proprietary bills did not pass. William Penn kept his colony, and the larger problem of whether Parliament or the King had final authority over the colonies was left to become an issue of the American Revolution.

231

[69] See, in that order: Sir Thomas Hammer to Matthew Prior, Sept. 2, 11, 1710, Historical Manuscripts Commission, *Calendar of the Manuscripts of the Marquis of Bath* . . . (London, 1904-08), III, 440-442; Powlett to Penn, Apr. 22, 1699, Penn-Forbes Letters, II, 79; Normanby to Penn, July 17, [1699?], *ibid.*, 72; Charles Cholmondeley to Harley, July 22, 1710, *Portland MSS.*, IV, 551; Earl of Scarborough to Penn, July 21, 1702, Penn-Forbes Letters, II, 98.

[70] It is clear that Penn's help was sought in these counties because of the strength of his own influence rather than the numerical strength of Quakers or dissenters in general. The ratio of nonconformists to conformists in all these counties was the same as the average for all of England—about 1 in 22; Lyon G. Turner, ed., *Original Records of Early Non-Conformity* (London, 1914), III, 142. Sussex, Gloucester, and Somerset had larger than average, and growing, Quaker congregations, but in Worcester and Wales the number of Quakers, never very large, was decreasing between 1690 and 1709; John S. Rountree, *Quakerism, Past and Present* (Philadelphia, 1860), 86.

Equality and Empire
The New York Charter of Libertyes, 1683

David S. Lovejoy*

HISTORIANS of colonial America have given over a good deal of space to the course of events between the founding of the colonies and the American Revolution. Through them we have learned much about how colonies were settled and developed and how they were expected to fit the demands of the emerging British Empire. What historians have found difficult to determine is how American colonists felt about themselves as British subjects outside the realm, and what they believed was the colonies' role within the empire. Such an inquiry is, of course, less difficult for the eighteenth century, particularly for the period just before the American Revolution. Events at that time at last forced the colonists to come to terms with the idea of empire and to set limits upon it and upon the power of Parliament in accordance with their own needs and historic assumptions. In the seventeenth century, colonial society was less mature, less stable, and less reflective about itself and its relationship to the Mother Country. No single momentous event like the Revolution united or crystallized colonial thought around definite political or constitutional theories. Rather, each colony went its way, influenced by its own peculiar political, economic, and religious circumstances on the one hand, and by the emerging, yet fitful, colonial policy on the other. At the same time, the English government had not yet determined precisely what the colonists' role was in the larger scheme. Crown, Parliament, and ministry after the Restoration had only begun to decide how their general conclusions about empire ought to be implemented.

Despite the unsettledness of the connection between colonies and Mother Country, certain events affecting individual colonies did produce in the seventeenth century reactions which help the historian determine what went on in the minds of the people, who they thought they were, and how they believed they stood in relation to England. A unique situa-

* Mr. Lovejoy is a member of the Department of History, University of Wisconsin. Mr. John C. Rainbolt of the University of Wisconsin assisted him in his research.

tion obtained in the colony of New York after the English conquest in 1664, and the New York colonists' response to it explains something about the colonial mind and gives a clue to what a particular group of American colonists had concluded about the imperial relationship.

I

On October 17, 1683, eighteen deputies from the settled areas of New York convened on Manhattan Island for a meeting of an assembly. They came from the city at the tip of Manhattan, down the Hudson River from Albany and Schenectady, from Long Island, Pemaquid in Maine, and the islands in the Atlantic now belonging to Massachusetts. After electing a speaker they drafted a charter or constitution, which described a structure of government and defined certain individual, civil, and political rights for the people who lived there. What was the significance of this assembly and in particular the charter it drafted? What does the charter tell us about these colonists' understanding of their rights within an emerging British Empire?

First of all, this was the first official legislature to meet in the colony of New York. Virginia was settled in 1607 and its first legislature met within twelve years. Massachusetts had enjoyed a legislature from the outset, Maryland almost from the start. But not New York which the Dutch had settled as early as the 1620's and the English had conquered in 1664. Under the Dutch, four successive directors had administered the colony, including Peter Minuit and Peter Stuyvesant, first and last. Each ruled with a council and no assembly. Government was arbitrary over a heterogeneous population of Dutch, Germans, Swedes, and a number of English from Massachusetts and Connecticut who settled on Long Island.

New Netherlands came to be a thorn in the side of good mercantilists in England and hungry colonists in America, both of whom saw their trade threatened, furs siphoned off to Holland, and expansion of New England blocked by foreigners at New Amsterdam and Fort Orange (Albany). After the Restoration of Charles II in 1660, broader and better defined ideas of imperial trade emerged in the minds of the English King, ministry, and Parliament. One of the early imperial schemes of the Restoration government was the conquest of New Netherlands. After Stuyvesant reluctantly surrendered his settlements to the English Royal Commissioners in 1664, Charles II gave the colony to his younger brother,

233

James, Duke of York, to govern as he pleased. James's pleasure was to rule New York through a governor and council.

The Duke's grant was a fat one. It initially included all of New Netherlands, Long Island, half of Connecticut, several islands off the coast of Massachusetts, part of what is now Maine, and all of what is now New Jersey. But the Duke's proprietary was different; unlike the proprietary of Maryland, and later proprietaries of the Carolinas, the Jerseys, and Pennsylvania, it had no representative assembly. There were several reasons for the omission. First, the Dutch had never had a legislature, and they were a large segment of the population. Secondly, and probably more important as things turned out, Stuart monarchs were suspicious of elected legislatures since they had never had any great luck with them in England, and James in particular thought them a nuisance. New Yorkers had to be satisfied with what were known as the Duke's Laws, a New England code arbitrarily adapted to proprietary circumstances. Richard Nicolls, a member of the Royal Commission charged with the conquest of New Netherlands and the Duke's first governor, ordered a convention in 1665 at Hempstead, Long Island, where elected representatives from the settled areas close by accepted, not without some protest, the colony's first set of laws. One cannot call this meeting an assembly, for it met only to approve the laws and then did not meet again. The Duke's Laws went into effect immediately, and the governor and council ruled with an appointed Court of Assizes to dispense justice. In 1665 the proprietary colony of New York was underway.[1]

II

Between 1665 and 1683 a good deal of protest arose against the handling of New York affairs. The lack of an assembly was a primary grievance. Most of the protests originated on Long Island where New Englanders were concentrated. Their arguments were based first on Governor Nicolls's promise—supposedly made at the time of submission to

234

[1] See *The Colonial Laws of New York from the Year 1664 to the Revolution . . .*, I (Albany, 1894), 1-71. Southhold's deputies came to the convention armed with instructions from their town meeting which demanded that no taxes be raised from them without their consent "in a general court meeting," but no regard was paid. Edmund B. O'Callaghan, *Origin of Legislative Assemblies in the State of New York . . .* (Albany, 1861), 9. O'Callaghan's study appears also as "Historical Introduction," in *Journal of the Legislative Council of the Colony of New-York [1691-1743]* (Albany, 1861), iii-xxvii.

the Commissioners—"of equall (if not greater) freedomes and immunityes then any of his Majesties colonyes in New England." To transplanted New Englanders, rights equal to or greater than those of other Yankee colonists must mean at the very least protection from arbitrary government by establishment of a representative assembly with the sole power to enact laws and levy taxes upon them. The Court of Assizes later denied that Nicolls made such a promise and informed Long Islanders that nothing was "required of them but obedience and submission to the Lawes of the Government."² A more vigorous protest complained that the inhabitants were "inslaved under an Arbitrary Power," and that Nicolls exercised more authority "than the King himselfe can do." The governor labeled this slander and high treason and reminded the colonists that the English Civil War, the "Late Rebellion," began "with the selfe same steps and pretences."³

Besides petitions and high words, protests also took other forms. In 1666 two constables in Southhold, opposed to the arbitrary method of taxation, refused to do their duty, and the sheriff issued a warrant to levy fines upon them. In the same town there was outright refusal by several people to pay their rates, even by some of the overseers who had agreed to the making of them. Petitions and protests got the Long Islanders nowhere, and they were branded "ill mynded people who take delight to breed disturbances and to infuse ill principles into the myndes of his Majesties good Subjects."⁴

In 1670, after Francis Lovelace had replaced Nicolls as governor, he and the council levied a new tax upon the inhabitants over and above the usual to defray the expenses of repairing Fort James on Manhattan. Huntington town meeting led the way and denounced the tax because it deprived people of the "liberties of english men." Besides, the meeting complained, the people of Huntington were busy with their own problems and would receive no benefit from a fort in New York City anyway. Jamaica people called the tax contrary to the "Laws of the nation"

² O'Callaghan, *Origin of Legislative Assemblies*, 5-11; E. B. O'Callaghan and B. Fernow, eds., *Documents Relative to the Colonial History of the State of New-York* (Albany, 1853-87), XIV, 632.
³ Richard Nicolls to John Underhill, May 7, 1666, *Documents of N. Y.*, XIV, 580.
⁴ The Governors Commission to Thomas Delavall Esquire Mr. Mathias Nicolls Secr. and Mr. Isaack Bedlow. etc., Mar. 9, 1671, in Victor H. Paltsits, ed., *Minutes of the Executive Council of the Province of New York* (Albany, 1910), II, 524-525; *Documents of N. Y.*, XIV, 578, 582, 584.

and doubted that the governor's commission permitted it. Already they were paying a penny in the pound to support the government; if the governor and council demanded money for the fort, they reasoned, they could also demand "what ills we know not tell thear be no end."[5] Flushing and Hempstead, along with Jamaica, held several town meetings and drew up resolves protesting the government's demands. These resolutions eventually reached the governor and council, who pronounced them scandalous, illegal, and seditious, demanded that they be "publiquely burned," and ordered that the "principall contrivers thereof be inquired into."[6]

During the Third Dutch War, 1672-74, the Dutch recaptured New York, and agitation, at least against the Proprietor's governor, ceased for a time. Re-establishment of Dutch rule, however, did not stop the settlers of East Hampton, South Hampton, and Southhold from petitioning King Charles about grievances sustained from both English and Dutch governments. What they objected to was interference with their whale fishery, first by "heavy taxes" under the English, higher than those in New England, without allowing them "any deputies in court," and then by arbitrary laws imposed upon them by the Dutch. The eastern Long Islanders claimed they had purchased their land thirty years earlier and that the land rightly belonged under the Connecticut patent from where most of them had come. If they could not be governed by Connecticut, they suggested the King might make them a "free corporation," a very unlikely possibility to say the least. The petition got as far as the Lords of Trade and doubtless died there.[7]

In the Treaty of Westminster which ended the war, the Dutch agreed to return New York to the English, and James dispatched Major Edmund Andros as governor to serve as his link with the colony. Agitation for an assembly continued. Andros gave the colonists no encouragement, but he did report to the Duke that taxes and customs might come easier if the colonists had a part to play in the way they were levied. The Duke, of course, wanted New York to pay its own way. He also wanted income from his colony, through revenue from customs duties. After all, what

[5] Charles R. Street, ed., *Huntington Town Records* . . . (Huntington, 1887-89), I, 163-164; Josephine C. Frost, ed., *Records of the Town of Jamaica, Long Island, New York, 1656-1751* (Brooklyn, 1914), I, 47-48.

[6] *Documents of N. Y.*, XIV, 646; *Min. of Exec. Council*, II, 485-487.

[7] W. Noel Sainsbury and others, eds., *Calendar of State Papers, Colonial Series, America and West Indies* (London, 1860—), *1669-1674*, #875, #875 I, pp. 380-381.

was a proprietary colony for if not to profit its proprietor? James considered Andros's suggestions and agreed that the colonists' desire for an assembly was "in imitacon of their neighbor Colonies"; but he refused to go along with Andros's suggestion. Instead James commended Andros for discouraging any idea of an assembly.

James gave several reasons for his refusal. It was outside Andros's instructions to grant an assembly, he said. There was no argument there. Redress against grievances was easily come by under the Duke's Laws as they existed; all the governor and council had to do was to rule according to the laws already set down. What is more, wrote the Duke to Andros, the Court of Assizes doubtless contained the same people who would be elected to an assembly anyway. Assemblies without proper restrictions "would be of dangerous consequence" and apt to "assume to themselves many priviledges which prove destructive to, or very oft disturbe, the peace of the government wherein they are allowed." Probably the Duke could have made no statements more clearly revealing his insensitivity to, and misunderstanding of, the colonists' sentiments and attitude toward government. A final remark did suggest that if Andros still believed an assembly would help, the Duke would consider proposals the governor might make.[8]

A specific incident in 1680 brought the whole issue to a head and indicated that opposition to arbitrary government was not confined to testy transplanted New Englanders. As one might expect, it was a money problem which precipitated this sharp turn in the history of the colony of New York. The Duke's customs rates and duties on trade ran for three-year periods, and the rates levied in 1677, out of which came the support for government, expired in November 1680. But just before the date of expiration, the Duke recalled Governor Andros to London to answer several charges, including one against the governor's handling of the revenue. Andros embarked for home without renewing the customs duties—leaving Lieutenant Anthony Brockholls in his place as deputy. When Collector William Dyer attempted to collect the customs, the merchants balked. Ships entered and cleared without paying rates. The council met but took no steps to continue the laws. Brockholls stood by helpless, watching the government's sanction crumble.[9]

237

---

[8] Duke of York to Andros, Apr. 6, 1675, and Jan. 28, 1676, in *Documents of N. Y.*, III, 230, 235.

[9] *Documents of N. Y.*, III, 221-223; Duke of York to Andros and Sir John Wer-

Collector Dyer bore the brunt of the people's pent up anger. They claimed that his attempt to collect the expired customs and the use of soldiers to assist him were violations of Magna Carta, the Petition of Right, several other statutes, and the honor and peace of the "King that now is." For maliciously exercising such "Regall Power," a grand jury formally charged him with being a "false Traytour" to the King and with subverting the "known Ancient and Fundamentall Lawes of the Realme of England." Once in court to reply to the charges, Dyer challenged the jurisdiction of the Assizes, claiming that both he and the court had commissions from the same source, James, Duke of York, and therefore the court could not try him. The court, fearing trouble with the Duke, agreed not to pursue the case but instead sent the collector to England where he might be proceeded against as the Crown directed. In London after the prosecutor failed to appear, the charges were dropped, and Dyer was advanced in his Majesty's service.[10]

238

William Dyer's trial in New York got a number of people excited. The lack of power to collect the customs and Dyer's attempt to do so without authority intensified demands for an assembly. The outspoken discontent made it clear that if the Duke wanted money, he would have to allow a legislature. Long Islanders no longer fought the battle alone; evidence of bad feeling among the people was widespread. The colony's Grand Jury, which had indicted Dyer, petitioned the Court of Assizes and summarized the protests of a good many when it complained of the insupportable burden which was thrust upon them all. In a very revealing document, the Grand Jury explained that the burden could only be removed "by sitting us upon Equall Ground with our fellow Brethren and subjects of the Realme of England In our Neighboring Plantacons." The only way to do this, of course, was to place the government in the hands of a governor, council, and assembly elected by the freeholders. Only by

den to Andros, May 24, 1680, *ibid.*, 283-284; O'Callaghan, *Origin of Legislative Assemblies*, 12-13.

[10] Proceedings against Mr. Dyer, Collector of the Port of New-York, and The Bill found against Capt. William Dyre, in *Documents of N. Y.*, III, 288-289 and *n*; The Bill or Accusacon against Capt. William Dyre found by the Grand Jury, in "Proceedings of the General Court of Assizes Held in the City of New York October 6, 1680, to October 6, 1682," in New-York Historical Society, *Collections*, XLV (New York, 1913), 11; Proceedings of the Court of Assizes, July 1, 1681, in *Cal. St. Papers, Col., 1681-1685*, p. 81; John West, Clerk of Assizes, to [Sir Leoline Jenkins], July 1, 1681, *ibid.*; Order of the Privy Council, Sept. 14, 1681, and Report of Sir John Churchill to the Commissioners of the Duke of York's revenue, Nov. 28, 1683, *ibid.*, pp. 115, 555.

this means could New Yorkers enjoy the good and wholesome laws of the realm. In a burst of eloquence the Grand Jury proclaimed: "Thereby wee may Bud Blossom and bring forth the fruites of a Prosperous and flourishing Government for want of which wee have Been (and yett are) in a most wythering and Decaying Condicon. . . ."[11]

The Grand Jury begged the Court of Assizes—which, if not a representative body, at least included settlers from several areas—to carry their case directly to the Duke and strongly urged sending a petition, which the Court agreed to do immediately. The Assizes's petition to James complained of "inexpressible burdens" and of the "arbitrary and absolute power" over the people which exacted revenue against their will. Even more forcefully than the Grand Jury, it hammered home the idea that English subjects, no matter where they lived, were equal as far as rights and treatment from government were concerned. Under present conditions as colonists they were "esteemed as nothing" and had "become a reproach" to their neighbors in the King's other colonies who, unlike New Yorkers, flourished under the protection of the King's "unparalleled form and method of government." What was practicable at home and in other colonies, that is, an "assembly of the people," was the "undoubted birthright" of all the King's subjects.[12]

Another incident occurred which pointed to similar conclusions about government. At Albany Collector Robert Livingston took John De Lavall to court in August 1681 for refusing to pay an excise on 510 gallons of rum he had unloaded and sold. At his trial De Lavall turned the court up-side-down by directing to it several searching questions. By what right did Livingston collect the excise, and, if by order of the governor, when did the King, Lords, and Commons give such power to the governor to levy taxes? If the excise was lawful, in what law could it be found? Not bound by the limits of a customs case, De Lavall asked, too, whether he and other colonists were considered "free born subjects of the king?" If not, he asked, "during which king's reign and by which act passed during such king's reign we were made otherwise than free?" These were touchy questions, and the red-faced court found it expedient to refer the case to the "supreme authorities" at New York.[13]

[11] N.-Y. Hist. Soc., Colls., XLV, 14-15.
[12] Ibid.; John Romeyn Brodhead, History of the State of New York, II (New York, 1871), 658.
[13] A. J. F. Van Laer, ed., Minutes of the Court of Albany, Rensselaerswyck and Schenectady, 1680-1685, III (Albany, 1932), 153-155.

With the customs uncollected, government in New York seemed to be grinding to a halt; the colony was losing its income needed for its support to say nothing of the money needed to pay what it owed to the Duke. Brockholls wrote to Andros in London describing how the merchants took advantage of the courts which were too frightened to carry out the deputy's orders. "Here it was Never worse," he declared, a government "wholly over thrown and in the Greatest Confusion and Disorder Possible."[14]

To add to Brockholls's worries, the Long Island towns grew increasingly restless. Several town meetings elected deputies and sent them to an extralegal convention at Huntington in late September 1681 where they consulted about their "Just liberties" and dispatched a petition to the deputy governor and Court of Assizes.[15] Brockholls and his court rejected the petition, reprimanded those who presented it, and sent them home with a warning to "Remaine in Quiett." The town meeting of Oyster Bay was not put off by such treatment and defiantly answered the court: "When the five men which ware the Representatives off longisland have Satisfacktion wee are willing to make payment of whatt Is Justly due as to the publick."[16]

Sometime before Dyer's unsuccessful attempt to collect the customs, Matthias Nicolls, secretary of the governor's council, sailed home to England to have a talk with the Duke. Nicolls was an old settler, having come to New York in 1664, and a very busy officeholder. What his mission was is not clear, but once in England he followed James to Scotland and doubtless explained to him just what the colony's financial problem was. In view of the circumstances in New York, he may very well have pled directly for an assembly.[17]

There can be no doubt that James changed his mind about a New York legislature for financial reasons. The government's recent failure to collect the Duke's customs was the second blow to his revenue within the space of a year or two. Even after James had in 1680 given over East and

---

[14] *Documents of N. Y.,* III, 289n.

[15] Benjamin D. Hicks, ed., *Records of the Towns of North and South Hempstead, Long Island, N. Y.* (Jamaica, 1896-1904), I, 385-386; John Cox, Jr., ed., *Oyster Bay Town Records* (New York, 1916-40), I, 245-246; Street, ed., *Huntington Town Recs.,* I, 315.

[16] N.-Y. Hist. Soc., *Colls.,* XLV, 17, 25; Cox, ed., *Oyster Bay Town Records,* I, 247.

[17] Wait Winthrop to Fitz-John Winthrop, Dec. 19, 1681, in Massachusetts Historical Society, *Collections,* 5th Ser., VIII (Boston, 1882), 424; Brodhead, *Hist. of N. Y.,* II, 335-336.

West New Jersey to proprietors, Berkeley and Carteret, New York had continued to levy customs duties on her neighbors' trade for revenue purposes. The New Jersey people complained, and James, in a surprise move, requested a legal opinion about his customs rights in New Jersey from Sir William Jones, former attorney general, prominent Whig lawyer, and a new member of Parliament in 1680. Shortly after Jones replied that James had no legal right to the customs of New Jersey, the Duke released fully both colonies to their proprietors. The loss to New York was estimated to be about one third of its trade, with, of course, a consequent sharp decline in its revenue. This was not the worst of it. Jones's opinion cast great doubt, even among the Duke's commissioners, upon James's right to charge customs at all, even in New York. And, what is more, if he continued to do so, whether legally or illegally, he would likely drive his colonists across the river to New Jersey where they would be free of his jurisdiction and his taxes.[18] It was doubtless these brute facts and maybe Matthias Nicolls's persuasive arguments which helped convince the Duke that the only way to make New York worth his time and effort was to grant an assembly, on condition, of course, that the people there agreed to support the government and to pay off the arrears accumulated since the disturbances began. His intent, he wrote to Brockholls, was to establish a government with all the "advantages and priviledges" which

241

[18] Sir John Werden to Sir Allen Apsley, Aug. 8, 1681, in *Documents of N. Y.*, III, 291; Mayor of New York to Werden, n.d., *ibid.*, 361. William Blathwayt to Lord Culpeper, Aug. 26, 1680, William Blathwayt Papers, XVII, Colonial Williamsburg, Inc., Williamsburg, Va. (microfilm, Wisconsin State Historical Society Library, Madison). For Sir William Jones's opinion, see George Chalmers, *Political Annals of the Present United Colonies* . . . (London, 1789), 619, 626; and Chalmers, *An Introduction to the History of the Revolt of the American Colonies* . . . (Boston, 1845), I, 150. Extract of a Letter from the Mayor of New York, dated the 13th May 1685, in William Hand Browne, ed., *Archives of Maryland*, V (Baltimore, 1887), 444-445. Why James should neglect his own legal advisers and ask for an opinion from Sir William Jones, ardent Whig and a leader in the drive to exclude James from the throne, is not altogether clear. For a partial explanation, see John E. Pomfret, *The Province of West New Jersey, 1609-1702* . . . (Princeton, 1956), 111-112, and *The Province of East New Jersey, 1609-1702* . . . (Princeton, 1962), 121-123. See also Mrs. Schuyler Van Rensselaer, *History of the City of New York in the Seventeenth Century* (New York, 1909), II, 203. Sir William Jones's stand against taxation without representation made him a champion among American colonists. See his opinion as attorney general respecting Virginia's attempt in 1675 to secure from Charles II a charter which would guarantee Virginians the right to tax themselves, in John Burk, *The History of Virginia* . . . , II (Petersburg, Va., 1822), Appendix, xl-xli. See also Cotton Mather, *Magnalia Christi Americana* . . . (Hartford, 1820), I, 162.

other American plantations enjoy, and "in all other things as nere as may be agreable to the laws of England." He may or may not have been believed when he added: "I seeke the common good and protection of that countrey and the increase of their trade, before my advantages to myselfe in the matter."[19]

III

James's new governor, Colonel Thomas Dongan, a Catholic, arrived in New York in August 1683 carrying instructions to call an assembly.[20] Dongan had not been off the boat very long before the people of Easthampton, probably unaware of the governor's intent, cornered him with a petition, citing fully all the arguments in favor of a colonial legislature. The arrangement made in 1664 between them and Richard Nicolls, they claimed, was a "compact" which they alone had fulfilled. They stressed what Long Islanders had tirelessly repeated: a wish for status equal to that of subjects in other colonies, claiming that their unequal condition deprived them of a fundamental privilege of the "English Nation." In short order the governor issued writs for an election of representatives.[21]

On October 17, 1683, less than two months after Dongan arrived, the first meeting of the New York assembly took place at Fort James. Long Islanders sent six deputies—two from each riding; New York City with Haerlem, four; Esopus (now Kingston) and Albany (including Rensellaerswyck), two each; Staten Island, Schenectady, Pemaquid, and the islands, each one. Eighteen in all, they were elected, directly or indirectly, by the freeholders, although in New York City, Pemaquid, and Schenectady the sheriffs "appointed" the freeholders who in turn elected representatives. As to who these men were, one can be reasonably sure of the identity of only about half of them.[22] Probably a majority were origi-

242

[19] Duke of York to Brockholls, Mar. 28, 1682, in *Documents of N. Y.*, III, 317-318; Werden to Brockholls, Feb. 11, 1682, in *Cal. St. Papers, Col., 1681-1685*, p. 197.

[20] *Documents of N. Y.*, III, 331-334.

[21] Easthampton petition is found in Benjamin F. Thompson, *History of Long Island . . .*, 3d ed. (New York, 1918), III, 637-640; O'Callaghan, *Origin of Representative Assemblies*, 14-17.

[22] For the various methods of electing representatives see the writs issued by Dongan in O'Callaghan, *Origin of Representative Assemblies*, 16-17. For names of some of the delegates see Marius Schoonmaker, *The History of Kingston, New York . . .* (New York, 1888), 75; Van Rensselaer, *Hist. of City of New York*, II, 259; J. W. Thornton, "Ancient Pemaquid: an Historical Review," in Maine Historical Society, *Collections*, V (Portland, 1857), 263-264; A.J.F. Van Laer, ed., *Cor-*

nally Dutch and not English.[23] Yet the Charter of Libertyes is very much an English document, which strongly suggests that the six Long Islanders and the few other Englishmen present took the lead over their Dutch colleagues in the task before them. Far better known than the names of the members is what they accomplished, for the result speaks for itself.

Of primary importance was the Charter of Libertyes and Priviledges which the members drafted as a frame of government protecting in no uncertain terms the colonists' individual liberties, the rights of property, and the right to consent to their laws and taxes. Even a quick reading of the Charter impresses one with the colonists' desire to guarantee for themselves rights English subjects anywhere ought to enjoy. Secondly, the very statement of these rights implied strongly that they had not enjoyed them under the Duke—that they, in fact, had been governed arbitrarily, setting them apart from his Majesty's subjects elsewhere.

243

First of all, the Charter set up a frame or structure, as the preamble stated, for the "better Establishing the Government of this province of New Yorke and that Justice and Right may be Equally done to all persons within the same."[24] Supreme legislative authority, under the King and the Duke of York, was to reside forever in "a Governour, Councell, and the people mett in Generall Assembly." Executive authority was lodged in a governor and council who were to rule "according to the Lawes." The Charter rescaled representation in the assembly by county, varying it from four deputies allowed from the city and county of New York to two from all other counties except Albany which might send three. Again the Charter explicitly stated that once these representatives met with the governor and council, they would forever be "the Supreame and only Legislative power under his Royall Highnesse." Bills approved by the legislature were to become laws and remain in force until vetoed by the Duke or repealed.

The framers of the Charter went out of their way to provide for the protection of individual liberties. The right to vote for representatives was guaranteed to the freeholders and freemen of any corporation, and the Charter defined a freeholder as anyone so understood according to

respondence of Maria Van Rensselaer, 1669-1689 (Albany, 1935), 127; and Edgar A. Werner, *Civil List and Constitutional History of the Colony and State of New York* . . . (Albany, 1889), 67.
    [23] John West to William Penn, Oct. 16, 1683, in Samuel Hazard, ed., *Pennsylvania Archives*, Ser. 1, I (Philadelphia, 1852), 80.
    [24] The Charter can be found in *Colonial Laws of N. Y.*, I, 111-116.

the laws of England—a clear case of equality there. The article guarantee-ing liberty of person, one of the most fundamental rights of Englishmen, came directly from Magna Carta, II, 39 and 40: "THAT Noe freeman shall be taken and imprisoned or be disseized of his Freehold or Libertye or Free Customes or be outlawed or Exiled or any other wayes destroyed nor shall be passed upon adjudged or condemned But by the Lawfull Judgment of his peers and by the Law of this province." From the Petition of Right of 1628 came a paragraph protecting New Yorkers from taxa-tion without representation. Another defended property rights and smacked generally of both Magna Carta and the Petition of Right. Other fundamental rights, such as trial by jury, no excessive bail, and guarantees against quartering troops in private homes in peacetime, were included— every one of which protected the colonists from arbitrary treatment and suggested that under the previous government they had been apprehensive of such rights.

244

Besides personal and property rights, the legislators wrote into the Charter provisions for a number of parliamentary privileges for their legislature, which would have allowed a remarkable degree of legislative independence and fortified it against encroachment from either Duke or governor. Triennial meetings were guaranteed, a right Parliament in England had had trouble securing only a few years earlier and then not honored by the Crown. Representatives were empowered to appoint times of their meeting and to adjourn from time to time and assemble again as they pleased. They were to be sole judges of the qualifications of their own members and could purge their house as they saw fit. Also assembly members and at least three servants each were to be protected from arrest going to and from and during their sessions. It is clear the New Yorkers thought of their legislature as a little Parliament and intended by such privileges to maintain its power, dignity, and prestige.

The longest section in the Charter was devoted to religion, and well it might be since New York contained a heterogeneous population, each part of which maintained its own church. Long Island was predominantly Puritan and Congregational. The Calvinist churches of the Dutch ap-peared throughout most of the colony, particularly in New York and Albany. A number of Germans, Swedes, and other Europeans supported churches of their own. The Duke's official party was divided between Catholics (Dongan and a few others) and the more numerous Anglicans. Considerable time was probably spent by the drafters in agreeing upon a religious policy. The Long Islanders may well have been a little stiff-necked about the whole thing, and although they went along with liberty of conscience for Christians, which was, of course, a practical necessity as it had been earlier, they saw to it that the Charter confirmed the supported churches in their Long Island towns as long as two thirds of each town meeting approved. Moreover, they got written into the Charter power to compel the minor third of each town to contribute to the church's support. Liberty of conscience for Christians, yes, but as far as the English towns of Long Island were concerned, the public worship of God would continue under majority control, and the ministers' salaries would come out of taxes as was the custom in New England. All other Christian churches within the colony the Charter confirmed generally allowing them to continue their privileges.

245

The Charter of Libertyes is strong evidence that a number of New Yorkers had a definite idea of the kind of government colonists three thousand miles from the realm ought to enjoy. But the very liberal aspects of the Charter might lead one to believe that political and constitutional principles were *all* the framers had in mind when they drafted it. It would be wrong to assume that the New Yorkers had inquired into their unequal condition in the empire and drafted a charter to correct it only from a dispassionate love of principle. New Yorkers were made aware of these inequalities by conditions which, they believed, affected their peculiar interests, for such inequalities frequently cost them money, deprived them of economic opportunities they believed they were entitled to, or discriminated against them by denying them rights which other English subjects enjoyed. That New Yorkers should express their discontent about these inequalities in political and constitutional terms is what one would expect. This is the way political and constitutional principles usually evolve or are developed. It must be remembered that English liberties protected property and economic opportunity as well as civil and human rights. Members of the assembly owned property, or they would not have been elected, and they represented people who owned property, people who could not otherwise have voted for them.

New York colonists were well aware that the power to tax is the power to control property, and the Charter placed this power in the hands of the new legislature. But even this guarantee, it seems, was not sufficient for colonists whose property heretofore had been subject to the whim of a proprietor. Before the Duke ever saw the Charter, the lower house had expanded the "Libertyes" of the constitution and tightened the representatives' grip on the taxing power. On the same day the Charter was agreed to, the assembly worded the first revenue act in a style which echoed the House of Commons' similar business. It was the "Representatives" of the province of New York, with the advice and consent of the governor and council, which gave and granted to the Duke the "dutyes and Customes hereafter Specified."[25] Although the Charter granted control over taxes to the legislature as a whole—governor, council, and deputies—the lower house, the freeholders' representatives, at the very outset, asserted the right to originate money bills, just as did the House of Commons.

Each settled area of the colony had its peculiar demands, and no doubt these were seriously considered by the deputies and councilmen who drafted the Charter and enacted laws under it. That the six Long Islanders looked to their own interests and found votes to support them is already evident in the Charter's confirmation of religious privileges. Even better proof of Long Island influence was the new legislature's immediate repeal of a law which had annually taxed Long Islanders' property to defray public charges. The reason given for repeal was that "provision is otherwise made" for the colony's income, and the provision, of course, was the new revenue law which taxed through customs and excise.[26] The shift of part of the burden of taxation from Long Islanders' real estate to the colony's trade certainly suggests that their interest was well served by the assembly.

No doubt there were differences of opinion among those who fashioned the Charter, and debates over its drafting must have reflected several definite points of view. But it must be remembered that it was acceptable to the council as well as the representatives of the freeholders. And Dongan's council was an appointed body containing six individuals whose careers in government hardly demonstrated a devotion to the rights of Englishmen and government by consent. Four of the six, including Brockholls, Dongan continued in office from 1686 to 1688, after the business of the Charter was forgotten; and, when New York joined the Dominion of New England, Edmund Andros appointed to his council five of the six, again including Brockholls.[27] It was against the likes of these, men

[25] Ibid., 116-117.
[26] Ibid., 124. See J. M. Neil, Long Island, 1640-1691: the Defeat of Town Autonomy (unpubl. M.A. thesis, University of Wisconsin, 1963), 95.
[27] O'Callaghan, Origin of Legislative Assemblies, 17; Werner, Civil List, 363-364; Documents of N. Y., III, 543.

246

who willingly accepted arbitrary roles as rulers of New York under both
Dongan and Andros, that Jacob Leisler revolted in 1689 in an attempt,
among other things, to break the oligarchy and distribute the privileges
of office and monopoly more widely, particularly to his own group.[28]
Two years later, when royal Governor Henry Sloughter settled the colony's government after Leisler's Rebellion, he recommended three of the
original six and one of the representatives of the 1683 assembly for seats
on his council as persons of "approved Loyalty and Integrity," which, in
light of the times, meant men who could be trusted to act with the royal
government.[29]

The assembly which drafted the Charter *elected* Matthias Nicolls, now
back from his mission to Scotland, its speaker. Nicolls, a trained lawyer
and very able public servant, was a prerogative man who had come to the
colony in 1664 as secretary to the Royal Commission and supposedly
helped to draft the Duke's Laws the next year. He had been hand-in-glove
with Governors Nicolls, Lovelace, and Andros; in 1680 he was both secretary of the council and a member of the Court of Assizes. He headed
Dongan's council in 1686 but died before Andros drew New York into
the Dominion. Owing to his close relationship with the proprietary government and his score or more years in vital offices, Nicolls was doubtless
the most influential member of the legislature of 1683 next to Dongan.
It is probable that he was more responsible than any other individual for
the form the Charter took.[30]

247

[28] For a recent interpretation of Leisler's Rebellion, see Lawrence H. Leder,
Robert Livingston, 1654-1728, and the Politics of Colonial New York (Chapel Hill,
1961), chap. 4.
[29] Werner, *Civil List*, 363-364; N.-Y. Hist. Soc., *Colls.*, XLV, 9; Sloughter to the
Earl of Nottingham, Mar. 27, 1691, in *Documents of N. Y.*, III, 756.
[30] For pertinent information about Matthias Nicolls, see Thompson, *Hist. of Long
Island*, III, 334-335; Brodhead, *Hist. of N. Y.*, II, 335-336; Leonard W. Labaree in
DAB s.v. "Nicolls, Matthias"; Samuel Maverick to the Earl of Clarendon, Sept. 1,
1663, in N.-Y. Hist. Soc., *Colls.*, II (New York, 1870), 57, and *Colls.*, XLV, 3;
Minutes of the Common Council of the City of New York (New York, 1905), I, 4,
19, 48-49, 66, VIII, 149; Richard B. Morris, ed., *Select Cases of the Mayor's Court of
New York City, 1674-1784* (Washington, 1935), 50; Secretary Nicolls to Colonel
Nicolls, Dec. 31, 1669, in *Documents of N. Y.*, III, 186; Governor Dongan's Report
on the State of the Province, *ibid.*, 417; Van Laer, ed., *Min. of Court of Albany*, III,
27; and Charles M. Andrews, *The Colonial Period of American History*, III (New
Haven, 1937), 116, 117. Andrews asserts that Nicolls was largely responsible for
drafting the Charter of Libertyes. For a different view, see Van Rensselaer, *Hist. of
City of New York*, II, 263-264; and Charles B. Moore, "Laws of 1683—Old Records
and Old Politics," *New York Genealogical and Biographical Record*, XVIII (1887),

John Spragge, who served on Dongan's and later Andros's Dominion council, was appointed clerk of the assembly which drafted the Charter, and during the year the Duke commissioned him secretary of the colony.[31] The failure of Dongan himself to veto the Charter (for reasons to be discussed later) is even surer evidence that those who controlled the government of New York had their own reasons for co-operation.

If such men as these were happy with the Charter, men who were firm supporters of any government, regardless of its principles, it must have been for reasons closely related to their own interests. Or to put it another way: if the Duke of York had decided upon representative government for New York, albeit as a last resort to secure its financial support, then that government ought to represent the interests of those who held positions of power. These men would mold the Charter in such a way that their particular needs might be reflected in the government the Charter established. While the new legislature afforded New York colonists treatment equal to what they believed other colonists and Englishmen at home enjoyed, at the same time it gave a smaller group of insiders a splendid opportunity to conduct the affairs of New York for their own good. The rights of Englishmen and colonial self-interest were peas of the same pod. But the whole scheme would mean little if the Duke failed to go along.

IV

The first step was to get the Charter past Governor Dongan who, as proprietary governor, was responsible for the Duke's interests. Fortunately, this proved to be no problem, and the reason may be that one of the first laws passed by the new legislature presented Dongan with a handsome sum of money, equal to a penny in the pound on all real and personal property belonging to freeholders and inhabitants.[32] Stephen Van Cortlandt of the council, who informally represented the huge Van Rensselaer estate in the new legislature, suggested that his constituents not oppose the move "as it is for the governor," implying that they could not afford

61. Rosalie Fellows Bailey, *The Nicoll Family and Islip Grange* . . . (New York, 1940), 9.

[31] Werner, *Civil List*, 363-364; *Documents of N. Y.*, III, 543; Commission from the Duke of York appointing John Spragge Secretary of New York, Jan. 27, 1683, in *Cal. St. Papers, Col., 1681-1685*, p. 378.

[32] *Colonial Laws of N. Y.*, I, 137-138; *Min. of Common Council of N.Y.C.*, I, 102. See again J. M. Neil, Long Island, 1640-1691, pp. 94-96.

to offend Dongan at this juncture since the Van Rensselaers were seeking at that very time his confirmation of a land claim.[33] The gift to Dongan was probably not considered outright bribery by the colonists but rather a "suitable returne" for the "many great favours" conferred upon them by the governor. Following Dongan's approval, the Charter of Libertyes was published at the City Hall on the last day of October 1683 in the presence of the governor, council, and representatives, the "Inhabitants having notice by sound of Trumpet."[34]

The second step was to obtain the Duke's approval. The Duke had agreed to grant an assembly if the colony would contribute the necessary financial support for the government and make up the arrears. At its first session the assembly levied ample taxes to carry the government's charges, but in doing so it stated that the revenue act was in consideration of the gracious favors extended to the colonists by the Duke—the favors included, of course, his future confirmation of the Charter already drafted, which, they claimed, restored their rights.[35] For granting an assembly the Duke received a sufficient revenue; for granting a sufficient revenue the New Yorkers hoped to secure approval of their very liberal Charter which put control of government in the hands of their legislature. There was a good deal of risk in this transaction on the assembly's part, but Dongan's immediate acceptance of the whole business was certainly encouraging.

Once the Charter became effective and the revenue assured, the scene shifted from the Duke's colony in America to London and the English court. After James's commissioners, who handled his colonial business, made a few suggested amendments respecting customs, James, in October 1684, one year after the drafting of the Charter, signed and sealed it and sent it to the Auditor to be registered with orders to dispatch it to New York.[36]

But this was as far as it got. Suddenly the Charter of Libertyes ran up against obstacles in England the New York colonists had neither knowledge of nor means to combat.

[33] Stephanus Van Cortlandt to Maria Van Rensselaer, Nov. 2, 1683, in Van Laer, ed., *Correspondence of Maria Van Rensselaer*, 132. See also pp. 7, 127.
[34] *Colonial Laws of N. Y.*, I, 137-138; *Min. of Common Council of N.Y.C.*, I, 99.
[35] *Colonial Laws of N. Y.*, I, 116-117.
[36] Sir John Werden to Dongan, Mar. 10, 1684, in *Documents of N. Y.*, III, 341; Duke of York to Dongan, Aug. 26, 1684, in *Cal. St. Papers, Col.*, *1681-1685*, p. 679; Memorandum, Oct. 4, 1684, *ibid.*, p. 695; *The Historical Magazine*, VI (1862), 233.

The final years of Charles II's reign, punctuated by the Exclusion Crisis, intrigue, and several tangled plots, left him bitter and inclined to reaction, even revenge, against Whigs, dissenters, and corporation charters, particularly that of the City of London, whose juries had thwarted his will. In the last three years of his life Charles surrounded himself with an inner group of favorites—Lords Sunderland, Godolphin, Jeffreys, and above all Lady Portsmouth—who, along with M. Paul Barrillon, the French minister, had the King's ear. This knot of advisers, often called the "French party," helped Charles steer an arbitrary course which resulted in more stringent policies toward the major issues of the 1680's. Charles died before the new plans jelled, but sufficient momentum was generated and strongly felt in the destruction of the London charter and in the sharp turn in the direction of colonial policy.[37]

In November and December 1684, three months before the King's death, Charles and the Privy Council did some very serious thinking about the colonies in America. In fact, steps toward reorganization of the colonies had commenced several years earlier with an attack upon the Massachusetts Bay Charter which was finally revoked in October 1684. In order to bring other colonial governments more closely under control of the King, Charles began actions against Maryland, the Carolinas, both New Jerseys, and Delaware; and James even agreed to surrender proprietary New York to the Crown.[38]

A major question before the King and Council, once the way was clear to consolidate New England under one head, was what kind of government it ought to have. Should the colonists retain their legislative assemblies, or should they be told what laws they might have by a governor and council as New Yorkers had been told since 1664? Discussion of this question in the Privy Council explains a great deal about the Stuart concept of empire and how Charles and James thought colonists ought to be governed.

It was Lord Halifax who brought the issue to a head when he spoke

[37] David Ogg, *England in the Reign of Charles II* (Oxford, 1934), II, chap. 17; J. P. Kenyon, *Robert Spencer, Earl of Sunderland, 1641-1702* (London, 1958), chap. 3; *Bishop Burnet's History of His Own Time . . .* (London, 1857), 390-391.

[38] For the attack upon the charter and proprietary colonies, see Philip S. Haffenden, "The Crown and the Colonial Charters, 1675-1688," *William and Mary Quarterly*, 3d Ser., XV (1958), 297-311, 452-466; *Cal. St. Papers, Col., 1681-1685*, passim; Blathwayt Papers, I, IV, and particularly Blathwayt to Governor Effingham, Dec. 9, 1684, in XIV.

very pointedly in defense of colonial assemblies at a Privy Council meeting in early December which both Charles and James attended. M. Barrillon got wind of the whole business—he may have attended the Council meeting—and reported to Louis XIV Halifax's argument. It was unquestionable, said Halifax, that "the same laws under which they live in England ought to be established in a country inhabited by Englishmen." He lectured the Council at length with a variety of reasons why "an absolute government is neither so happy nor so stable as that which is tempered by laws and sets bounds to the authority of the prince." He ended his appeal with the plain declaration "that he could never like to live under a King who should have it in his power to take at pleasure the money out of his pocket." But Halifax was opposed by all who heard him, especially Lord Jeffreys, who replied that when it came to a question of the King's prerogative "whoso capitulateth rebelleth"—that the very attempt to define the function of the sovereign was equivalent to revolution. Ignoring Halifax's appeal, the Privy Council resolved that a governor and council alone should rule New England, "accountable only to his Britannic Majesty." Halifax paid for his boldness, for the Duke of York used the occasion to undermine Charles's confidence in Halifax by arguing that it was dangerous to share secrets of government with a man so critical of the King's prerogative. M. Barrillon reported to Louis that Lady Portsmouth and Sunderland were pleased with Halifax's defeat, and that both agreed their plans, which aimed at eliminating Halifax and persuading the King to assert his prerogative, were going nicely.[39]

The thinking of Charles, James, and the Privy Council about colonial government in late 1684 was certainly inimical to the kind of charter New Yorkers had drafted for themselves. Despite James's agreement to it in October, the Charter had not yet been returned to New York. Moreover, it would not be. Charles died in February 1685 and James, who had even stronger convictions about the prerogative, succeeded him as king.

In the meantime the Lords of Trade had decided to submit the New York Charter to scrutiny, doubtless persuaded to it by the abrupt change in colonial policy and probably by James himself. The re-appraisal resulted in what the scrutinizers called "Observations," and these clearly pointed

---

[39] Barrillon to Louis XIV, Dec. 7, 1684, in Charles James Fox, *A History of the Early Part of the Reign of James the Second* . . . (London, 1808), Appendix, vii-ix; Louis XIV to Barrillon, Dec. 13, 1684, *ibid.*, ix; H. C. Foxcroft, *The Life and Letters of Sir George Saville, Bart., First Marquis of Halifax &C.* . . . (London, 1898), I, 427-429.

out to all who read or heard them the true nature of the Charter: that
it granted to New Yorkers rights and privileges not just equal to those
enjoyed by English subjects in other colonies but doubtless greater than
any other colonists enjoyed. The observers agreed that under the Charter,
inhabitants of New York would be actually governed according to the
laws of England, not merely as close to them as their colonial conditions
might permit. This was a "Priviledge" not granted to any of the King's
colonists in America. Further, the words of the Charter lodging the supreme legislative authority in the governor, council, and the "People" met
in general assembly, represented an innovation and were found in no
other colonial constitution or charter. The observers pointed out several
other differences. The governor was much too dependent upon the council, more so than any other governor in America—which may help to
explain the New York council's willingness to approve the Charter. It
was true that the King was supposed to call Parliament in England at
least once every three years, but to require that the legislature of New
York have triennial meetings would be to put a greater obligation on
that government than "ever agreed to in any other Plantation." Moreover,
such a privilege had been rejected in other places "notwithstanding a
Revenue offered to induce it"—a revealing admission at least. Since the
governor, council, and representatives under the Charter were the supreme
and only legislative power of New York, the observers asked, would not
such power seriously "abridge the Acts of Parliament that may be made
concerning New York?" Doubtless the New Yorkers would have agreed
that this was precisely the case.[40]

The New York Charter, the government it established, and the differences between them and what existed in other colonies were fully and
finally discussed at a meeting of the Lords of Trade on March 3, 1685,
with James II, the Earl of Sunderland, and Lord Godolphin all present.
The conclusion reached was simple and to the point: "His Majesty doth
not think fitt to confirm the same." The government of New York, it
was agreed, would "be assimilated to the Constitution that shall be agreed
on for New England, to which it is adjoining."[41] Two days later James II
wrote to Dongan announcing his accession to the throne and that New

252

York was now a royal colony attached to the Crown. He ordered Dongan to hold the line as it was and to follow former instructions. Tell my subjects, he wrote, that the colony and its affairs are now committed to his Privy Council and they "may shortly expect such a gracious and suitable return by the settlement of fitting privileges and confirmation of their rights as shall bee found most expedient for Our service and the welfare of Our said Province."[42] More than a year later the colonists learned just what James meant, for in May 1686 he wrote fresh instructions to Governor Dongan declaring the New York Charter "disallowed . . . Repealed, determined and made void." The governor and council, however, were to continue the duties and impositions which were levied under the Charter until they decided otherwise upon taxes sufficient to support the government. In addition, all other laws passed by New Yorkers under the short-lived government were to remain in force as long as they were not contrary to the governor's instructions.[43] The colonial assembly met in October 1685, but Dongan found "weighty and important Reasons" for proroguing it to the next year. In September 1686 repeal of the Charter was read to the governor's council, not to the whole legislature, along with Dongan's new commission and instructions. The Charter assembly never met again.[44]

Whether New Yorkers believed they had been tricked is not known. Certainly it must have appeared to some that the Duke permitted an assembly so that it might vote funds on its own terms; and once it had done so, he abolished the legislature and retained the tax laws. But probably the Duke was not quite so bold-facedly disingenuous. The New York Charter ran up against sharp Stuart reaction to Whiggism and republicanism which had its certain effect on imperial policy. In fact, the Charter was scrutinized for the last time at a crucial turning point in colonial policy which hinged on revocation of the Massachusetts Bay Charter and the decision to unite New England under one government. Begun by Charles, the new policy was strenuously pursued by James once on the throne, and the result was the Dominion of New England to which New York was added in 1688. With these plans materializing in London, no wonder James lost sympathy for the New York Charter which granted

---

[42] Ibid., 360-361.
[43] Instructions, ibid., 370; James II's Commission to Dongan, ibid., 378.
[44] Min. of Common Council of N.Y.C., I, 166-167, 180; Minutes of Council of New York, Sept. 14, 1686, in Cal. St. Papers, Col., 1685-1688, p. 242.

his colonists a status not only equal to that of other colonists but surely
even more advantageous. What is more, if the Lords of Trade accurately
understood the Charter, it gave to New Yorkers the same laws Englishmen enjoyed. And all of this was to become fact at the very time the
Crown had decided to rule over half of the American colonies with little
or no regard for the rights of Englishmen, let alone Englishmen's laws.
The Dominion of New England under Andros proved that colonists
enjoyed only the rights a Stuart king wished to give them, and despite
the efforts of New Yorkers, these did not include representative government.

254

It is clear that New York colonists, at least those who drafted the
Charter and approved of it, were vitally interested in the rights of Englishmen as they defined them, and the use of Magna Carta and the Petition
of Right was proof that they knew them pretty well. New Yorkers demanded rights equal to what they believed other colonists enjoyed and
saw no reason why these should not be equal at the same time to those
of Englishmen at home. Although they were colonists of a proprietary
government, they made it known that they did not regard themselves
subordinate or inferior to his Majesty's other subjects anywhere. Their
concept of empire demonstrated a strong belief in equality among its
members as far as government, rights, and opportunities were concerned.
And the idea of equality they hoped to fix with a permanent charter
which would guarantee it to them. This was a bold interpretation of empire in 1683, particularly in view of the fact that the Crown, Parliament,
and Proprietor were only beginning to decide what rights colonists ought
to have, and what they decided was a far cry from what New Yorkers
assumed to be true.

In the eighteenth century most provincial assemblies in defense of
self-interest and colonial rights steadily encroached upon the prerogative
of the Crown and usurped authority from the King's governors. When
in the 1760's Parliament and King challenged these assumptions, Americans were forced to define their ideas and concluded that, as equal members of the Empire, they ought to enjoy equal rights with Englishmen.
Ahead of their time, seventeenth-century New Yorkers tried in one fell-
swoop to do the same thing and set themselves up with the rights of
Englishmen protected through a fundamental law of their own making.
Most Americans did not fully contemplate for almost another century
an empire so firmly based upon the idea of equality.

THE GLORIOUS REVOLUTION AND
THE PATTERN OF IMPERIAL RELATIONSHIPS

L A W R E N C E   H .   L E D E R *

For students of British and British American history, the year 1689 is of major importance. To Englishmen it stands for the Glorious Revolution and the triumph of parliamentary authority over Stuart absolutism; to Americans it signifies the end of one period and the beginning of another, although precisely what ended and what began has never been clearly defined. Certain it is that Americans for a generation reverently referred to "the late happy revolution" as a touchstone in their political arguments. Perhaps our own lack of understanding stems from too close an inspection of the events in each colony with their diverse local experiences and a failure to see in the Glorious Revolution the blending of these events into a common pattern, into the imperial structure of the eighteenth century.[1]

The year 1689 marks the attainment of a level of maturity by certain mainland colonies, and with it the accumulation of problems, tensions and frustrations, all of which were unleashed by William of Orange's invasion of his father-in-law's kingdom. Five of the mainland colonies celebrated their sixtieth anniversaries within a few years of 1689 — Massachusetts, New York, Maryland, Connecticut, and Rhode Island — and only the latter two passed that anniversary peacefully. They could do so because, thanks to the actions of their neighbors, they fell heir to a peaceful solution of their problems.

Massachusetts, New York, and Maryland were not as lucky, and the overthrow of James II triggered the violence built up within the structure of each colony. Indeed, they might well have undergone violent upheavals whether or not James' throne was challenged, for the causes of the rebellions in

---

* Professor Leder is chairman of the Department of History at Louisiana State University in New Orleans.

each of these colonies had little to do with the Glorious
Revolution, although the consequences for each were clearly
shaped by it. Each had accumulated a backlog of perplexing
problems or had posed against it insuperable obstacles. In
all three colonies, those discontented for whatever reason
flocked to the banner of William of Orange, hailed his
revolution as "glorious," and promptly identified their local
causes with his. The only question unanswered was whether
William of Orange, or more properly William III, would
concur in those identifications.

256

Bostonians by 1689 were still battling to determine who
would rule the erstwhile Bible Commonwealth — the old-
line Puritan leadership or the Crown. This was not a religious struggle, but a political one, although all controversies
in New England seemed to be couched in theological terms.
It was a constitutional problem of the nature of the empire.
The Bay Colony, with the passage of years, had become increasingly independent of royal authority; by 1660 it was
practically a self-governing commonwealth. After the restoration of Charles II, this independence was challenged — first
by a royal commission sent in 1664 to compel the colony to
acknowledge the Crown's authority, and second by Edward
Randolph who appeared on the scene in 1676 as a sort of
avenging angel to force conformity to the Navigation Acts.
Neither effort met with much success.

As the conflict between the Crown and the Puritan leadership deepened in the 1680's, many in the colony whose
interests were more commercial than theological began to
ponder the consequences of this dispute. The Bay Colony
depended for its livelihood on trade, and the possible results
of the colony's obstinacy were frightening to the merchants.
They were forced to take action, but their decision came
too late. By the time they had turned to the idea of supporting conversion of Massachusetts to royal status in the
mid 1680's, the Crown had already determined upon more
than mere surrender. The Charter was dissolved, the government assumed by the Crown, and the imperial bureaucracy
began to fashion a new approach to imperial organization.

Massachusetts was remodeled by its absorption into the
Dominion of New England, the elimination of any representative legislature, repression of town meetings, attacks

upon the validity of the colonists' land titles, and introduction under royal protection of the detested Church of England. These measures inflamed the populace and made the merchants rue their decision to surrender to royal authority. The rebellion was ready to move; all that it lacked was the spark. The news of William of Orange's landing at Torbay provided that, and the people of the Bay Colony re-opened the questions of colonial self-government and imperial relationships.

Little similarity existed between the Massachusetts and New York situations even though both were incorporated into the Dominion of New England. The former Dutch territory had different problems: first, the underlying tension created by the transformation of a Dutch trading company outpost into a ducal proprietary and then into a royal colony; second, the imposition of a rigid governmental framework which destroyed the flexibility essential in any growing society by eliminating the channels through which one group can strive peacefully to displace another in the continuing struggle for power.

The quarter century following the English conquest of 1664 was clearly a transitional period in New York. As things English gradually supplanted those of Dutch origins, there were bound to be points of dispute and areas of discontent, and these were accentuated by the economic decline that began in the 1670's and continued throughout the period. Colonial authorities ascribed the depression to various causes and sought to alleviate it by the creation of monopolies and the transmission of appeals to London, but without any noticeable improvement in the colony's economy.

The desire of the proprietor, the Duke of York, heir presumptive to the throne, to make his colony financially self-supporting if not profitable complicated the colony's economic distress. His goal became less attainable by the mid-1680's as Anglo-French hostilities erupted, but the Duke's fiscal hopes continued unabated. He finally authorized a legislative assembly solely in the hope that the people would assume a greater financial share of maintaining the colony.

These rapid alterations and these uncertainties made for a fluid situation in which a group of shrewd politicians gained power, governmental offices, and prestige. But their rise was

257

challenged by another group standing on a slightly lower
rung of the ladder, and these potential aristocrats forced the
Duke's hand in the matter of a legislative assembly. To them,
it offered a logical path for advancement. But once the Duke
of York became James II of England in 1685, he no longer
needed the colony's financial aid. The Assembly was abolished and the colony was incorporated into the Dominion.
Those already in power found themselves confirmed in their
places, but those still seeking recognition were blocked. The
path to preferment no longer lay in local agencies of government, but in the autocratic machinery of the Dominion at
best, or in the complex bureaucracy of Whitehall at worst.

The question in New York was not one of self-government
versus Crown authority, but rather who would rule under
the King's aegis. The repressed ambitions of a number of
New Yorkers determined the leadership of the rebellion
once William of Orange made his fateful decision, and once
the Bostonians took the initiative by shattering the Dominion. New Yorkers hailed the Glorious Revolution and nursed
the hope that the new monarch would extend the rights of
Englishmen to this distant corner of the empire.

Further southward in the proprietary of Maryland another
set of problems evoked different responses. The crucial complaint was the Charter granted to the first proprietor in the
1630's which created a reservoir of anachronistic feudal
privileges. The Council served as the bulwark for protecting
the proprietor's legal rights against the assaults of the Assembly which sought to win the same parliamentary rights for
itself that had been wrested from unwilling English monarchs in the earlier seventeenth century. Moreover, the vast
majority of Protestants resented the extensive power of the
small minority of Catholics, and this gave a unique religious
flavor to the Maryland situation.

Maryland differed from Massachusetts and New York, too,
in that the discontented oftentimes allied themselves with
royal officials and supported royal policy as a tool with which
to bludgeon the proprietor. This alliance, albeit an un-
easy one, would soon prove too powerful for the Baltimores.
When word reached Maryland of the overthrow of James
II, and when the proprietor seemingly failed to provide for
the colony's formal acceptance of the new monarchs, the

rebels immediately seized their opportunity to cast the proprietor into the same role as the deposed King, overthrow proprietary rule, and align themselves fully with the imperial bureaucracy.

The different backgrounds and problems of each colony resulted in sharply different immediate results, but a remarkable uniformity developed as the final revolutionary settlement. The rebel leadership in all three colonies had thrown themselves wholeheartedly behind William's cause and urgently prayed that he accept their particular causes as his own. To each situation the monarch and his bureaucrats reacted differently.

The rebel leaders of Massachusetts divided into two overlapping camps, the merchants and the old oligarchy. The religious group fervently hoped for a restoration of the colony's former charter and favored immediate resumption of the old governmental forms as though the Dominion had been nothing more than a passing nightmare. They prepared indictments of the Governor-General, Sir Edmund Andros, and the other royal officials, and prepared to return them to England for trial.

The merchant leaders of the Bay Colony cooperated halfheartedly with these plans. They also wanted self-government, but not in the hands of the religious oligarchy. They understood the need to accommodate the colony to the plans of the imperial bureaucracy, but they hoped at the same time to moderate those plans and to salvage some control for themselves. When the revolutionary settlement was forged in Whitehall by the same imperial authorities who had earlier created and managed the Dominion, it was a compromise effected along the lines of the merchants' hopes. The colony had a representative legislature, but one elected on property rather than religious qualifications; it had a governor, but one appointed by the Crown rather than elected, and he had a veto power over the election of the council. The monopoly of the righteous had been broken, and the colony would veer in the future more and more toward a mercantile entrepot rather than a Godly City on a Hill.

New York's problems were resolved with much less felicity. The avowed aim of the rebel leaders had been to break the power monopoly held by a handful of the aristocracy. During the rebellion itself, they seized the chance to wreak their vengeance upon former officeholders for past insults, thereby creating bitter animosities which colored New York's politics for decades. The old leadership, temporarily displaced, utilized its contacts with the imperial authorities and insured its eventual return to power. When the new royal Governor, Henry Sloughter, arrived, he immediately imprisoned the rebel leaders, tried them for treason and murder, and executed the two most important, Jacob Leisler and his son-in-law Jacob Milborne, before royal clemency could be sought.

260

The New York rebels met with no sympathy in London because their plans did not mesh with those of the imperial bureaucracy. Unless the old guard leadership in the colonies had opposed or interfered with plans for enhancing royal control, there was no reason to abandon them. In Massachusetts the Puritans had committed this sin and were dropped in favor of the new merchant oligarchy; in New York the old leadership had been complaisant, had gone along with the Dominion, and were now willing to support whatever scheme was concocted in Whitehall. Thus there was no transfer of power in New York to a new class or generation, and the New York rebellion failed.

The only significant accomplishment in New York — and this was not a direct consequence of the rebels' actions — was the re-establishment of a legislative assembly. This would later permit a more conventional challenge to the authority of the old guard and a gradual, peaceful transfer of power. But until that happened, the fight within the colony would be hard, bitter, and long. New York's split into two warring camps permitted the Governors sent from England to use the situation for their personal benefit during the next two decades. Not until Robert Hunter's arrival in 1710 did the colony acquire a Governor strong, honest, and shrewd enough to place the colony's welfare foremost, break with the old patterns, and end the factional bickering.

In Maryland, the consequences of the revolution differed dramatically from that in either Massachusetts or New York. The primary ambition in the Bay Colony had been to restore self-government, in New York to transfer power to a new group, but in Maryland it was to destroy the proprietary power. To accomplish this, the Maryland rebels sought a closer unity with the Crown as the lesser of two evils and, as a consequence, that colony came closest to meeting the desires of the imperial authority. It was the only colony in which the revolution successfully achieved all its goals.

When the Maryland rebels petitioned the Crown to recognize their coup, eliminate proprietary authority, and convert the colony into a royal one, their wishes became royal commands. The Attorney-General of England began proceedings to deprive Baltimore of his charter, and the Crown assumed governmental authority in the colony, leaving the land title vested in the proprietor. Within the colony, the assembly made a clean sweep of the statute books, eliminating objectionable laws, established a more harmonious relationship with the Indians, and attacked the financial practices of the proprietary group. This shift in power resulted from Whitehall's recognition that the rebels' ambitions coincided at the moment with the Crown's policy of centralization. The consequent harmony was short-lived, for in the eighteenth century the Marylanders split with royal authority over financial matters and imperial restrictions, but for the moment the alliance held and the rebels were triumphant.

Out of the maelstrom of revolutions emerged several lessons for imperial administrators. The Dominion was dead as a device to curb the individuality of the colonies, and future schemes for imperial unification met with chilled responses from Whitehall. Colonial cooperation replaced imperial coercion as the established goal in the first half of the eighteenth century. Moreover, the imperial authorities recognized the inadvisability of imposing alien forms upon British subjects. From 1689 on each royal colony — and conversion of colonies to royal status became a fixed principle of policy — had a standard set of governmental institutions: a royal governor, an appointed council, and an elected assembly. This uniformity of institutional organization carried with it the premise that the rights of Englishmen followed the flag to the far corners of the empire. And future arguments over governmental power and imperial relations would be predicated upon the implications of this touchstone of political faith.

Neither of these lessons, of course, affected the substance of bureaucratic thinking about the role and nature of empire. No change took place on this score from the days of Charles II and James II except for agreement that the methods of those monarchs were wrong. The passage of the Navigation Act and the creation by royal warrant of the Board of Trade and Plantations, both in 1696, spelled out imperial policy anew. These were among the most important political and administrative decisions to emerge from the Glorious Revolution because they enhanced royal authority in the colonies at the same time that parliamentary authority within England was greatly expanded.

A dichotomy developed, one which created little difficulty until the 1760's when Parliament sought to correct its oversight by extending its control to the colonies more directly. This would shatter the revolutionary settlement of 1689, it would wrench apart the pattern of empire created by the Glorious Revolution. The events of 1689 defined the rights and relationships of the members of the eighteenth century empire, and Americans had accepted and even revered that definition. Suddenly in the 1760's it was assaulted and the empire as the Americans understood it was in jeopardy.

------

1 This paper was originally delivered at the Mississippi Valley Historical Association meeting in Omaha, May 1962, and has since been revised. It is an attempt to put into perspective the recent scholarship on the political transition in the American colonies between the seventeenth and eighteenth centuries. Among the recent literature is Michael G. Hall's *Edward Randolph and the American Colonies, 1676-1703* (Chapel Hill, 1960) which considers all of the colonies, but places special emphasis on Massachusetts. It supplements two other important studies: Bernard Bailyn's *The New England Merchants in the Seventeenth Century* (Cambridge, 1955) and Viola F. Barnes' *The Dominion of New England* (New Haven, 1923). For the New York story, Jerome R. Reich's *Leisler's Rebellion: A Study of Democracy in New York, 1664-1720* (Chicago, 1953) presents an interpretation which is contradicted by Lawrence H. Leder, *Robert Livingston, 1654-1728, and the Politics of Colonial New York* (Chapel Hill, 1961). Two significant articles on the background of the rebellion in New York are Bernard Mason's "Aspects of the New York Revolt of 1689," *New York History*, XXX (April, 1949), and Lawrence H. Leder's "The Unorthodox Domine: Nicholas Van Rensselaer," *ibid.*, XXXV (April 1954). The Maryland story has received less detailed treatment, but Wesley Frank Craven's *The Southern Colonies in the Seventeenth Century* (Baton Rouge, 1949) summarizes the older scholarship on the origins of John Coode's movement, while Michael G. Kammen's "The Causes of the Maryland Revolution of 1689," *Maryland Historical Magazine*, LV (December 1960) provides a new analysis. David S. Lovejoy's introductory material to the section on "The Glorious Revolution in America: The Crisis of 1689," in Leonard W. Levy and Merrill Peterson,

eds., *Major Crises in American History: Documentary Problems* (2 vols., New York, 1962), I, 3-54, suggests the growing interest in this topic. A new volume of sources on the Glorious Revolution in Massachusetts, New York, and Maryland is Michael G. Hall, Lawrence H. Leder, and Michael G. Kammen, eds., *The Glorious Revolution in America: Documents on the Colonial Crisis of 1689* (Chapel Hill, 1964).

A Quantitative Approach to the Study of the Effects of British Imperial Policy upon Colonial Welfare: Some Preliminary Findings*

HISTORIANS have long debated whether the American colonies on balance benefited or were hindered by British imperial regulation. George Bancroft thought the regulations worked a definite hardship on the colonies. George L. Beer believed these regulations nicely balanced and that the colonies shared in the general advantages. Lawrence Harper, in a now classic article, actually attempted to calculate the cost and found that British policies "placed a heavy burden upon the colonies."[1] Oliver Dickerson wrote that "no case can be made . . . that such laws were economically oppressive,"[2] while Curtis P. Nettels, writing at the same time to the same point, stated: "British policy as it affected the colonies after 1763 was restrictive, injurious, negative."[3] It is quite evident that a difference of opinion exists among reputable colonial historians over this important historical issue.

In this paper an effort is made to meet this issue head on. I shall attempt to measure, relative to a hypothetical alternative, the extent of the burdens and benefits stemming from imperial regulation of the foreign commerce of the thirteen colonies. The main instruments of this regulation were the Navigation Acts, and we shall confine our attention to evaluating the effect of these Acts upon colonial welfare. Various other imperial regulations such as the Rev-

* The paper is a progress report on one aspect of a larger study of the effects of British imperial policy upon colonial welfare. All computations in this study are preliminary and subject to revision. I have benefited from conversations with many persons, especially Douglass C. North and James Shepherd. The former was especially helpful in pointing out several errors in a previous draft. Since I did not take all his advice, he is not responsible for any errors that may remain. J. N. Sharma and James Livingston served ably as my research assistants. The National Science Foundation provided support for the project on which this paper is based. Due to space limitations an appendix explaining how the calculations were made has been deleted, but it is available to the interested reader from the author.

[1] "Mercantilism and the American Revolution," *Canadian Historical Review*, XXIII (Mar. 1942), 3.

[2] *The Navigation Act and the American Revolution* (Philadelphia: University of Pennsylvania Press, 1951), p. 55.

[3] "British Mercantilism and the Economic Development of the Thirteen Colonies," JOURNAL OF ECONOMIC HISTORY, XII, No. 2 (Spring 1952), 114.

enue Acts, enacted after 1764, the modification of naturalization
and land regulations, the interference with colonial issues of paper
money, and the various regulations discouraging manufactures will
not be dealt with in this paper. The assumption is that the direct
effects of these regulations upon the economic welfare of the American colonists were insignificant compared to the effects of the Navigation Acts.[4]

The hypothesis of this paper is that membership in the British
Empire, after 1763, did not impose a significant hardship upon the
American colonies. To test this hypothesis I shall endeavor to bias
the estimates against the hypothesis, thus not attempting to state
what actually would have happened but only that it would not have
amounted to as much as my estimate. The end result will, therefore,
err on the side of overstating the real costs of the Navigation Acts
to the thirteen colonies.

The traditional tools of economic theory will guide the prepara-
tion of these estimates. Two series of estimates will be prepared
where possible: one, an annual average for the period 1763-1772,
based upon official values; the other, for the single year 1770. The
official trade statistics for the year 1770 have been adjusted to make
them more accurate.[5]

I

*Is it legitimate for the historian to consider alternative possibilities to events
which have happened? . . . To say that a thing happened the way it did is
not at all illuminating. We can understand the significance of what did happen
only if we contrast it with what might have happened.*

MORRIS RAPHAEL COHEN[6]

All attempts at measurement require a standard to which the
object being measured is made relative or compared. In the case
of this paper, the colonies either on balance benefited or were bur-
dened by British imperialism, relative to how they would have
fared under some alternative political situation. The problem is to
pick the most probable alternative situation.

[4] The effects of British regulations not considered in this paper will be taken
into account in the larger study now in process.
[5] The statistics on colonial exports have been adjusted in a manner suggested by
James Shepherd and used by him in preparing his balance of payments for the
colonial period. Imports, due to a lack of prices, were adjusted by the Schumpeter-
Gilboy price index.
[6] Quoted in Robert W. Fogel, *Railroads and American Economic Growth* (Baltimore: Johns Hopkins Press, 1964), p. 17.

The only reasonable alternative in this case is to calculate the burdens or benefits of British regulation relative to how the colonies would have fared outside the British Empire but still within a mercantilist world. Considered within this political environment there is little doubt that prior to February 1763, when the Treaty of Paris was signed, the American colonies on balance benefited from membership in the British Empire. Before that date, the colonies were threatened on two sides by two superior colonial powers. C. M. Andrews has pointed out that, before 1763, in addition to remaining within the protection of Great Britain, the American colonies had only one other alternative: domination by another European power, probably France or Spain. Clearly, from a colonial point of view, belonging to the British Empire was superior to membership in any other.[7]

The French and Indian War ended the menace of foreign domination through the cession to Great Britain of Canada by the French and of Florida by Spain.[8] Immediately, thereupon, several Englishmen voiced their fears that these spoils of victory, by removing the foreign threat, made inevitable the independence of the American colonies.[9] Even the French Foreign Minister, Choiseul, lent his voice to this speculation when, soon after the Treaty of Paris, he predicted the eventual coming of the American Revolution. In 1764, Choiseul went so far as to send his agents to America to watch developments.[10] Knollenberg has pointed out that English suspicions of a desire for independence on the part of the colonies do not prove that the suspicions were well founded.[11] They do, however, suggest that an independent America was, by 1763, a distinct possibility; and thereafter the American colonists possessed another alternative to membership in a European empire. This alternative was an independent existence outside the British Empire but still within a mercantilist world.

The alternative situation that I shall employ to calculate the economic effects of the Navigation Acts after 1763 is that of a free

---

[7] JOURNAL OF ECONOMIC HISTORY, XII (1952), 114.
[8] In 1790, nearly 80 per cent of the residents of the United States traced their origin, or that of their ancestors, to the British Isles.
[9] Bernhard Knollenberg, *Origin of the American Revolution: 1759-1766* (New York: Collier Books, 1961), p. 18.
[10] Max Savelle, "The American Balance of Power and European Diplomacy, 1713-78," in Richard B. Morris, ed., *The Era of the American Revolution* (New York: Columbia University Press, 1939), p. 162.
[11] Knollenberg p. 19.

and independent thirteen colonies outside the British Empire. This
new nation would, therefore, be subject to most of the same restrictions hindering foreign nations attempting to carry on commerce
with the eighteenth-century British Empire.[12]

II

*Had the wealth and economic potential of the thirteen Atlantic colonies
depended solely on farming, their growth history might have paralleled that
of many another slowly developing agricultural settlement. However . . . an
indigenous commercial economy developed, unique in colonial history and
conducive to sustained growth.*

GEORGE ROGERS TAYLOR[13]   267

This "unique" commercial economy developed within the British
Empire subject to the rules and regulations of the Navigation Acts.
The American colonies in a sense grew up with the empire, which
after the successful conclusion of the Seven Years' War in February
1763, was the wealthiest, most populous colonial empire in the
world. It included the kingdom of Great Britain and Ireland with
the outlying islands of Europe; trading forts on the Gold Coast of
Africa; enclaves in India, and some minor islands in Asia; Newfoundland, Hudson Bay, Nova Scotia, Quebec, the thirteen American colonies, East Florida, and West Florida on the continent of
North America; the Bahamas, Bermuda, Jamaica, Antigua, Barbados, and the Leeward and Windward groups of minor islands
in the West Indies, as well as the settlement of Belize in Central
America.

The American colonies by 1763 formed the foundation of Great
Britain's Atlantic empire and had become, as a group, England's
most important commercial ally.[14] The basis of this commerce was
a vigorous colonial export trade. The total exports in 1770 amounted
to £3,165,225. Trade with Great Britain and Ireland accounted for
50 per cent of colonial exports. The West Indies trade constituted
another 30 per cent, and commerce with southern Europe and the
Wine Islands, another 17 per cent. Trade with Africa and South
America accounted for most of the residual.

The colonists, of course, used their exports to purchase imports.

---

12 This was certainly the case after the American Revolution.
13 "American Economic Growth Before 1850: An Exploratory Essay," JOURNAL
OF ECONOMIC HISTORY, XXIV, No. 4 (Dec. 1964), 435.
14 B. R. Mitchell, *Abstract of British Historical Statistics* (Cambridge [Engl.]:
University Press, 1962), p. 312.

They were Great Britain's most important customer and Great Britain their most important supplier. The British Isles shipped to the American colonies in 1768 (a year for which a detailed breakdown is available) £2,157,000 worth of goods, or nearly 75 per cent of all colonial imports, which totaled £2,890,000. Of this, £421,000 were British reexports from northern Europe.[15] The West Indies, the other important source of imports, accounted for 20.5 per cent of the colonial imports; southern Europe and the Wine Islands, 2.9 per cent; and Africa, a little less than 2.0 per cent.

The thirteen American colonies carried on this foreign commerce subject to the constraints of a series of laws designed to alter the trade of the British Empire in the interests of the mother country.[16] This commercial system can be viewed as being made up of four types of laws: (1) laws regulating the nationality, crews, and ownership of the vessels in which goods could be shipped; (2) statutes regulating the destination to which certain goods could be shipped; (3) laws designed to encourage specific primary industries via an elaborate system of rebates, drawbacks, import and export bounties, and export taxes; (4) direct prohibition of colonial industries and practices that tended to compete with English industries or to harm a prominent sector of the British economy or even, occasionally, the economy of a British colony.[17] These laws, it should be stressed, did not regulate the American colonies alone, but with occasional local modifications applied equally to the entire British Empire.

The laws regulating the nationality of vessels were designed to insure a monopoly of the carrying trade of the empire to ships of the empire. In the seventeenth and eighteenth centuries the freight factor on goods traded internationally probably averaged at least 20 per cent, and these laws were designed to insure that this revenue stayed within the empire.[18] The Navigation Acts also insured,

[15] The values of imports are the official values f.o.b. Great Britain. For that reason, they are probably approximately 10 to 20 per cent too low. Import figures for 1768 were used because detailed breakdowns for 1770 were unavailable when this paper was written.

[16] Sir William Ashley thought the regulations of English mercantilism were pious formulas nullified in the actual world of commerce by fraud and evasion when they existed contrary to national commercial habits. Studies by Lawrence Harper have indicated that the burden of the Navigation Acts was in fact felt in transatlantic commerce.

[17] The Molasses Act of 1733 was a law enacted in the interest of the British West Indies. This law taxed foreign molasses sufficiently to make the molasses of the British West Indies competitive. The law was, however, widely evaded.

[18] Export commodities shipped to the West Indies were reputed by one source to be worth £ 275,000 when they left the American colonies and £ 500,000 when

to the extent that they were effective, that England would be the entrepôt of the empire and that the distributing trade would be centered in the British Isles.

The commodity clauses of these various regulatory Acts controlled the destination to which certain goods could be shipped. These enumerated commodities generally could be shipped only to England. The original list contained tobacco, sugar, indigo, cotton-wool, ginger, fustic and other dyewoods. Later, naval stores, hemp, rice, molasses, beaver skins, furs, and copper ore were added. The Sugar Act of 1764 added coffee, pimiento, coconuts, whale fins, raw silk, hides and skins, potash and pearl ash to the list. In 1766, the law was amended to prohibit the direct export of any colonial product north of Cape Finisterre.

There were exceptions and compensations to these commodity clauses which benefited the American colonies. Rice, after 1730, could be directly exported south of Cape Finisterre and, after 1764, to South America. Tobacco was given a monopoly in Great Britain, as its local cultivation was prohibited. While the list appears extensive, of the enumerated commodities only tobacco, indigo, copper ore, naval stores, hemp, furs and skins, whale fins, raw silk, and potash and pearl ash were products of the thirteen colonies, and only tobacco, rice, and perhaps indigo and naval stores could be considered major exports of the colonies that later became the United States.

An elaborate series of laws was enacted by the English Parliament to encourage specific industries in the interest of a self-sufficient empire. These included preferential tariffs for certain goods of colonial origin. A distinctive feature of these laws was an elaborate system of rebates and drawbacks to encourage the exports of certain commodities from England and extensive bounties to encourage the production of specific goods for export to Great Britain.

Most enumerated goods benefited from a preferential duty. These goods were thus given a substantial advantage in the markets of the mother country. Goods receiving preferential treatment in-

they arrived in the West Indies. The freight factor is thus over 30 per cent. The return trip saw excess cargo capacity and therefore lower rates. The freight factor on the return trip was but 5 per cent. Herbert C. Bell, "West Indian Trade before the Revolution," *American Historical Review*, XXII, No. 2 (Jan. 1917), 273-74.

cluded cotton-wool, ginger, sugar, molasses, coffee, tobacco, rice, naval stores, pitch, rosin, hemp, masts, whale fins, raw silk, potash and pearl ash, bar and pig iron, and various types of lumber. Certain of these goods also received drawbacks of various amounts upon their reexport from Great Britain. Foreign goods competing in the English market with enumerated colonial commodities were thus subject to a disadvantage from these preferential duties.

A system of bounties was also implemented to encourage the production of specific commodities in the colonies or to allow the British manufacturers to compete with foreign exports in the colonial markets. The production of naval stores, silk, lumber, indigo, and hemp was encouraged in the colonies with bounties. In the mother country the manufacture of linen, gunpowder, silks, and many nonwoolen textiles was encouraged by a bounty to allow these products to compete with similar foreign manufactures in the colonial markets.

Certain of the colonial commodities favored by legislation were given what amounted to a monopoly of the home market of the mother country. The colonial production of tobacco, naval stores, sugar and sugar products was so favored. In the case of tobacco, the major share of total imports was reexported, so the local monopoly proved not a great boon.

In economic terms, the Navigation Acts were designed to insure that the vast bulk of the empire's carrying trade was in ships owned by Englishmen. The design of the commodity clauses was to alter the terms of trade to the disadvantage of the colonists, by making all foreign imports into the colonies, and many colonial exports whose final destination was the Continent, pass through England. The effect was to make colonial imports more expensive and colonial exports less remunerative by increasing the transportation costs of both. Finally, through tariff preferences, bounties, and outright prohibitions, resources were allocated from more efficient uses to less.

I shall approach the problem of assessing the overall effect of the various British regulations of trade by considering their effect on the following aspects of the colonial economy: (1) exports of colonial products; (2) imports into the colonies; (3) colonial foreign commerce; and (4) colonial shipping earnings. An assessment will then be undertaken of compensating benefits arising from

270

membership in the British Empire. Finally, an attempt will be made to strike a balance on the total impact of British imperial policy upon the colonial economy.

III

The enumeration of key colonial exports in various Acts . . . hit at colonial trade both coming and going. The Acts . . . placed a heavy burden upon the colonies.

LAWRENCE HARPER[19]

In spite of the extravagant language that has been used to condemn the system, the grower of enumerated commodities was not enslaved by the legal provisions of enumeration . . . . Enumeration clearly did not hamper the expansion of the tobacco raising business in America . . . . It has been assumed by many writers that enumeration imposed a serious burden upon rice planters. The ascertainable facts do not support this assumption.

OLIVER DICKERSON[20]

271

The export trade between the colonies and the mother country was subjected to regulations which significantly altered its value and composition over what it would have been if the colonies had been independent. The total adjusted value of exports from the American colonies to Great Britain in 1770 was £1,458,000, of which £1,107,000, or 76 per cent, were enumerated goods. Such goods were required to be shipped directly to Great Britain. The largest part, 85.4 per cent, of the enumerated goods was subsequently reexported to northern Europe and thus when competing in these markets bore the burden of an artificial, indirect routing through England to the Continent. The costs of this indirect route took the form of an added transhipment, with the consequent port charges and fees, middlemen's commissions, and what import duties were retained upon reexport. The enumerated goods consumed in England benefited from preferential duties relative to goods of foreign production. A few of these enumerated commodities also were favored with import bounties.

The additional transport costs borne by enumerated goods upon their reexport had the effect of lowering the prices received by the colonial producer and depressing the quantity exported. In economic terms, the world market price as shown in Graph 1 would, in the absence of regulation, be P_2 and exports would be Q_2. The

---

[19] *Canadian Historical Review*, XXIII (1942), 3.
[20] Dickerson, p. 33.

effect of the additional cost of shipment through England is to raise the price to the consumer to P_3. Colonial exports, consequently, are reduced to Q_1. Therefore, both consumers and producers suffer from the enumeration of colonial exports whose final destination is not England.

272

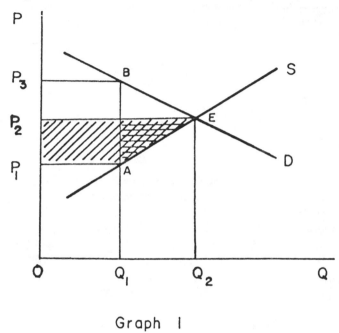

Graph I

The incidence of this burden depends upon the elasticities of supply and demand for the product. The direct cost to the producer as shown in Graph 1 is the unit burden times the quantity produced $(P_2P_1 \cdot Q_1)$.[21] The burden on the reduced output is equal to the return that would be earned on the additional output over what the resources would earn in their next-best alternative. This cost is illustrated by the shaded triangle in Graph 1 and represents the sum of the direct and indirect burdens.

In order to calculate the direct burden borne by the colonial producers of enumerated goods that were reexported from England, we need to know three separate time series. In the case of tobacco, we need to know the world market price in a European port, the

[21] Since most tobacco was exported, exports for all practical purposes equal output or production.

price actually received in the colonies, and the actual reexports of tobacco from England—all three of which are readily available.[22]

The price that would have existed in the colonies in the absence of enumeration can be estimated, given the above information. It was estimated by dividing the observed Amsterdam price of Virginia tobacco before the Revolution by the ratio of Amsterdam to Philadelphia tobacco prices after the Revolution.[23] The postwar ratio of prices reflects the advantages received by the colonists by shipping directly to northern Europe rather than indirectly through England. This procedure provides us with an estimate of the price of tobacco in the colonies (P_2 on Graph 1) had tobacco not been subject to enumeration. The difference between the estimated price (P_2) and the actual price (P_1) is the unit burden suffered by reexported colonial tobacco.

Calculated in this manner, the price of tobacco in 1770 colonial America, had the colonies been independent, would have been over 49 per cent higher than it actually was. The average price for the decade 1763-1772 would have been 34 per cent higher than was actually recorded. These higher prices indicate that tobacco planters suffered a burden on the tobacco they actually grew in 1770 of £262,000 and, for the decade, an average annual burden of £177,000.

The direct burden is only a portion of the total colonial loss due to enumeration. The hypothetical higher tobacco prices would certainly have stimulated an increase in the supply of tobacco. Assuming that a 1 per cent increase in price would generate a 1 per cent increase in supply, the resulting increase in supply would have been about 39,000,000 pounds in 1770, or an annual average of 29,000,000 pounds for the decade.[24] The loss to the colonies of this foregone

273

---

[22] For Philadelphia prices, Anne Bezanson, *et al.*, *Prices and Inflation during the American Revolution: Pennsylvania, 1770-1790* (Philadelphia: University of Pennsylvania Press, 1965). For a European port, Amsterdam prices have been used as found in N. W. Posthumus, *Inquiry into the History of Prices in Holland* (Leiden: E. J. Brill, 1946). For tobacco quantities, see *Historical Statistics of the United States, Colonial Times to 1957* (Washington: U. S. Government Printing Office, 1960), series 230-37, p. 766.

[23] Albert Fishlow, discussion of a paper by Gordon Bjork, "The Weaning of the American Economy: Independence, Market Changes, and Economic Development," JOURNAL OF ECONOMIC HISTORY, XXIV, No. 4 (Dec. 1964), 565.

[24] This amounts to assuming an elasticity of supply of one. This is probably optimistic, since the average exports of tobacco between 1790 and 1793 were 28 per cent greater than the average for the period 1763-72 and 41 per cent greater than for 1770. This suggests on a crude base an elasticity of supply between .8 and .9. Bjork also found that tobacco prices after the Revolution rose sharply.

output is the calculated value of the shaded triangle in Graph 1, which is £64,000 for 1770, or an average of £30,000 for the decade.[25] Thus, the total burden on tobacco amounts to £326,000 for the year 1770, or an average of £207,000 for the period 1763-1772.

The calculation of the encumbrance suffered by rice proceeded in the same manner as the calculation of the burden on tobacco, except that Charleston prices were used instead of Philadelphia prices since South Carolina was the center of colonial rice production. The burden on the price of rice reexports was calculated to be an appreciable 105 per cent. This amounted to £95,000 in 1770, or £110,000 average for the decade 1763-1772.[26]

The indirect loss attributable to the expected increase in rice exports with the increase in price amounted to £25,000 for 1770, or an average of £29,000 for the longer period. In the case of rice, an elasticity of supply of .5 was assumed, due to the limited area of southern marshlands suitable to the cultivation of rice. The whole burden on rice products totaled £120,000 for 1770, or an average of £139,000 for the period 1763-1772.

Tobacco and rice together accounted for the vast bulk of the enumerated products that were reexported and therefore bore most of the burden. If we apply the weighted average of the tobacco and rice burden to the remainder of enumerated reexports, and adjust for the expected increase in supply, we obtain an estimated additional burden of £53,000 for 1770, or an annual average of £35,000 for the ten-year period.

However, to arrive at the total burden on enumerated exports we must allow for the benefits that colonial exports received from preferential duties or bounties. Most enumerated commodities benefited from one or the other: beaver skins, furs, and copper ore appear to be the only exceptions. Enumerated goods consumed in Great Britain amounted to £161,570 in 1770, or an average of £126,716 for the decade. The average preference amounted to 38 per cent of the price of enumerated products consumed in the

274

---

[25] The indirect burden suffered because of the loss of exports is calculated as the unit burden times the increased output that would have been exported, divided by two.

[26] For rice, the prices are to be found in Arthur H. Cole, *Wholesale Commodity Prices in the United States, 1700-1861, Statistical Supplement* (Cambridge: Harvard University Press, 1938). The rice estimate was made on the basis of but one observation in the colonial period (1760). The author considers the rice estimate optimistic.

mother country.[27] Again, assuming an elasticity of supply of one, we find that in the absence of these preferential duties the first-order effects would result in a decline in the amount of these enumerated commodities consumed in England of about £61,000 for 1770, or an average of £48,000 for the decade. The benefit of preferential duties to the colonists is the gain enjoyed by those exports that would have been sent to England in the absence of preferential duties had the colonies been independent (or £38,000 in 1770 and £30,000 average for the decade) plus the gain on the commodities actually sent that would not have been sent to England had the colonies been free. This amounted to £17,000 in 1770, or £9,000 as the annual average between 1763 and 1772. The benefit accruing to the colonies from preferential duties thus totals £55,000 for 1770, or £39,000 for the decade average.

275

TABLE 1
NET BURDEN ON COLONIAL FOREIGN COMMERCE

	1770	1763-1772
Exports		
Tobacco	£ 326,000	£ 207,000
Rice	120,000	139,000
Other	53,000	35,000
Burden	499,000	381,000
Preference	55,000	39,000
Bounty	33,000	35,000
Benefit	88,000	74,000
Imports		
Burden	121,000	144,000
Net burden on foreign commerce	£ 532,000	£ 451,000
	or	or
	$ 2,660,000	$ 2,255,000

In addition to preferential duties, the Crown annually spent large sums in the form of bounties to promote certain industries. The recorded bounties for the year 1770, for instance, totaled £47,344.[28]

---

[27] The average preference was figured from statistics presented in tables 2 and 3, found in Lawrence Harper, "The Burden of the Navigation Acts on the Thirteen Colonies" in Morris, ed., *Era of the American Revolution.*

[28] Recorded bounty payments for the decade 1763-72 averaged:

Indigo	£ 8,065
Naval stores	32,772
Lumber	6,557
Total	£ 47,394

These payments were designed to divert resources from more efficient uses into industries where they were employed less efficiently but where, for political purposes, they were thought better occupied. Thus it was better to obtain naval stores in the American colonies at a higher cost than to rely upon foreign imports. Part of the bounty, therefore, was a payment for the inefficient allocation of colonial resources and was no gain to the colonies.

The calculation of the approximate proportion of these payments that exceeded the amount required to pay the cost of the inefficiency is not difficult. Since in every case Great Britain continued to import substantial amounts of these commodities from foreign as well as colonial sources, the demand for bountied goods from the colonies can reasonably be assumed to have been perfectly elastic. That is, the colonies could have sold as much of these goods in England as they desired without lowering the market price. This is shown in Graph 2 as a horizontal demand schedule (*D*) and *OB* is the market price of the commodity.

The effect of a per-unit bounty is to increase the supply of the commodity; this is shown as an increase in the quantity supplied from Q_1 to Q_2. The net benefit to the colonies of the total bounty (shown on Graph 2 as the area *ABCD*) is the shaded portion of

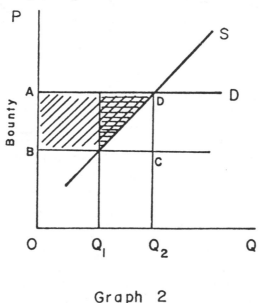

Graph 2

that rectangle. The total bounty payment less the cost of an inefficient use of resources (the unshaded area of the rectangle *ABCD*)
gives the net benefit, which must be less than the bounty payment.
In order to measure the actual benefit derived by the colonies from
the bounty payments we need know only the percentage of the market price represented by the bounty and the elasticity of supply of
the commodity.'

The export of colonial naval stores was stimulated by bounty payments in significant amounts. The average for the decade 1763-1772
totaled £33,000, and for the year 1770 the payment amounted to
£29,803. The average bounty amounted to about 28 per cent of
the price; therefore, assuming an elasticity of supply of one, the
bounty was responsible for roughly 28 per cent of the exports of
naval stores to Great Britain. Figured on this basis, the net gain
to the colonists from the bounty on naval stores was 86 per cent of
the payment.[29] This amounted to an average of £28,000 for the
decade, or £26,000 for the single year 1770.

277

The second largest bounty payments were for the production of
indigo; in 1770 this amounted to £8,732 and for the decade an
average of £8,065.[30] Evidently, the indigo bounty not only stimulated increased output but was responsible for the entire output,
since the production of indigo in the colonies disappeared after independence. Therefore, the net benefits of the indigo bounty are derived by calculating the value of the triangle as shown in Graph 3. In

[29] The gain to the colonists from the bounty payments was figured in the following
manner. The gain is in two parts. First, the unit bounty times the quantity that
would have been produced without the bounty gives us the clear gain. In order to
find that portion of naval stores that would have been produced without the bounty,
we assumed a supply elasticity of one, reckoned the percentage of the price of
naval stores that the bounty represented, and thus easily estimated that portion of
the supply of naval stores for which the bounty was responsible. The other part
would have been produced anyway; on this portion the full amount of the bounty
was clear again. On the part stimulated by the bounty, only one half was gain to
the colonists.

[30] This figure is taken from reports by the London Custom House, retained in
Treasury 38, Vol. 363, Public Record Office, London, as originally stated in Dickerson, p. 28, and is accurate. Lawrence Harper "Navigation Acts" (cited in n.27)
uses a figure of £ 23,086. While the Dickerson figure may possibly exclude some
payments, the Harper figure is calculated on the basis that all indigo received the
bounty, which was not the case. Lewis Grey quotes a British official to the effect
that about seven eighths of the indigo exported from South Carolina received the
bounty, but much less deserved so, being poor in quality. On this basis the payments could have reached as high as £ 20,000 a year. Lewis C. Grey, *A History of
Southern Agriculture* (Washington: Carnegie Institution, 1933), p. 292.

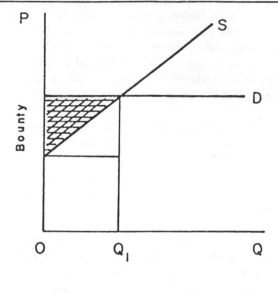

278

Graph 3

the absence of the bounty, no indigo would have been exported. The effect of the bounty was to stimulate an export equal to Q_1. The net gain to the colonists from the indigo bounty at best is equal to, and is probably something less than, one half the amount of the bounty. We estimated that 50 per cent of the bounty payment for indigo was gain for indigo producers—gain they would not have enjoyed if the colonies had been independent. This totaled £4,400 in 1770, or £4,000 as the annual average for the decade.[31]

The importation of colonial lumber into Great Britain also received a bounty which, according to Beer, totaled £6,557 in 1769.[32] Sufficient data are not available to allow a calculation of the gain to the colonists from this payment, but it appears that the bounty was just sufficient to pay the added cost of shipping lumber to England. This payment was necessary to divert lumber from the West Indies, which was the colonies' natural market, and to attract it to England. It appears justifiable to assign the entire payment

[31] Figured on the basis of an annual bounty of about £ 20,000. Then around £ 10,000 would have been the value of the bounty to the producers of indigo.

[32] George Louis Beer, *British Colonial Policy, 1754-1765* (New York: Macmillan, 1907), p. 224.

as the cost of a less efficient use of resources. Nevertheless we shall
include 50 per cent as a net gain to the colonists, which amounts to
£3,300.

The total net gain to the colonies from the bounties paid for
colonial products was, therefore, £33,000 in 1770 and an average
of £35,000 for the decade. Our analysis of the effect of the Navigation Acts on colonial exports has included the burden on exports,
the benefit of the preferential duties, and the net gain from bounty
payments. The sum total of these burdens and benefits is a net
burden upon exports of £411,000 for 1770. The average annual
burden for the decade 1763-1772 was calculated to be £307,000.   *279*

IV

The extra expense of importing competitive European products from Eng-
land acted as a protective wall which permitted increases in English prices.
. . . Those [statistics] which exist tend to confirm . . . the theory that trans-
shipment was costly.

LAWRENCE HARPER[33]

The clauses of the Navigation Acts that sought to make England the chief
source of supply for manufactured goods were not burdensome . . . . There
was a distinct effort to make the British market attractive to colonial pur-
chasers.

OLIVER DICKERSON[34]

British law required that the colonies purchase their East Indian
and European goods in England. The colonies actually purchased
three quarters of their imports from the mother country, of which
about 20 per cent were goods originally manufactured in Europe
or Asia. These imported goods also bore the burden of an indirect
route to the colonies, analogous to that borne by tobacco destined
to be consumed in Europe. This burden was reflected in higher
prices for goods of foreign manufacture in the colonies than otherwise would have been the case.

Our method for calculating the burden borne by colonial imports
of foreign manufactures is similar to the method used to calculate
the cost of enumeration on colonial goods reexported to Europe.
Two commodities, tea and pepper, for which both colonial and
Amsterdam prices are available, were selected as our sample.[35]

---

[33] "Navigation Acts," p. 36.
[34] P. 70.
[35] Colonial prices are to be found in Bezanson and Amsterdam prices in Posthumus.

Tea and pepper accounted for about 16 per cent of the value of foreign goods imported into the colonies through England. The price that would have obtained in the colonies had they been independent was calculated for these goods exactly as in the case of tobacco. The alternative prices of these commodities, according to our estimates, would have averaged 16 per cent lower than they in fact were.[36] Thus, the colonists paid more for their imports of foreign origin than they would have paid had they been independent.

The colonies actually imported foreign goods to the average value of £412,000 for the decade 1763-1772 and of £346,000 for the single year 1770. The burden on the goods, according to our measurement, averaged £66,000 for the decade, or £55,000 for 1770. However, the burden on imports should not be calculated on the basis of foreign goods alone. The burden should also be calculated on goods of English manufacture which were made competitive in the colonial markets by virtue of the artificially increased cost of foreign goods forced to travel an indirect route to the colonies.

The bounty laws benefiting English manufactures which were designed to make English goods competitive with those of foreign manufacture give us a clue to the identity of these English manufactures. If goods of English manufacture required a bounty to compete with similar foreign goods suffering the handicap of an indirect shipment, then the colonists, if independent, would have purchased foreign instead of English goods. Thus, some English goods actually purchased by the colonists would not have been purchased if the colonies had been independent.

Linen was the most important of these goods; the list also included cottons and silks. The colonies thus paid more for most nonwoolen textiles than they would have if they had existed outside the British Empire. The additional monetary loss resulting from the purchase of English rather than foreign goods was calculated to average £73,000 for the decade or £61,000 for 1770 alone.[37] The colonists thus paid a total of £116,000 more in 1770 or £139,000 average for the decade for their imports than they would have if independent. If we assume, for convenience, a price elas-

---

[36] Bjork, JOURNAL OF ECONOMIC HISTORY, XXIV, (1964), 554, found that goods of foreign manufacture (his Index A) fell dramatically in price after the Revolution, while goods in which Britain had a comparative advantage fell little if at all in price (his Index B).

[37] This loss was calculated by taking the percentage unit burden on the price of such imports times their total value.

280

ticity of demand for imports of one, the colonists would have spent the same amount on imports but they would have received more goods for their money.[38]

The results of this preliminary investigation into the effects of the Navigation Acts upon the foreign commerce of the American colonies are found in Table 1. The result is an overall burden for the year 1770 of £532,000, and an average of £451,000 for the decade.

V

The fact is that colonial shipowners suffered, directly, and colonial ship-owners, indirectly, under the Navigation Acts.

LAWRENCE HARPER[39]

Instead of being oppressive the shipping clauses of the Navigation Acts had become an important source of colonial prosperity which was shared by every colony. As a device for launching ships these clauses were more efficient than the fabled beauty of Helen of Troy's face.

OLIVER DICKERSON[40]

The purpose of the various clauses in the Navigation Acts dealing with shipping was to insure that ships built and manned by Englishmen monopolized this aspect of the foreign commerce of the empire. Colonial vessels, for all intents and purposes, were considered English and shared in the benefits of the monopoly.

Calculation of the resultant colonial benefits was hampered by a lack of available data; therefore, the conclusions should be considered tentative. The estimate was constructed in the following manner: an estimated percentage of the total tonnage entering and clearing colonial ports in 1770 that was colonial owned was calculated from the American Inspector General's ledger. Using an estimated average earnings per ton, it was possible to approximate the shipping earnings deriving from the foreign commerce of the American colonies.[41] The total earnings from shipping the foreign commerce of the thirteen colonies were calculated to be £1,228,000, of which 59.4 per cent, or £730,000, was earned by American vessels.

The next question considered was what these earnings would

---

[38] The consumer surplus lost to the colonists because of higher import prices could be easily calculated in the Hotelling-Harberger manner.

[39] *Canadian Historical Review*, XXIII (1942), 4.

[40] P. 32.

[41] See James Shepherd, "Colonial Balance of Payments," p. 691, for a discussion of how this estimate was obtained.

have been had the colonies been independent. Using as a guide what actually did happen between 1789-1792, after the Revolution but before the outbreak of the war in Europe, I found that the colonies' share of the trade carrying their own commerce declined from 59.4 per cent to 53.2 per cent. On this basis, their shipping earnings in 1770 would have been £653,000 instead of £730,000—a difference of £77,000.

However, as we have seen, had the American colonies been independent their volume of foreign commerce would have been greater. Their ships would have carried a portion of the increased amounts of tobacco, rice, and other exports that would have been shipped, as well as a portion of the larger volume of imports.'

282

My calculations suggest that the volume of shipping required to carry this additional output would have amounted to over 53,000 tons. If American vessels had carried the same percentage of this increased volume as they carried of the total volume in 1789, their earnings in 1770 would have increased to over £742,000—or a little more than they in fact were during the late colonial period. The composition of the trade, however, would have been different.[42]

Thus, it seems fruitless to do more with the effect of the Navigation Acts upon shipping earnings until we know more about shipping rates before and after the Revolution. The best guess, at this time, is that on balance the colonial shipping industry neither gained nor lost from the Navigation Acts.

VI

Indeed, the question ought not be separated from the larger one of the savings offered Americans by the military and naval protection of the British.

STUART BRUCHEY[43]

The main obligation of the mother country to its colonies in a mercantilist world was to provide protection. In this area lies the significant benefit to the colonies from membership in an empire. The empire of course also performed certain administrative functions for the colonies from which they benefited.

[42] Colonial vessels probably would have carried relatively less of the trade with the West Indies, assuming that (as happened after the Revolution) they were excluded from the British West Indies. However, they would also presumably have carried relatively more of the transatlantic trade.

[43] *Roots of American Economic Growth* (New York: Harper and Row, 1916), p. 74.

Great Britain in the defense of the empire could provide for the protection of the American colonies at very little additional expense to itself. That is to say that the colonies, if independent, would have had to expend more resources in their own defense than did England, just to maintain the same level of protection. Our estimate of the value of military and naval protection provided by the British to the colonists, since it is based in part upon actual British expenditures, is therefore too low.

The value of British military protection was estimated as follows. Great Britain, before 1762, maintained a standing army in America of 3,000 officers and men. After 1762, the size of this troop complement was increased to 7,500 men.[44] These troops were garrisoned throughout the colonies, including the frontiers where they served as a defensive force against the incursions of hostile Indians. Each man stationed in America cost the mother country an average of £29 a year, or annually a total expense of at least £217,500.[45]

283

The colonists constantly complained about the quality of the "redcoats" as Indian fighters. Furthermore, they believed the larger standing army in the colonies after 1762 was there not primarily to protect them but for other reasons. However, they found after independence that a standing army of at least 5,000 men was required to replace the British.[46] Thus the benefit to the colonies from the British army stationed in America was conservatively worth at least the cost of 5,000 troops, or £145,000.

Another large colonial benefit stemmed from the protection offered colonial shipping by the British navy, which included the Crown's annual tribute to the Barbary powers. The ability of the British navy to protect its merchant ships from the ravages of pirates far surpassed anything a small independent country could provide. This the colonies learned to their sorrow following the Revolution.

The value of such protection would be reflected in the rise in marine insurance rates for cargoes carried by American vessels after independence. Unfortunately, until research in process is completed, I do not have sufficient data to directly calculate the value of the protection of the British navy in this manner.

However, this benefit can be tentatively measured in an indirect

44 Knollenberg, p. 34.
45 Great Britain, *House of Commons Journals*, King George III, Vol. XXXII (1768-1770), sessions no. 1768, 1803.
46 *Historical Statistics*, p. 737.

manner. Insurance rates during the 1760's on the West Indies trade one way averaged about 3.5 per cent of the value of the cargo.[47] Rates to England were higher, averaging 7 per cent. These rates on colonial cargoes existed while colonial vessels were protected by the British navy. During the French and Indian War, the risk of seizure increased the rates to the West Indies, which rose steadily until they reached 23 per cent, while rates to England climbed as high as 28 per cent,[48] indicating the influence of risk upon marine insurance rates.

The colonists upon obtaining their independence lost the protection of the British fleet. Insurance rates, as a result, must have increased over the prerevolutionary levels. To estimate the approximate rise in insurance rates, we calculated the percentage decline in insurance rates for American merchant vessels following the launching in 1797 of three frigates which formed the foundation of the small, eighteenth-century American navy.[49]

The percentage difference between the rates on an unprotected merchant marine and those charged on the merchant fleet safeguarded by our small navy was applied to the insurance rates prevailing before the Revolution. The weighted difference in rates between a barely protected merchant marine and a totally unprotected one was slightly over 50 per cent.

Applying this percentage to existing prerevolutionary rates, it appears that the average cargo insurance rate, if the colonies had been independent, would have been at least 8.7 per cent of the value of the cargo instead of 5.4 per cent, a difference in rates of 2.7 per cent. Figuring this increase in insurance charges on the value of colonial cargoes in 1770 gives a low estimate of the value derived from British naval protection of £103,000. Three ships were not the British navy and could not be expected to provide equal protection. Marine insurance rates thus probably increased more than 2.7 per cent. An estimate that rates doubled does not seem unreasonable and would raise the annual value of naval protection to £206,000.

The estimate of the value of British protection for the American colonies is thus made up of the adjusted cost of the army in the

[47] Harold E. Gillingham, *Marine Insurance Rates in Philadelphia, 1721-1800* (Philadelphia: Patterson & White, 1933), pp. 18, 64.
[48] *Ibid.*
[49] Charles Goldsbourgh, *The United States Naval Chronicle* (Washington, 1824), pp. 109-10.

colonies, £145,000, plus the estimated value of naval protection for the merchant marine of £206,000. The estimated total value of the protection afforded the colonies by their membership in the British Empire was thus calculated to be at least £351,000.

By way of a check upon this estimate, the Government of the United States, during its first nine years under the Constitution, found it necessary to spend annually an average of $2,133,000, or £426,600, for national defense.[50] This included the purchase of arms and stores, the fortification of forts and harbors, and the building and manning of a small navy. In addition, an independent America had to bear the expense of conducting an independent foreign policy. The support of ministers to foreign nations, the cost of negotiating and implementing treaties, the payment of tribute to the Barbary nations, all previously provided for by Great Britain, now had to be borne by the independent colonies. These expenses alone cost the United States, during the last decade of the eighteenth century, annually over £60,000.

After achieving independence, the United States found it necessary to spend annually about £487,000 to provide certain functions of government formerly provided by Great Britain. This suggests that our estimate of £351,000 for the value of British protection to the American colonists is too low. It is doubtful, in the light of history, whether the new nation was able to provide this type of governmental services of equal quality to those furnished by the British. If not, even the £487,000 a year understates the value of governmental services supplied by Great Britain to her American colonies.

285

VII

For reasons which have been explained more fully elsewhere we shall reject Beer's claim that there was no exploitation.

LAWRENCE HARPER[51]

Exploitation . . . by the home country is an economic myth.

OLIVER DICKERSON[52]

My findings with reference to the effect of the Navigation Acts upon the economy of the thirteen colonies indicate a net burden of £532,000, or $2,660,000, in 1770. The average burden for the

---

[50] U.S. Congress, *American State Papers, Finance*, III, 14th Cong., 1st sess., 63, 69.
[51] *Canadian Historical Review*, XXIII (1942) 2.
[52] P. xiv.

decade 1763-1772, based upon official values, was somewhat lower — £451,000, or $2,255,000. These estimates are near the lowest estimates made by Harper and seem to strengthen his case that exploitation did exist.[53]

Considering for a moment only the value of the losses on colonial exports and imports, the per capita annual cost to the colonist of being an Englishman instead of an American was $1.24 in 1770. The average per capita cost for the decade based upon official values was a somewhat lower $1.20. The benefits per capita in 1770

TABLE 2
SUMMARY OF THE RESULTS

	1763-1772	1770
Burdens		
Burden on colonial foreign commerce	£ 451,000 or $ 2,255,000	£ 532,000 or $ 2,660,000
Burden per capita[a]	$ 1.20	$ 1.24
Benefits		
Benefit of British protection	£ 351,000 or $ 1,775,000	£ 351,000 or $ 1,775,000
Benefit per capita	$ .94	$ .82
Balance[b]		
Estimate 1	$ −.26	$ −.42

[a] Population for the decade average was figured to be 1,881,000, and for 1770 to be 2,148,000.
[b] The balance was obtained by subtracting the per capita benefits from the per capita burden.

were figured to be 82 cents, and for the decade 94 cents. Subtracting the benefits from the burdens for 1770 shows a per capita loss of 42 cents. The estimate for the decade shows a smaller loss of 26 cents a person. It is unlikely, because of the nature of the estimating procedures employed, that these losses are too low. Conversely it is not at all improbable, and for the same reasons, that the estimated losses are too high.

Suppose that these findings reflect the true magnitude of the cost

[53] Harper estimated that the burden on tobacco, rice, European goods imported, and the benefits of bounties together added up to a burden of between $2,560,000 and $7,038,000. Harper's estimate of the loss on tobacco and rice really measured the area $(P_1.A.B.P_3)$ in Graph 1 rather than $(P_1.A.E.P_2)$, which is the correct area. However his lower estimate is rather close to ours.

of the Navigation Acts to the thirteen colonies. The relevant question becomes: How important were these losses? Albert Fishlow stated at last year's meetings that he believed that the average per capita income in the 1780's "could not have been much less than $100."[54] George Rogers Taylor, in his presidential address, hazarded a guess that per capita income did not grow very rapidly, if at all, between 1775 and 1840.[55] Therefore, assuming that average per capita income hovered about $100 between 1763 and 1772, what would it have been had the colonies been independent?

The answer is obvious from Table 2: it would not have been much different. The largest estimated loss on this basis is .54 of 1 per cent of per capita income, or 54 cents on a hundred dollars. Suppose for a moment that my estimates are off by 100 per cent; then, in that case the largest burden would be slightly more than 1 per cent of national income. It is difficult to make a convincing case for exploitation out of these results.

ROBERT PAUL THOMAS, *University of Washington*

[54] JOURNAL OF ECONOMIC HISTORY, XXIV (1964), 566.
[55] *Ibid.*, p. 429.

Nieu Amsterdam, about 1673, by Peter Schenk. Courtesy of the New-Y
Historical Society, New York City.

London Merchants, the New York Market, and the Recall of Sir Edmund Andros

By ROBERT C. RITCHIE

A desire for personal gain and the economic needs of the colony led New York's governors to favor the Dutch mercantile community until English interests and imperial interests forced a confrontation. Robert Ritchie is Assistant Professor of History at the University of California, San Diego. His monograph, "The Duke's Province: A Study of Politics and Society in New York, 1664-1691," won the New York State Historical Association Manuscript Award in 1975.

During the second half of the seventeenth century English foreign commerce experienced a sustained growth. A major factor in this boom was the rapid increase of colonial trade. It was inevitable that increasing numbers of English merchants were drawn to this trade and that they would consequently try to gain a stronger voice in shaping Imperial policy. Their influence did not stop in England as they were quite willing to interfere in colonial politics to achieve their goals. A good example of this can be seen in the part taken by London merchants trading to New York in effecting the Duke of York's administration of his colony. Their activities led to the recall of Sir Edmund Andros, an event usually explained by pointing to Andros' inability to increase revenues, or his harsh treatment of Governor Carteret of New Jersey, or other complaints lodged by his enemies. However, there is much to suggest that the recall was engineered by the English merchants fighting for a foothold in New York.[1]

1. Ralph Davis, "English Foreign Trade, 1660-1700," *Economic History Review*, 2nd series, VII (1954-55), 150-166. Two works hint at the role of the merchants: John R. Brodhead, *The History of the State of New York, 1609-1691* (New York,

Prior to the English invasion of 1664 the Dutch West India Company and the independent merchants of New Amsterdam and Albany had developed a widespread trading network, the chief strength of which was its connection with Amsterdam.[2] This great entrepôt supplied them with inexpensive manufactured goods which enabled them to open new markets. First, they developed the Indian trade based on furs, New Netherland's only important export item. Second, they initiated an active commerce with the Chesapeake Bay and New England colonies. The Chesapeake trade brought in tobacco, a very important commodity in their European trade. Even further afield, in the Dutch Caribbean colonies of Surinam and Curaçao, they traded for sugar, dyes, and other exotic goods. They also bought slaves to supply the increasing demand for labor in the tobacco growing areas.[3]

The expanding trade of New Netherland inevitably attracted the attention of English policy makers. After 1660 the Council on Plantations received a series of reports complaining that the cheapness of Dutch goods subverted English trade in New England and in the Chesapeake Bay colonies. It appeared that the Dutch might drive English goods from North America—a threat that neither English merchants nor royal officials concerned with trade and

---

1853), II, 342–43, and Jeanne G. Bloom, "Sir Edmund Andros: A Study in 17th Century Colonial Administration," (unpublished Ph. D. dissertation, Yale University, 1962), 34–9. Brodhead merely mentions the hindering of English merchants, while Bloom states that John Robinson, William Pinhorne and Robert Wooley accused Andros of possible misdeeds. Both also stress the problem of provincial revenues. The latter argument receives primacy in Charles M. Andrews, *The Colonial Period of American History* (New Haven, 1957), III, 100; and Wesley F. Craven, *The Colonies in Transition, 1660–1713* (New York, 1968), 204. Maria van Rensselaer, *History of the City of New York* (New York, 1909), II, 203–05 and Herbert L. Osgood, *The American Colonies in the Seventeenth Century* (New York, 1904, reprinted 1957), II, 130–31, accept the multiple charges made against Andros by John Lewin. Osgood incorrectly identifies Lewin as a London attorney instead of a merchant.

2. On the development of the New Netherland economy see, Van Cleaf Bachman, *Peltries or Plantations: The Economic Policies of the Dutch West India Company in New Netherland, 1623–1639* (Baltimore, Maryland, 1969), and Thomas J. Condon, *New York Beginnings: The Commercial Origins of New Netherland* (New York, 1968).

3. The "Gideon of Amsterdam" arrived just prior to the English conquest with 290 Africans. Amsterdam Notarial Archives, 3189, N. 8, March 23, 1666, Queens College Library, Queens, N.Y. Hereafter cited as Not. Arch.

revenue could afford to ignore.[4] The upshot was the
invasion and conquest of New Netherland in August, 1664,
and the creation of a new proprietary colony for James, the
Duke of York and Albany.

The governors of New York confronted a difficult
dilemma in the years after 1664. Policy demanded that
New York be made part of England's trading sphere, but
there were very few English merchants, and the local Dutch
merchants remained tied to established trade patterns. Their
relatives, friends, partners, and affection for their homeland
kept them oriented towards the Netherlands. To disrupt
this pattern meant stopping the flow of manufactured
goods to the colonists. Should this occur, the disorders
that might follow among the overwhelmingly Dutch
population would endanger English control. The surrender
agreement recognized these problems. The Dutch were
permitted to continue their trade with the Netherlands for
six months.[5] Even the Dutch West India Company was
allowed to retain all of its property and the power to collect
customs on goods shipped from the Netherlands. It was
expected that these privileges would soon be ended as
English merchants entered the market.

Unfortunately, English merchants were not immediately
attracted to the New York market, which meant that the
first English governors, unwilling to be dominated by
Boston, were forced to rely on the Dutch mercantile
community.[6] Two other factors furthered this alliance.
First, New York was the base for the only English garrison
in North America, but the inefficient English bureaucracy
did not provide dependable support, and in order to meet
the garrison's expenses the governors had to rely on local

291

4. A typical anti-New Netherland polemic is Samuel Maverick's letter to the Earl
of Clarendon, n.d., (probably winter 1661–62), New-York Historical Society
Collections (1869), 19–22.

5. "Articles of Capitulation" in Edmund B. O'Callaghan and Berthold Fernow,
eds., *Documents Relative to the Colonial History of the State of New York* (Albany,
New York, 1856–87), II, 250–53. Hereafter cited as *N.Y. Col. Docs.*

6. The merchants' lack of interest was probably a result of the depression accompanying the second Anglo-Dutch war and the lack of contacts with New York.
For the war see Charles Wilson, *Power and Profit: A Study of England and the
Dutch Wars* (London, 1958), 90–126. Complaints about the slump in New York were
widespread. See, for example, Nicolas van Ruyven to Peter Stuyvesant, August 7,
1666, and Richard Nicolls to Lord Arlington, November 12, 1667, *N.Y. Col. Docs.*,
II, 472–73; III, 167–68.

taxation.[7] Customs were the most lucrative local tax and customs were dependent on trade. Secondly, the governors appointed by the Duke of York were all career army officers. Notoriously impecunious as a group, they naturally sought to further their fortunes while in office. Before Edmund Andros arrived in New York in 1674, these factors had already established a pattern of relationships which, because of its profound influence upon Andros' career, must be examined in more detail in the administrations of his predecessors, Richard Nicolls (1664–1668) and Francis Lovelace (1668–1673).

Confronted with the depression caused by the second Anglo-Dutch war, Richard Nicolls had a difficult course to chart in order to revive prosperity. In his letters he insisted that the English government send goods to New York immediately, and he warned Secretary of State Lord Arlington that if the government failed to do so, Dutch vessels would continue to supply the needs of planters from Long Island to the Delaware River. Such an event would throw away the fruits of England's conquest. Nicolls' pleas for English goods yielded a small return. During his four years in office only one ship bound for New York is recorded in the London port books.[8]

While pleading with England, Nicolls turned to the local merchants in a way that reflected a lack of faith in the government's willingness to help him. He first made many of the Dutch merchants denizens, a status that allowed them to trade in areas under English control. In the crucial area of trade with Amsterdam, Nicolls decided to stand by the Dutch merchants. He permitted Cornelius Steenwick, a prominent merchant, to bring cargoes from Holland for

292

7. The Treasury only agreed to pay £1,000 a year in 1674. William Shaw, ed., *Calendar of Treasury Books Preserved in the Public Record Office, 1660–1718* (London, 1904–57), III, Part I, 59, 81, 465. This was clearly insufficient as salaries alone totalled £2,062 in 1674. *N.Y. Col. Docs.*, II, 220. The only disbursements from this grant that are recorded were military supplies worth £905. Colonial Office Group, Class 324, Piece 4, fol. 45, Public Record Office. Hereafter cited as CO. and PRO.

8. Nicolls to Arlington, October, 1664, *N.Y. Col. Docs.*, III, 68–70. Nicolls demanded goods be sent by May, 1665. The nature of the port books and the loss of so many other customs records does not preclude other ships from sailing to New York. But for the period December 1665 to September 1668 only the "William and Mary" is registered as sailing to New York. Exchequer, Class 190, Pieces 50/5 and 52/1, PRO. Hereafter cited as E190.

one year. His reason was that trade "is the only means of supporting the Government, and the welfare of the inhabitants."[9] Nicolls also worked to weaken the trading rights of the Dutch West India Company—an action designed to please the local mercantile community. He thus refused to enforce the company's six-months grace period on customs by allowing the *Unity* of Amsterdam, homeward bound with a load of tobacco, to leave port without paying the company.[10] Ultimately, the surrender article relating to the Dutch West India Company was abrogated and the company lost its rights to collect customs, to trade and, finally, all of its property in New York.[11] Thus encouraged, the magistrates of New York City, who were mostly independent merchants, promised the Duke of York "great revenues" from trade.[12]

As English trade lagged, Nicolls went much further in his support of the Dutch. He proposed a plan to circumvent the newly-enacted Navigation Acts. Under his plan, four to six Dutch ships would sail directly from New York to the Netherlands each year, thereby avoiding the new regulations. Peter Stuyvesant, on behalf of the New York community, supplemented Nicolls' letter with petitions to York and King Charles.[13] He requested special treatment on the grounds that the merchants of New York would be ruined if their trade with relatives and friends in the Netherlands suddenly ended. If they were denied their request, the Indian trade would suffer from the lack of proper trade items leading to a possible take-over of the

9. *Colonial Records, General Entries, 1664-65.* New York State Library *Bulletin,* History, No. 2 (Albany, 1899), 183-85. Permits to Steenwick and his partners December 13, 1664, *Ibid.,* 137, 148-49.

10. Order, October 25, 1664, *Ibid.,* 122-23. Nicolls kept the English customs collector from collecting customs also and in this order he admits that it is against the Navigation Acts to do so but justifies it on the basis that it is necessary to encourage the people.

11. Order on the payment of duties, November 26, 1664, *Ibid.,* 133-34. The property of the company was seized December 24, 1664, *Ibid.,* 140-41. On December 29 all magistrates were ordered to turn in a true account of the company's property, *Ibid.,* 142-43.

12. Magistrates of the city of New York to the Duke of York, November 22, 1664, Berthold Fernow, ed., *The Records of New Amsterdam from 1652-1674* (New York, 1897), V, 160-61.

13. Nicolls to Lord Arlington, April 9, 1666, *N.Y. Col. Docs.,* III, 113-15. Stuyvesant to York, n.d., *Ibid.,* 163-64. Stuyvesant to King Charles, October 23, 1667, *Ibid.,* 164-65.

fur trade by the French. The Dutch also needed a supply of their own agricultural implements in order to continue farming because Dutch and English agricultural practices were so different. Stuyvesant concluded by stating that without a minimum of two supply ships annually, the Dutch would be forced to abandon New York.

Perhaps alarmed about the possible advantages to the French and the depopulation of New York, the Council for Trade supported the petitions. In 1667 it recommended that three ships be permitted to sail between the Netherlands and New York annually for seven years. The Privy Council then issued an Order in Council to this effect on October 23, 1667. This concession proved short-lived, however. The end of the second Anglo-Dutch war (and the subsequent trade revival) in 1668 reinforced the hostility of the English customs farmers who wanted to end this special privilege. The Council for Trade, concerned because English merchants were withdrawing from North America on account of competition from cheap Dutch goods, agreed. The Order of 1667 gave way before a new one prohibiting trade between the Netherlands and New York after November, 1668.[14]

This created immediate problems for the New York Dutch merchants. Under the 1667 Order, seventeen merchants had gone to Amsterdam to trade. Cornelius Steenwick and Peter Stuyvesant were particularly hard hit. They had apparently cornered the market in the proprietary permits required and had sold them to other Dutchmen. The new order invalidated the permits, thus severely injuring the sellers and buyers alike. The Dutch merchants promptly appealed to King Charles, requesting that the blow be softened by a grant of one last shipment to New York City. The King approved the petition as an act of kindness towards his new subjects.[15]

14. Report of the Council, October 17, 1667, *Ibid.*, III, 165-66. Order in Council, October 23, 1667, *Ibid.*, 166-67. Council of Trade to the King, n.d., *Ibid.*, 175-76. Order in Council, November 18, 1668, *Ibid.*, 177-78.

15. Contract February 27, 1668, Not. Arch. 2784, N. 492, 494. Petition, December 11, 1668, *N.Y. Col. Docs.*, 178-79. Order in Council granting this request, December 11, 1668, *Ibid.*, 179. Some of the merchants were left stranded. On March 14, 1669 ten New York merchants requested Jacques Cousseau of New York City, then in England, to approach York or the King to allow them to go home on a New England ship. Not. Arch. 2788, N. 507, 376-77.

The merchants continued their attempts to gain special privileges. In 1669 Governor Francis Lovelace sent the Reverend Aegidius Luyck, his factor, to England to consult with his friends about legalizing New York's trade with the Netherlands. Luyck failed to discover any means of carrying on a direct legal commerce. This reduced the Dutch traders to the ruse of ordering their captains to go from port to port in England in an effort to get clearances to sail to New York without paying statutory duties. Some preferred smuggling to the stopover in England and the duties usually extracted.[16] But most decided to conform to the new situation and make the best of it.

295

Though failing to gain special privileges in England the governors of New York aided the merchants of New York City in achieving another major goal. Control over the economy of the province was of prime importance to the merchants, and the structure of New York politics facilitated their ambitions. The Duke's Laws of 1665 created a highly centralized, authoritarian government with no popularly-elected assembly as existed in the other colonies. Power lay with a governor who administered the colony with the aid of a council of his own appointees.[17] Influence with the governor was crucial, and the merchants were able to acquire it for two reasons already mentioned—the greed of the governors and the necessity they were under of supplying the needs of the garrison.

Francis Lovelace's regime provides a good case in point. He arrived in 1668 determined to enrich himself, and had before him the example of his predecessor, Nicolls, who returned home after four years in New York with debts of over £8000.[18] To avoid a similar fate Lovelace brought with him his brother Thomas, a merchant, on the premise that to fully profit from his office the experience of a commercial man was essential. The brother bought land cheaply on Staten Island, the Delaware River, Esopus, and New York City, and used Lovelace's position to encourage

16. Not. Arch. 3493, N. 289. *Ibid.*, N. 336. In one instance William Darvall unloaded part of his cargo at Shelter Island before proceeding to New York City. *Ibid.*, 3284, N. 92.

17. Craven, *Colonies in Transition*, 73–75.

18. Record Book of the Duke of York's Commissioners of Revenue, Add. MS. 7091, foll. 40–41, Cambridge University Library, Cambridge.

immigrants from Bermuda to settle on his property.[19] They entered trade, for which they built a ship named *Good Fame*, shortly after arriving in New York. They then sold shares in the *Good Fame* and used the proceeds to acquire shares in at least two other vessels, the *Duke of York* and the *Hopewell*. Thus equipped, they entered into agreements with various New York Dutch merchants who served as their factors in a large trade to Amsterdam.[20] Eschewing trade with England, Lovelace thus tied his fortunes closely to those of the local merchant community.

Lovelace revealed a particular partiality towards the Dutch. Whereas Nicolls had never put a Dutchman on the council, Lovelace appointed two of the old merchant elite, Cornelius Steenwick and Cornelius van Ruyven. Perhaps he thought that the passage of time since the conquest allowed overtures to the Dutch community that Nicolls had feared to make. Whatever the reason, though he kept the Dutch in a minority on the council and on the aldermanic board of New York City, Lovelace did allow them an influence not granted earlier.[21]

English officeholders were drawn from two groups— one consisted of military officers, friends, relatives and officials who came over in the entourage of the governors;

19. Testimony of Thomas Lovelace (1674), Rawlinson A, 173, foll. 185-86, Bodleian Library, Oxford University, Oxford. Fernow, *Records of New Amsterdam*, VI, 286-88. Samuel Hazard, et al., eds., *Pennsylvania Archives* (Harrisburg, Pa., 1852-1949), 2nd Ser. V, 651-52. The plans for the immigrants were discussed by Lovelace in a letter to the Governor of Bermuda, June 3, 1669, *N.Y.Col. Docs.*, XIII, 424-26.

20. Samuel Maverick reported to Richard Nicolls that the ship was costly to build, October 15, 1669, *Ibid.*, III, 185. Lovelace owned part of one vessel with Thomas Delaval, the customs collector, and the latter's son-in-law William Darvall, a prominent merchant. Lovelace to Richard Nicolls, May 19, 1672, Coventry Papers, LXXVI, fol. 257, Longleat House, Wiltshire. Dutch merchants in Amsterdam and Leyden were his partners in the other venture. Not. Arch. 3502, N. 320. For some of Lovelace's trade activities see New York Colonial MSS. XXII, foll. 115, 116; XXIV, foll. 115, 127, 169, 102. New York State Library, Albany. Hereafter cited as N.Y. Col. MSS. Not. Arch., 3504, pt. 1, N. 339; 3496, pt. 2, N. 295; 3206, N. 21, N. 22; 3207, N. 25. Isaac Bedloo was commissary to the garrison besides being Lovelace's factor. As such he was given access to the public treasury to such an extent his accounts became inextricably mixed with those of Lovelace and the government. See *N.Y. Col. Docs.*, II, 651, N.Y. Col. MSS, XXII, foll. 115, 116, and Orders, Warrants, Letters, MSS, II, foll. 233, 234. New York State Library, Albany. Hereafter cited as OWL.

21. The composition of the city government was compiled from the annual October elections in Fernow, *Records of New Amsterdam*, V, VI, *passim*. For the councillors see S.C. Hutchins, *Civil List and Forms of Government of the Colony and State of New York* (Albany 1869), 17-18.

the other was comprised of the few English merchants in the city. Many of the first group, such as Thomas Lovelace or the collector, Thomas Delaval, entered trade. Here their interests linked with those of the English merchants. A common bond linking these groups to the Dutch was a desire to strengthen the position of New York City in the economy of the colony. And Lovelace's interest was to help them toward this goal.

Two examples show the success of the merchants. First, Lovelace aided the merchants in their victory over their rivals in Albany. The Albany "handlaers," or fur traders, had a monopoly over the vital fur trade and they marketed directly in the Netherlands, bypassing New York City whenever they could. Frederick Philipse petitioned against Albany's monopoly on behalf of the city's merchants. He argued that if the monopoly continued, the merchants of Albany would dominate the trade of the entire Hudson River Valley and thus impoverish the main city of the colony. Lovelace responded to the petition on June 27, 1670, when he issued an order that required goods going upriver to be loaded and to pay customs in New York City before continuing in vessels owned by freemen of the city. In the same year, Lovelace also banned overland trade with New England, thus plugging the only remaining loophole. The Albany merchants retained the fur trade, but they had to do their exporting and importing through New York City.[22]

The city merchants won their second victory by gaining a monopoly over the export of wheat and wheat products. These commodities were significant items in the growing trade with the tobacco and sugar colonies of the South and West Indies. The city merchants moved to gain control over these vital exports in 1671 when the wheat harvest failed. Crops had failed before, in 1666 and 1667, at which time Nicolls had imposed an embargo on the export of wheat and its products.[23] In 1671, however, the city fathers called

297

22. July 7, 1668, Fernow, *Records of New Amsterdam*, VI, 138–41. Victor H. Paltsits, ed., *Minutes of the Executive Council: Administration of Francis Lovelace, 1668–1673* (Albany, 1910), II, 522–23. *Ibid.*, I, 56–58. For the importance of this overland trade to New England fur traders see Bernard Bailyn, *The New England Merchants in the Seventeenth Century* (Cambridge, Mass., 1955), 60.

23. Jeremias van Rensselaer to Jan Baptist van Rensselaer, October 25, 1666, A.J.F.

the bakers before them. Asked if it was feasible to export grain, the bakers replied that if exports were allowed there would be no bread in the city by summer. They requested an embargo on wheat grain but not on flour or breadstuffs. Their reason was humane: to protect the livelihood of the coopers and other "mechanics" in the city who processed wheat or made containers for shipment. The mayor and aldermen reported their concern to the governor and the council who responded by banning the shipment of wheat while allowing the export of bread and flour only if it was done from the city.[24] Protests against this order were

van Laer, ed. and trans., *Correspondence of Jeremias van Rensselaer, 1651-1674* (New York, 1932), 387-89; same to same, June 16, 1670, *Ibid.*, 422-25.

24. Testimony of the bakers, March 7, 1671, Fernow, *Records of New Amsterdam*, VI, 286-88. Order barring export of grain, Paltsits, *Minutes of the Executive Council*, I, 80, 519-20.

Sir Edmund Andros. From Winsor, Narrative and Critical History of America.

immediate but unavailing as the outlying communities bitterly objected to a policy which gave special privileges to the city merchants. A normal harvest in 1672 spurred the protesters and brought about limited grain exports. An exception to the rules for wheat sales gave "strangers" in New York City a right to purchase wheat at six pence below set rates, thus encouraging the export trade. The city advantage reappeared, however, when the harvest failed in 1673 and the 1671 orders were again placed in effect.[25]

Lovelace's actions relative to the fur and wheat trades worked to ensure the position of the New York City merchants at the expense of other communities in the colony. His operating premise seemed to be that what was good for New York City and for his own pocket was good for New York.

Events beyond the governor's control soon ended his happy situation. The old trade rivalry between England and Holland intensified once again and led to open warfare. A Dutch naval squadron, sailing home in 1673 after a successful raid in Virginia, stopped to take on water at Sandy Hook. Lovelace was away in Connecticut at the time, and the Dutch residents welcomed the opportunity to return to the shelter of their "Patria." They "capitulated" on the grounds that the city had no defences against the squadron. On his return Lovelace became a prisoner before being sent back to England in disgrace.[26]

The war also damaged Lovelace's trading interests and those of Steenwick, Philipse and Delaval. Their ships in

25. A typical complaint against the new policy was made by Jeremias van Rensselaer to his brother, Richard, August 25, 1671, Laer, *Rensselaer Correspondence*, 439–42. Not only were the protests ignored, but the embargo was continued because more and more ships were coming to the city for cargoes of bread and flour which were selling at high prices. *Ibid.*, 520–21. For the orders on wheat exports see Paltsits, *Minutes of the Executive Council*, I, 88–91, "Colonial Records of the State, 1664–1673." Appendix G in the New York State Historian's *Annual Report* (1896), 175–80, and finally the order of April 29, 1673, Paltsits, *Minutes of the Executive Council*, I, 175–77. At about the same time the monopoly was strengthened by an edict restricting the inspection of all wheat exports to New York City. *Ibid.*, 184–87. At the same meeting of the council it was noted that Lovelace's own wheat had sold well in Boston.

26. C. De Waard, ed., *De Zeewusche Expenditie naar De West Onder Cornelis Eventsen Den Jonge, 1672–1674* ('S-Gravenhage, 1928), 38–40. The Dutch farmers who first contacted Evertsen complained of the misuse of taxes and non-payment of government debts. *N.Y. Col. Docs.*, II, 578–79. See also John R. Brodhead, *The History of the State of New York, 1609–1691* (New York, 1853), II, 204–08.

Amsterdam were quickly confiscated and the Dutch government in New York seized Lovelace's and Delaval's estates.[27] The irony, undoubtedly lost on those with confiscated property, was that neither England nor the Netherlands really desired another war, and peace was quickly restored. After approximately one year, New Netherland was returned to English control.

300   The war's end brought Sir Edmund Andros to New York. An army officer like his predecessors, he was just beginning his long career as an imperial bureaucrat. Initially Andros kept the Dutch out of his government. However, he later reversed himself and brought Dutchmen into the council. Ultimately, Frederick Philipse and Stephanus van Cortlandt, two members of the mercantile elite, were to become his chief allies. Both had close ties to a network of influential Dutch families, thus tying Andros to the nascent New York establishment.[28] Like his predecessors, Andros inhibited efforts by settlers from Long Island and the Hudson and Delaware River valleys to share power and profit with New York City.

While Andros did not engage in commerce so openly as Lovelace, he too used his position to enhance his fortune. His purchases of land in the Delaware River Valley were a matter of public record, but his mercantile affairs are shrouded in controversy. What can be ascertained is that he had a sloop, the *Mary*, which engaged in a coastal trade as far afield as Virginia. On one occasion he also sent a cargo to England. The other records of his activities derive mainly from his detractors, who charged him with

27. Francis Lovelace to Governor John Winthrop Jr., June 26, 1672, Paltsits, *Minutes of the Executive Council*, II, 739. William Darvall to Robert Wooley, September 20, 1673, *N.Y. Col. Docs.*, III, 206. Darvall reported that the English in New York had to swear on oath to the Dutch government or else suffer confiscation. Thomas Lovelace's testimony, Rawlinson A, 173, fol. 186, Bodleian Library, Oxford University. Petition of Delaval, Additional MS, 18, 206, foll. 61–62, British Museum. Hereafter cited as BM addl. MS. Cornelius Darvall, brother of William, made a futile attempt to gain a return of his family's seized goods. Not. Arch., 1523, N. 606.

28. During Andros' administration the council consisted of officials and New York City merchants. Hutchins, *Civil List*, 18. Cortlandt and Philipse were the only Dutch members of the council, but their influence on Andros was notorious. Jasper Dankaerts wrote that "he (Philipse) and the governor are one." Burleigh J. Bartlett and J. Franklin Jameson, eds., *Journal of Jasper Dankaerts, 1678–1680* (New York, 1913), 238.

running a retail store of his own and engaging in a foreign trade with Amsterdam through Frederick Philipse and Stephanus van Cortlandt. As will be shown, Philipse and Cortlandt received special privileges in trade that indicate a unique relationship with Andros. In light of this evidence, and with what else is known, it would not be unreasonable to believe the detractors.[29]

Andros followed his predecessors in advancing the interests of the New York City merchants. He wrote to York requesting a direct legal trade with Amsterdam or else permission for New York vessels to go to outports where they could be cleared without landing their goods or paying customs. York's secretary, Sir John Werden, told him to drop both ideas as neither the Navigation Acts nor the customs collectors would permit such schemes.[30]

301

In New York, Andros was unhampered by higher authorities in regulating the local economy. He made New York City the sole port of entry for imports, returned Albany to its position as merely a fur trading base, confined the packing and bolting of flour and the export of wheat products to the city, and hampered the entry of European goods from Boston into New York. Once again the merchants triumphed over their fellow colonists.[31]

Heartened by Andros' support, the mercantile establishment resumed its familiar trading patterns after the war. A regular shuttle of two to four ships sailed to and from Amsterdam with stops at Dover or Falmouth coming and going to pay duties and meet English trade regulations. Frederick Philipse, the single most active merchant, used Falmouth almost exclusively. Because Falmouth was a seldom-used outport, one assumes he found amenable

---

29. OWL, III, foll. 290, 293, *N.Y. Col. Docs.*, XII, 545–56. 571–72. N.Y. Col. MSS, XXVI, fol. 43; XXVII, fol. 6; XXVIII, fol. 89; XXIX, fol. 69. Jameson, *Journal of Jasper Dankaerts*, 244–45. "Mr. Lewin's Report on the Government of New York", *N.Y. Col. Docs.*, III, 302–08.

30. Werden to Andros, January 28, 1676, *N.Y. Col. Docs.*, III, 236–38. Werden also dissuaded Andros from allowing Margareta Philipse (wife of Frederick) from buying a Dutch ship and engaging in trade in England. *Ibid.*, 246–47.

31. OWL, III, foll. 25, 173, 184. Proclamations made November 30, 1674 and March 6, 1675, Mayor's Court Minutes, MSS, II, no foliation. Queens College Library Microfilm, Queens College, New York. Randolph's Report on New England, October 12, 1676, C.O. 1/37, fol. 240. *N.Y. Col. Docs.*, XIII, 534; XIV, 730–31. N.Y. Col. MSS, XXVI, fol. 122; XXIX, fol. 19.

customs collectors there.[32] The New York City-Amsterdam trade could have continued to grow and thrive except for one factor—the entrance of London merchants into the New York market.

Despite the marked expansion of English commercial activity after 1660, direct trade with New York had been rare. Only two ships are recorded as sailing from London to New York between 1664 and 1674. After 1674, however, there was a veritable invasion with at least fifty merchants entering the trade, notably William Antelby, Thomas Crundall, Gerrard Dankheythusen, William Depeyster, Edward Griffeth, Thomas Hart, John Harwood, Benjamin Hewling, John Lewin, Edward Man, Samuel Swinock, Gerrard Vanheythusen, and Robert Wooley.[33] There is no evidence to indicate the reasons for their sudden interest in New York. It may be that after the Treaty of Westminster turned New York over to England once and for all, they decided to challenge the Dutch merchants. They did not blindly enter the market, as almost all of them had traded regularly with Boston prior to 1674. No doubt they heard from their relatives, friends or factors of the whale oil, foodstuffs, furs, and tobacco exported from New York.[34]

In some cases it appears that Dutch mercantile families merely extended their base of trade. William Depeyster represented his family's interests in London. His brother Samuel and another relative, Peter, maintained the family interest in Amsterdam while Abraham Depeyster, their cousin, watched over affairs in New York. William shipped English cargoes to New York to supplement the goods sent from Amsterdam, giving the family a three-cornered network.[35] Other families which copied this pattern were the

302

32. Dover port books from 1671–1680, E 190/663-2, 5, 6; 664-2, 14, 17; 665-4, 11 and Falmouth 1043-14, 16; 1044-12, 18.

33. For trade between 1664 and 1674 see E 190/50-5, 53-6. For the new pattern of trade and the men involved see E 190/63- 8; 62-1, 5; 66-5; 80-1; 89-10; 91-1, PRO. Some of these merchants also registered goods in Dover. See port books listed in note 28.

34. For the importance of Boston see, Curtis P. Nettels, "Economic Relations of Boston, Philadelphia and New York, 1680-1715," *Journal of Economic and Business History*, III (1931), 185-215. To trace London's trade to New England prior to 1673 see E 190/52-1; 53-6; 50-5; 62-1, 5; 63-8.

35. The Dutch branch of the family is frequently mentioned in Not. Arch., 3295, N. 97; 3217, N. 39; 3322, N. 103; 3332, N. 289. The heirs of William Depeyster

Darvalls and the extended Dankheythusen-Vanheythusen-Lodwick families.[36] A corollary to this trade was the entrepreneural activity of Nicholas Cullen and Mathew Chitty. Cullen was a merchant in Dover who handled the affairs of many New York merchants who trans-shipped through Dover. He and his partner, Chitty, entered the New York market through their Dutch contacts.[37]

Samuel Swinock entered the New York market through an arrangement with Thomas Delaval, the ex-customs collector. When Delaval returned to England in 1673 to get compensation for the goods seized from him by the Dutch, he met Swinock. The latter was willing to extend him credit and ship sizeable quantities of goods, for when Delaval died in 1683 he owed Swinock £1,687 sterling.[38] A similar example was that of Edward Griffeth who met Jacob Milborne after the latter was exiled from New York for creating dissension in the Dutch Reformed Church and arguing with Andros. On at least two occasions, Milborne returned to New York as Griffeth's factor.[39] John Harwood merely extended his New England trade with the aid of his relatives who had settled in New England, and his partnership with Hezekiah Usher, a prominent New

303

---

were his trading partners Samuel, Peter and Abraham. The codicil relating to the latter granted him £1,000 after he had made all of his returns. Prerogative Court of Canterbury Probate 11/369, p. 36. Hereafter cited as PCC.

36. Dankheythusen's extensive family is outlined in his will, PCC, Probate 11/414, p. 59. Examples of the Darvalls' trading activities are in Not. Arch., 3236, N. 62; 3224, N. 637; 3502, foll. 617-18. Their ships also stopped in Dover and London, E 190/663-2, 6; 664-2, 17; 80-1. William Darvall became mayor of New York City and was a councillor from 1676 to 1680. Hutchins, *Civil List*, 17-18. Herbert L. Osgood, et al., eds., *Minutes of the Common Council of the City of New York, 1675-1776* (New York, 1905). I, 1-2.

37. Abraham Depeyster and Jacob Leisler were named in Cullen's will as executors of Cullen's gifts to the Dutch Churches in New York City and Albany, PCC, Probate 11/438, p. 113. Cullen was associated with Mathew Chitty in a number of deals with Frederick Philipse and Depeyster, Not. Arch., 3403 (no number designated); 3302, N. 97. Jacob Leisler acted as Chitty's attorney in New York City. Mayor's Court Minutes MSS, V. fol. 45. Cullen's ventures are frequently recorded in the Dover port books E 190/667-7; 668-4; 669-16.

38. Delaval returned to England after the Dutch conquest of New York in 1673. His goods were seized by the Dutch because he was an official in the government. He petitioned the Duke of York for compensation. BM addl. MS, 18, 206, fol. 61 verso-62 verso. Delaval's estate is discussed by James Riker, *Revised History of New Harlem* (New York, 1904), 809. His will, PCC, Probate 11/372, p. 17.

39. Chancery, Class 7, piece 576/37, PRO.

England merchant. Through these contacts he corresponded with Robert Livingston, to whom he rashly sent
valuable cargoes.[40]

Many English merchants ventured into the New York
market without local contacts, and had to rely on a factor
or a New York merchant. The role of one of these local
merchants, John Winder, is revealed in a famous post-
humous law suit. After Winder's death, his widow married
John Palmer who had arrived in New York from Barbados
in 1674. In the summer of 1679, John Ward of London
sued Palmer for debts owed by Winder. An account of
Winder's estate exhibited in the case reveals that Winder
carried accounts for some very active "new" merchants
(John Lewin, Mathew Chitty, John Ward, Robert Wooley)
and some less active ones as well (Alderman Francis
Warner, John Jackson, Sir Henry Tufts). All were trading
in New York through Winder.[41] Others also entered New
York trade in this manner, according to the records of
a special tax levy. On October 31, 1676, the mayor's council
issued a special order warning twenty-five individuals to
pay their taxes prior to leaving New York. Twenty-three
of the twenty-five were English and nine are readily
identifiable as London merchants. Some were men of
substance: John Robinson, George Heathcote, Edward
Griffeth, James Lloyd and John Robson had estates
valued at £2,000, and those of Thomas Thatcher, Robert
Sanford and Abraham Whearly were valued at over £500.[42]
These were substantial assessments in New York then, and
they indicate the impact of the new merchants on the
province's market. As a result, clashes ensued between the
newcomers and the local merchant community in which
some Englishmen were roughly handled. Andros chose to

40. John Harwood's will, PCC, Probate 11/380, p. 72. On Usher see, Bailyn, *New England Merchants*, 135-37. At the time of Harwood's demise he had an outstanding stock of £5,000 with Usher. On his dealings with Robert Livingston see, Lawrence H. Leder, *Robert Livingston, 1654-1728, and the Politics of Colonial New York* (Chapel Hill, N.C., 1961), 46-51, 110-11.

41. John Lewin and Mathew Chitty had the largest account, £1442. Mayor's Court Minutes, MSS, V. foll. 211—12. This case became the first appeal to the Crown from New York. Paul M. Hamlin and Charles E. Baker, *Supreme Court of Judicature of the Province of New York, 1691-1704* (New York, 1959), I, 9-10, 425-27.

42. Osgood, *Minutes of the Common Council*, I, 9, 25-26.

The Stadt Huys of New York in 1679. Lithograph by G. Hayward. Courtesy of the New-York Historical Society, New York City.

maintain his established alliances rather than formulate new ones with strangers.

The first English merchant to feel the brunt of Andros' wrath was George Heathcote, a familiar figure in New York who had hitherto been left alone. He first appeared in New Amsterdam to trade in October, 1661. In time he developed an extensive trade and bought property in Albany, on the Delaware River, in Southhampton, Long Island, and in New York City. A Quaker, Heathcote had a strain of anti-authoritarianism that put him in jail in Boston for refusing to remove his hat before Governor Bellingham.[43] During the summer of 1676, Heathcote was

43. For Heathcote's activities in New York see *N.Y. Col. Docs.*, XIII, 485; E.B.

charged with trading illegally in Albany after trade there had been restricted to freemen of Albany. Heathcote protested the charge because he owned property in Albany and thought himself to be a resident. He made the mistake of confronting Andros in the customs house to plead his case. During this confrontation, he broadened his complaint to state that there were so many cheap Dutch goods in Albany which had not been cleared in England that he could not sell his goods and so was denied "ye Privileges of an English man." Sheriff Thomas Ashton of New York City formally complained to Andros that Heathcote had defamed the city's good name and demanded his censure. For his temerity, Heathcote was arrested and brought before a specially convened court of assize. In court he vainly pleaded not guilty to a charge of "scurrillous speech" and was fined £20 plus costs. The fine was large but the court costs were an incredible £61.5.6. After a number of conciliatory petitions the fine was suspended, but the court costs remained.⁴⁴

John Robinson was the next victim. He made the mistake of testifying at Heathcote's trial in support of the contention that Albany was flooded with cheap Dutch goods. Just before the trial, perhaps in an attempt to influence Robinson's testimony, William Dyre, the customs collector, took him to court for payment of £97 in duties for which Dyre had given him credit. A year later he was foolish enough to repeat Heathcote's mistake of telling Andros that there were illegal Dutch goods in Albany. He quickly abased himself before the mayor's court and escaped a fine, but he did not escape punishment. Andros exacted

306

O'Callaghan, ed., *The Documentary History of the State of New York* (Albany, 1850-51), II, 304; N.Y. Col. MSS, XXX, fol. 215; Joel Munsell, ed., *Collection of the History of Albany From Its Discovery to the Present Time* (Albany, 1865), III, 135, note 2. The incident with Bellingham is related in George Wooley, *A Two Years Journal in New York* (London, 1701), 177. Heathcote left New York for Pennsylvania where he died in 1710. He left his estate to his cousin, Caleb, who had a long career in New York politics. Dixon R. Fox, *Caleb Heathcote: Gentleman Colonist, the Story of a Career in the Province of New York, 1692-1721* (New York, 1926.)

44. October 26, 1676 Mayor's Court Minutes, MSS, III, foll. 104-5. His trial was held before a special court of assize, October 25-27, 1676, N.Y. Col. MSS, XXV, foll. 234, 237. George Heathcote to Andros, October 26, 1676, *Ibid.*, fol. 241. Proposals of George Heathcote, December 12, 1676, *Ibid.*, fol. 156. On the same day his fine was suspended, *Ibid.*, fol. 157.

his revenge by denying Robinson permission to trade in Albany.[45]

Andros finally overreached himself in the case of Edward Griffeth, and it was Griffeth who precipitated his recall. Griffeth's experience was similar to that of Heathcote and Robinson. In 1677, he complained about the preferential treatment given the New Yorkers in customs collection and also alleged that in being shut out of the Albany trade he was denied his rights as an Englishman. He was tried for acting in "derogation and contempt of the King's Authority" and fined £20.[46] Griffeth, unlike the others, sought revenge. When Andros returned to England for a five-month visit during the winter of 1677–1678 to receive his knighthood and attend to family business, Griffeth's family began a legal attack against the governor. Andros left England before the evidence and witnesses could be gathered, but a group of merchants, led by Griffeths, tried to delay his departure through a petition to the Duke of York, requesting that Andros be detained until the witnesses and evidence arrived from New York.[47] Their request was denied. Nonetheless, their petition exposed to view the friction between the merchants and Andros. They charged Andros with (1) violating the Navigation Acts by allowing a direct commerce with the Netherlands that avoided paying customs; (2) granting special privileges to individuals such as Philipse; (3) controlling the trade of Albany in order to favor a few friends; (4) intervening in the collection of customs to aid

307

---

45. Robinson was the only merchant to testify in favor of Heathcote's charges. *Ibid.*, foll. 234, 221. Dyre demanded the £97 at the behest of Andros. The hearing was held October 10, 1676, Mayor's Court Minutes, MSS, III, fol. 96. It appears that Robinson also charged Andros specifically with bringing over Dutch goods in the ship *Unity* of Amsterdam. N.Y. Col MSS, XXVI, foll. 30, 39. Order suspending Robinson's right to trade, August 8, 1678, *Ibid.*, XXVII, fol. 176. There were others who were punished for "contempt." James Graham was fined £12 and Richard Mann £2 for their opinions. Mayor's Court Minutes, MSS, IV, foll. 178, 188, verso. For other actions against the new merchants see Robert Story v. Sir Edmund Andros, *Ibid.*, foll. 300–01. William Darvall even arranged to have a cargo unloaded on Shelter Island as he feared Andros would seize it —which in fact he did. Not. Arch., 3284, N. 92.

46. Griffeth's trial, October 19, 1677, Mayor's Court Minutes, MSS, IV, foll. 334–35.

47. "Articles of Complaint against Edmund Andros by Thomas Griffeth, Henry Griffeth, John Harwood and others," May 10, 1678. Massachusetts and New York Misc., MS. 91.1, Massachusetts Historical Society, Boston, Mass.

his friends; (5) carrying on a private trade of his own. Accompanying these complaints about trade were others touching different aspects of Andros' administration. Andros was accused of manipulating trials and, in one instance, throwing John Robson (a merchant) in jail without a trial or hearing. Taxes were diverted from the garrison for Andros' private use and were also manipulated to dissuade English merchants from trading. Last, and not least, Andros had interfered with the practice of religion and had subjected the English to public humiliation by punishing them on a Dutch whipping post. In sum, his administration was oppressive and tyrannical. His actions had put a damper on further English immigration and created such outrage among the people that they would not defend the colony.

The Duke's response to this petition has not survived, perhaps because he was preoccupied with his own future in the midst of such events as the popish plot and the Exclusion Act crisis. York's own troubles are germane in another way, for he tried to placate his enemies through changes in policy. For example, in 1680 he accepted Sir William Jones' opinion that it was illegal for New York to charge customs in New Jersey.[48] It was during this same period that he decided to recall Andros.

On May 24, 1680, York and his secretary, Sir John Werden, sent letters informing Andros of the decision.[49] The letters stated that the primary reason was to ascertain the true revenues of the proprietary. Both men went on to urge Andros to return home quickly to defend himself against individuals who were trying to blemish his record. There were "suggestions of y'or favoring Dutchmen before English in trade . . . , or delaying ships unduly for private reasons, or admitting Dutch ships immediately to trade with you, or trading in ye names of others."[50] Werden, in a later letter, specifically cited the complaints of Griffeth as influencing his recall.[51]

48. For this controversy see John E. Pomfret, *The Province of East New Jersey, 1609-1702* (Princeton, 1962), 121.

49. York to Andros, May 24, 1680, *N.Y. Col. Docs.*, III, 283. Werden to Andros, *Ibid.*

50. *Ibid.*

51. *Ibid.*, 286.

York did not stop at simply recalling Andros; he
appointed an investigator to go to New York to examine
the situation, and the influence of the merchants can
be seen in the man appointed—John Lewin. No stranger
to New York, Lewin had traded to New England and
New York where he occasionally joined with Robert
Wooley, one of the most active of the new merchants.
Together they had purchased a house in New York City
from John Robinson.[52] Lewin's commission empowered
him to investigate all aspects of trade and revenue
collection, and the detailed set of instructions added to
it leaves the impression that the Duke's suspicions of
Andros were growing.[53] There is also reason to believe that
the Duke of York was sensitive to an appeal touching
his own interests. New York had never been a profitable
venture for the Duke; indeed, it produced only losses.
If Andros was allowing illegal trade with the Netherlands
and allowing friends to bring in duty-free cargoes, an end
to such practices might turn into revenue for the proprietor.
Thus, the appointment of Lewin, who was no neutral,
went beyond a simple desire to placate English merchants.

309

Lewin arrived in New York in October, 1680, and spent
the next year fulfilling his orders. While he was doing
so, he had new things to consider. New York was shaken
by a tax revolt, the direct result of Andros' failure
to promulgate a new ordinance on taxes before going
to England. The consequence was that after November 1,
1680, legal sanctions for the taxes ceased.[54] On May 9,
1681, a ship from London landed its cargo without
paying customs and Dyre promptly seized the merchandise.
Shortly thereafter collector William Dyre was sued for
detaining the goods, and then for high treason.[55] Dyre

---

52. For Lewin's and Wooley's trading activities see, E 190/52-1; 63-8; 62-1, 5; 66-5;
96-1; 53-6. They were involved in a long court proceeding from 1676 until
1679 when it finally went to England on appeal, N.Y. Col MSS, XXV, fol. 706,
XXVIII, foll. 134, 138, 174; XXIX, foll. 2, 8, 9, 15, 18, 19. Their purchase of a house
is recounted by I.N. Stokes, *The Iconography of Manhattan Island*, 1498–1909
(1916–28), VI, 133.

53. Lewin's commission and instructions May 24, 1680, *N.Y. Col. Docs.*, III, 279–80.

54. York to Andros, May 7, 1677, *N.Y. Col. Docs.*, III, 246.

55. Dyre was first charged April 26, 1681. Mayor's Court Minutes, MSS, V, fol. 267.
The charge of treason stems from Dyre's collecting duties after his legal authority
for doing so elapsed. He was thus violating the royal monopoly of customs.

had a reputation for harassment which was given appropriate recognition in a poetic attack made in Boston:

> Yr Brother Dyre hath the Divell played,
> Made the New Yorkers at the first affraide,
> He vapoured, swagger'd, hectored (Whoe but hee?)
> But soon destroyed himself by villaine.[56]

The man who carried the case against Dyre was Samuel Winder. He and twenty-one other unnamed witnesses testified at a grand jury hearing that Dyre had "Traitorously Maliciously and Advisedly used and Exercised Regall Power" by imposing illegal customs. The grand jury found for the bill, and the court of assize summoned Dyre to trial. He challenged the court's authority to try the case and, after debating this point, the court sought the easy way out by referring the case to England.[57] This step in itself dramatized the disarray in the colony and seemed to justify the description of it as "a government wholly overthrown and in the greatest confusion and disord'r possible."[58]

Lewin, meanwhile, collected evidence and testimony, chiefly in New York City and Albany. The leading Dutch families in both cities did not welcome him as we know from a letter written by Stephanus van Cortlandt to his sister, Maria van Rensselaer:

Capt. Lewin does not go up [the river] to deprive anyone of his rights, or to abridge the same, but to inquire into the Duke's revenues and the situation of the trade and commerce in his highness' territories, and also to inquire whether anyone has any complaints against Governor Andros, . . . I hope you will guard yourself, . . . also admonish Mr.

56. "Randolph's Welcome Back Again," January, 1680, Robert N. Tappan and A.T.S. Goodrich, eds., *Edward Randolph: Including his Letters and Official Papers from the New England, Middle and Southern Colonies in America* (Boston, 1898-1909), III, 61.

57. Winder was acting as attorney for Edmund Gibbons. Dyre had detained a cask of rum to force Gibbons to pay customs. At this time Dyre was mayor of New York City which complicated the suit. The aldermen still made him post a £300 bond when he missed his first trial date. Mayor's Court Minutes, MSS, V, foll. 270-73. The proceedings of the grand jury and the special court of assize, June 29-July 2, 1681 can be traced in the New-York Historical Society, *Collections*, (1912), 8-15. The assize tried to return the case to the mayor's court which refused to reconsider its decision as it had no jurisdiction over capital crimes. New-York Historical Society, *Collections* (1893), 425-26.

58. Anthony Brockholls to Sir John Werden, September 17, 1681, *N.Y. Col Docs.*, III, 289.

Martin Gerritsz (von Bergen) when he is in discourse with Capt. Lewin and mention is made of the governor, not to say anything to the detriment of Sir Edmund, but to say that all he did was for the best interest of the entire province, for they intend . . .[59]

Unfortunately, several lines are obliterated after "for they intend . . . ."

In New York City Lewin met with open obstruction. Frederick Philipse complained to the mayor's court that Lewin was collecting depositions illegally. The court decided that he had acted contrary to law in administering oaths, thus producing "confusion" and "disorders" in his proceedings.[60] Andros' deputy, Captain Anthony Brockholls, refused to intercede against Lewin no matter what the court decided. Against this background Lewin completed his report and returned to England with a document as much political as it was fiscal.[61]

Andros, for his part, must have expected to return quickly to his duties. He had left Brockholls in temporary charge, while conferring on Lady Andros powers of attorney.[62] In England, however, he was forced to undergo a hearing which, although conducted on favorable terms, did delay his return. The hearing began in December, 1681, with John Churchill, the Duke's solicitor-general, presiding. Edward Antill and a Mr. Robinson represented the merchants. William Dyre and Mathias Nicolls, long the secretary of the proprietary, represented the government.[63] Lewin and Andros were the chief protagonists.

The trial focused upon Lewin's report which, in its general tenor and its particulars, was an attack on Andros and Dyre. Lewin accused them of withholding tax records, creating others especially for him, and keeping no records of tax disbursement. He also repeated the charges made

311

59. April, 1681, A.J.F. van Laer, ed., and trans., *Correspondence of Maria van Rensselaer, 1664–1689* (Albany, 1935), 48.

60. Philipse made his charge September 13, 1681. Osgood, *Minutes of the Common Council*, 1, 87. The court met to discuss it, September 15, 1681, *Ibid.* Werden ordered Andros to make sure Lewin had power to administer an oath. He left for England without doing so, thereby hampering the investigation. *N.Y. Col. Docs.*, III, 284.

61. Lewin's report, *Ibid.*, 302–08.

62. Brockholls was put in charge by direct order of the Duke, *Ibid.*, 283. Mrs. Andros returned to England, November 1681. Van Laer, *Correspondence of Maria van Rensselaer*, 52–54. Power of attorney, N.Y. Col. MSS, XXVI, fol. 151.

63. The report of the hearing, *N.Y. Col. Docs.*, III, 314–16.

by Griffeth that the entry of illegal goods was common, as was the practice of not charging full duties on imports. Those behind the illegal trade were Andros, Philipse and Cortlandt. In addition, Lewin charged that Philipse and Cortlandt were Andros' covert trustees in trade. For these services they had been allowed to conduct an illicit trade with the Netherlands and given special treatment at the customs house. Those who were not friends of the governor had been forced to pay the full amount of the customs, and their goods were commonly held in the customs house to hinder their trade. These practices were particularly aimed at English merchants, and knowledge of this had indeed hindered English immigration. In sum, Lewin reported that New York was dominated by cronyism, cheating, lying, arbitrary procedures and corruption, all of which he laid at Andros' feet.

312

Andros denied everything. Neither side was governed by the rules of evidence because the hearing was not judicial in nature. Andros made use of this fact to brush aside the charges and extol his own accomplishments. Though Churchill exonerated Andros and Dyre, they were not restored to their offices in New York; that, at least, was a victory for the merchants. Moreover, Dyre still had to free himself from the formal charges made against him and Andros was bedevilled by litigation, especially from the persistent Griffeth.[64] Ultimately, both were successful not only in overcoming their legal difficulties, but also in continuing their careers. Andros was appointed governor-general of the Dominion of New England, and Dyre the surveyor-general of colonial revenues.

During the hearing and its aftermath affairs in New York drifted. Taxes went uncollected and the special legislation which favored New York City was ignored. Released from the thrall of city merchants, Albany and Long Island went their own way, with Brockholls incapable of mastering the contending interests now freed

---

64. Wait Winthrop reported to his brother, Fitz, on December 19, 1681 that Andros was bedevilled in the courts, *Winthrop Papers*, IV, Massachusetts Historical Society, *Collections*, XLVII (Boston, 1882), 423–24. Andros petitioned the Duke for relief from arrests and law suits and York ordered his solicitors to take charge. BM addl. MS, 24, 928, fol. 14. Dyre's troubles can be traced in *N.Y. Col. Docs.*, 318–21. Griffeth's suit was in Chancery for years, see Chancery 7/576/37 and Chancery 33/259.

from restraint.[65] With near anarchy in New York and a still precarious situation in England, the Duke of York sought a solution to the problems of his proprietary. His decision was to grant New York an assembly, a body he had hitherto regarded as an anathema. His willingness to grant one at this time reveals the difficulty of his position.[66]

This remarkable episode shows the power of the London merchants in New York affairs. On breaking into a new market they found an entrenched oligarchy relying for its trade goods on a foreign government. They first challenged this oligarchy on the local level, and when they met with resistance they quickly turned to London to press their cause. There they pressured the Duke of York to recall Governor Andros and send out an investigator who was one of their own. These actions created such a vacuum in New York that the colony went without a stable government for three years. This situation, precipitated by the withdrawal of Andros, combined with the Duke of York's own political difficulties, caused York to reverse a long-standing policy and create a representative body to participate in governing the proprietary. These events were unforeseen by the merchants but were, nevertheless, a result of their interest in the New York market. Of greater importance to the merchants was that with Andros out of the way they could concentrate on trade. In 1682 five ships sailed from London to New York City to exploit the new market.[67]

The impact of the English merchants was, therefore, considerable. Resolutely determined to create favorable market conditions in North America, the merchants of London were a formidable interest group in imperial affairs. In committees of Parliament, the chambers of Whitehall, and colonial customs houses the merchants had power enough to shape both commercial and political relationships in the formative years of the Empire.

313

---

65. For a discussion of Brockholls' difficulties see Brodhead, *History of New York*, II, 347–69.

66. York to Andros, April 6, 1673, *N.Y. Col. Docs.*, III, 230 and York to Andros, January 28, 1676, *Ibid.*, 235.

67. E 190/106–1.

THE
Pennsylvania
Magazine
OF HISTORY AND BIOGRAPHY

Laws and Governments proposed for West New Jersey and Pennsylvania, 1676-1683

EDWARD BILLING AND WILLIAM PENN, the Quaker promoters of two mid-Atlantic colonies created in the reign of Charles II, seized the opportunity to draft laws and regulations for their settlers. "The Concessions and Agreements of the Proprietors, Free-holders and Inhabitants of the Province of West New Jersey in America," probably drawn up in 1676, was carried over to Burlington where the manuscript is still cherished.[1] By March 1677 over one hundred fifty signatures had been appended to it. Billing's was the first, Penn's the fourth, with many signers in London and others already in the colony. No plans for the colonies are "as worthy of study" as these, averred one scholar; another wrote that they reflected "a kind of wisdom and justice that is anything but doctrinaire," distinguishing them from

---

[1] The Concessions (cited in text by chapter) are taken from *The Papers of William Penn, I, 1644-1679*, eds. Mary Maples Dunn & Richard S. Dunn (Philadelphia, 1981), 387-410, which reprints it from the Ms at Burlington, N.J. The editors make no absolute decision about authorship. *The West Jersey Concessions and Agreements of 1676/77, A Round table of Historians* (Trenton, 1979) offers six short talks on background, authors, relationship to other colonial agreements, authorship, date, ideas and principles.

such schemes as those for Carolina in 1669, Pennsylvania in 1682, and East New Jersey in 1683.[2]

The Frame of the Government of the Province of Pennsylvania, in America Together with certain other Laws Agreed upon in England, by the Governor and divers freemen of the aforesaid Province was published in London in 1682 shortly before William Penn first visited the colony. In December he presented to the Assembly at Upland or Chester "The Great Law or Body of Laws of the Province"—hereafter it was frequently called his "Code."[3] These productions obtained for the author a European reputation as a legislator. Charles de Secondat, Baron de Montesquieu (1689-1755) dubbed him Lycurgus, though as one commentator has remarked, this was a singularly inept description of so lenient a lawgiver.[4] Both William Penn and Edward Billing have been credited with the authorships of the Concessions, whose contents seem nearer the context of Billing's earlier life and previous writings than that of the much younger Penn. Analysis of the Concessions and Penn's *Frame* reveals two differing attempts to implement a few of England's mid-century legal reforms as well as the transfer of everyday juridical English customs to the new settlements overseas.

315

Change in government and law was much debated in the seventeenth century, not only in British territory, but in countries like France and Denmark. In France, for example, Jean Baptiste Colbert (1619-1683) improved, among other legislation, the civil code and appointed a commission anticipating, but not implementing, a digest similar to that achieved by Napoleonic statesmen. In 1660, Denmark's king dismissed the traditional Gothic estates, established an absolute monarchy, and then produced a book of laws admired, even by severe critics of the new establishment like Algernon Sidney (1622-1683)[5] and Robert Molesworth (1656-1725). The latter, in *An Account of Denmark* (London: 1694), declared that the Danes enjoyed laws "that for Justice, Brevity, and Perspicuity,. . .exceed all that I know of in the World." They were

---

[2] John E. Pomfret, *The Province of West New Jersey, 1609-1702* (Princeton: 1956), ch. 6, 86-102.

[3] Text of Penn's Frame and laws, *Statutes at Large of Pennsylvania, I, 1680-1700*, compiled by Gail McKnight Beckman (New York, 1976). Frame and laws cited page; numbers; "The Great Law," first version, in Beckman pp. 128-135, as "Code" by chapter.

[4] *D.N.B.* life of Penn by Ramsey MacDonald.

[5] Algernon Sidney, *Discourses Concerning Government* (London, 1698), ch. III, sect. 26.

grounded in equity, written in the tongue of the country, and com-
prehensible without the aid of counsel or attorney. Suits were quickly
settled; few lawyers were required.[6]

The English had long boasted of the rule of law under which they
lived, but had also discussed possible amendment and reduction into
briefer and simpler form.[7] Yet the long struggle between the Stuarts
and the people was ostensibly chiefly to obtain recognition of rights
often claimed to be traditional. By the end of the seventeenth century, to
be sure, their definition and confirmation was accomplished. They were
briefly: no taxation without representation; frequent parliaments; no
standing army in times of peace, the right to petition the crown; and
protection in the courts—by Habeas Corpus, production of adequate
testimony, trial before a jury of the vicinage, and the prohibition of
excessive bail and cruel or unusual punishment. Protestants after the
Revolutionary Settlement enjoyed a modicum of religious liberty and
considerable freedom of speech and press.[8] But no overall rectification
of law was then attempted, although certain constitutional changes effected by the Long Parliament before hostilities erupted in 1642, for
example, the abolition of Star Chamber, were retained. The disuetude
into which the Court of Wards had fallen during the wars and some
regulation of usury were confirmed by statute at the restoration of
Charles II in 1660. The right to the writ of Habeas Corpus was affirmed in 1679. But even much desired and comparatively unrevolu-
tionary practice was annulled by the returned Cavaliers: the ballot
ceased to be used in the Commons, and Latin and French were again the
usage of the courts, English not becoming the official language until
1731. The achievement of the century was clarification, a monarchy
limited by law and a more powerful parliament less frequently challenged by king or would-be reformer, rather than overt legal rectification.

Yet major and minor innovation was the subject of much paper shot:

316

[6] Robert Molesworth, *An Account of Denmark* (London, 1694), ch. 15, 232-233.
[7] William Penn, *England's Present Interest* (London, 1675, ed. used 1698), 85, "a ruling by
law"; James Harrington, *The Political Works*, ed. J.G.A. Pocock (Cambridge, 1977),
"Aphorisms Political," III, 762. Harrington insisted that England was not governed by arms,
but by a government by laws, though "imperfect, or ineffectual laws."
[8] *English Historial Documents, 1660-1714*, ed. Andrew Browning (London, 1953), prints
the achievements of the Revolution—juries, 85-89; Habeas Corpus, 92-96; Bill of Rights,
122-128.

pamphlet warfare proliferated even as war began but especially in the years between the virtual defeat of the King in 1647 and the Cromwells' supremacy. Moderate proposals, like those of 1653 in the report of a commission presented by Matthew Hale (1609-1676),[9] or in *England's Balme* (London: 1656), by William Sheppard (1595-1674)[10] were ignored either through a general indifference in spite of the articulate minority, or because of persistent, if not obtrusive opposition, from vested interests.

Not surprisingly then much more revolutionary suggestions received less attention than they may have deserved. Tracts expressed the aspirations of Sectaries, Levellers, and others. These questioned the structure of church and state, a matter of concern of course both to the Republic set up in 1649-1653, and the Protectorate, 1653-1659. Further they attacked the whole system of justice. Chancery, court of equity and other widely unpopular institutions were to be abolished or entirely reconstituted. Emphasis was to be laid on local, elective bodies and officials, rather than on the expensive complex at Westminster. The legal process was to be public, with the accused allowed to plead his own cause if he wished, and able to demand the presence of at least two witnesses to his presumed guilt. Freedom of worship was, in varying degrees, permitted, and ecclesiastical jurisdiction diminished or discarded. Punishment was examined and in general greater leniency was advocated: reduction of the death penalty, retribution to the robbed, injured or bereaved, as well as amelioration of the deprivations inflicted upon the next of kin of suicides and those executed. Jails were to be clean and jailers forbidden unjust exactions. A registry of transactions in real property was to be kept; conditions of land tenure drastically revised.[11]

Overseas the complexity of English law was necessarily less; few

317

---

[9] The Hale Commission is reprinted in *Somers Tracts* (London, 1809-1815) VI, 177-245 from *Several Drafts. . .*(London, 1653). Mary Cotterell, "Interregnum Law Reform, the Hale Commission of 1652," *English History Review* 88 (April, 1968), 689-704.

[10] Nancy Matthews Arson, "William Sheppard, Law Reformer," a thesis submitted to the University of Maryland in 1974—forthcoming from C.U.P. I was graciously allowed a photocopy.

[11] David Veall, *The Popular Movement for Law Reform, 1650-1660* (Oxford, 1970); Blair Worden, *The Rump Parliament, 1648-1653* (Cambridge: 1974, paper 1977), 105-118; *Select Essays in Anglo-American Legal History*, 3 v. compiled by a committee of the Associations of American Law Schools (Boston, 1907-1909) I, iv; R. Robinson, "Anticipations under the Commonweath of Changes in the Law," 467-491. These are useful on proposals and reformers but the literature on any one group, e.g., the Levellers, is enormous.

lawyers emigrated, process was almost perforce in English, and the courts more localized. The common law prevailed, but where conditions required changes, legislation was expected to be approved, revised or rejected in London. During the vicissitudes of the Interregnum, and the comparitive inertia, save for a few exceptional years, of most officials responsible for imperial policy under Charles II, and until the appointment of sixteen commissioners and a new Council of Trade in 1696,[12] experiment seemed feasible. Men like John Locke (1632-1704), Anthony Ashley Cooper (1621-1683), first Earl of Shaftesbury, *318* and others tried to bring it about. Such experiments as were contained in the West Jersey Concessions and Penn's arrangements for Pennsylvania will be discovered here to have some unique qualities.

Billing and Penn present in most respects striking contrasts. Penn is the more familiar personage, though like him Billing seems to have been of gentle birth and well educated. Both Quakers were doubly motivated in colonial purpose by the wish for a refuge from religious persecution and by personal financial exigency. Billing, of Cornish origins, was born about 1623.[13] In 1657 he was a cornet or second lieutenant in the army of George Monck (1608-1670) in Scotland. Before that year no listing of his name has yet been discovered in the records of university, Inns of Court, or army. *A Word of Reproof* (London: 1659), a tract sometimes attributed to him, suggests its author's involvement in 1650 at the battle of Dunbar, and experience before that at Oxford. The rank of cornet after seven years service seems low; *A Word of Reproof* may not be his. George Fox (1624-1691),

---

[12] Browning, *Documents*, 542-544, Order establishing a Council of Trade naming sixteen commissioners to it.

[13] Billing, Bylynge, Bylling—he used all spellings, himself—is not noticed in standard biographical dictionaries though the typescript "Dictionary of Quaker Biography," found at Friends Library, London, and Haverford College has a useful note on Billing to which Frederick B. Tolles contributed. Pomfret, n.2, above, is inclined to follow *Essays in Honor of Rufus M. Jones, Children of Light*, ed. Howard E. Brinton (N.Y.: 1938) where no. IV "The Problem of Edward Bylynge" contains much information: i, 83-106; Violet Holdsworth, "His connection with Cornwall" provides, besides a genealogical table, much about the family: ii. John L. Nickalls, "His Writings" attributes the Concessions to him and also *A Word of Reproof*. In Nickalls revised ed. of *The Journal of George Fox* (Philadelphia, 1975) a note, p. 320, identifies the maiden name of Lilias as Hepburn. Nickalls is followed on authorship of the Concessions by H.N. Brailsford, *The Levellers and the English Revolution* (Stanford, 1956) and by Christopher Hill, *The World Turned Upside Down* (N.Y., 1972).

travelling in the north in the fall of 1657, met both Edward and, separately, his then estranged wife, Lilias (d. 1674). The Quaker convinced them both and brought about reconciliation between them. Billing left the army, moved south and thereafter operated a brewery in Millbank not far from the meeting held at the house of Stephen Hart (fl. 1659) in New Palace Yard, Westminster.

With others Billing signed the 16 April 1659 petition urging Parliament to relieve the sufferings of Quakers.[14] In the October of that year, during the anarchy prevailing after the fall of Richard Cromwell (1626-1712), protector since the death of his father Oliver (1599-1658), the book collector George Thomason (fl. 1666) purchased *A Mite of Affection manifested in 31 Proposals. . .for a Settlement in this Day and Hour of the World's Confusion* (London: Giles Calvert, 1659). This work, to be discussed later, bears a close relation to the Concessions.[15] Monck's soldiers, by now in London, on 6 February 1659-1660 rudely entered Hart's house and so roughly treated both men and women worshiping there, amongst them the Billings, that the diarist, Samuel Pepys (1633-1703) expressed sympathy, and the General forbad repetition of such affrays.[16]

Harassment of Quakers by fine and imprisonment continued under Charles II; Billing, never one to suffer quietly, wrote vividly of persecutions endured. *An Alarm to all Flesh* (London: Robert Wilson, 1660) by E.B. began "Howle, howle, shriek, yell and roar. . .ye sensual, Earthly Inhabitants of the whole Earth," and a little further on declared "Edward Billing," a prisoner afraid of no man (p. 9). This was followed by *Words in the Word to be read by Friends,* written in the Gatehouse prison by E.B. in 1661, urging tradesmen not to encourage luxury by selling the superfluous. *A Faithful Testimony* (London: for the Author, 1664) addressed Episcopalian persecutors about "the un-

319

[14] *The Clarke Papers,* ed. C.H. Firth, III (London: 1899), a newsletter, p. 100, identifies one of the signers as Cornet Billing.

[15] *A Mite of Affection* (hereafter *A Mite* and ch. quoted) is reprinted in *Early Quaker Writings,* ed. Hugh Barbour and Arthur Roberts (Grand Rapid, Michigan, 1973), 407-421; on 411 Monck's army marched south 1659-1660, not 1660-1601 as stated.

[16] Haverford Quaker Collection has a photo-copy of a Swarthmore MS, V. 93 where a letter attributed to Billing describes the affair. *The Diary of Samuel Pepys,* ed. R. Latham & Wm. Matthews (Berkeley: 1970) I. 44. Pepys' other references to Billing show him jeering at a republican M.P. about the coming restoration, 50, talking with the Diarist who found him "a cunning fellow," 279, and Billing upbraiding Pepys about naval mismanagement, VIII (1974) 349.

natural Act" (p. 4), that is 13 & 14 Car II.c.1—against Quakers denying them the rights of Englishmen, established in Magna Carta. Billing described indignities like mouths stuffed with rolled-up hankies, the canes and cudgels used, as well as the faulty legal process in the Old Bailey where but one witness was called. Justice was continually abused. Punishment was very severe. *A Certaine Sound* (London: 1665), described infections incurred in filthy confinement and insisted that no similar banishment or death was suffered by Roman Catholics (p. 12). In a tract of 1678, *A Copy of a Letter*, Billing denied dubbing the Pontiff "Anti-Christ" or "Whore of Babylon," but emphatically questioned his claims to dominion over body and soul. [17]

Energetic and knowledgeable, Billing was also, by March 1674, deeply in debt through, he declared, the extravagance of his recently deceased wife. [18] The extremity of the laws against Quakers imposed on him must have greatly added to his burden. [19] To remedy his money troubles, he and another ex-Cromwellian soldier turned Quaker, Major John Fenwick (1618-1683)[20] in 1674 purchased from John, Lord Berkeley, (d. 1678) West New Jersey, an area bestowed upon that nobleman ten years previously by James, (1633-1701) Duke of York. The partners soon quarrelled about their respective shares. Penn, Gawan Lawrie (d. 1687) and Nicholas Lucas (1607-1688), appointed by the Society of Friends to arbitrate, awarded Fenwick one tenth, and the remainder to Billing. Fenwick promptly made his way to Salem in the new colony; Billing never crossed the Atlantic, dying in London in January 1687, aged sixty-three. In his last years he was at odds with the West Jerseymen over the hereditary proprietoryship finally granted him by Charles II. Since the purchase itself could confer no ruling powers, until then Billing's position had been dubious, and the Concessions of no legal standing. But Penn and Robert Barclay (1648-

---

[17] All Billing's known tracts are in the Haverford College Quaker Collection, including the rare *A Word of Reproof* graciously sent in photo-copy from the Clements Library, Ann Arbor, Michigan. *A Copy* of a letter [to the pope] *Harleian Miscellany*, 12v. (London, 1810) VIII, 436-440. *The Case put and Decided*, tracts of the Billing, Budd-Jenning dispute (reprinted Philadelphia, 1880).

[18] HMC 70, *Pepys MSS* (London, 1911), 268, March 1674.

[19] The letter to Arlington printed in *State Papers relating to Friends 1654-1672*, ed. Norman Penney (N.Y.: 1913), 307.

[20] Robert W. Harpee, *John Fenwick and Salem County in the Province of West New Jersey, 1609-1700* (Salem, N.J., 1978).

1690) also close to James, persuaded the Stuart brothers to remedy the anomolous position of the owner by appointing Billing governor and confirming this by patent in 1683. Billing having already received the assurance of authority, dispatched Samuel Jenning (d. 1708) in 1681 as deputy. That deputy found the inhabitants furious for the Concessions had promised only elective officials. Additional controversy about Billing's acceptance of the King's mandate embittered matters, and the constitutional situation remained unclear even after Billing's death, until the province passed under royal control in 1702.[21]

The Penns[22] were a family from Minety in Gloucestershire. The elder William (1621-1670) took to the sea and fought in the naval wars of the forties and fifties in Irish and Carribean seas. Sympathetic to the Stuarts and angry over his treatment by Cromwell, he quarrelled with him and lived from 1656 until 1660 on those Irish estates with which his services had been rewarded. At the restoration of Charles II, ownership of those estates was confirmed, he was knighted, and he rejoined the navy becoming a favorite colleague of James. His son William was born in London in October, 1644, carefully educated and, when religious dissidence ended his few months at Oxford, was sent abroad for travel and further study at Saumur, a center of moderate Calvinism, where he lived with the famous theologican Moses Amyraut (1596-1664). Back in England, his formal instruction, if it ever began at Lincoln's Inn, was ended by the Great Plague which in 1665 closed metropolitan institutions. Dispatched to Ireland to care for the family property young William Penn met, probably for the third time, the Quaker Thomas Loe (d. 1668), and sometime in 1667, became a Friend. Suffering severe persecution in spite of the family position, he thereafter vigorously wrote and preached his faith both in England and western Europe. Records of arguments in tract and courtroom reveal Penn's familiarity, perhaps gained in the enforced leisure of prison life, with traditional legal literature; this expertise not only resulted in the important decision about the independence of the jury in Bushell's Case

321

---

[21] Pomfret as cited *passim;* tracts in *The Case Put and Decided.*

[22] The best so far among Penn's many biographers is Catherine Owens Peare (Philadelphia, 1957) though occasional inaccuracies mar the text, and the index has omisions. An early life by Samuel Janney (Philadelphia, 1852) is good. A brief assessment of Penn's eighteenth-century reputation may be found in Caroline Robbins, "The Efforts of William Penn to lay a foundation for future ages," *Aspects of American Liberty* (Philadelphia, 1977), 67-80.

of 1670,[23] but in the tenor of *England's Present Interest* (London: 1675), other polemics, and eventually in the laws devised for Pennsylvania.[24]

The Stuarts liked not only the Admiral but his son. Penn was thus able at times to mitigate the lot of fellow Quakers as well as his own. Through Charles and James he acquired, as a result of a petition to them the previous summer, an American domain by the charter of 4 March 1681. Penn's influence with James, who succeeded his brother in 1685, was widely noticed and later caused considerable embarrassment. After that monarch fled to France late in 1688, Penn experienced frequent interrogations, brief imprisonments, and the loss for two years of his province. Retreat in the face of varied attacks from those who suspected him of Jacobitism served, at least temporarily, to lessen the esteem in which members of the Society of Friends had held him; for the duty of early Quakers was, as Barclay had declared in *An Apology* (c. 1678), to face up to persecution.[25]

The son of a courtier welcome in royal circles, Penn had a large acquaintance outside the religious group for which he so devotedly exercised himself. Powerful persons of the ruling class, to which he, as the proprietor of a large colony belonged, came to his aid on many occasions: after the Glorious Revolution, in connection with the recovery of Pennsylvania, and when he proposed a Union of American settlements. Such people received his appeals when he feared that the new board or council of trade threatened the proprietory colonies, and assisted his release from a debtors' prison where the persistent claims of his former steward's family for sums owed or said to have been owed to Philip Ford had placed him in 1708.

Penn's friendship with James II raised the question of his loyalty to William and Mary in his day and has also continued to evoke varying theories. Quite certainly James and Penn were sympathetic towards nonconformists to the established church of England, the King because

322

---

[23] Reports of the trial of 1670 have frequently been reprinted: conveniently in *The Witness of William Penn*, ed. Fred B. Tolles & E. Gordon Alderfer (N.Y.: 1957), 87-105: additional information is in *The Papers of William Penn* I, 171-180.

[24] Besides *England's Present interest*, reports of the trial, *England's Great Interest in the Choice of the New Parliament* (London, 1679), Penn wrote on liberty of conscience and the Frame and laws but other political works (outside maintenance of rights and urging freedom of worship) are relatively few.

[25] Robert Barclay, *An Apology for the True Christian Divinity. . .Of the people called Quakers* (c. 1678; edition quoted London, 1780), 507-512.

of the afflictions suffered by Catholics, Penn because of the persecution of his own and other sects. Evidently Gulielma Penn and Queen Maria D'Este were on good terms; indeed some have suggested the Penns visited her and James in their French exile. Penn was greatly indebted to the Stuarts, and evidently believed James sincere in his protestations about toleration. But James did not heed his advice about Oxford or the trial of the bishops and their intimacy may have been exaggerated. Though frankly admitting to questioners, his obligations to the late king, Penn would not have engaged in armed conspiracy to overthrow the new government in England. In the present connection the rela-   *323* tionship would simply demonstrate that Penn was not anti-monarchical in sentiment. And aristocratic friends do not seem unnatural to a man of a family always of the gentry, and moderately prosperous, who had recently risen into society's upper echelon.[26] Penn's Quaker friends also helped him, but in him, the odd mixture of religious and social or secular has seemed to some students inconsistent or inexplicable. Penn wrote no tracts advocating republican sentiments.

The West New Jersey Concessions embodying much of the republicanism of *A Mite of Affection*, certainly owed many of its assumptions to this 1659 tract. If Billing, as seems likely, wrote both, this poses no problem. Billing, an adult during the Interregnum and a soldier in Monck's army, was exposed to levelling and other political novelties. Penn, on the other hand, was but sixteen when he entered Oxford after his father's warm reception by Charles II. Though there is evidence of early religious inclination and experience, Penn shows little political or legal predisposition before his conversion to defend himself and his friends. Even then, he chiefly stressed those juridical claims made by most Englishmen and eventually protected by the Bill of Rights in 1689. He and William Meade (1628-1713), co-defendents in 1670, quoted Magna Carta with equal ease. Penn adding the witticism that their judges made the great document "a nose of wax."[27]

To the traditional rights of Englishmen Penn added liberty of con-

---

[26] The letters for the most part still on microfilm at HSP illustrate his wide acquaintance with the nobility. Alison Olson, "William Penn and the Politicians," *WMQ* ser. 3, 8 (1961), 176-195, is useful on Penn's non-partisan preference among correspondents and Ian Steele, "Board of Trade, 1699-1702," *WMQ*, 3 ser. 23 (1966), 596-619, though not specific on Penn, illuminates his concerns in those years.

[27] *The Witness of William Penn*, 102.

science, a fundamental property or propriety. This interpretation was also mooted by men like his friend George Villiers (1628-1687), second Duke of Buckingham, who declared 16 November 1675,

> There is a thing called *Property*, (whatever some men may think) that the People of *England* are fondest of. It is this that they will never part with, and that His Majesty in His Speech has promised to take particular care of. This, my Lords, in my Opinion, can never be done, without an *Indulgence to all Protestant Dissenters*.

324 Perhaps the Duke derived this concept from *The Great Case of Liberty of Conscience* (London: 1670). Penn was to defend him in 1685 when under attack because of his support for the dissenters. Even in ostensibly political tracts written after the dissolution of parliament urging the election of men like Sidney for the new Commons, in the hope that they would repeal the penal laws, Penn seldom took a partisan or innovative stance on issues other than religious liberty and the legal injustice often inflicted during the enforcement of persecution by officials oblivious to the rights of Englishmen.[28]

Commentators and biographers have often conceived of Penn as republican and thus a possible author of the Concessions in 1676, attributing the changed pattern of the Frame and laws to growing conservatism. Scrutiny of *A Mite of Affection* and the Concessions finds in them much that seems closely affiliated with reforms proposed during the period of experiment in the Commonwealth rather than the Restoration. Nothing in Penn's writing indicates any knowledge of the literature of innovation. He signed and must have read the Concessions. Anything he later decreed about debtors, punishment, the use of English in court, to cite but a few examples, might well have been prompted by the Concessions. No contemporary attributed the Concessions to his pen; on the contrary, the angry colonists in Jersey referred to it as Billing's composition.[29] Five years separated the Concessions from the arrangements for Pennsylvania. One provides almost manhood suffrage, absolute liberty of conscience, a yearly rotation of office, almost all holders of it to be elected; the other prescribes a tri-partite scheme of government, a governor endowed with consider-

[28] *State Tracts. . .*Printed in the Reign of Charles II (London, 1689), 62. On the defence of Buckingham, see M.M. Dunn, *William Penn* (Princeton, 1967), 145-147; *The Witness*, 75; *Fruits of Solitude*, I, 330-369.

[29] See n. 17, *The Case put*.

able power over appointment, a council or second chamber and an assembly chosen for a three-year term by voters qualified by property holdings. The constitution of East New Jersey of whose twenty-four proprietors after 1683, Penn was one, followed a similar plan save in the multiplicity of proprietors.[30]

Not only the supposed authorship of the Concessions, or a major part in it, but also the existence of ideas publicized in the *Oceana* (London, 1656) of James Harrington (1611-1677) in the proposed constitutions for the colonies established during the reign of Charles II, have suggested republicanism.[31] Harrington's work had added to the already considerable familiarity in England with the "famous Venetian System." But by no means all admirers of Venice were classical republicans. Thomas Sheridan (fl. 1661-1703), secretary to James II in exile, included in *A Discourse of the Rise and Power of Parliaments* (London, 1677) not only a recognition of the Venetian government, but a readiness to adapt many of its practices to the improvement of English institutions.[32] Penn's inclusion then of the ballot, rotation in office, a separation of initiative from confirmation of legislation, and a double vote for the chief executive, did not make him a republican. As noticed, both constitutions set up in Pennsylvania and East New Jersey resembled the English as much as the Venetian form. The Concessions included the ballot, rotation in office, and the seven appointed to guard the "fundamentals" *(Con.* 14) against treasonable alteration; these provisions also mirrored the Italian state and differed from other colonies in franchise, selection of officers, and a uni-cameral legislature. The West New Jersey province offered, therefore, in spite of imperial ties, a republican, almost levelling experiment. The settlers felt this experiment had been betrayed by Billing's acceptance of the royal grant.

Among sectaries, republicanism also occasionally implied some egalitarianism, but Quakers, in spite of their acceptance of the ministry of women, denied levelling aspirations. They deplored undue luxury,[33]

325

[30] John E. Pomfret, *The Province of East New Jersey 1609-1702* (Princeton, 1962) *passim*, and the early constitution in *Archives of New Jersey I,* 1621, 1687, ed. Wm. A. White (Newark, 1880).

[31] Besides Pomfret on West New Jersey, H.F. Russell Smith, *Harrington and his Oceana* [1914] N.Y.: 1971) ch. VII, 152-184, deals with Carolina, the Jersies and Pennsylvania, placing great emphasis on Penn's republicanism.

[32] Thos. Sheridan, *A Discourse passim*, pp. 24, 31, 58, 70, 234.

[33] *The Select Works of Wm. Penn* in 3 v (London, 1825, reprint, N.Y., 1971) I, "No Cross, No Crown," Part I, ch. xii on avarice; xiv, 441-461 on luxury; *Fruits of Solitude*, II, 227.

but Penn's *Advice to his Children* (London, 1726) and *Fruits of Solitude* accepted the existence of a structured society, and outlined the duties of the various categories of rank ordained by the Almighty in all nature, including mankind. [34]

Analysis of the documents for these Quaker colonies brings out nuances of approach. What is apparent is that Billing, author of *A Mite of Affection*, whatever help he later obtained from trustees, was largely responsible for the Concessions. Penn, writing only a few years later with the thoughtfulness and hesitancy shown in the various drafts of 1681-1682, and in spite of the advice offered by republicans like Benjamin Furly (1636-1714) and Sidney, was undoubtedly the chief architect of the government and laws of Pennsylvania. Some repetition will be inevitable here in relating the schemes for the provinces to each other and to suggestions of the turbulent but fruitful years which proceeded them. That repetition will also emphasize both Penn and Billing's anticipation of those rights of Englishmen defined by the end of the century, and enumerated more than sixty years later as natural rights by revolutionary Americans.

A Mite of Affection assumed a republic. The magistrate was to have no coercive power whatever in religious matters (*A Mite*, 1). Government was to be decentralized; much administrative authority was to rest in local, elected bodies representing community units, after a re-organization of county, hundred and parish on Harringtonian lines (*A Mite*, 14). No office could be held more than one consecutive year (*A Mite*, 30). The general parliament or assembly, when elected, should be annual (*A Mite*, 27). No provision was made for protector, governor or executive council. Juridical proposals will be considered later in discussions of those in the concessions and the Code.

Such a tract naturally related to contemporary English conditions as well as to reforms put forward by a variety of persons. Rejecting servile and copyhold tenures, "badge or yoke of the conquest," land ownership should be adjusted to the general well-being and everyman's due property (*A Mite*, 6). A court of record—that is, a register—was to be set up in each county (*A Mite*, 9). Apprentices and those who had attained to knowledge of their craft should not be prohibited by any

---

[34] Penn's *Advice to his Children* written c. 1699, posthumously published, 1725; and *Fruits of Solitude* I, 199, 207, II, 255-268; Barclay *An Apology*, 516.

326

pretended charter from pursuing their occupation (*A Mite*, 22). King's Bench prison was to be abolished (*A Mite*, 17). Any people unjustly excluded from civil and military positions by the "late single person," obviously Oliver Cromwell, should be restored to his place (*A Mite*, 26). Persecutors were to have no role in government (*A Mite*, 4). Images in churches, presumably any remaining by 1659, were to be removed. Here, as well as in the prohibition of cards, dice and other profane pastimes, the puritan rather than the Leveller speaks (*A Mite*, 20, 21). Sequestered estates of royalists were to be used for the care of the maimed, or for the families of those killed in the late wars; any overplus was to help defray public expenses (*A Mite*, 24). Assistance to the indigent, of course, partially echoes the traditional poor law (*A Mite*, 19). Free trade (*A Mite*, 28), and standardized weights and measures throughout the British Isles were to unite England, Scotland and Ireland (*A Mite*, 23).

327

A Mite of Affection expressed hopes for England in 1659; arrangements proposed for West Jersey and Pennsylvania, 1676-82, included chapters relevant only to the New World including fair relations with the indigenous inhabitants, and good understanding between white and red man (*Concessions*, 25, 26; *Code*, 18). The sale of spirituous liquor to Indians was forbidden. Penn's attempt to acquire some skill in their language and benevolent intentions were long remembered and respected by the tribes.

New colonies perforce regulated acquisition and use of land: price, dues or rents paid, and the interval allowable between sale and settlement. The first twelve chapters of the Concessions dealt with these, and outlined projected streets and highways. Parts of Penn's Frame, laws and Code were likewise concerned, but with the difference that the Charter granted him wide powers and privileges as Proprietor. Quit rents were to be the source of much friction between the Penns, their agents and the purchasers and occupiers down to the Revolution of 1776, while this problem was of little consequence in New Jersey.

As already suggested, the political assumptions of Penn and Billing were very different. Both endorsed the juridical rights demanded by Englishmen and allowed considerable freedom of worship. Billing's acceptance of an hereditary proprietorship challenged the levelling concepts implied in the Concessions. In the later history of Jersey and Pennsylvania, royal action and recalcitrant colonists changed some of the early arrangements. Many innovations were short-lived.

Rotation in office in West Jersey was annual; in Pennsylvania service was for a three-year stint, for Councillors has been noted; moreover, the absence of a chief executive in the plan of 1659 as well as in that of 1676 contrasted with the powers Penn enjoyed. Both the council and assembly in Pennsylvania were elected, but only the former could initiate legislation. The assembly obtained this function by the Charter of Liberties in 1701, signed as Penn departed from his second and last brief visit. The West Jersey body, on the other hand, determined its own times of meeting and adjournment, delegating certain of its members to carry on during the suspension of session. It also appointed important officers like the chief justice. The assembly could bring forward any grievance or problems the members or their constituents wished to consider, though these must not attempt to change the "fundamentals" laid down in the first chapters of the Concessions.

In Penn's province an affirmation of fidelity to the Proprietor and his family was demanded of officials. The owners of East New Jersey made all appointments that did not infringe the right there of self-governing boroughs. In all three colonies voting was originally by ballot, marriage legally a civil ceremony and freedom of worship, at least to the god-fearing, was assured.

The Concessions and Penn's Code differ on religious liberty. *A Mite of Affection* declared that the magistrate had no authority in the matter. All believers in Jesus Christ were to enjoy independence of worship, and none with faith in the eternal and ever-living God could be excluded from peaceful habitation. No forced payment towards support of any minister was allowed (*A Mite*, 1). Chapter 16 of the Concessions reiterated even more strongly the sentiment expressed in *A Mite*, and did not require any expression of Christian belief. Penn's Code, on the other hand, though permitting freedom of worship to all Christians and believers in God, limited office to trinitarians. Strict Sabbath observance was also commanded. (*Code*, 1, 2).

Quaker practice as well as Leveller prejudice outlawed the use of oaths in *A Mite* (2) and prompted the provision in the Concessions (c. 18 & 20) for averment and solemn declaration. Penn prohibited swearing, probably including in that term not only official oaths but everyday blasphemy (*Code*, c.3). He also made the Quaker calendar legally acceptable (*Code*, 41). Puritan and Quaker ideology was responsible for the ban on "profane pastimes" as noted in *A Mite*, ignored in the Concessions, but listed at length in the Code (c. 29-30), along

328

with penalties for clandestine marriage (*Code*, 9-14). Penn also legislated in some detail against malicious and seditious speech, defaming and clamorous railing (*Code*, 31-34). Such interest may have been partially stimulated by reaction against the vices and loose talk of the Stuart court. Penn regulated the price of beer and ale, forbad unlicensed taverns, and ruled that meals served to travellers and stabling for hoses, should be of fair quality and reasonable cost (*Code*, 40). Thus he, unlike the authors of Concessions and *The Fundamental Constitution of East New Jersey*, was aware of a variety of both social crimes and everyday needs.   *329*

Crime was followed by punishment, the nature of which greatly interested many thinkers during the Interregnum distressed by the often savage penalties then imposed. *A Mite* specifically forbad the death penalty for theft (*A Mite*, 7). The Concessions on the other hand seemed more anxious that civil and criminal trials should be fair "as far as in us lies, free from oppression and slavery (*Con*. c.23). The day of execution for those convicted of capital offences was left to the general Assembly to determine as they in "the wisdom of the Lord shall judge meet" (*Con*. 31). Appeal, unavailable for criminal offenses in England, was thus possible (*A Mite*, 11). In Pennsylvania the only capital crimes were murder and treason. Penn listed fines and terms of imprisonment of varying severity and length for many transgressions (*Code*, 9-17, etc.). *A Mite* left the nature of the penalty to the decision of the jury, then to elected justices, and by them to an "unconcerned person" (11 & 12); the *Code*, to the magistrate where not otherwise defined (ch. 66). Part of the property of the convicted should go to the family and part to that of the victim (*A Mite*, 16; *Con*. 30; *Code*, 7). *The Concessions* (30) also provided that the estate of a suicide should devolve on the family, a concession later allowed in Pennsylvania. Restitution was decreed for the victims of certain offences (*Con*. 28, 30; *Code*, 20, 22, 44, etc.).

The plight of the debtor in England was notorious, at least from the sixteenth to the nineteenth century, when Dickens made it generally and unfavorably known to those who, by chance, were not already cognizant of it. The rich, to be sure, sometimes welcomed the confinement that wealth could always ameliorate in order to avoid paying creditors. The moneyless man was imprisoned, often abruptly, and was thus rendered powerless to work off his obligations. *A Mite* (17) not only proposed forcing the well-to-do to pay up, but also made it possible for those able and willing to work to discharge their debts. *The Concessions* devoted one of the longest chapters (18) to this matter. Due notice of process was to be given, allowing time sufficient for travelling the necessary distance to court. Should property be found sufficient to pay the debt, this should be confiscated for the purpose. On the other hand, if the testimony of honest compurgators proved the debtor without the wherewithal, he should be discharged forthwith. Penn ruled that debts should be paid, but in cases where legal issue existed, and land owned had been purchased before the contraction of debt, then "all goods and one half the land" should be exempted from seizure (*Code*, 61). Furthermore, he suggested the possibility of full and free discussion about debts owed or claimed between defendent and plaintiff (*Code*, 49), a reflection of favored Quaker practice.

In *A Certaine Sound* Billing vividly portrayed the noxious conditions of the prisons in which he and his fellows were incarcerated. Save for those, like Penn himself in 1708, who were able to improve personal indignities, inmates found all jails dreadful and badly in need of that overhaul, only seriously undertaken largely at the instigation of John Howard (1726-1790) more than a century later. *A Mite* declared that prisons should be warm and clean and condemned the impoverishment caused by exacting jailers (*A Mite*, 18). *The Concessions*, though against payment of fees to officials (*Con.* 22), neglected the subject of jails as such. Penn limited costs, declaring that all charges should be made public and rated as low as possible (*Code*, 47-48). Rooms should not be rented to inmates and should be clean. Prisoners should be allowed to provide themselves with necessities (*Code*, 63). All prisons should be workhouses for felons, thieves, vagrants and loose livers (*Code*, 64). The term "houses of correction" (*Code*, 24) was intended literally to stress the remedial purpose of confinement. Possibly Quakers had noticed the purpose of the Corporation of the Poor in London in the 1650's to prepare indigent children and vagrants for usefulness in society.[35] Those jailed through the testimony of false informers could obtain damages from their accusers (*Code*, 65).

The law's delays had long been criticized. Speedier and cheaper justice was desired by all at the mercy of the legal process. The bewildering divisions of function and power of the Westminster Courts,

[35] Valerie Pearl, "Puritans and Poor Relief," in *Puritans and Revolutionaries: Essays presented to Christopher Hill*, ed. Donald Pennington and Keith Thomas (Oxford, 1978), 206-232.

the existence of ecclesiastical tribunals, of Chancery, and of the legal
role of the houses of parliament, all contributed to unnecessary and
expensive proceedings. Much of this system was not established overseas. Many eccentricities of the English system never developed in
America. Decentralization, as promoted in tracts like *A Mite of Affection*, was forced by circumstance upon the colonies. The absence of
many professional lawyers before the eighteenth century served to keep
costs down and proceedings simple, if occasionally chaotic. The early
role of those few men of law in the colonies was largely in office. Among
colonists in Pennsylvania and West New Jersey, Robert West and
William Bacon were said to have been of Middle Temple; attornies like
Thomas Rudyard, briefly deputy governor of East New Jersey, were
sometimes credited with helping write the early drafts of laws. Thomas
Story and David Lloyd, the latter chief instigator of Pennsylvania's
Judiciary Act of 1701, learned law not at the Inns of Court, but under
London barristers. [36]

331

Besides endorsing traditional juridical rights, both the Concessions
and the Code protected testimentary arrangements, and the situation of
indigents and orphans (*Con*. 29; *Code*, 53-56) in an attempt to avoid
those lengthy proceedings for which Chancery was notorious. A saving
of legal fees was made possible by settlement out of court, Quaker
fashion (*Con*. 21; *Code*, 49,62) and by the right to plead one's own case
without professional aid. Frequent jail delivery was decreed (*A Mite*,
12; *Code*, 45 & 62). Legal officials were to be popularly elected in West
New Jersey (*Con*. 41). In Pennsylvania nominations were gathered
locally but the final choice, at least at the upper level, was by the executive. All these regulations, the emphasis on low and publicly ad-
vertised fees, and the openness of the courts were designed to keep
expense to a minimum (*Con*. 22, 23; *Code*, 42).

Another obstacle to prolonged litigation was the Register of legal
transactions, in land, often proposed but never implemented in Stuart
England. *A Mite of Affection* (9) proposed one; the Concessions provided that such was to be kept both in the Province and in London (*Con*.
24). The Code legislated for a record, not only of transactions in land,
but also of births, deaths, marriages and the hiring of servants. The
wages of these last were to be reported (*Code*, 52-57).

[36] Search of geneological works like *Passengers and Ships prior to 1684* compiled by Walter L.
Sheppard (Baltimore: 1970) turns up remarkably few lawyers even in the city later proverbially
famous for its men of that occupation—Philadelphia.

In a new colony it was especially important that the law should be known as widely as possible. *A Mite of Affection* had complained of laws the accused neither knew nor had heard of, often in a language he did not understand. It proposed, as other contemporaries had unsuccessfully done, bringing out a simpler digest in English (*A Mite*, 8). The Concessions, anxious for familiarity with law as well as for the avoidance of alterations in the fundamentals, ruled that The Agreements should be read twice a year at the beginning and dispersal of the Assembly, and displayed in every common hall of justice where they were to be read four times a year (*Con.* 13-15). The Code stipulated the use of English in all juridical proceedings, which should be readily understood and speedily administered (*Code*, 45). When printed the laws should be read in schools (*Code*, 70). All laws thus designated referred of course to those drawn up specifically for the colonies or especially appropriate for them.

332

The laws and governments set up in West New Jersey in 1676-1677 and Pennsylvania in 1682 have been discussed here as they were offered to the colonists; unlike Billing's tract of 1659, they had therefore a brief period of actual testing. They have been discussed as written and as part of the appropriate general context. To summarize, however succinctly, the working out of the experiments over the nearly quarter of a century when they were ostensibly still in some kind of working order is too complex a task. Courts, schools, towns and counties had yet to be created, some almost at once, others not for a time. Quarrels about Billing's changed status, wrangles in Pennsylvania for more power for the assembly and few obligations to the Proprietor, and developments in the English government and policy make the story of law reform a separate chapter in colonial history. Innovative measures were sometimes reversed, and civil organization grew. The population increased and became more diverse. By 1705 even toleration was diminished, though still greater than in most other areas. Punishment inflicted was more severe. Herbert William Fitzroy makes a dismal story of deterioration in the eighteenth century as Pennsylvania attempted to bring the criminal law code into conformity with English practice.[37] Whatever the case, after 1776 men began to see a need for law reform and

---

[37] Herbert William Fitzroy, "Crime and Punishment in Pennsylvania," PMHB, LX (1936), 202-269; West Jersey John M. Murrin and F.R. Black, "The Fate", "The Ideas and Principles of the Concessions and Agreements" in *The West Jersey Concessions and Agreements*, a round table, 42-49.

studied the work of Cesare Beccaria (1738-1794) and John Howard. Philadelphia built the Walnut Street prison; other states followed with their own improvements. How much the legend of the great legislator, or of the reputation of the Concessions and Agreements influenced post-revolutionary endeavor is difficult, if not impossible to determine. Yet even a tradition of liberty, justice and equality has its value in the history of freedom.

Bryn Mawr College   CAROLINE ROBBINS

333

The publisher and editor gratefully acknowledge the permission of the authors and the following journals and organizations to reprint the copyright material in this volume; any further reproduction is prohibited without permission:

The American Historical Association for material in *The American Historical Review*; The Academy of Political Science for material in the *Political Science Quarterly*; *The Economic History Review* for material in *Economic History*; *The Huntington Library Quarterly*; The Economic History Association for material in *The Journal of Economic History*; *The William and Mary Quarterly*; *Military Affairs*; *Business History Review* and the President and Fellows of Harvard College for material in the *Review*; The New-York Historical Society for material in their *Quarterly*; The New York State Historical Association for material in *New York History*; The Historical Society of Pennsylvania for material in *The Pennsylvania Magazine of History and Biography*.

Contents of the Set